Handbook of Special Librarianship and Information Work

7th edition

Edited by Alison Scammell

 THE ASSOCIATION FOR INFORMATION MANAGEMENT

Published by Aslib, The Association for Information Management.

ISBN 0 85142 398 1

Aslib, The Association for Information Management, founded in 1924, is a world class corporate membership organisation with about 2000 members in some 70 countries. Aslib actively promotes best practice in the management of information resources, represents its members and lobbies on all aspects of the management of and legislation concerning information at local, national and international levels.

Aslib provides consultancy and information services, professional development training, conferences, specialist recruitment, Internet products, and publishes primary and secondary journals, conference proceedings, directories and monographs.

Further information is available from:

Aslib, The Association for Information Management
Staple Hall
Stone House Court
London EC3A 7PB

Tel: +44 (0) 171 903 0000
Fax: +44 (0) 171 903 0011
Email: *aslib@aslib.co.uk*
WWW: *http://www.aslib.co.uk/*

Listing of editions

First published 1955
Second impression 1956
Second edition, completely revised, 1962
Second impression, with minor corrections, 1963
Third edition, completely revised, 1967
Second impression 1968
Fourth edition, completely revised, 1975
Second impression 1977
Third impression 1978
Fifth edition, completely revised, 1982
Sixth edition, completely revised, 1992
Seventh edition, completely revised, 1997

Contents WITHDRAWN

CASE STUDIES

Biographical Notes

JIM BASKER

Jim Basker is Manager, Information Services at the Chartered Institute of Bankers. He runs a department of 11 serving a membership of 70,000 from new shopfront premises in Bishopsgate, London, and is part of a team transforming the CIB into the leading provider of financial services education and training. He has played an active part in professional information groups in the City since moving from the University of Portsmouth in 1989, where he was Business Faculty Librarian, among many other duties, for 11 years. A graduate of Oxford, Sheffield University Department of Library and Information Services and of London, his first challenging job was at Leeds, where he was a pioneer of study skills courses at the Brotherton Library.

BRIDGET BATCHELOR

Bridget Batchelor is one of the two partners of Harwood Associates. Originally a Civil Servant, from the late 1970s her jobs increasingly involved persuading people that being customer-focussed was the only effective way to do business. A career change into marketing followed. The two strands came together in her appointment as Marketing Manager for PSA Projects during its preparation for (successful) privatisation. She introduced commercial marketing techniques throughout the business, prepared marketing and communications strategies and raised awareness of modern marketing practice through top management seminars. Harwood Associates specialises in people, particularly in the professions, who are starting to market themselves in a structured way for the first time. Clients have included Aslib, BNFL plc, the Business Information Network, Drake Beam Morin plc (outplacement consultants), TFPL Ltd, The Technology Partnership plc (high-tech research consultants) and Winters (City accountants); a range of UK Government Departments including Environment, Health, Trade and Industry; several parts of MOD; the Inland Revenue; and the Northern Ireland Government Library Service.

BOB BATER

Bob Bater qualified as a chartered librarian in 1978 after a start-up career in industrial chemistry. Working as Technical Librarian of an international firm of consulting engineers, and later in document management at British Aerospace, increasing contact with computers convinced him that the information profession and the technology could either compete or co-operate. Preferring co-operation, he migrated to information technology in the mid-1980s and spent more than eight years as Information Systems Manager with the NHS Training Division. A founder member of the Aslib Information Resources Management Network, Bob's main focus now is on building effective business solutions, integrating technological components with the disciplines and techniques of information science within an overall information management framework. He entered the uncertain but exciting world of independent consultancy in late 1994, and formed InfoPlex Associates with two colleagues specialising in IT training and IT systems management respectively.

PHIL BRADLEY

Phil Bradley is an independent consultant in the area of IT in libraries. He comes from an information background, having worked for the British Council and SilverPlatter Information. He teaches, lectures and consults widely in the areas of CD-ROM technology and the Internet. Phil is on the Board of Directors of CD-ROM SPAG and on the Management Committee of UKOLUG (UK Online User Group). He is the author of a number of books, and has contributed chapters to others. His home page on the Internet is at *http://www.philb.com* and you are encouraged to visit it to obtain more information about him, his clients and his publications.

GRAHAM CORNISH

Graham Cornish studied theology and history at Durham and library & information science in Liverpool before joining the (now) British Library in 1969. He has held a variety of posts in different parts of the Library ranging from storage and retrieval to administration and research. Since 1983 he has been responsible for copyright issues within the BL and since 1986 has managed much of the BL involvement in IFLA. He is a member of the UK

Library Association Council and Chair of the International Sub-Committee. He has been elected a Fellow of both the Library Association and the Institute of Information Scientists. He has published numerous journal articles and nine monographs, especially on copyright, document supply, audio-visual materials, services of the visually impaired and national libraries. He is closely involved in six EU projects on electronic copyright management and advises Luxembourg on copyright and libraries.

J. ERIC DAVIES

Eric Davies is a member of Faculty in the Department of Information and Library Studies at Loughborough University. His recently completed doctoral research featured several aspects of data protection management. Prior to his current appointment he spent over 25 years in academic library management. He also has experience of public and special libraries. His main interests lie in strategic management of academic libraries, the impact of IT on management, scientific and technical information users and sources, and information skills training and development. He has been active in professional association affairs for many years and has in the past served on the governing Councils of both the Institute of Information Scientists and the Library Association. He has published widely on a variety of professional topics and delivered numerous conference papers and workshop presentations.

ALAN GILCHRIST

Alan Gilchrist set up his own consultancy practice in 1977, after leaving Aslib. Since then he has undertaken well over a hundred projects in the public and private sectors in the UK and abroad. He is a founder member of both the UK based CURA Consortium, and GAVEL g.e.i.e., a European consortium of information management consultants. He is a member of the Advisory Board of the International Society for Knowledge Organization; Chairman of the F.I.D. Special Interest Group on Organizational Excellence; and Editor of the *Journal of Information Science.*

PETER GILLMAN

Peter Gillman, ALA, MSc, FIInfSci, FRSA, is an independent freelance consultant specialising in information management. Most of his working life has been concerned with information services, libraries, and the products and technologies that support them. His career as a consultant began when he joined the Aslib Research and Consultancy Group in 1982. In 1985 he and two colleagues founded The Information Partnership. His work as a consultant has spanned all types and sizes of organisation. Wherever practicable he has championed the understanding of the user/customer viewpoint and needs as being the things that should determine how services are developed and delivered. Peter edited *TIP Applications* for the ten years of its life. He now edits *Aslib Proceedings*; and provides a regular column on IT in library and information services for *IT Link*. He is presently studying for a research degree at the School of Library, Archive and Information Studies at UCL, where he is an external lecturer.

TRACY GRIFFIN

Tracy Griffin graduated from the London School of Economics and has a post-graduate qualification in information science from Manchester Polytechnic. She has managed enquiry services for over six years, starting her career with the Export Market Information Centre at the Department of Trade and Industry. Tracy has considerable experience of the financial sector having worked at the Building Societies Association/Council of Mortgage Lenders and the financial services group within the management consulting arm of Coopers and Lybrand (where she was also involved in their knowledge transfer initiatives). She has also worked at the Business Consulting division of Arthur Andersen. Since May 1997, she has been the Information Manager at the LEK Partnership with particular responsibility for developing their knowledge sharing capabilities.

DAVID HAYNES

David Haynes is the Director of David Haynes Associates which provides management consultancy services in all aspects of information management. David is an information consultant with extensive experience of library, information and records management assignments for organisations in the public and private sectors. He has worked for several different United Nations Agencies and the European Commission. He formerly worked for Aslib and before that for Pira, the Printing Industries Research Association. He has published extensively and has a particular interest in electronic records management.

COLIN HEWSON

Colin Hewson is Information Systems Officer at Incomes Data Services. He was formerly Librarian at the Association of Commonwealth Universities, which he computerised using CAIRS-IMS and then CAIRS-TMS software. From 1994-95 he was seconded to a 3-person team responsible for computerising the Commonwealth Universities Yearbook. Subsequently he developed an in-house OPAC for searching both Yearbook and bibliographic data. For several years he has led workshops and seminars at the annual CAIRS User Group Conference.

SUSAN HILL

Susan Hill has been associated with the information profession since the early 1970s and has developed extensive contacts with library and information professionals, both throughout England and Europe as well as her home country of New Zealand. In 1994 she launched, and has rapidly developed, Instant Library Ltd - the information management services consultancy in Loughborough, England. She also heads up the London recruitment arm of Instant Library. Susan is an active member of the Institute of Information Scientists, currently on Council, the core Management Committee and is Chair of the Membership Development Committee. She has lectured at every library and information school in Britain and helped validate courses. Susan has given many papers at conferences and seminars, in the UK and abroad, run workshops, and written articles mainly on topics relating to professional and personal development, recruitment and selection, and also the future of the profession

GEORGE MCMURDO

George McMurdo works as a lecturer in information studies at Queen Margaret College, Edinburgh. He is professionally a librarian and an information scientist. Past work has been in libraries and computerized information systems, in the UK and abroad. Present work and research interests include computer-mediated communication systems, database management systems, and computer graphics. He currently helps administer the Mailbase electronic discussion list LIS-IIS which is about information science matters.

DAVID NICHOLAS

David Nicholas is Senior Tutor for Research at the Department of Information Science, City University. Previously he was MA Course Tutor at the University of North London. His principal research and teaching interests are in the fields of end-users, on-line searching and information needs. He has undertaken research into end-users since first obtaining a British Library grant to study the impact of end-use on the information profession in 1986: the project was 'Information seeking in an information society: end users'. This project was followed by another BL funded project: 'Online searching at the House of Commons'. Journalists, politicians, financiers and academics have been among the end-user groups studied. Current research concerns include the Internet and its impact upon key information communities, and the consumer end-user.

CHARLES OPPENHEIM

Charles Oppenheim is Professor of Electronic Library Research at De Montfort University, Milton Keynes and Director of De Montfort University's International Institute for Electronic Library Research. He is a Fellow and Past President of the Institute of Information Scientists. He is also Vice President of Aslib. He is a frequent contributor to the professional literature, a well known public speaker and is on the editorial board of a number of professional journals. He is Editor in Chief of a refereed journal, Aslib's *International Journal of Electronic Library Research*, which started publication in 1997. He is one of the UK's representatives on the European Commission's Legal Advisory Board. His professional and research interests include: ethical issues of information; patents; the Internet; copyright; liability for information provision; information policy; online; CD-ROM and real time financial information; data protection; the economics of information; and the information industry. Charles was a member of FIGIT (Follett Implementation Group for Information Technology) and is a member of FIG (Follett Implementation Group), both committees of the Higher Education Funding Councils. He was also the Specialist Adviser to the 1996 House of Lords Select Committee into the Information Superhighway.

PAUL DAVID POLLY

David Polly is a palaeontologist and is the Web administrator for the Natural History Museum. He received his PhD from the University of California at Berkeley in 1993 and was a visiting Assistant Professor at the University of Michigan before coming to the NHM in 1996. In 1993, as a graduate student at Berkeley, David started the Museum of Paleontology World Wide Web server and has since been continually involved in Museum Internet activities. David is currently working as part of a large team—including Ray Lester, Len Nunn, Neil Thomson, Colin Curds, and many others—which is developing a multi-media database system for the Natural History Museum.

LYNDSAY REES-JONES

Lyndsay Rees-Jones is a Professional Adviser for Special Libraries and Information Services at the Library Association. She previously worked at National Grid Plc as Librarian & Information Officer and during that time was an active member of the UK Serials Group. She has worked in a number of other special library and information environments and has gained experience in all aspects of library management including establishing, developing and restructuring library services.

ALISON SCAMMELL

Alison Scammell is an independent information management consultant specialising in user needs studies and library and information strategies. She combines her commercial consultancy with academic research at De Montfort University's International Institute for Electronic Library Research. She is also researching a PhD at the Institute, studying the information needs of teleworkers in the computing, media and financial services sectors. She has recently been involved in a JISC funded project to examine the organisational and cultural change effects of electronic information. Alison Scammell has had a long career in special libraries having spent seven years managing the information service at the Building Societies Association/Council of Mortgage Lenders. She has also worked at a merchant bank, a management consultancy, a government department and the House of Commons. Alison Scammell can be contacted at *alison@ zayin.demon.co.uk.*

MARCUS SPEH

Dr Speh is Senior Advisor Corporate Information Technology at Shell International, where he is leading the global knowledge management program. Before that, he was Director of Knowledge Management at Andersen Consulting. He came to Andersen Consulting after an academic career in theoretical physics and some involvement in the early developments of the World-Wide Web. He can be reached on the Internet at *marcus@courage.demon.co.uk*.

PHIL SYKES

Phil Sykes originally trained as a lawyer before becoming a librarian. He has worked at Leeds Polytechnic, Hatfield Polytechnic and now manages "the ARC" at Liverpool John Moores University, an innovative resource centre which provides a "converged" computing and library service. His main professional interests are in staff management and motivation, liability for information provision, the convergence of academic support services, and electronic information provision. He has recently set up two projects under the "eLib" programme, funded by JISC, which explore the issues surrounding electronic supply of course readings.

STELLA TRENCH

Stella Trench is Vice President, Corporate Research & Development at AIG, a multinational insurance and financial services company, where she has worked for nearly eight years. The department provides desk research and information, analysis, primary market research and client database management services to the group. Stella manages the European branch of the R&D service (which she established) and is also responsible for special international projects within the department. Prior to AIG, Stella was Manager of the National Library and Information Service at Grant Thornton, Chartered Accountants. She has also worked at Reed International and GEC Avery. Stella has been involved with the Special Libraries Association at Board Level for several years. She has also been involved in the City Information Group, is a member of the Library Association, the Institute of Information Scientists and the Market Research Society. She has contributed to courses and conference sessions run by TFPL, the London Business School and the SLA.

IAN WATSON

Ian Watson is Manager of Information Services at Scottish Media Newspapers, the Glasgow-based publisher of The Herald and the Evening Times, which has been acquired by Scottish Television. Responsibilities include the development of electronic text and picture databases and the provision of reference and research services to journalists. A graduate of Glasgow (Political Economy) and Sheffield (Information Studies) Universities, he has previously worked with the Turing Institute (an artificial intelligence research centre) and the Planning Exchange (a centre for information on environmental and economic development). Both posts involved the management of electronic databases and the development of fee-based information services. He is a member of the Institute of Information Scientists, in which he has participated as a member of Council and extensively at branch level. Other activities include writing a regular column for Aslib's *Managing Information* on the information society and the occasional lecture to information science students.

ANNE WEIST

Anne Weist is currently working as the Forest Healthcare Trust Librarian, Medical Education Centre, Whipps Cross Hospital, London. She has also worked on secondment to the North Thames (East) Regional Library Unit. She has also worked as the HIV/ AIDS Information Officer, Wessex Regional Health Authority and at the Help for Health Trust, Winchester. Her professional interests include: CAL development in postgraduate medical education, promoting the use of the Internet among Health Care Professionals, and improving information retrieval skills. Anne is currently a member of the Health Libraries subgroup of the Library Association.

LEONARD WILL

Leonard Will acted as technical consultant to the Public Record Office for the library automation project. He is an independent consultant in information management, specialising in the organisation of information in libraries, museums, archives and records management systems. Previously Head of Information and Research Services in the City University Library, London, and Head of Library and Information Services at the Science Museum, he now works in partnership with his wife, Sheena, under the business name Willpower Information. He is a Chartered Librarian and a Member of the British Computer Society. The Willpower Information WWW site is at *http://www.willpower.demon.co.uk*, the email address is *L.Will@willpower.demon.co.uk*.

Introduction

Alison Scammell

In the five years since the publication of the last edition of the *Handbook*, the information scene has been completely transformed. The phenomenal growth of the Internet has accelerated the move towards a more electronic information environment and the digital culture is gradually pervading all aspects of everyday life. There is a general consensus that we are now on the brink of a new information age.

Many crucial aspects of information management are currently in a transitional phase as the forces affecting the supply, organisation and delivery of information adjust to the new digital paradigm. Paradoxically, the extraordinary technological advances and the sheer volume of information now available on a global scale are causing a return to the basic principles of information management. Many of the functions associated with traditional library procedures are being re-examined in the context of today's information imperatives and are proving to be of fundamental importance.

As the new information era unfolds, special libraries and information centres are taking centre stage. More and more organisations are recognising the value and importance of information as a crucial resource. Companies are being re-structured into 'learning organisations' where a high premium is placed on the expertise and knowledge of people and the specific ways in which they handle and communicate information. These developments are offering a whole host of opportunities for special information managers who are rapidly having to re-invent their roles and are consequently enhancing their status as key players in the emerging knowledge economy. By enlisting our users as stakeholders in the information enterprise we can encourage a positive information culture which can be harnessed to the overall objectives of the organisation and, ultimately, to its success.

This edition of the *Handbook* has been completely revised and up-dated to reflect the new demands being placed on the special information service. The contributors comprise a blend of practitioners, academics and consultants. This eclectic mix of styles and attitudes represents an holistic approach to special information work in the late 1990s, providing a synthesis of hands-on, front-line experience with in-depth research and analysis.

The *Handbook* is intended as a general primer for all those interested in special information work. It brings together in one single reference source a guide to the central concerns of the special information management functions, skills and activities as we approach the millennium. Inevitably, the chapters deal with a selective range of issues. There are also obvious difficulties in keeping up-to-date with current developments in such a fast changing field and so I have tried to put the emphasis on procedures and good practice rather than to focus too heavily on specific systems and products. Getting the balance right is a formidable task. By including a number of case studies, demonstrating some of the practical and political problems of implementing new technology, I hope I have provided guidance that will be of more enduring value.

I would like to thank all the authors, not just for their whole-hearted contributions to the book but also for their numerous suggestions, advice and brainstorming sessions. I would particularly like to thank the case study authors for participating so enthusiastically, both in their respective information endeavours and by sharing these experiences in print.

The Role of the Special Librarian in the Electronic Era

Alison Scammell

INTRODUCTION

There can be no doubt that the information environment is becoming increasingly digital. However we define the 'electronic era' it is hard to conceive of a special library or information centre today which deals exclusively in hard-copy material. We have had a long time to get used to the idea of computers in libraries and a fundamental reassessment of the role of the information profession has been underway since the introduction of online databases in the 1980s. The dramatic growth of the Internet in recent years has accelerated the pace of change and the debate over the role and future of the information intermediary has intensified.

This chapter is not concerned with academic arguments about whether or not electronic information will dominate or whether print media will become obsolete. The assumption is still that hard-copy material will continue to be used, in varying degrees, for a very long time. Neither is this a discussion about the electronic library, a concept that is hard to define and remains as controversial as the idea of the paperless office. Indeed there is now talk about exploring and developing the concept of the 'hybrid library', which could be defined as a combination of electronic and print products, all united by a common electronic catalogue with consistent cataloguing and search mechanisms.[*]

The aim of this chapter is to look at the ways in which the electronic environment is generally evolving, the changing functions of the special information service and some of the skills required to do this work.

---

[*] *I am grateful to Charles Oppenheim for suggesting this as a possible definition.*

3

ORGANISATIONAL CHANGE

A discussion of the transformation of the special library needs to be done within the wider context of organisational change. The last 15 years or so have seen the rapid acceleration of change within all types of organisations accompanied by a publishing bonanza of texts by 'management gurus'. The enduring preoccupation with flatter, less hierarchical organisational structures discussed by writers such as Handy[1] and Kanter[2] has been embraced enthusiastically in the library and information science literature although these structures may be less prevalent in corporate and institutional environments than might be desired. More adverse effects of organisational restructuring have resulted from the business process re-engineering and accompanying downsizing, which has occurred throughout all sectors. This has taken its toll on information departments, which have often been in the front line for cutbacks or even outright closure. One legacy of this restructuring process is that information centres are left struggling to meet increased demands for a service with reduced resources.

Technology has been an important driving force for change. The wholesale integration of information technology into mainstream organisational routines has affected everyone. A fully networked organisation is considered to be a powerful way of fostering more collaboration and co-operation between individuals, reshaping work styles and improving communication flows. Many organisations are moving strategically towards a more digital culture. At one extreme is the computing industry where a combination of flexible working routines, advanced telecommunications and high end office technology is seen as an important investment in developing a more customer-centred approach. This is resulting in a growing community of remote, distributed and mobile workers with an increasing reliance on a predominantly electronic information infrastructure.

THE ELECTRONIC ENVIRONMENT

In special information units the traditional online databases and familiar CD-ROM products have been joined by the Internet and World Wide Web (WWW), electronic journals, groupware, e-mail and intranets. Technology is advancing at a phenomenal pace and information managers face a relentless deluge of new electronic products and services on the market. Every month the computer magazines herald the promise (or threat) of a new computing standard, wonder product or a batch of software upgrades.

Special libraries are now routinely using electronic tools to manage library procedures. Internet resources are available for acquisitions, order processing, cataloguing and serials management. Publishers and vendors can be located via their Web pages and orders placed using e-mail. Resource sharing, co-operative cataloguing and access to central authority control files are procedures that can more easily be streamlined using online resources. Directories, bibliographies, catalogues, reviews, tables of contents and press releases are all available online. Serials subscription agents can be contacted via their Web sites and can provide a wider range of regularly up-dated resource management data for customers, such as subscription price projections. Price checks, order processing and claims can all be dealt with much more speedily. Enquiries can be taken and answered via e-mail, reducing delays for urgently required results and the Internet provides a convenient first stop reference point for a whole range of queries. Electronic document delivery services offer an efficient and speedy alternative to more traditional interlibrary loan procedures providing a range of different solutions to complement material held in-house.

The value of electronic information is that it can be easily shared, distributed, updated, manipulated and rapidly searched. A feature of the current electronic environment is the apparently seamless way in which resources are networked and accessed across different computing platforms, and a substantial research and development effort is being concentrated in this direction. The emphasis, therefore, is on sophisticated behind-the-scenes technology to produce powerful results while simultaneously enabling easy search procedures at the system's interface. In developing facilities geared towards improving end-user access the goal is therefore to 'minimise the skill but maximise the power'.[3] An example of the technology used to achieve this is the Z39.50 protocol which allows searching on a variety of different databases (with different structures) using the same set of commands. The World Wide Web currently represents the single most important common interface from which to access a diverse and disparate range of information. A major feature of the commercial online sector in recent years has been the rush by providers to produce Web-based versions of their products, seen as a crucial prerequisite in tapping the lucrative end-user market.

In an electronic environment, information can take many forms and is hard to define. We can no longer regard a document in simple terms as a static, single physical entity (which at one time would have been a book or a journal article). Information cannot necessarily be considered as a complete, finished piece of work that can easily be catalogued, classified and consigned to a collection. Information held in electronic form can be several things at once, a multimedia fusion not just of sound, text and image but animation, video clips, software applications and real time discussion.

Barker[4] has identified three types of document for use in a digital resource: static, dynamic and living. Static documents are the most basic, they contain fixed information and never change their form (such as 'traditional' online data). Dynamic documents also contain fixed information but are able to change their outward form, the way embedded material is presented to users (such as multimedia CD-ROMs). Living documents are able to change both their form (outward appearance) and their embedded information (such as information contained on the Web).

Hypertext has brought several new dimensions to the information seeking process by establishing both interactive and non-linear approaches to accessing data. One important characteristic of the emerging electronic market place is that products and services are appearing which are being specifically designed for electronic use rather than having direct hard-copy equivalents or even originating with a print version. The increasing popularity of multimedia and growth of hypertext applications means that a direct hard-copy equivalent is often not feasible.

INTRANETS

For many organisations, particularly in the corporate sector, the electronic information infrastructure is being built around groupware products or around the intranet (an internal version of the Internet). The appeal of intranets is that they provide a single central information store and encourage communication flows throughout the organisation. Information can easily be shared and disseminated to large groups of people dispersed across different sites, even across national borders. There is the potential to link every desktop in the organisation irrespective of which computing systems are in use. At ICL for example, the intranet can be accessed by any of the company's 23,000 employees in 80 countries.[5]

A vast range of internal company information can be held on the intranet. At a basic level this could include internal telephone lists, procedures manuals, organisational charts and other personnel documentation, the type of information which is almost impossible to keep up-to-date using hard-copy formats. More advanced information handling scenarios are also feasible. At Glaxo Wellcome the intranet provides a means of performing very visual tasks where sophisticated graphical manipulation of data is required and the provision of internal online laboratory manuals can ensure that safety information remains completely current and can be rapidly searched.[6]

The value of an intranet is that it can integrate in one central source a combination of internal, external, formal and informal information. This is an important consideration in the corporate sector where informal information sources are rated so highly. Positive communication flows are encouraged and interaction between colleagues and project teams is seen as a valuable way of creating a shared knowledge base for the organisation. There is a suggestion however that because intranets are a 'productive layer in knowledge economy engineered organisations'[7] they are less likely to be really successful in strictly hierarchical organisational structures.

Intranets are relatively cheap and easy to develop because they use the existing technology of the Internet (the same TCP/IP protocols, use of HTML, Web browsers and search engines). Above all, the intranet provides a managed information environment in stark contrast to the chaos of the Internet. As intranet technologies mature, the focus is moving away from the technical aspects of implementation and development to consideration of the management of information and end-user applications. This is seen as crucial to the overall success of the intranet and an area for which the information unit is ideally suited. Information professionals are becoming Webmasters and intranet co-ordinators, combining technical expertise with information management ability.

ELECTRONIC JOURNALS

Electronic journals are a good example of the kind of multimedia products likely to feature more prominently in the special information service. Although the number of electronic journals is accelerating at a fast rate, there is clearly some way to go before the full benefits of this new medium are fully exploited. Many of the titles currently available are simply electronic versions of titles already in hard-copy form and the multimedia potential has not been fully developed. Inevitably this will change as new products appear and parallel publishing declines. Attitudes to electronic publishing are also affecting their development. Authors are still generally reluctant to regard electronic journals as carrying the same authority as traditional print-based titles and publishers are concerned about rights issues and pricing mechanisms.

There is no doubt that electronic publishing offers enormous potential for information delivery. As well as providing search facilities, the inclusion of hypertext links to external sources can transform a journal into a vast databank of navigable information. Links can be included to a range of external sources in addition to links within the journal itself (such as to previous editions of a specific column, hotlinks to notes or references and subject threads linking themes across different issues). Instant feedback, real time discussion or electronic conferencing is also possible. The production of full colour graphics may be a cheaper option for an electronic product than is currently possible in hard-copy form. There is the potential for creating multimedia essays combining sound, animation and video clips. Software applications could be included to perform data analysis or demonstrate scientific principles. Integration of different products can further enrich the information base by, for example, linking different reference works such as dictionaries and encyclopaedias and a number of such products are currently available.

THE INFORMATION SERVICE

It is common to refer to the paradigm shift occurring in libraries as they move from a holdings environment to an access one. There are a number of concerns associated with this shift, not least a change in the perception of the library's value, which has traditionally been judged by the size of its physical collection. This will need to be addressed by ensuring the information service maintains maximum visibility within the organisation. Electronic tools provide a pivotal means of achieving this and information units are investing substantial resources in establishing and developing a Web or intranet presence.

Another concern is that an access-based environment will undermine the user's preference for browsing (although it could be argued that the hypertext-based facilities of the WWW offer the ultimate browsing environment). The growing number of full-text sources (including books) available electronically, and the sheer range of information available for immediate desktop access may provide some compensation.

The direct access of electronic resources by end-users and the consequent decline of intermediary searching (a process that began with the introduction of online databases) has been boosted by the end-user potential of the Internet. Disintermediation, a term borrowed from other industry sectors (where technology has eliminated the need for a middleman) has received an enormous amount of attention in the library and information science literature. Most of the debate has centred on the positive aspects this change will have in providing new training and consultancy roles. One example of the positive approach to this issue is the concept of 're-inter-mediation'[8] that will be required from information specialists as they re-invent their roles to accommodate and support an entirely new set of user needs.

There is a growing consensus that it is desirable to be working towards a scenario where the end-user has convenient and easy access to a vast array of high quality information sources and can be empowered to develop their own information literacy. This should be achieved within the context of managed information structures supported by highly trained information professionals. Parallels can be drawn here with the way in which resources have been channelled into designing OPACs with the primary intention of empowering end-users to become self sufficient in their information searching. Information professionals can play an important role in assisting users to perform their own information seeking, by training, advising on systems and products, providing user documentation and online support and performing more complex search routines. Maintaining their searching proficiency in a scenario involving reduced mediated searching will be a challenge for information staff, but will be an essential part of their continuous professional development.

The timely delivery of extremely current information has always been a crucial factor in the special information unit and in contrast to public and academic libraries, large book collections have often been inappropriate. Special libraries have always dealt with a diverse range of non-book information and material, most of which is inherently suited to electronic formats. The basic functions of information management have therefore not changed radically from more traditional scenarios. The primary function of the special information manager must be to meet the information needs of the users and the key procedures to achieve this still involve the selection, organisation and dissemination of resources.

Selection of information

Selection of information remains a key function of the information unit whether hard-copy or electronic resources predominate. In an electronic environment this becomes a formidable task because of the enormous choice of material on offer and the existence of a global information market place. Many of the problems currently associated with the selection process stem from the fact that electronic publishing is still in a transitional, experimental phase and a number of legal, technical and pricing issues have yet to be resolved. Until accepted economic models for pricing of electronic information have emerged, information managers will need to deal with a complex set of pricing strategies making the comparison between suppliers and products a particularly difficult task.

Document delivery issues need to be considered as an essential part of this whole acquisitions management procedure. At a basic level there are numerous problems associated with accessing and/or downloading material from a network. Special browsers or software (such as Adobe Acrobat) may be needed to read material in its original form or a vital dimension of the information may be lost.

On another level, interlending issues and use of third parties will need to be considered in the context of which material needs to be borrowed or bought outright; for example, whether you are paying for the continued or repeated use of the data or for once only use (and also the precise proportion of a book or journal being accessed). Whether the information needs to be kept indefinitely and how electronic information should be stored and archived, involves the consideration of technical and physical preservation issues as well as cost and resource management implications; for example, an archive may be maintained by the publisher or document supply service.

These procedures are likely to remain problematic and complex for a long time and as market conditions and technical possibilities change, so too will the information management options. A new set of skills are likely to be required. Transaction management (using specifically designed software) may be needed to deal with the elaborate costing and copyright process involved in accessing, storing and preserving electronic documents. Negotiation skills will be important in dealing with a range of different vendors and a degree of legal expertise will be required to cope with contractual issues, copyright, data protection and information liability matters.

The sheer range of media complicates the selection function. Similar information may be available in many different ways and comparisons need to be made both between competing products in the same medium as well as across different formats. Inevitably there will need to be tradeoffs between a whole range of measures such as overall usability, accessibility, currency, cost and content. A range of complementary sources may be required, for example, using online databases to update material supplied on CD-ROM and using the Internet to update online data. Existing resources need constant evaluation to ensure they continue to fulfil important user needs criteria.

New electronic products on the market are likely to require different equipment or enhancements to existing hardware, such as memory upgrades or more sophisticated monitors. Multimedia products require more complex hardware solutions and these considerations need to be taken into account in selection and procurement decisions. The information professional will need broad ranging technical skills to assess and evaluate appropriate system requirements for new electronic information products. The need to anticipate future needs becomes more urgent in an electronic information context where the pace of change has such a profound impact.

Evaluating products and services in a fast changing market place will require a combination of skills involving technical and searching expertise, awareness of changing user and organisational information requirements, subject knowledge, familiarity with sources and financial management. It is harder to assess the authority of a data source in an environment where there is an abundance of free material competing with established commercial services. One of the major debates about the value of Internet-based information is its integrity. The reliability of sources is less certain in an electronic era when anyone can publish, than when a smaller number of established publishers were operating and material was subject to editorial scrutiny and peer review (although of course many electronic journals are subject to the same peer review process as print-based versions). Trusted, reliable sources of data are absolutely vital in a special information context where such a high premium is placed on the quality and authority of information.

Evaluation and selection have been highlighted as forming the cornerstone of the OMNI (Organising Medical Networked Information) Project's approach to organising Internet materials.[9] Many of the librarians participating in this project considered evaluation of Internet resources as a new topic for which they did not possess the requisite skills. This is an example of how traditional library skills need to be up-dated and applied in a new context. Evaluating Internet resources may be considered to be very different to selecting traditional library material as networked resources do not have a common set of features such as statement of responsibility, introduction or preface (although there is currently considerable debate on how such resources can be standardised). A comprehensive set of evaluation guidelines has been produced by the OMNI team and form some of the earliest examples of Internet resource evaluation criteria.[10] These guidelines provide a useful checklist which could be applied in a wider context and cover a whole range of selection criteria such as scope, audience, authority, provenance, coverage, accuracy of information, currency/frequency, uniqueness, accessibility, usability, design/layout and user support.

In compiling subject gateways, resource sharing may become an attractive option, especially for small information units or one-man bands. Electronic information can be easily shared and creative ways can be explored to achieve this, such as developing joint Internet resource products. Co-operative partnerships between different information units in similar fields can encourage a whole range of reciprocal arrangements, enhancing the quality of service provision for all parties and reducing overall costs.

Organisation of information

The emphasis in a traditional print-based library is on the physical organisation of the internal collection. In the access scenario a new dimension has been added, the need to manage and control the vast range of external information resources. Internet search engines vary from the classified structure of Yahoo! to the more advanced Boolean search facilities of Alta Vista, but are all hampered by the fact that the Internet provides such an overwhelming mass of disorganised information and they are proving to be an unsatisfactory way of accessing the Internet.

Consequently, information professionals are returning to basic principles of subject classification and retrieval, authority control and thesaurus construction as a means of developing systems to filter the vast range of information now on offer. The importance of indexing is being acknowledged as a vital alternative to free-text approaches ("an unindexed library is not information at all, it is noise"[11]). Knowledge of thesaurus construction and classification schemes is as important in an electronic scenario as in traditional print collections.

Subject mapping of electronic information can take different forms. The compilation of Internet resource guides to meet the specific subject bias of the organisation can provide an easy and effective way for users to access the most appropriate information sources. In contrast to the American dominated information of the Internet, a UK bias can be emphasised. This can take a more structured approach and at the top end of the scale are the subject gateways (referred to earlier) such as EEVL,[12] SOSIG[13] and OMNI[14] which have been developed as part of the eLib research programme.[15] These resources all use classification schemes to provide a structured subject approach to managing material. Although primarily designed to meet the information needs of the academic and research community these gateways have a much wider application and the lessons learned from developing such metadata (information about information) can be of value in compiling systems to meet local needs.

On a smaller scale, special information units can devise similar resource mapping tools. The importance of these services is that they provide access to quality resources where material has been critically evaluated, selected and filtered. The organisation's intranet is an ideal mechanism for mounting a subject gateway to both external and internal resources and provides the users with a 'first stop' search approach. However, establishing and developing these services is very labour intensive and needs to be managed effectively. In order for the service to remain of value, links need regular review and maintenance to ensure they are kept up-to-date. Increasingly such routine procedures such as 'link checking' are likely to be automated but a substantial amount of human intervention will inevitably still be required.

These services can also be a valuable mechanism for staying in touch with remote and distributed users. Feedback on the service should be encouraged and is easily arranged by including e-mail forms for users to suggest new resources or comment on existing ones. One advantage of electronic information services is that they can be monitored more easily than hard-copy collections and usage data can be collected automatically.

There is a need to devise practical retrieval mechanisms for managing internal information. Document management in an electronic environment may require specialised software with 'version management' facilities to handle the dynamic qualities of 'living' information which is subject to more frequent amendment than hard-copy material. Various scenarios have been envisaged for enabling effective retrieval mechanisms at the document creation stage and, within an organisation, protocols and standards could be developed to achieve this. For example, authors could be encouraged to apply indexing standards to their work, assisted by expert systems to automate this function. Systems of applying subject authority control can be applied to either internal or external information sources to translate the users' natural terminology to the vocabulary used by the system as effortlessly as possible.

Existing information systems may need to be retuned to cater for the quite different requirements of a user group operating in a distributed environment. OPACs may need to be redesigned, interfaces will be needed to the disparate and diverse information systems and media. One starting point for a new systems approach is to focus on the concept of 'organisational usability' within a digital information environment as outlined by Kling and Elliott.[16] The dimensions of organisational usability they provide emphasise the ways computer systems can be fully integrated into the work practices of organisations and include:

- "Accessibility - Ease with which people can locate specific computer systems, gain physical access and electronic access to their electronic corpuses. This dimension refers to both physical proximity and administrative/social restrictions on using specific systems.

- Compatibility - Level of compatibility of file transfers from system to system.

- Integrability into work practices - How smoothly the system fits into a person's or group's work practices, including access to complementary computing resources (i.e. communication lines, scanners, printers) to facilitate work flows - how people actually prefer to work.

- Social-organisational expertise - The extent to which people can obtain training and consulting to learn to use systems and can find help with problems in usage.

- Reliability - System should be reliable with easy recovery from common problems (with the possible assistance of support staff)."

These aspects of usability point to the importance of taking a broad-based view of systems in an organisational context rather than a narrow focus on the user interface. They demonstrate the importance of taking an holistic approach to identifying users' needs in designing library and information services. The users' information seeking process needs to be examined to ensure the system is operating effectively at all levels.

The accessibility of a system varies with a person's experience and expertise with the necessary platforms, as well as their access to specific databases or resources. General system availability and institutional regulations regarding use of a resource is also a factor to take into account; for example, pricing mechanisms may considerably affect accessibility. A database that is apparently 'free' at the point of end-use is more accessible for individual users than a service requiring advance booking, permission or billing/cost centre administration.

Compatibility is an important consideration where the retrieval of files in text, graphics, audio or animation format are in common use and the ease with which they can be processed, imported or exported affects the overall success of the system. Use of electronic information systems needs to be capable of being integrated into the work routines and habits of users but they may even go beyond this and be responsible for changing work processes and organisational culture altogether. Systems also need to be able to cope with a range of different searching skills, accommodating both the novice and advanced searcher.

Dissemination of Information

Dissemination is a vital component of information management and provides a crucial value added aspect to the information delivery procedure. The dissemination of information in an electronic environment provides some exciting opportunities and challenges for the information unit. Use can be made of the organisation's intranet as well as the company's Web site to distribute information, and the information centre should invest time and resources into establishing its own home pages for this purpose. Current awareness and alerting services can be performed in real-time unhampered by the production delays associated with print-based services. Summaries, synopses, commentaries and bulletins can be easily downloaded from original sources (depending on copyright restrictions) and posted on the library's home page with hotlinks to the full document. The advantages of disseminating information in electronic format is that it can so easily be reformatted and repackaged, providing an important value added service.

Presentation, editorial and design skills are all very important and the number of training courses aimed at information professionals reflects the growing importance of these areas. Librarians are becoming publishers as well as organisers of information. Electronic house journals and magazines can be developed and managed by the library. This could be used to encourage interaction between different parts of the organisation and to explore new ways of communicating. Electronic discussion lists and forums can also be used to disseminate information both internally and externally and are particularly useful for sharing resources with similar organisations or industry groups.

Delivery mechanisms feature more prominently in a fully networked environment and output can be tailored to cater for the specific requirements of individual users. For example, online search results may need to be downloaded directly into groupware for automatic internal re-routing among project group members. A fully developed intermediary function can mean that the library develops the expertise (using the most appropriate electronic tools and software) to provide the end-user with the means and advice to access a variety of different information formats. One current common example of the type of delivery problem encountered by end-users is in accessing material in different formats. Although the software is often provided by the information source, it can be time-consuming or complicated to download. The information section can provide advice, assistance or additional software or perform the procedures instead.

The selective dissemination of information (SDI) is a function of the information service that has been a feature of library computer systems for many years and is only really practical on a large scale if automated. Internet based SDI services are now taking the form of 'intelligent' search agents or 'knowbots', performing regular information trawling of specific subjects (they are considered 'intelligent' if they can recognise and then adapt to the user's changing subject interests). Several variations on this theme are possible, one example is a personalised daily newspaper compiled from different sources and featuring selected subject areas.

The information intermediary's role in managing these services will include evaluating, installing, road testing and programming or 'training' these facilities. Providing effective dissemination services will still require a familiarity with our users, their environment, work styles, and information seeking habits. This will need to be matched by a comprehensive knowledge of information products, services and systems. We will become mediators between the end-users, the resources and the overall objectives and strategies of the organisation.

THE USERS

Underpinning the entire selection, organisation and dissemination functions of information management will be the understanding of the precise needs of our users. The users themselves are ambivalent about using electronic information. There are fundamental human/computer interaction issues influencing the use and take up of electronic information sources. Although there is a marked preference for reading hard-copy material, users want to be able to access up-to-date information easily and quickly and at times they find most convenient. User needs must be assessed on a regular basis and reasons for non-use of information systems must also be explored and analysed.

The user training and consultancy role is likely to increase in importance. We need to play a major role in enabling users to enhance their information literacy and to increase their searching proficiency. Searching support can be provided in several ways, through training as well as using documentation (both in online and hard-copy formats). Help desk approaches to support may become more appropriate in a distributed scenario where more users are accessing systems remotely. Information professionals will need to find ways of remaining in touch with these unseen clients and new relationships will need to be forged. Reconfiguring system support to be really effective in a distributed network may require even more complex solutions. One approach is to facilitate ways in which users can learn from each other using 'collaborative browsing' techniques supported by an interface which provides a visualisation of the search process, allowing search histories to be stored, manipulated and communicated to other searchers.[17]

INFORMATION SKILLS

There have been many attempts to define the core skills or competencies of information professionals in the future and many of these analyses of information skills highlight the need for both professional and organisational/personal competencies (the general management skills that are not specific to the information profession).[18, 19] Both the Institute of Information Scientists[20] and the Special Libraries Association[21] have compiled skills criteria and the results of a 1997 survey of the information professional is also available.[22] These core information skills and competencies are summarised below.

Professional information skills

- Identifying, anticipating and analysing user and organisational information needs
- Technological skills
- Subject expertise
- Knowledge of disparate information resources and how to access/integrate them
- Familiarity with research methods
- Ability to evaluate information

- Ability to organise and store information for effective retrieval
- Ability to add value to information: presentation, editorial and publication skills
- Knowledge of delivery mechanisms and means of disseminating information
- Training, education and consultancy skills
- Knowledge management
- Knowledge of legal, economic and political aspects of information.

Management skills

- Understanding the organisational culture
- Strategic planning
- Financial management
- Human resource management
- Project management
- Change management
- Communication skills
- Marketing skills
- Vision and creativity
- Liaison and negotiating skills.

There is a danger in being too specific in defining information skills and roles because of the need to keep pace with the demands of a fast changing technology and continually reshaping organisational structures. Indeed, it could be argued that individual job descriptions will become less rigidly defined as the combined skills of the project team are valued more highly than the contribution of a single individual. Information managers are more likely to require a broader range of overlapping skills as demarcation lines become increasingly blurred. The skills required to manage information on the organisation's intranet for example may be a combination of document management, knowledge management, information retrieval and records management expertise. Information professionals will also need to become more involved in the software design stage of their information tools, liaising between the users and the software developers.

The multidisciplinary nature of the digital environment involves a converging set of technologies and skills and requires more routine liaison with different players such as the IT specialists, system designers, publishers and other information providers. There may be lessons to be learned here from the academic sector where a greater dependence on electronic information is resulting in the convergence of the university library and IT department (although in many examples the experiment has not been successful and has resulted in diverging the two functions). Information professionals need to learn coalition-building skills to ensure these new relationships develop constructively and successfully. Organisational and general management skills are more important in a fast changing world and are necessary if the information function is to continue to play a key role.

CONCLUSION

The electronic era provides some exciting challenges and opportunities for re-orienting the special information workplace. We will always need to define our roles in a much wider context than the current information and library scene. Trends in management fashions, corporate and organisational culture and global developments are all significant. We are experiencing a period of fundamental technical, political, social and economic change and the corporate map is being constantly redrawn.

Special libraries are progressing towards an electronic information culture in different ways and at different speeds. This is being influenced by a number of different organisational and commercial pressures and is not necessarily part of an overall coherent strategy. In this respect special librarians may be at more of a disadvantage than their colleagues in the academic sector, where the introduction of an electronic culture is occurring within the context of a long-term structured programme of research and development. Of course, the entire information community will benefit from these developments but in the short term special information managers may feel they are struggling to innovate and experiment in a haphazard and insular way. One solution may be to forge more alliances and embark on joint ventures to provide reciprocal services. This will provide an opportunity to tap into wider networks of expertise outside the parent organisation. It is also important that information staff participate in the activities of professional associations and special interest groups in order to play an active role in planning for the future.

Above all, we should remember that we all have a part to play in shaping the information scene of the future for the benefit of everybody, and we can take direct responsibility for this on an individual level. As Professor Tom Wilson has said, 'we cannot all be 'movers and shakers' but we can be nudgers!'[23]

REFERENCES

1. Handy, C. *Beyond certainty*. Arrow Books, London (1996).

2. Kanter, R.M. *The change masters: corporate entrepreneurs at work*. Routledge, London (1992).

3. Pollit, S. et al. View-based searching systems: progress towards effective disintermediation. In *20th International Online Information Proceedings*, edited by D.I. Raitt and B. Jeapes, Learned Information Ltd, Oxford (1996).

4. Barker, P. Living books and dynamic electronic libraries. *The Electronic Library*, **14** (6) 1996, 491-501

5. Bird, J. Switching on to intranets. *Management Today*, December 1996, 78-80.

6. Wodehouse, Lord. The intranet: the quiet (r)evolution. *Aslib Proceedings*, **49** (1), 13-19.

7. Fishenden, J. Managing intranets to improve business process.1996. Aslib Proceedings, **49** (4), 90-96. Web version located at: *http://www.geuze.demon .co.uk/aslib.htm*

8. Crane, D.J. Creating services for the digital library. In *20th International Online Information Proceedings*, edited by D.I. Raitt and B. Jeapes, Learned Information Ltd, Oxford (1996).

9. OMNI Annual Report 1996, Web version located at: *http://omni.ac.uk/general-info/annual-report/ar96-fin.html*

10. OMNI guidelines for resource evaluation, Web version located at: *http://omni.ac.uk/agec/evalguid.html*

11. Brown, A. Immersion in a sea of words, *Wired*, July 1996, 70-74, 104.

12. EEVL Web site home page located at: *http://eevl.icbl.hw.ac.uk/*

13. SOSIG Web site home page located at: *http://sosig.ac.uk/*

14. OMNI Web site home page located at: *http://omni.ac.uk/*

15. eLib Web site home page located at: *http://ukoln.bath.ac.uk/ services/elib/*

16. Kling, R. and Elliott, M. Digital library design for organizational usability. *SIGOIS Bulletin*, **15** (2) (1994).

17. Twidale, M.B. and Nichols, D.M. Collaborative browsing and visualization of the search process. *Aslib Proceedings*, **48** (7/8), 177-182.

18. Ojala, M. Core competencies for special library managers of the future, *Special Libraries*, **84** (4) (1993), 230-234.

19. Corrall, S. Information specialists of the future: professional development and renewal. In *Information superhighway: the role of librarians, information scientists, and intermediaries, 17th International Essen Symposium,* edited by A.H. Helal and J.W. Weiss. Essen University Library, Essen, (1995).

20. Institute for Information Scientists. Criteria for information science, located at *http://carduus.imi.gla.ac.uk/Members.html*

21. Special Libraries Association. Competencies for special librarians of the 21st century, May 1996, located at: *http:// www.sla.org/professional/competency.html*

22. FID/MIP. *Results of FID's survey of the modern information professional*, located at: *http://fid.conicyt.cl:8000/mip08.htm*

23. Wilson, T. *The role of the librarian in the 21st Century,* keynote address for the Library Association Northern Branch Conference, Longhirst, Northumberland, 17th November 1995, located at: *http://www.shef.ac.uk/uni/academic/I-M/is/lecturer/21stcent.html*

Analysing the Organisation's Information Needs

Peter Gillman

INTRODUCTION

This chapter should be understood to be about the information needs of organisations as expressed through the information needs of the individuals working in them. It is not about the extent or means by which those needs are met. The information needs of individuals, considered as parts of functional groups and measured against the needs of those groups, forms the organisation's information needs.

Fashions change. At one time it was conventional to ignore users' information needs, and to concentrate on information usage studies. There was considerable professional debate about the merits or otherwise of the approach. Current thinking tends to see the need for both viewpoints: the specific needs of individuals may or may not be met through corporate resources; and usage studies only examine the extent to which whatever resources are provided are used. Of necessity the two views are so closely inter-related that to attempt to isolate them will lead only to a partial understanding of information requirements.

The synthesis of the two viewpoints has led to the development of the information audit as a tool to measure information requirements, the availability of resources, and how the resources are delivered ('tuned') to meet the requirements.

Information, it can be argued, has a value in itself and its worth cannot be objectively measured. This obscures the many ways in which information impacts on its users and their communities. It also obscures the fact that the value of information for any one user or group of users is completely bound to the form and extent to which it is available at the point of need. This chapter will discuss how the impact can be assessed and what techniques are available to help accomplish this. The value of information is supplied by the context of its delivery. Evaluation means establishing that value, and to do that therefore means establishing the context. The question of value is not about establishing the cost of information provision, but the value of what it does.

Information needs are all needs, expressed by all qualified users. In theory, therefore, all sorts of information should be considered. In practice there are many specialised information types (such as financial data) that are best provided by expert groups. This chapter is therefore confined to the types of information likely to be dealt with by the expert group of information professionals.

The chapter is written from the practical viewpoint of consultancy (rather than research) where the investigator is contracted to provide an answer within a fixed time. This is close to the circumstances of staff carrying out their own investigation. Of necessity this approach means that the full rigour of statistical and investigative methods are not used. The outcome may be less thorough than would be required for published research, yet is most likely to suit the needs of managements that require rapid results and often find it hard to take a long view on problems.

The example of a hypothetical electronic engineering business, *E-build Ltd*, manufacturing circuit boards for sale to system builders, will be used as required throughout this chapter to illustrate the various points.

ORGANISATION FUNCTION AND STRUCTURE

The process of analysing the information needs of an organisation must be preceded by an understanding of these key points:

- The purpose of the organisation
- The extent and limits of the organisation
- The information culture within the organisation
- Type of information to be analysed.

Taken together these provide the framework within which data can be collected and analysed. There is no context-free information use model that can be generated or applied.

The purpose of the organisation

Evaluation of an organisation's information needs means finding out the extent to which the needs fit with the purpose of the organisation. Therefore an evaluation can only be carried out if:

- There is a stated purpose against which activity can be measured
- It is possible to collect and analyse information usage, provision and delivery data that is relevant to the purpose.

Common errors in approaching the evaluation of information systems are generally to do with one of these two aspects. Either the organisational purpose is not clearly stated and understood; or the data collected are not the ones that are needed.

It is possible for staff and management to have quite different ideas about what an organisation exists to achieve, how it operates, and how it measures itself. Extreme examples exist of senior managers taking visitors on 'shop floor' tours and describing to them processes and procedures that have not been carried out for years. For this reason the statement of purpose must be derived from discussion with all possible levels of staff, none of which can be assumed to have the monopoly of the correct view.

Many organisations have been through the process of producing mission statements intended to encapsulate the reason for the organisation's existence. A mission statement does not, however, say what the goals of the organisation are, nor how corporate resources will be deployed to meet these goals, nor how achievement of goals will be discerned or measured. Mission statements are frequently intended for publication in an annual report; and to give employees and staff some form of coherent statement of common purpose. The larger and more complex the organisation, the more diffuse the statement. Mission statements are therefore almost useless as an exposition of corporate purpose outside the narrow boundaries of internal and external public relations.

The chief executive of a commercial enterprise may take a more focused view of purpose: anything that enhances the profitability by either reducing costs or increasing effectiveness. This is a valid view, yet it does nothing to establish why and how the organisation functions.

As an investigation progresses through an organisation, with the same question posed about purpose, the answers will vary. People very close to the processes of data collection and entry are likely to have very local and pragmatic views. Senior management will often lack the fine detail, but should have a more strategic viewpoint. 'Purpose' therefore is going to be tightly bound up with the level and type of responsibility of the person questioned.

The organisation being addressed for the purposes of analysis is the level of unit (for example a Division or Branch) which can be seen as a whole, with a distinct and measurable purpose.

The purpose of an organisation can be expressed in terms of a statement of intention for such an organisation, supported by figures indicating how resources will be deployed to achieve the purpose, and how attainment of the target will be discerned and measured. The purpose of the library service in *E-build Ltd* might be expressed as:

- Providing technical literature (such as reports, journals, product and parts catalogues, component performance reports, technical memoranda, data sheets) to manufacturing, research and development areas
- Providing competitor, product and market analyses and supporting material to marketing areas
- Providing systems and services to service the needs of these areas in ways which best suit their requirements.

These sub-purposes can be measured in various ways, as will be shown further on in the chapter.

Errors in defining the purpose

Errors in understanding the purpose of an organisation are, surprisingly, quite common; and it is for a very obvious reason. The chief executive (or whatever the person at the head is called) of an organisation should see all parts of it as contributing to a common goal. However it is often unclear just what that goal is. There is no single purpose of a local authority library service, for example. It may be stated in terms of processes - to lend books and recordings to local residents. It may be in more intellectual terms - to raise standards of literacy and an awareness of information resources. It may be stated in terms of compliance - because it is required by law. It will largely depend on the point of view of the individual concerned. The same argument can be applied to any organisation.

Furthermore the view of the purpose will depend upon where in the organisation, laterally and vertically, the individual is. A database administrator or print-room operator would be unlikely to have the same view of purpose as would the chief executive or members of the Board of Directors. To make the point even more forcibly, it would be almost impossible to state a purpose for a country's government that could be recognised and agreed by all subjects or citizens. Even within one ruling party the frequency of cabinet and parliamentary splits and disputes shows the difficulty of finding any common purpose.

In many cases it is quite likely that the 'purpose' will actually be the thing for which the penalties of non-achievement are the most severe. Thus in the pharmaceutical industry generally, the purpose of records management is to avoid the penalties associated with being unable to prove compliance with all the stages of drug development and testing.

In any area of subjectivity the answers will only be as good as the quality of questions asked. A process of review and cross-checking should ensure that the statement of purpose is a true reflection of the organisation.

The extent and limits of the organisation

For a large and complex organisational structure it will be necessary to break the structure down to smaller, more functional units in order to be able to make useful measurements. There can be no rigid rules about how small the units ought to be: it is entirely dependent upon organisational complexity. That in turn is largely a function of the extent to which decision-making and accountability is devolved or centralised. A rule of thumb is to see whether a measurable statement of purpose can be produced. The level at which it is possible, is the level at which the activities of information use data can be collected and analysed.

The implication is that for a large and complex organisational structure there may have to be a number of analyses carried out. If the level of organisation chosen is, for example, the whole of a multinational chemical manufacturer it will be impossible to derive any useful figures supporting information use except at a level of abstraction too high to produce figures that can be analysed. In such a case the analyst might go down through the organisation to below the Divisional level, perhaps even looking at separate work-groups.

E-build Ltd has a fairly conventional structure, with divisions for finance, administration, marketing, research and development, production etc. A statement of purpose covering the whole company is at too high a level of abstraction for meaningful data collection. It is necessary to look to the Divisions, at least, in order to find out how each one supports the whole enterprise.

This support can be measured in terms of the contribution that each Division makes to the overall profitability. A cross-check is possible, in that the revenue of the company is, in part, spent by the Divisions in carrying out their work. Thus a relationship can be established between the cost of having each Division and the contribution it makes to revenue income. It is essential however to ensure that cost/benefit is not looked at crudely: an expensive research and development activity may produce no revenue at all and yet without it there is no product stream to manufacture and sell. A common error in downsizing is to miss this connection and fail to see that some support activities are better described as enabling activities: their outcome is to assist other activities to take place.

An information culture within the organisation

Corporate downsizing, one of the popular business activities of the mid-1990s, has led to the complete or partial destruction of many information units. This is largely because they have been viewed as activities that consume revenue while generating none in return. It is axiomatic that the returns from investment in effective information provision are generally down-stream (i.e. they are not immediate) and are quite hard to attribute to specific activities or services. It is also axiomatic that the people who decree downsizing are not information service users, and generally have left the organisation or moved on by the time the real consequences of the lack of organised information provision become apparent.

It is notable that while information management as a whole is particularly susceptible to corporate death through carelessness because it cannot be shown to make a direct contribution to the revenue stream, the same is not true of the considerable IT investment that many organisations make. The lack of a direct connection with revenue is there, but IT is generally well insulated from investment cutbacks.

An organisation with an information culture is one which understands:

- The cost of acquiring, managing and delivering information
- The cost to corporate operations of not recognising or optimising the function of information flows
- The value of organised and integrated information flows
- That these costs are not directly equivalent; that is, the opportunity costs of not having access to information resources cannot be compared directly with the costs of information resource acquisition and management.

Costs cannot be set against the value of organised and integrated information flows in the manner of an equation. It is in the nature of an information culture to understand that these things are different; it is in the nature of corporate downsizers to ignore this.

The pervasiveness of an information culture can be measured by the extent to which it is recognised, as part of the normal operation of the business, that the value of information can only be established at the point at which it is used. The key to evaluating, or assessing the value of information provision is therefore the context of use. Information has value only when it is used. An apple lying on a shelf has potential energy released by falling, but the value decreases as the apple deteriorates; a book on a shelf or a record in a database has potential value released by use but the value deteriorates as the information ages. Value arises at the point of use, and is determined by how closely what is available fits what is needed.

An information culture cannot be produced, it has to arise from the efforts of individuals. The culture is established when the individuals' efforts are seen as a co-ordinated whole which has the effect of raising the level of corporate performance by a large step - perhaps an order of magnitude. Such a culture, based on the effective utilisation of resources and their deployment to benefit the whole organisation, can probably only take root when it has top-down support from the highest levels.

COMPONENTS OF AN INFORMATION SERVICE

An information service is a mixture of:

- A stated purpose for the overall service and the components of it, covering the various target user groups and how and why they are to be supported
- A deliberate policy covering the types and forms of material to be collected, organised, and made available, and the suitability of those types and forms for the purposes stated
- Coherent and integrated organisation of information acquisition, management and delivery systems
- Data interpretation, or the packaging of information to fit particular needs
- Accessibility to the target groups in appropriate ways.

These things are all largely within the control of the provider of the service.

It is implicit here that there is (or should be) a symbiotic relationship between users, their needs, and the means by which the needs are satisfied. This establishes users, resources, needs, delivery mechanisms, collection policies and all other aspects of an information service as also being components of it.

Types of information to be analysed

Information is not an homogenous whole. What is information at one point (because it has value to the user) is of no value at another point, where it does not offer benefit.

To be of value information must:

- Meet the subject interest of the user
- Be at a level of detail that matches the requirement
- Be delivered in a form which fits the user's requirements
- Be delivered in a time-scale that fits the user's requirements.

Clearly this shows that in *E-build Ltd*, 200 bibliographic citations in response to a request for details on the middle-European market for floating-point arithmetic processors, is not satisfactory. Nor is it enough to answer a request for statistical information with a table when what the user requires is a graph to put on a overhead projector slide in the next 10 minutes.

Both of these responses are answers: neither has provided information.

An evaluation of information needs must consider the four points above as an integral part of the problem.

E-build Ltd might use a matrix to codify and define the components of its service as in Figure 1 overleaf.

On examination of this first draft, many of the rows and columns in the matrix are not particularly helpful: they are the wrong sorts of categories. This may be because they are too broad, or because they ignore the different roles that people play in the working environment. How these problems are dealt with will be shown later.

CHARACTERISTICS OF USERS

Users of services are almost exclusively outside the control of service providers. In most cases providers can only react to what users want. To provide a user-oriented service means offering one that takes account of this variability and lack of control. Users of information services have these characteristics among others:

- Each will perform a number of different roles in a working environment
- They come from a wide range of backgrounds
- They bring different levels of understanding and ignorance with them
- They will each do a huge number of different things with the resources they find
- They are not predictable in their needs, expectations or levels of experience and understanding
- They do not, in general, fit any predetermined patterns (although they may fit one or two criteria)
- They have choice over whether or not to get information, and from which sources
- They may choose to (and are allowed to) go without information.

Although all of these factors are important, a) is worth a special mention. Individual members of an organisation may be designated as market researchers, systems analysts, finance managers etc. These are job titles, but are not really descriptive of what the individuals concerned actually do. In all three of those jobs there is a strong element of research. Each is also involved with financial budgeting and control. Each also carries out some degree of administration. Practically every function within an organisation is also carried out, to a greater or lesser degree, by every person in it. The difference between a technical research worker and a market analyst can be expressed as the degree to which each undertakes research, or market study, or any other function.

Users Resources	Product Marketing	Competitor Analysis	Market Analysis	Product Research	Product Development	Manu-facturing	Engineering Control
Technical Reports				X	X		X
Journals	X	X	X	X	X	X	X
Product Catalogues				X	X		
Parts Catalogues				X	X		
Component Performance Reports				X	X		
Technical Memoranda				X	X	X	X
Data Sheets				X	X		
Market reports and surveys	X	X	X				
Competitor reports		X					
Databases	X	X	X	X	X		
Market Intelligence	X	X	X				

Figure 1 - Resource and user matrix: Forms of information packaging and functional user groups

This understanding is important in refining the matrix of Figure 1. As it stands, the user groups that head the columns are functional divisions or structural groupings, they are not descriptions of the way people work. The matrix refinement recognises this by abandoning the functional groupings and instead concentrating on roles which are types of work that individuals carry out.

The result of the refinement can been seen in Figure 2, together with a similar refinement of the resource types, which is discussed below. The refinement of the user groups has apparently left some titles unchanged, this is because they are also valid descriptions of activities. What is key here is that the titles should no longer be taken to refer to parts of the organisation or to jobs, but to individual working activities.

CHARACTERISTICS OF INFORMATION RESOURCES

Information resources, as described in Figure 1, are a mixture of presentation and delivery formats (journals and databases), content (market reports and technical memoranda) and subject (parts catalogues). In fact all of these categories overlap. Analysis of the problems of information supply will be made easier if the distinctions are disentangled.

The physical forms can be separated from the type of content to give a more understandable picture of needs and resources. Figure 2 shows the position for *E-build Ltd* when the resources are defined in terms of content alone.

Information resources come in a variety of physical and logical forms including:

a)   Single articles

b)   Collections of articles (conference proceedings, journals)

c)   Books (which may include the content of a) and b) above)

d)   CD-ROM (which may include the content of a), b) and c) above)

e)   Online databases (which may include the content of a), b) and c) above)

f)   Pages and screens from Internet World Wide Web pages (which may duplicate e) above)

g)   Microforms

Users / Resources	Primary Research	Secondary Research	Market Analysis	Product Marketing	Product Development	Manu-facturing	Engineering Control
Product Evaluations		x	x	x	x		
Component Evaluations	x	x			x	x	x
Parts lists		x				x	x
Review articles			x	x	x		
Technical articles	x				x		x
Internal Technical Notes	x					x	x
Component Specific-ations and Performance Data		x			x	x	x
Market reports and surveys			x	x	x		
Competitor reports	x	x	x				
Market Intelligence	x	x	x				

Figure 2 - Revised user and resource matrix:
Classes of information and types of usage

h)   Data-sets on disk.

All of these will also be seen to cover all subject aspects as well. It is necessary to tease out the differences when assessing information needs. This is dealt with in more detail later under 'Information audits'.

The different physical forms are important because they are used in different ways; some are more appropriate than others to particular circumstances; some are accessible only under specific conditions; and so on. The search functionality offered by the CD-ROM or online version of a full-text journal cannot be compared to manual searching and scanning; while the portability of the printed version cannot be compared to that of the screen-based one. The versions address quite different needs and these should be recognised.

Subjects are obviously important, and should be seen to include level of presentation and viewpoint. An undergraduate-level textbook on circuit design is not a substitute for the performance data sheet of an integrated circuit. When collecting data by interview or questionnaire, it will be found that it is often easier for respondents to identify subject areas than it is for them to recognise physical forms of delivery.

DATA COLLECTION

At the commencement of an evaluation a statement of purpose and aims for the investigation should be prepared, which should be agreed by all concerned parties. The statement can include a description of the data to be collected and how they will be analysed. This sort of statement forms the Terms of Reference that would be produced for a project. The statement should be used in surveys and interviews to establish the context for respondents.

The principal means of data collection are by direct observation, interviews with individuals or with groups, surveys and questionnaires, and statistics. There are circumstances where only one of these is needed, but they are rare. More likely three or more will be used. Apart from making a more complete picture this can have the effect of cross-checking the analyses.

Observation

Direct observation is the process of watching how users behave in relation to information resources. This can include watching (and counting) the use made of journals as they are consulted in stacks, and taping or transcribing reference requests and interviews. Observation is time-consuming and is frequently undertaken only in order to cross-check statistics, or to provide an opportunity to conduct brief on-the-spot interviews with a sample of users.

The results of direct observation are unlikely to be of much benefit on their own.

Individual interviews

Interviews with individuals are usually semi-structured: that is, the interviewer has a list of questions to be asked, but these are gone through discursively and not in the manner of a checklist.

Interviews of information needs will normally be centred upon the individual's work, what information resources are used as input to that, how they are sought, how they are delivered, and time-scales and critical features of delivery. It is also usually appropriate to find out whether the interviewee produces any information outputs that are used by others; and whether the interviewee directs the information activities of other staff in any way.

Individual interviews are often not practical in very large organisations, because of the time taken to gather enough representative views. In such circumstances individual interviews are usually conducted with staff who have been identified as being key in terms of their knowledge of the functioning of some part of the organisation. These interviews produce results which are then used as a pointer to other aspects of the investigation.

Interviews that are conducted on the assumption that information is what is printed and packaged as books and journals, are unlikely to yield good results. Non-information professionals do not think in this way, and questions posed should concentrate on the subject and level. Discussion on the physical form of delivery arises when that topic is introduced deliberately.

Group interviews

Group interviews work best where the interviewees have some common thread of interest, on which they are all likely to have different viewpoints. Interviewees need not all be of the same rank or level although obviously mixing very senior and very junior staff in the same group is unlikely to provide much useful output.

It is possible for one interviewer to run a group interview with up to 12 people. If possible have someone present who can take notes, it should be made clear to all concerned that these are not minutes of the meeting. The interviewer should describe how the data collected are to be analysed and presented.

Some care must be taken in laying down rules for the group: each interviewee should be allowed a period of time (say 10 minutes) to describe briefly their job responsibilities, and their information requirements. This process can be followed by opening up the discussion to everyone, but under the control of particular questions to which answers are required. These might include questions on access or availability, completeness and currency of resources etc.

A particularly valuable part of a group interview is the opportunity it presents for attendees to discover that they have similar or overlapping interests, and to share experiences on how sources for these are found and used.

The comments on assumptions mentioned earlier under 'Individual interview' about what information is, are equally valid here and should be carefully observed.

Surveys and questionnaires

Surveys and questionnaires are notoriously difficult to structure. There are many books covering the techniques of surveys, their messages should be clearly understood. The processes of designing and developing questions and how they are to be answered calls for many skills. Badly structured questionnaires will produce bad answers at best, and very few of them at worst.

A survey is often used to supplement other activities such as interviews. Psychologically it gives users the opportunity to be consulted. More practically, a survey demonstrates that action is being taken, and provides some weight of authority for the investigation. This should not be jeopardised by its being badly organised.

If a survey is conducted in parallel with an interview programme, then both activities should be seeking the same sort of answers. It may be necessary however to process the results separately, since interview results may arise from discussion, while questionnaires are usually completed without the benefit of further guidance.

Evaluation using statistics

It is quite common to evaluate services in terms of the numbers of users, numbers of enquiries, numbers of searches, numbers of documents retrieved, numbers of pages photocopied. These figures have some limited value in supporting bids for staffing levels; and in comparing figures for different years. But the use is very limited. Raw statistics (rather than performance measures or indicators) say nothing about whether particular levels of activity are appropriate. In each case, to get some idea of value, it is essential to ask additional questions that help to make sense of the statistics.

Commonly statistics are kept to show levels of activity (processes). But processes are only the means to carry out the wider tasks (purposes). The processes should only be used in reporting and evaluating if they are matched with measures or indicators of purpose.

Statistics with meaning

The following examples show how process statistics from the information service of *E-build Ltd* may be made more useful by adding some operational context.

Numbers of users

How many are there from each Division or department? How many should there be? What is the figure, expressed as a percentage of all potential users? What is being done to bring in current non-users? How much is known about how/why the service is used (or not used)? What are the competitive or alternative sources of information available that may affect numbers?

Number of enquiries

Irrespective of how many, are they the sort of enquiries that the service is supposed to be good at handling? How many arise because of user mis-understandings of the purpose of the service? Are the enquiries relevant to the work of the parent organisation? Are the enquiries at the right level to make best use of resources?

Numbers of searches

Are search subjects relevant to the business of the parent organisation? Were searches conducted to good effect? Were the appropriate databases and services used? Did the users have enough training to use the databases intelligently?

Number of documents retrieved

How much material does it take to provide the answer? Are all of the documents original and important, or are many of them derived from the same few sources? Are the sources, and the authors, the most authoritative or relevant ones?

Numbers of pages photocopied

This is wholly a measure of process. The purpose must be assessed in the same way as looking at numbers of searches and enquiries. What did the copies support? Were they a suitable way to answer the enquiries posed? Did enquirers need or want copies of source material? Was the material wanted available in other formats?

Errors of data suitability

Data used for an evaluation may be analysed because it is available, and not because it is actually suited to the purpose. Common problems are that the wrong things have been measured, that the measures are too specific or restricted, or that they do not tell enough of the story. The following examples illustrate this:

a) A database evaluation was performed on the basis of counting the cost of collecting records (all-in cost, equipment, staff, premises). This figure was divided by the number of records to give a notional cost per record. The figure was hugely sensitive to the overall number of records and the collection and maintenance policy for the database, which could vary the number of records. It was also sensitive to marginal changes in operating costs.

b) In an information service with multiple service points, a count was made of the number of accesses per service point. On the basis of this, an apportionment of total operating costs was made across all the points in proportion to the number of accesses on each. The apportionment was very sensitive to the number of outlets, their locations, and the service policy on access and availability; but these things were not considered or included.

c) An evaluation was made of the cost/effectiveness of a single database used to support part of the work of an organisation. This total cost was then taken to be typical for all such operations and the figures were extrapolated to all other similar databases that were maintained. Some of these other databases seemed to be very cost-effective as a result, while others seemed to be expensive out of all proportion to their apparent value.

d) 'Bean counting': this is the recording of copious statistics on each and every process, without setting these against any purpose. Bean counting allows large volumes of important-looking statistics to be presented, but usually fails to convey any useful sense of meaning or relevance.

It has already been stressed that it is important to look at what is supported or enabled by the activity: that will give several clues as to what information should be collected; and how it should be analysed and interpreted.

In the instance of point a) above, a revised version of the evaluation took this approach:

• Look at what activities are supported, and the cost to each of them of getting the same information elsewhere

• Establish an understanding of meaningful user groupings, by reason for access and level of access

• Assess the amount of usage by each of these groups of users, across all outlets

• Apportion the total cost of the database operation in proportion to user group levels as a measure of the extent to which each user group is supported

• Review the user groups and see whether the level of support is adequate or suitable for its needs.

Other approaches that might have been suitable for particular purposes would have looked at user groups, numbers of records aimed at those groups, and numbers of accesses by the groups. More sophisticated counting would look at the usage of actual records. How this could be done would depend upon a mix of data richness, indexing, and transaction logging.

Many library management systems, search engines and browsers also provide access and usage statistics. In large organisations these figures can be attributed to Divisions or other functional groups through some form of account identifier. Office automation systems frequently have some form of traffic volume counter. The figures from such sources can be valuable in two ways: to help plan short-term staffing rosters and resource availability; and in conjunction with some form of needs analysis, to show how system and electronic resource usage compares with other types of resource.

Transaction volumes should not be confused with measures of effectiveness, because they are only counts of processes, and do not explain purposes.

DATA ANALYSIS

The analysis of needs data can be as complex as the means for its collection. The essential problem seems quite simple: to collate and correlate information on needs in such a way as to be able to draw useful conclusions from the results.

The data on individuals' information requirements should have been collected in a way that does not bias them towards commenting only on what is already provided. This means that the data must show what information users require for their jobs; not what they think of what is already available.

The first step in analysis is to collate the data on all the different types of information that have been noted. The data may come from interviews, surveys and questionnaires. One method of analysis is to collate the material in a word processor, using a different numbered section for each topic. Then under the heading for each topic can be entered the comments made about it, together with a note of the name and functional group of whoever has made each comment. The same material can alternatively be collated in a database, or in a spreadsheet. The important consideration is that it should be possible to bring together similar comments on similar topics so that an organised picture of needs becomes apparent.

The comments should be edited to ensure that each type of comment is captured just once, with a note against it of the user groups concerned.

Several matrices can now be compiled. One is to list all of the subject topics (e.g. parliamentary debates, standards, data sheets) on one axis, and all of the means of delivery on the other. The means of delivery include online text and references delivered to the workstation, online access available at some central point, hard copy for reference, photocopies supplied, telephone or fax response, etc. The cells (where topics and means of delivery intersect) contain the names of the user groups requiring that form of service. This version of the matrix is useful for assessing relative demand for different methods of delivery, and can be used to evaluate the present mix of services provided.

Another form of the matrix is to plot the topics on one axis, against the user groups on the other. In this case the cells will contain the information about means of delivery. This version of the matrix is used to show the types of service that should be provided for each user group.

The matrices to be used for analysis will depend upon how service developments or enhancements are to be planned and responded to.

It should be noted at this point that the means of delivery should be logged even though they may not be feasible, or legal. Thus a high level of demand for regular photocopies of copyright-protected material may not be legally met unless some form of licence agreement is made with the rights holder. The level of demand, and the means to satisfy it or permit it to be carried out, are quite separate issues.

Use of the matrix

Figure 2 represents an improved way of looking at the information usage by staff in *E-build Ltd*. Matrix analysis is a useful tool because it gives a structure within which a complex problem area can be broken down into its various components. There are many applications of the idea that can be used to help understand information needs and provision.

Information service non-users

There are two groups of non-user of information services that can be noted in *E-build Ltd*. The first is the group who are deliberately excluded. The second is the group of information users who do not draw on the service.

Excluded users

The information service's statement of purpose does not cover providing a service to finance, personnel (Human Resources), sales, administration, office services, and a number of other likely groups. This is an approach that many information service providers feel unwilling or unable to take, instead they follow the line that no user should ever be turned away. If that is to be the policy of the service, it should be recognised that effective analysis of it becomes almost impossible, since the only criteria for providing service is that it is requested. Coherent planning of resources and systems of delivery is impractical.

If certain groups can be excluded from the user base as a matter of operational policy, then a version of the matrix may be used to determine how these potential users may be provided with alternative services.

Service non-users

These are the staff who clearly fall in to the user categories being considered, but obtain the resources and services they require elsewhere. For an organised information service they are often the most intractable group to investigate. This is an area where the information service staff are poorly placed to research the problem, since they may be a literal part of it. In this case external advisers or consultants can investigate the circumstances of non-use and will frequently unearth reasons for it that demonstrate that the formal information service has a poor understanding of the critical information needs.

A variation of the matrix deals with this non-user population. The matrix can be used to plot the information needs that ought to be required by various users groups; and through analysis of usage records and other transactional data, establish the proportion of usage to non-usage.

A critical point here is that 'non-user' refers to someone not utilising the formally-provided resources. They may be getting equivalent (or more appropriate) services through other agencies such as local, university and business school libraries, online databases and professional institutions. The reasons why these parallel activities take place should be of great concern and interest to anyone investigating information needs.

Internal information flows

Matrix analysis with the same set of user groups on each axis can be employed to plot the interactions between functional groups. The interactions are likely to be expressed as figures representing volumes of data, but they may also be indicators showing the direction of flow.

Matrices of this type are time-consuming to produce, but they have great value in the process of investigating the nature of the flows. Functional groups can be shown a 'picture' of their interactions with other organisational groupings and be invited to comment on them. This level of discussion has been known to reveal previously hidden flows and patterns quite different from those that might be expected.

The information-flow matrix is frequently used as the second stage in a data collection exercise.

INFORMATION AUDITS

An information audit has a different purpose from a financial audit. A financial audit is about establishing whether cash flowing in and out of some defined area of business has been accounted for adequately. It does not mean whether the money was spent to good effect, or whether it was spent appropriately. A financial audit is concerned with verifying that there is a secure trail linking all aspects of income and expenditure. It is the accountability (the extent to which the cash flow is documented) that is at issue.

An information audit is a different matter, as it looks at things the other way round. Given a cost for a resource, how has it been deployed? Over the life of the information contained in the resource, how has that been used? It is important here to distinguish between simple counts of activity (so many books lent out over such a period) and trying to measure the effectiveness on behalf of the user of each of those loans. An information audit is about purpose, not process. Purposes are expressed in terms of the wider business activities that they support; processes in terms of what has to be done to achieve the purposes.

It is also important to choose with care the area of business to which the audit will be applied. To measure the whole of an activity against the whole of its parent organisation is a task doomed to become bogged down in an intractable morass of unreconcilable data. It is preferable to choose one functional area of service at a time, and then concentrate on understanding its nature. Matrix analysis will help to target the investigation.

The field of the information audit does not ignore cost, but tries to take it in to account as only one factor. Information is 'soft' in the sense that cost is quite easy to establish, but benefit is not. Cost can be quantified (hence budget exercises) but benefit gained or lost is largely a non-numeric measure and so conventional accounting leaves it out altogether. This can be seen in the development of business cases for new systems. Actual costs are derived and projected; benefits are expressed in terms of better working, integrated access etc. The information profession is relatively poorly served with the means to evaluate non-numeric measures of performance.

The techniques of audits

There is no single method of carrying out an audit. There is certainly no single algorithm into which all figures are plugged, and which produces a single answer as a result. What there is, is a range of techniques that can be used to develop an understanding of elements of the problem. Skill and professional judgement are required to supply the context.

There are three things that need to be understood as being in an interlinked relationship: the mission of the overall organisation; the objectives of the users in the area under consideration; and the information service in its widest sense (staff, stock, services, processes) as it applies to those users.

An idealised picture of the findings of an audit might look something like Figure 3.

In reality one or more of the circles is distorted at the expense of the others. There are several things that you are trying to spot in an audit:

- Area A shows the extent to which the information service interacts with external information resources. Does area (A) lie wholly within the circle defining the total organisation? (This can only be true if there is no interaction of this library with other organisations, through interlibrary loans or networking - an unusual and unhealthy situation.)
- Area B shows the extent to which users interact directly with external information resources. Does area (B) lie wholly within the circle defining the total organisation? (Possible, if it is an internal service function, but this needs to be understood.)

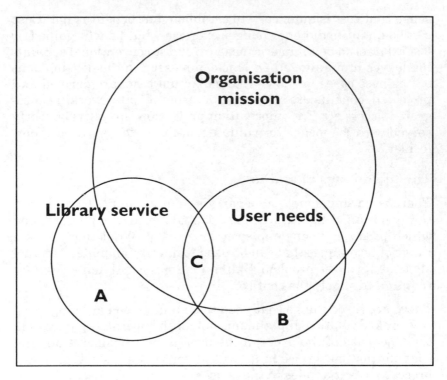

*Figure 3 - Inter-relationship of mission, needs
and information provision*

- If all information functions within the total organisation are plotted, is area (C) the same size as the circle of information services? It should be.

Situations may be found where one circle is bloated at the expense of the others; or where each circle overlaps only one other. In these circumstances there is something seriously wrong with either the analysis or the organisation (or both). Careful investigation will be required to verify the findings and the analysis.

Matrix analysis in an information audit

An information audit can use a version of matrix analysis to understand user needs, which are one of the main inputs to the audit. Provided they are expressed as kinds of information and not kinds of resources, they make an effective starting point.

An example of the application of this technique would be to plot, on the vertical axis of the matrix, the range of needs expressed by information users in a large organisation. The horizontal axis will be for the Divisions or locations in which the users work. A tick in a cell where location and need intersect show whether or not a particular service is required by anyone at that location. The needs are those established as the result of a needs analysis without any guidance as to what is or is not actually available.

In the same manner as with the earlier matrix examples, this one needs an alternative version, to show what the situation should be. Here a critical problem becomes apparent. The difference between what is and what should be indicates the extent to which information provision is seen by users as effective in having something to offer. The matrix will have some spaces where there should be ticks, and vice versa. If there are many empty cells then it will be presenting a picture of provision that is not geared to user needs. Thus the use of this particular baseline for an audit will show a very poor correlation between requirements and resources.

Resources available and needed

The second input to the audit process is the resources. As before there are two routes from which to choose: the resources actually available, and those that might be made available.

The process of analysing either of these routes is broadly similar. It is to map, or plot, the contents and means of delivery against the requirements. That is easily said, but not so easily done. In practice the outcome of the analysis is a series of subjective statements about needs and resources backed up with specific examples. This should not be surprising given the earlier statements about the differences between a financial audit and an information one.

The understanding of resources is a complicated area. Some of the complexity can best be illustrated by an example. In many organisations it is common to find several areas that have a critical requirement for parliamentary information. This may be limited to information on proceedings of the House of Commons, or to information on legislation and regulations. *Hansard, Justis Parliamentary* and the Chadwyck-Healey product are all obvious contenders, but each has particular strengths and weaknesses in terms of coverage. The means of technical delivery are also different. The information service can perhaps have just one of these to meet all levels and types of need. How can its suitability be related to user requirements? Part of the work of an audit would be to document conflicts like this and find a means of demonstrating them. In the case of parliamentary information this could be shown as a table. On one axis will be the list of requirements: statutory instruments, legislation in force, text of debates in the House, legislation in progress and so on. On the other axis will be the various competing resources. The cells in the table will be used to indicate whether each resource can answer each need. It is very likely that for complex resources such as those exemplified here, some of the needs will be partially met. If this is the case, a scoring system will be used to show the extent to which resources meet requirements.

The requirements, as expressed by users, may include technical matters such as delivery mechanisms. It is important to include these since a requirement to have searchable full-text of debates delivered to a workstation clearly cannot be met by the purchase of Hansard in printed form.

It is quite possible for an audit conducted along these lines to show that many resources provided are not at all suited to the key demands placed upon them.

Frequency and means of access as needs

The audit should reveal user requirements related to expected frequency of access to resources, the need for immediate or delayed access, and for how far back coverage is required. Different groups will have quite different 'packages' of requirements, and it will be necessary to analyse each in turn. The process of analysis will take data about the existing resources and establish how they match each individual criterion in turn. It may be necessary to use a scoring or ranking system to show the extent to which the resources meet each criterion.

It is very possible that each user group will have identified a specific (but different) need for the same resource, this is unlikely to be satisfied by the one and only offering of it that is provided. The uncomfortable outcome may be (in the example of parliamentary information) that all three products are required to meet the spread of needs. This presupposes that it has been established that the user needs have been found to fall within the organisation's statement of purpose. Obviously only requirements that are within that are evaluated.

A further example of this approach is the analysis that was carried out for a group of scientific laboratories. Each of 24 specialist databases available to the scientists to support their work was examined in turn. Through a series of interviews followed up by checklist questionnaires, over 100 of the scientists were asked about their needs for various types of information. Each type was to be scored, ranking its importance to the individual on a four-step scale from 'high' to 'low', frequency of requirement on a four-step scale from 'continually' to 'never', and delivery via self-service arrangements, or through an information intermediary.

The criteria used were currency (how up to date) and coverage (how extensive) to graph a rectangle that described each database. Over the graph was plotted another rectangle that showed importance against frequency, on the same scale. The result was 24 graphs demonstrating the extent to which what was provided met what was needed. The results were, for the most part, quite alarming. Need and provision, were about as different as could be contrived.

This approach worked very well for its particular circumstance, but the method might be suspect in other cases. This simply illustrates the point that the outcome of an information audit is the analysis of evidence, and not the end-product of a set of fixed techniques. An audit involves applying a range of techniques, the results of which will aid understanding. The audit is not in itself the understanding.

The audit in the planning process

An information audit is mostly qualitative and not quantitative. There are no simple numbers that say 'good' or 'bad': the outcome of the audit is an overall statement of how organisational information needs are perceived and met. Neither is the audit an end in itself. It should be the start of a further process of reviewing needs and service provision in order to bring them more in to line with each other.

The outcome of an audit can be to demonstrate a gap between the aspirations of management and the actuality of the business. How this is done will depend upon the nature of the organisation. One approach is to weight user requirements with factors indicating the extent to which each requirement is critical to the functioning of the organisation. If intelligently applied this approach can be used to show the short and medium-term effects of reductions in journal acquisition, provision of online services and similar activities which are often the targets of cost reduction.

An audit, built on a sound analysis of information needs, allows organisational efficiency and effectiveness to be set against capital and revenue costs.

The Subject Approach to Managing Information

Alan Gilchrist

INTRODUCTION

"On those remote pages it is written that animals are divided into (a) those that belong to the Emperor, (b) embalmed ones, (c) those that are trained, (d) suckling pigs, (e) mermaids, (f) fabulous ones, (g) stray dogs, (h) those that are included in this classification, (i) those that tremble as if they were mad, (j) innumerable ones, (k) those drawn with a very fine camel's hair brush, (l) others, (m) those that have just broken a flower vase, (n) those that resemble flies from a distance."

Thus the Argentinian author Borges, himself a librarian, in his essay *The Analytical Language of John Wilkins.* It epitomises well the problems faced by people in their attempts to arrange and describe what they know. These attempts have continued since the beginning of civilization; through Aristotle and Bacon, the 19th century architects of bibliographic classifications, and into the 20th century with the advent of computer-based information retrieval and more latterly the phenomenal burgeoning of the Internet. And yet, for all our ability to generate, replicate, store and transfer terabytes of binary code we are still faced with the problem of effectively and efficiently finding information in that welter of data; and of transmuting that information into knowledge. One cynic has described the Internet as a huge dark warehouse containing all the world's books to which the subscriber is given a key to the front door and a lighted candle. In time, matters are likely to improve as advances in natural language processing (NLP), artificial intelligence (AI) and neural networking are translated into the practical reality of commercially viable search engines and intelligent agents. Research scientists at London's Imperial College recently unveiled Magnus, a piece of electronic wizardry with an advanced ability to learn, such that it can link objects to their names, learning the meaning of words.[1] But even computers have to learn, and the intelligent agents referred to above will go through that process and become capable of analysing not only documents themselves but what man knows about those documents and has been recorded.

At a more mundane level, Milstead has defended the thesaurus (which will be discussed later in this chapter) against those who say it is dead technology by posing and answering a question:

"How will thesauri be used in the year 2000 and what will they look like?.... Their uses in information storage and retrieval will be quite different, as they are blended into systems of machine-aided indexing and text retrieval - systems in which the boundaries between the 'thesauri' and other semantic tools are vague, and which aid the user far more in defining the search than is commonly the case today."[2]

So, until such mentefacts as intelligent agents become ubiquitous, organisations around the world will continue to need to arrange physical items in useful sequences, manipulate their electronic surrogates in computers, and describe those items in natural language.

It is particularly difficult to pull together the apparently disparate threads in the area of information retrieval which seem to be opening up again in the late 1990s. And yet, there are perhaps some fundamentals which should not be overlooked either because they are visible in currently used and viable schemes, or because they might be deployed to good effect in some of the newer schemes which, it might be agreed, rely too much on the magic of technology.

This chapter, then, is largely about some of those fundamentals; and its title is chosen with care. It is not about information retrieval *per se*, or the building of databases and the use of specific software packages. Rather, it attempts to review some of the practicalities in order that readers may discern some pathways through the jungle. Two of the most basic fundamentals are proposed in the next two brief sections.

THE INDEXABLE ITEM

There was a time when the indexable item was predominantly the book and a book on, say, astronomy would be firmly placed on a shelf marked 'Astronomy' along with other books on the same subject. Nowadays, particularly with computerised records and electronic documents we must think of the indexable item as being any entity we wish to describe in order that we may be able to find it again. Consequently, indexable items will include documents (books, reports, patents, correspondence); artefacts (such as may be stored in museums or spare parts storerooms); pictures and videos; people (e.g. employees or customers); sound recordings; and websites. Furthermore, indexable items may be parts (e.g. chapters, committee decisions or collections of any of the above, yes, even parts of people - consider medical records); or collections of items and also surrogates of the above (e.g. bibliographic records, iconic representations etc.). This is now referred to in computing terms as 'granularity'.

An important aspect of this fact is that, with increasingly sophisticated client/server architecture, it is becoming possible to search through a range of databases with the same query in order to retrieve a set of answers relating to different media. For example, the recently amalgamated services of the British Broadcasting Corporation's Information and Library Archives facility is working on a front-end capability that will help users in just this way. A programme maker researching for a programme on BSE will be able to retrieve stills and videos, sound recordings and transcripts, background material; the names of politicians and scientists involved in the debate and what they said; the contract details concerning the commissioned programme and even (less directly) some appropriate background music.

What, whereof, where (and even wherefore)

In systems analysis, one often comes across a series of W words, Which, Why, Who etc. It is no different in information analysis where there are three important questions to be asked concerning an indexable item: What is it? What is it about? Where can one find it? The connected answers to these three questions are necessary and should be sufficient to support effective retrieval. To these three questions could be added a fourth: What is the purpose of the indexable item? It could be argued, in these days of full-text retrieval that the answers to these questions merge; but there may also be surrogates of the document held elsewhere as external pointers to that document or the document itself may be a surrogate of the original which the user may want to consult (where, for example, the text has been scanned into the system).

CATALOGUING

Traditionally, the task of describing what a document is has been that of cataloguers, who record the details of a document which can be extracted from what the document says about itself, such as author, date of publication, number of pages etc. Given the range of document types in the bibliographic domain, particularly with the arrival of multimedia, this is a complex and an important area of bibliographic control. Consequently, it has become increasingly formalised in the larger systems, particularly those employing MARC type formats. The formalisms used in such systems are laid down in the *Anglo-American Cataloguing Rules*[3]. Much progress is being made internationally in 'Universal Bibliographic Control', and a recent development has been the establishment of the Anglo-American Authority File [4] whereby the major bibliographic libraries in the UK, North America and Australia will share a common authority file to standardise on names. Interestingly, this will be extended to the control of allocated Library of Congress Subject Headings (see below). These facilities, together with Cataloguing in Publication (CIP) - the provision of cataloguing information printed in the document itself, i.e. prior to publication - provide useful information for many libraries, both in the public and private sectors.

The importance of descriptive cataloguing should not be overlooked in subject access, though the full records made possible by the AACR2 will not be appropriate for smaller collections. Indeed, it is possible to use AACR2 at different cut-off levels; and there is also a British Standard on minimal cataloguing [5]. Again, the technology has made all this so powerful and is still making advances as electronic documents become more common. Some of the suppliers of text retrieval software, for example, support searching on variable fields within the document identified by a Standardised General Mark-up Language (SGML). Another area of development, very akin to the cataloguing task is in the standardisation of metadata formats [6]. Metadata is data about data, but unlike the conventional catalogue card may, like SGML, be embedded in the electronic document itself.

Purpose and design

Vickery[7] enunciated the purposes of retrieval languages over 25 years ago and they need very little modification. In edited summary, he said they may:

- Provide for the selection of items on the basis of the existence of character strings
- Provide for the selection of a set of items likely to be relevant to a particular topic - the function of specific reference
- Provide for the selection of a group of items lying within a certain subject field - the function of generic survey
- Provide for the sequencing of a set of selected records according to probable relevance to a particular topic - by means of some ranking device
- Provide for the ordering of a group of items into a meaningful sequence
- Give aid to searchers in their choice of search terms - the function of thesauri.

Nowadays, retrieval systems may be able to provide all or most of the above within one package, supported in different ways by the retrieval language elements provided.

The retrieval system designer should also consider the system parameters before setting out to build the system and procure equipment. Such parameters will include, for example:

- Subject field or fields covered
- Type of material to be stored for access; full text or records
- Quantity of material
- Language aspects
- The users; direct access or through intermediaries
- Available system resources
- Hardware and software.

Performance

Closely associated with purpose and design is consideration of the required performance of the system and this will have a direct impact on the choice or design of retrieval language. Possibly the criterion which comes readily to most people's minds is 'response time', normally regarded as the time the system takes to respond to a keyed-in query. In fact, the response time can also be regarded as the whole of the time taken from the formulation of a request by the searcher to the point of satisfaction; and this is clearly related to the efficacy with which the retrieval language facilities support the searcher, including such aspects as the explicit logic of the language, the ease of selection and manipulation of the search terms, and of search strategy modification.

However, the two criteria of most significance are recall and precision, first proposed by the Cranfield Project almost 40 years ago[8]. These are:

- Recall: the ratio of relevant items retrieved to the relevant items not retrieved
- Precision: the ratio of relevant items retrieved to the irrelevant items retrieved

Here, the efficacy of the retrieval language can be of paramount importance, and it will be seen later in this chapter how different aspects of the language can be used to affect recall or precision, the two having, in broad terms, some inverse relationship. It is worth noting that in most online systems (i.e. those using iterative interrogation) increasing precision is very obvious to the searcher, but the recall ratio may be impossible to judge.

CLASSIFICATION

The discussion of classification seems to have produced more heat amongst librarians in the past than any other, but the arguments now seem to have diminished, for two main reasons:

- The supremacy of the Dewey Decimal Classification, and to a lesser extent the Library of Congress Classification
- The almost exclusive use of word based systems in searching online systems.

However, classification remains a natural and necessary technique, is still being developed in formal systems, and can be seen in many manual filing systems and as providing the structure of many of the more explicitly logical thesauri.

The purpose of classification is quite simply to bring together those things which are alike, and to separate those which are not. As such it is one of the most basic logics we possess in learning, understanding and arranging our world.

Enumerative classification

The first great bibliographic classifications were enumerative in that they divided the universe of knowledge into a number of categories and then by successive division, listed all the subordinate topics. It was important to try to ensure that each class so created was comprehensive in that it contained all the possible members (even though in practice one member might often be 'Other...') and also that each class was mutually exclusive. In practice, such classifications have two major drawbacks. The first is that, being bound to a notation which 'locks' members of classes into their hierarchies, it is impossible to predict subject explosions such as have happened with computers and polymers. Additionally, because of the process of hierarchical division and the order in which the divisions are effected often being unhelpful, even seemingly arbitrary to at least some users, the schemes were found to be inflexible. Anybody who has grappled with somebody else's filing system (in a filing cabinet or a PC) will be aware of these problems, as most are built in this way.

Analytico-synthetic or faceted classification

A significant advance was made in bibliographic classification when it was realised that it was the 'characteristic of division' that was most important in the construction of classification schemes and that schemes would be far more flexible and hospitable to new concepts if they were arranged in this way. Simply put: instead of dividing, say, literature first by form, then period, then language as might be done in an enumerative scheme; the characteristics form, period and language were used as it were in parallel. Hence the expression analytico-synthetic whereby a subject domain can be analysed into its constituent concepts so that they can be synthesised in such a way as to define more complex topics. Note that complex hierarchies are still perfectly containable within facets. Figure 1 shows an extract from the *ROOT Thesaurus* of the British Standards Institution.[9] It is from the classified display and shows the concept 'Threaded fasteners' which fits into a hierarchy of 'Fasteners' and 'Mechanical components' within the main category of 'Mechanical engineering'. It can be seen that 'Threaded fasteners' are further divided (*By thread position*) into 'Internal-thread fasteners' and 'External-thread fasteners', and the former divided again by the characteristics of configuration, purpose and head shape. In this last instance, it is

N   Mechanical engineering

NR/ NX	**Mechanical components** (continued)
NWF/ NWY	**Fasteners** (continued)
NWG/ NWI	**Threadless fasteners** (continued)
NWI	Nails (continued)
NWI.F	Wire nails (continued)
NWI.FF	Pins (nails) (continued)
NWI.FFP	Panel pins
NWI.FT	Sprigs
NWI.I	Cut nails
NWI.ID	Cut floor brads
	=Brads
	=Floor brads
NWI.IN	Clasp nails
	=Cut clasp nails
NWI.L	Annular nails
NWI.N	Drive screws
	=Helically-threaded nails
NWI.NW	Twisted-shank nails
NWI.R	Staples (nails)
NWI.W	Clout nails
	=Slate nails
NWI.WI	Tacks
NWJ/NWM	**Threaded fasteners**
	*<Threaded components NWB/NWD
	*-Threads NWC/NWD
	(By thread position)
NWK	Internal-thread fasteners
NWK.K	Sockets (threaded)
NWK.N	Nuts
	*-Locknuts NWM.CC
NWK.NC	Wing nuts
NWK.NE	Cap nuts
	=Cover nuts
	=Dome nuts
NWK.NG	Anchor nuts
	=Floating nuts
	=Press nuts
NWK.NJ	Tee nuts
	(By configuration)
NWK.NN	Flanged nuts
	Flanges NKT/ NKU
	(By purpose)
NWK.NS	Special purpose nuts
	(By head shape)
	(Synthesize, for example)
NWK.NW	**Hexagonal nuts
	-Nuts NWK.N
	+Hexagonal-head fasteners NWR.B
NWL	External-thread fasteners
NWL.B	Bolts
	*>Rock bolts RIY.IF
NWL.BB	Load-indicating bolts
NWL.BD	Foundation bolts
	=Rag bolts
NWL.BH	Friction-grip bolts
NWL.BJ	Double-ended bolts
NWL.BL	Shrouded bolts
NWL.BN	Banjo bolts
	=Hollow bolts
NWL.BP	Anchor bolts

Figure 1 – Extract from the ROOT *Thesaurus
of the British Standards Institution*

not necessary to re-enumerate all the possible shapes as these are listed elsewhere.

This advance was so significant that the Dewey Decimal Classification is increasingly introducing facet analysis into its revision work; and the same technique is often used *ab initio* in the construction of thesauri. It is also clearly more conducive to computer manipulation.

When facet analysis was introduced to the UK in the years after World War 2, it evinced much interest and activity, particularly amongst members of the Classification Research Group. (See, for example [10, 11, 12, 13, 14, 15]). One major tangible outcome was the ongoing second edition of the Bliss Bibliographic Classification (see below) while another, more abstract, was the concept of fundamental categories. Vickery, by analysis of a number of special schemes, showed that all were based on a set or subset of categories which could be expressed in a general way. [15] This approach has been found to be most helpful by subsequent compilers of classification schemes and thesauri. A later version, taken from Aitchison and Gilchrist[16] is illustrated at Figure 2. As can be seen, the list is itself a classification into Entities, Actions, Space and Time but any of the classes or sub-classes might be given more prominence and the list adapted appropriately to the situation and purpose.

Notation

Within classification debates, notation also attracted much heated attention. Nowadays, with computer processing and online retrieval it also has diminished somewhat in importance. Obviously, the fundamental purpose was to reflect the structure of the classification so that books could be arranged logically on shelves and catalogue cards in drawers.

With the advent of computers it was thought that coding (i.e. notation) would become more significant but in practice it was found that bibliographic classification was too cumbersome to be efficient in early computers and the idea was speedily overtaken by the manipulation of keywords (the birth of the thesaurus).

More recently, there has been some revival of interest because of the increasingly faceted nature of modern classification schemes and their gradual 'thesaurification'. The notation is thus more capable of reflecting the structure of the scheme within compu-

Entities (things, objects)
    (Abstract/ concrete)
    Abstract entities
    Concrete entities
        Naturally occurring substances
        Artefacts (man-made)

    (By function)
    Agents (Performers of action - inanimate and animate)
    Patients (Recipients of action - inanimate and animate)
    End-products

    (By characteristics)
    Properties
    Materials, constituent substances
    Parts
    Whole entities
    Complex entities

Actions
    Processes (internal processes, intransitive actions)
    Operations (external, transitive actions)
    Complex actions

Space

Time

In addition, Kinds or Types; Systems and Assemblies; Applications and Purposes of the above categories.

Figure 2 - General subject headings for a classification scheme

terised systems[17]. One useful aspect of notation remains and this is the fact that it is language-independent; a fundamental of the original Universal Decimal Classification. More recently it can be seen to be of obvious importance in such schemes as the Combined Nomenclature - the commodities classification scheme used by many of the world's customs authorities.

UNIVERSAL CLASSIFICATION SYSTEMS

Dewey Decimal Classification

The *Dewey Decimal Classification* system, first published in 1876 and now in its 21st edition, is the most widely used in the world [18]. It has become a *de facto* standard for the major bibliographic systems because of its promulgation through the MARC systems of the world. Because of this, and coming latterly into the ownership of the Online Computer Library Center (OCLC) it is now vigorously overcoming three fundamental deficiencies:

- Its enumerative nature
- Being confined, unnaturally, to nine major categories
- Its Anglo-American bias.

These are being tackled by facet analysis and the wholesale revision of complete schedules. The recent appearance of DDC21 on a CD-ROM running under Windows will do much to enhance its reputation and usability.

Universal Decimal Classification

The *Universal Decimal Classification* (UDC) was derived from the 5th edition of Dewey in 1905 with the express purpose of arranging a 'universal index on recorded knowledge', which itself did not survive. However, the classification did, and was particularly intent on elaborating the schedules dealing with science and technology which made it popular with special libraries where it was very widely used in Europe, particularly in the old USSR. and the Eastern European countries.

Latterly, partly because of its over elaborate international revision committee structure and partly because of the dominance of Dewey, the scheme has somewhat fallen into decline though revisions continue to appear, mainly in English[19] but also in French, Spanish, Dutch, Japanese and a number of other languages.

At its prime, it was a most elaborate scheme, having many more classes than Dewey and being available in many languages. The original plans to establish a truly multilingual system based on a common notation was never fully realised, though an electronic master file is now available from the UDC Consortium at its offices in The Hague. The Consortium was set up following the relinquishing of control by the Fédération Internationale de l'Information et Documentation (FID), and comprises five major UDC publishers and FID itself.

Other promising signs are to be found in the work of Riesthuis[20] who has worked on the automated thesaurisation of UDC schedules, and of Williamson[21], who has shown how the UDC could adopt and adapt the Bliss Classification revision work.

Library of Congress Classification

This classification was established for the Library of Congress between 1899 and 1920 specifically for its own collection, though it has since been adopted by many university libraries. It is enumerative and, being highly specific, is somewhat unwieldy. There are 21 main classes, each with its own index. The only way of accessing the entirety is thus through the Library of Congress Subject Headings, which by definition is closely related to the Classification.

Bliss Bibliographic Classification

The first edition of the *Bibliographic Classification* appeared in several volumes between 1940 and 1955. The second edition, edited by Jack Mills and Vanda Broughton has been appearing as separate main classes since 1977[22]. The second edition is highly faceted, and though not widely used, is an important source of subject analysis which has been used in the creation of, for example, structured thesauri[23].

SUBJECT HEADINGS LISTS

Most classifications require a natural language entry point. Originally, alphabetically arranged subject headings, enriched by cross references, would guide the reader to the appropriate shelves. It was Dewey who introduced the idea of the relative index so that books could be shelved in the order suggested by the classification's notation. Then, alphabetical subject headings lists were derived from the main classifications; and today, the best known is the *Library of Congress Subject Headings* (LCSH), now in its 19th edition[24]. Along with Dewey this has become a *de facto* standard for bibliographic control in the Anglo-American and other national systems. It is in a permanent state of revision with candidate terms being offered continuously by a large number of collaborating libraries. It is becoming increasingly thesaurised and thus more flexible in synthesis.

THESAURI

The name Roget is most closely associated with the thesaurus. This device, originally created in 1736 is used by writers everywhere to recall the word that is wanted but has slipped from mind;

but it is often forgotten that the 'synonym clusters' are based on a clever classification of abstract concepts (see Figure 3).

Index

Soliloquy *soliloquy* 585n.
　　　dramaturgy 494n.
solitaire *card game* 832n
　　　gem 844n
solitary
　　　uncomformable 84adj.
monological
　　　alone 88adj.
oneself, say to
　　　wanderer 268n.
　　　solitary 883n.
　　　friendless 883n.
　　　unsociable 883adj.
solitude *unity* 88n.
　　　desert 127n.
　　　seclusion 883n.

Text

585 Soliloquy
N. *soliloquy*, soliloquium, monologue,
　　　monody; apostrophe; aside
soliloquist, soliloquizer, monologist,
　　　monodist
Adj. *Soliloquizing* etc. vb.;

Vb. *Soliloquize*, talk to

oneself, say aside, think aloud;
apsostrophize, pray to, pray
aloud; answer one's own
questions, be one's own inter-
locutor; talk to the four walls,
address an empty house, have
oneself for audience.

*(Reproduced from Roget's Thesaurus of English Words and Phrases
by kind permission of the Longman Group)*

Figure 3 - Example from Roget's Thesaurus

More recently, and spurred by the advent of the computer, a new type of thesaurus was created for the purposes of indexing the scientific and technical literature. One of the first major thesauri was compiled by the American Institute of Chemical Engineers in 1961, but the one that possibly had the widest early influence was that created by the American Engineers Joint Council in 1964[25], (with a later edition produced by the US Department of Defense). This huge work, consisting of some 17,800 terms, a further 5,550 entry terms leading to the preferred terms and involving a complex network of relationships contained over 162,000 line entries. Thirty years later, it still provides a model for probably the most popular thesaurus format. The EJC Thesaurus was a controlled vocabulary; that is to say, a set of prescribed (and proscribed) terms that both document analysts and searchers were obliged to use in order to match search statements put to the system at the query stage with sets of terms assigned at the indexing stage.

More recently still, with the advent of full text systems, end user searching and often the elimination of controlled indexing, there has been a reversion to the Roget approach in the construction of search thesauri or the utilisation of semantic tools. Thus, some software packages provide the facility for the automatic invocation of synonyms (sometimes referred to as a thesaurus facility);

Preschool education
- **MT**   1.30 Educational systems and levels
  - **FR** *Education prescolaire*
  - **SP** *Educacion preescolar*
- **SN**   Education in nursery schools or kindergarten up to the age of five
- **BT1**   **Educational levels**
- NT1   Child rearing
- NT1   Early childhood education
- NT1   Preprimary education
- RT   Nursery schools

Preschool pupils
- **USE**   **Preschool children** (1.55)

Presentation:
- **Cultural property presentation** (3.10)
- **Statistics presentation** (2.15)

Preservation:
- **Archive records preservation** (5.35)
- *Book preservation*
  - **USE Document preservation** (3.10)
- **Cultural property preservation** (3.10)
- **Document preservation** (3.10)
- **Food preservation** (6.35)
- *Historic cites preservation*
  - **USE Preservation of monuments** (3.10)
- *Historic monuments preservation*
  - **USE Preservation of monuments** (3.10)
- *Historic sites preservation*
  - **USE Preservation of monuments** (3.10)

Preservation of monuments
- **MT**   3.10 Cultural policy and planning
  - **FR** *Conservation des monuments*
  - **SP** *Conservacion de monumentos*
- **UF**   *Historic cities preservation*
- **UF**   Historic monument preservation
- **UF**   *Historic sites preservation*
- **BTI**   **Cultural property preservation**
- RT   Archaeology
- RT   Architect restorers
- RT   Architecture
- RT   Buildings
- RT   Historic cities
- RT   Historic monuments
- RT   Preservation of works of art
- RT   Restoration
- RT   Urban planning

Figure 4 - Alphabetical listing of thesaurus headings

1.30 Educational systems and levels

Educational levels
NT1 Higher education
   UF Postsecondary education
   UF Tertiary education
   UF Third stage education
   UF University education
NT1 **Preschool education**
  NT2 **Child rearing**
    UF Upbringing
  NT2 **Early childhood education**
    UF Infant education
  NT2 **Preprimary education**
    UF Kindergarten
NT1 **Primary education**
   UF Elementary education
NT1 **Secondary education**
  NT2 **Lower secondary education**
    UF Intermediate education
  NT2 **Upper secondary education**
    UF Sixth forms

Educational systems

  UF National educational systems
NT1 **Adult education**
   UF Polyvalent adult education
  NT2 **Consumer education**
  NT2 Parent education
  NT2 Workers education
NT1 Mass education
NT1 Private education
   UF Fee paying schools
   UF Independent schools
   UF Private schools
NT1 **Public education**
   UF Public schools
   UF State education
   UF State schools
NT1 **Traditional education**
  NT2 Islamic education
NT1 'Womens education
  NT2 Girls education
    UF Girls enrolment

Extension education
  UF Educational extension

NT1 **University extension**
   UF Extramural teaching
Formal education
   UF School systems
NT1 **Basic education**
   UF Fundamental education
NT1 **Coeducation**
NT1 Compensatory education
NT1 **Correctional education**
   UF Prison education
NT1 **General education**
   UF General Studies
NT1 **Migrant education**
   UF Migrant child education
   UF Nomad education
  NT2 **Refugee education**
NT1 **Mobile educational services**
   UF Mobile classrooms
   UF Mobile schools
NT1 **Outdoor education**
NT1 Part time education
   UF Part time courses
NT1 **Rural education**
NT1 Special education
   UF Handicapped education
  NT2 **Education of the blind**
  NT2 Education of the deaf
NT1 Technical and vocational education
NT1 Urban education

Nonformal education
NT1 Community education
   UF Social education
NT1 **Family education**
  NT2 Home education
    UF Home instruction
NT1 **Lifelong education**
   UF Continuing education
   UF Continuous learning
   UF Permanent education
  NT2 **Informal education**
    UF Informal learning
  NT2 **Recurrent education**
NT1   Out of school education
   UF Parallel schooling

Figure 5 - Heirarchical listing of subject classifications

Flammable materials TLS
= Inflammable materials
< Materials by property and purpose
*- Fire risks GOC
*- Flammability DED.Q

Flange facings NKU.X
> Full-faced flanges
- Flanges
- Flat-face flanges
- Raised-face flanges

Flange bobbins WPL.L
< Bobbins

Flanged connections
= Flanged fittings NKS/ NKV

Flanged fittings NKS/ NKV
= Flanged connections
= Flanged unions
< Pipe fittings
> Bolting
- Flanges

Flanged nuts NWK.NN
< Nuts
*- Flanges NKT/ NKU

Flanged pipelines
Cast-iron pipelines NLC.C

Flanged unions
Flanged fittings NKS/ NKV

Flanges NKT/ NKU
= Pipe flanges
> Backing flanges
> Blank flanges
> Bossed flanges
> Clamping flanges
> Connecting flanges
> Detachable flanges
> Hub-type flanges
> Integral flanges
> Lapped flanges
> Loose flanges

> Neck flanges
> Plain flanges
> Rotating flanges
> Safety flanges
> Screwed flanges
> Slip-on flanges
> Socket flanges
> Welded flanges
- Flange facings
- Flanged fittings
*- Flanged nuts NWK.NN
*- Rigid couplings NQQ.CK

Flanges NKT/ NKU
+ Elliptical shape ATE.SF
=** Oval flanges NKU.U

Flanges NKT/ NKU
+ Steels UN/ UP
=** Steel flanges NKT.R

Flannel WMJ.D
< Woven fabrics

Flannelette WMJ.E
< Woven fabrics

Flap valves
- Check valves NJQ.X

Flare stacks ROB.C
< Chimneys

Flares GVJ.JP
< Alarm systems
*- Marine signalling devices QFM

Flash apparatus
- Flash equipment LQG.F

Flash equipment LQG.F
= Flash apparatus
< Photographic lighting equipment
> Electronic flash equipment
> Photo-flash lamps

Flash guide numbers LPX
- Photography

Figure 6 - The alphabetical sequence

some provide a complete Roget-type thesaurus for consultation; while others are loading complete dictionaries and glossaries, some of which are integrated into the retrieval process so that queries are automatically expanded.

Thesaurus elements

The elements of a thesaurus consist of preferred terms or descriptors, which may consist of one or more words; and non-preferred terms, lead-in terms or non-descriptors which are referred to the preferred terms. The reciprocal relationship between preferred and non-preferred terms is usually indicated by the symbols USE/UF (i.e. USE/Used For). Other relationships are normally confined to the hierarchical: Broader Term/Narrower Term (BT/NT); and the associative Related Term (RT/RT). Again, these relationships are reciprocal. There may also be included, where useful, Scope Notes (SN) which add guidance on the meaning, scope and use of certain terms.

It was mentioned above that the two most useful measures of retrieval performance are recall and precision, and a range of devices in the indexing language are designed to affect these two measures; the most common of which are shown below

Recall devices

- Control of word form (word order, grammar, number etc.)
- Identification of synonyms and near-synonyms
- Hierarchical relationships (allowing searching to be broadened)
- Associative relationships (allowing searching to be extended).

Precision devices

- Specificity of the indexing language
- Coordination
  - Pre-coordination (compound terms)
    Post-coordination (combination of terms in searching)
- Hierarchical relationships (allowing searching to be narrowed)
- Identification of homographs (words with more than one meaning).

Thesaurus structure and display

Broadly speaking, there are three major types of thesaurus, from the point of view of their structure and corresponding display.

EJC type

The principal display in this type is the alphabetical sequence, which lists the preferred and non-preferred terms, together with their hierarchical and associative relationships. Figure 4, taken from the recently revised second edition of the *UNESCO Thesaurus* [26] also includes a permuted index of compound terms, normally displayed separately (see the entry in the Figure under 'Presentation').

This type of thesaurus is also often supported by a loose classification of the terms, used without a complete notation and solely for the purpose of providing an overview of the subject domains included in the whole work. Figure 5, also taken from the UNESCO Thesaurus, shows a category headed '1.30 Educational systems' and a number of levels, in which can be found 'Prescribed education' the first entry in Figure 4.

Note also from Figure 4 that French and Spanish equivalents are shown; and these are also listed in their own alphabetical sequences showing only the equivalents in the other two languages.

Thesaurofacet type

This was the creation of Jean Aitchison and her team at the former English Electric Company in the UK, representing a significant development in thesaurus compilation [28]. Influenced by the work of those referred to above in the use of analytico-synthetic classification techniques, Aitchison brought together the faceted classification and the thesaurus in a one-to-one correspondence. Here, the systematic display is the dominant feature from which the indexer and searcher alike can quickly gain a view of the structure, scope and logic of the scheme; the alphabetical sequence providing an index to the schedules. Figure 1, taken from BSI's *ROOT Thesaurus* [9] shows part of the faceted classification. Figure 6 shows part of the alphabetical sequence, from which it can be seen that 'Flanged nuts' is a narrower term to 'Nuts' (indicated by the language-independent symbol <) and related to 'Flanges' (indicated by *- , where the asterisk denotes that the relationship straddles two hierarchical chains).

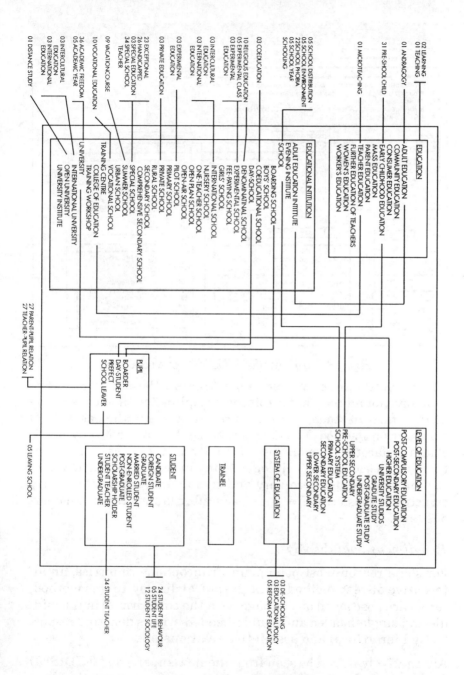

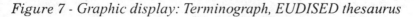

Figure 7 - Graphic display: Terminograph, EUDISED thesaurus

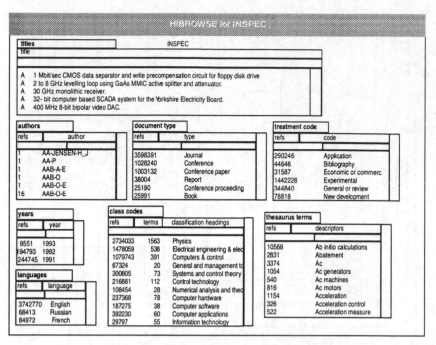

Figure 8 - HIBROWSE for INSPEC top level screen

Unfortunately, many people embarking on thesaurus construction have found the Thesaurofacet discipline too time-consuming at the start-up stage; and have preferred to use the easier EJC compilation method. This is regrettable, because not only is the Thesaurofacet style more 'user-friendly' but it is easier to maintain, because of its explicit logic. Many practitioners have found, to their cost, that a necessary and complete overhaul of a poorly structured thesaurus five years, say, after launch can be an onerous task.

Two-dimensional display

For some reason most popular in Francophone countries, an alternative display method is the graphical display. In this method, terms are positioned on the page with the core term(s) in the middle and single-headed and double-headed arrows denoting respectively hierarchical and associative relationships.

Alternatively, as can be seen from the now superseded EUDISED Thesaurus[27], clusters of terms are displayed showing relationships within the graph as well as outside to terms found in other graphs (see Figure 7).

Computer displays

In principle, any of the above three displays can be replicated on a computer screen. In practice, the EJC alphabetical is probably the most common, and the one adopted by several of the suppliers of thesaurus management software. Others use the *de facto* file management format, wherein clicking on a file (representing a descriptor) will open up the next hierarchical level.

Pollitt [29] has demonstrated operational systems wherein descriptors, other key words, and supporting information such as frequency of occurrence are presented in the form of pick lists.

This approach is based on the justifiable belief that people find it easier to select words than to have to remember them. Figure 8 shows an example of such a display produced for the INSPEC database.

The possibility of displaying semantic maps on the screen in two and even three dimensions has attracted much interest but the size of the normal computer screen is a deterrent, so that at present most displays are linked to simple tree structures.

Construction

There are several works available which deal with indexing languages and their construction.[16, 30, 31, 32, 33, 34]

The major steps are:

Subject field definition: in which the core and fringe areas are identified within the overall boundary

Selection of concepts and terms: by the scanning of published material including classification schemes and thesauri, dictionaries and glossaries, and other printed sources rich in terminology and definitions. Also useful is the analysis of questions put to the system as these should reflect the language of the users. A standard technique is to 'free index' a representative sample of material in the database allocating candidate terms to the broad initial categories. It is important to be able to identify the concepts underlying the words, because meaning exists only at that level. To give an obvious example: a rubber bone is not a bone.

Imposition of structure: where the most rigorous and productive technique is facet analysis, discussed above. Once the terms collected have been sorted into broad categories so that an outline or skeletal structure has been created, the terms can be further analysed into facets relating to their characteristics (as illustrated in Figure 1).

In thesaurus terms, hierarchical relationships should be either genus/species, whole/part or instance (e.g. Indian Ocean as an instance of an ocean). Associative relationships are somewhat harder to define, but it is here that the facet analysis will help. Equivalence relationships will include both true synonyms, and near synonyms, where for the purposes of retrieval it is not useful to draw a distinction between two or more terms, or where one is so specific that it can be subsumed under its generic term with no loss in performance.

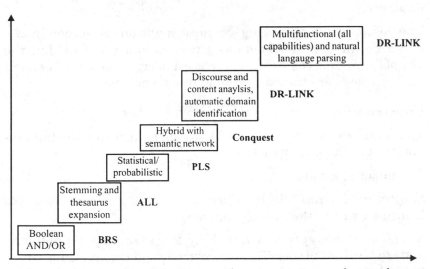

Advancing components and systems with representative product in class

Figure 9 – Progression of technical features over time

Word form control: whereby nouns are preferred as descriptors and adjectives and adverbs are proscribed unless part of compound terms; plurals are preferred to singulars where the objects referred to are countable; direct entry is preferred to indirect.

Precoordination level : which is perhaps the most contentious aspect of thesaurus compilation. The *ISO Standard* [34] states that a descriptor should represent a 'unit concept', but this is often not easy to do in practice, and a pragmatic approach may be preferable. If users favour a compound term which is not strictly a unit concept, then this should be taken into account; for example the term 'doctor-patient communication'.

NEW PARADIGMS

The preceding sections discussed the subject approach within the context of intermediation where the librarian or information scientist has total or partial control over indexing and the interpretation of the indexing language, if not its compilation. However, for years, researchers, notably the late Gerard Salton, have been investigating automated processes based on the use of such techniques as artificial intelligence (AI) and natural language processing (NLP). A basic assumption behind such research is that the database itself contains all the information needed for automatic analysis to be able to support retrieval, undertake automatic indexing and abstracting, generate a database-specific thesaurus, or extract information according to defined parameters.

Statistical analysis of the co-occurrence of words in a text have been shown to be extremely effective "either to rank documents based on their similarity to the query or on an estimate of the probability of their relevance to the query, where both query and document are treated as collections of numerically weighted terms." [35]

Linguistic analysis covers a range of techniques from word stemming to disambiguation based on semantic and syntactic analysis of the document.

The emerging technology will combine these techniques to create 'vector space indices'; wherein "the data generated by these algorithms are analysed and mapped onto an imaginary hypercube where each concept or information element is given a weight and a direction. The resulting index structure has a number of remarkable properties that can be exploited when a user wants to extract information from the domain of information." [36]

The goal behind all this work is to emulate the way in which humans process text. It has been shown by scientists in the field of psycholinguistics that this is done on at least six levels:

"Morphological: (the word bits, elephant vs. elephants, legal vs. illegal etc.)

Lexical (the word forms themselves)

Semantic (various meanings associated with the word or phrase)

Syntactic (the ordering, US invades Panama, vs. Panama invades the US)

Discourse (all the material we derive above the word and sentence level such as the referral further on in an article to information provided at the beginning; and on the difference between definitive information related to the past, and predictions and expectations in the future)

Pragmatic (that which we know, above the text; if you say the third world, or NATO countries, I know what you mean; this is world knowledge, expected from others with whom you are communicating.")[37]

Figure 9 gives one view of the advance of retrieval techniques [37]. In practice, though some software products are beginning to emerge with the most advanced capabilities shown in Figure 9, their application still needs very significant computer power involving parallel processing. However, there are now many software packages that employ a certain amount of statistical analysis, natural language processing, semantic network support and relevance ranking.

A number of search engines has also been developed for use on the Internet. Typically, such Internet agents will first define a Webspace (e.g. any documents in the HTTP space, the FTP space or the Gopher space, i.e. sites using one of these protocols). They will then extract the most information rich parts of each document (e.g. title, headings and subheadings, first 20 lines and the 100 most important words - this last being derived from a weighting algorithm which considers word placement and frequencies among other factors) [38]. Many of the commercial Internet providers give access to a number of different search agents.

EVALUATION

It was the Cranfield experiments in the late 1950s [8] that set the benchmark for the testing and evaluation of indexing languages and measures of recall and precision are still used. A descendant of Cranfield is to be found in the series of Text REtrieval Conferences (TREC) [39, 40]. In practice, TREC is a shared resource, funded by the US Government which allows anybody who wishes to join the club to test their retrieval packages or functionalities against a large common corpus of documents and a test set of queries. Though individual packages are ranked, the main interest is in the general findings from TREC which seem to favour statistical techniques in relation to full text document retrieval; and the helpfulness of relevance feedback. However, one of the principal participants in TREC has said:

"Although these tests are on a larger scale then earlier tests, they still involve limitations. More importantly, it is too easy in DR [Document Retrieval], and hence in TR [Text Retrieval], to intuit wrongly that things do or will work well, whether these are old approaches, old approaches dressed up in shiny modern technological guises, or truly new approaches. It is essential to test, test and test again." [35]

In Internet searching, it is acknowledged that recall is not a problem, but that precision is often very poor; and this situation is greater exacerbated the greater the recall. Consequently, in the construction of intranets it is becoming attractive to use a combination of Internet agents to achieve high recall and subsequently a tailored database search engine to improve precision.

CONCLUSIONS

The evolution of indexing languages and their application has moved from the physical arrangement of physical items and their surrogates, through content analysis, assignment of descriptors and manipulation of search keys, to the automated processing of full text. However, it is in the nature of evolution that different phases can coexist for considerable periods of time. Libraries will continue for the foreseeable future to arrange their books by classification schemes first devised in the 19th century but continuously revised. Other document collections will continue to be indexed and/or searched with the aid of thesauri and semantic networks. Meanwhile, rapid developments will continue to be made in automated text processing and as integrated advanced packages approach maturity, some of the functionalities will be assimilated by other (probably smaller) niche supliers of text retrieval software.

The problem facing today's information manager lies in how best to orchestrate some selection of these techniques in his or her information systems. It is likely that some, or even most of the techniques discussed above will be used either separately, or in combination. What is certain is that information retrieval is concerned with what is, somewhat misleadingly, referred to as 'natural language', and that its manipulation still involves as much art as science in application. The paper cited above [37], which looks into the future (already here of massive computer power and advanced text processing techniques) also has this to say:

"Unfortunately, we also see short-sighted efforts to eliminate the experienced search intermediary from some organisations, a loss whose long-term implications can be severe, but difficult to measure."

The most effective information systems, then, are likely to be those that combine the best of human skills with the best use of computers, and which use the most appropriate mix in content analytical processes.

REFERENCES

1. Scientists offer computer with mind of its own, *Guardian*, 17.12.96, p.4.

2. Milstead, Jessica L. Invisible thesauri : the year 2000, *Online & CD-ROM Review*, **19** (2) 1995, 93-94.

3. Gorman, Michael and Winkler, Paul W. (eds) *Anglo-American cataloguing rules*. Library Association and American Library Association, London and Chicago (2nd edition).

4. Danskin, Alan. The Anglo-American Authority File: an idea whose time has come? *ICBC,* **25** (3) July/September 1996, 57-59.

5. British Standards Institution. BS 5605: 1990 Recommendations for citing and referencing published material.

6. Heery, Rachel. Review of metadata formats, *Program,* **30** (4) October 1996, 345-373.

7. Vickery, B.C. Structure and function in retrieval languages, *Journal of Documentation*, **27** (2) June 1971, 69-82.

8. Cleverdon, C.W. and Mills, J. Testing of index language devices, *Aslib Proceedings,* **15** (4) April 1963, 106-130

9. British Standards Institution. *ROOT Thesaurus,* 2 vols, BSI, Milton Keynes (1985, 2nd edition).

10. Classification Research Group. The need for a faceted classification as the basis of all methods of information retrieval, *Library Association Record*, July 1955, 262-268

11. Foskett, A.C. *The subject approach to information*, Bingley, London (1996, 5th edition).

12. Maltby, A. Faceted classification. *In*: Bakewell, K.G.B. *Classification for information retrieval,* Bingley, London, (1968).

13. Foskett, D.J. *Classification and indexing in the social sciences,* Butterworth, London (1974, 2nd edition).

14. Vickery, B.C. *Classification and indexing in science,* Butterworth, London (1975, 3rd ed).

15. Vickery, B.C. *Faceted classification. A guide to the construction and use of special schemes,* Aslib, London (1960).

16. Aitchison, J. ,Gilchrist, A. and Bawden, D. *Thesaurus construction: a practical manual,* (3rd edition in preparation), Aslib, London.

17. Drabenstott, Karen Markey. Experience with online catalogs in the USA using a classification scheme as a subject searching tool. *In*: Fugmann, Robert. *Tools for knowledge organization and the human interface*, Indeks Verlag, Frankfurt Main (1990).

18. Mitchell, Joan S. *et al* (eds) *Dewey Decimal Classification and Relative Index,* 4 vols, Forest Press, Albany, New York (1996, 21st edition).

19. British Standards Institution. *Universal Decimal Classification*, English text, Parts I and II, BS1000M, BSI, Milton Keynes (1985-88, International Medium Edition).

20. Riesthuis, G. Thesaurification of the UDC. *In*: Gilchrist, A. and Strachan, D. *UDC: Essays for a new decade,* pp. 85-97, Aslib, London (1990).

21. Williamson, N. Restructuring UDC: problems and possibilities. *In*: Williamson N. and Hudon, M. (eds) *Classification research for knowledge representation and organisation. Proceedings of the 5th International Study Conference on Classification Research, 1991*, Elsevier, Amsterdam (1992).

22. Mills, J. and Broughton, V. *Bliss Bibliographic Classification*, Butterworth, London (1977, 2nd edition).

23. Aitchison, J. Bliss and the thesaurus: the Bibliographic Classification of H.E. Bliss as a source of thesaurus terms and structure, *Journal of Documentation*, **42** (3) September 1986, 160-181.

24. Library of Congress. *Subject headings*, 4 vols, Library of Congress, Washington (1996, 19th edition).

25. Engineers Joint Council. *Thesaurus of engineering and scientific terms: a list of scientific and engineering terms and their relationships for use in a vocabulary for indexing and retrieving technical information*, EJC, New York (1964).

26. *UNESCO Thesaurus. A structured list of descriptors for indexing and retrieving literature in the fields of education, science, social and human science, culture, communication and information*, UNESCO, Paris (1995, 2nd edition).

27. Viet, Jean. *EUDISED multilingual thesaurus for information processing in the field of education*, English version, Council of Europe, Paris, Mouton, Strasbourg (1973).

28. Aitchison, Jean, Gomersall, A. and Ireland, R.*Thesaurofacet : a thesaurus and faceted classification for engineering and related subjects*, English Electronic Company Ltd, Whetstone, Leicester (1969).

29. Pollitt, A. Steven *et al.* HIBROWSE for bibliographic databases, *Journal of Information Science,* **20** (6) 1994, 413-426.

30. Batty, C.D. Thesaurus construction and maintenance survival kit, *Database,* **12**(1) February 1989, 13-20.

31. Lancaster, F.W. *Vocabulary control for information retrieval*, Information Resources Press, Arlington, VA (1986, 2nd edition).

32. Svenonius, E. Design of controlled vocabularies in the context of emerging technologies, *Library Science with a Slant to Documentation and Information Technology,* **25** (4) 1988, 215-227.

33. Orna E. Build yourself a thesaurus. A step by step guide, Running Angel, Norwich (1983).

34. International Standards Organisation. *Guideline for the establishment and development of monolingual thesauri*, ISO 2788, ISO, Geneva (1986, 2nd edition).

35. Lewis, David D. and Sparck Jones, K. National language processing for information retrieval, *Communications of the ACM*, **30** (1) January 1996, 92-101.

36. Arnold, Stephen E. *Publishing on the Internet : a new medium for a new millenium*, Infonortics, Calne, Wiltshire (1996).

37. Weiner, Michael L. and Liddy, Elizabeth D. Intelligent text processing, and intelligence tradecraft, *The Journal of AGSI*, July 1995.

38. Fah-Chun Cheung. *Internet agents: spiders, wanderers, brokers and bots.* New Riders Publishing, Indianapolis (1996).

39. Harman, D.K. Review of TREC, *Information Processing and Management,* **31** 1994, 271-290.

40. Sparck Jones, Karen. Reflections on TREC, *Information Processing & Management,* **31** (3) 1995, 291-314.

FURTHER READING

Ashford, John and Willett, Peter. *Text retrieval and document databases,* Chartwell-Bratt, Bromley, Kent (1988).

Blair, D.C. *Language and representation in information retrieval,* Elsevier, Amsterdam (1990).

Dubois, C.P.R. The use of thesauri in online retrieval, *Journal of Information Science,* **8**(2) 1984, 63-66.

Foskett, A.C. *The subject approach to information,* Bingley, London (1996, 5th edition).

Kemp, Alasdair D. *Computer based knowledge retrieval.,* Aslib, London (1988).

Meadow, Charles T. *Text information retrieval systems,* Academic Press Inc., New York (1992).

Rowley, J.E. *Organising knowledge : an introduction to information retrieval,* Gower, Aldershot, (1987).

Salton, G. and McGill, M.J. *Introduction to modern information retrieval,* McGraw Hill, New York (1983).

Tenopir, C. *Full-text database retrieval performance.*

Resourcing the Information Centre

Jim Basker

INTRODUCTION

Mission statement, vision and strategy – for three years

The vision of the organisation is very important to the information service because it confers legitimacy. Examples include: "'in the new Europe XXX plc will lead the market", or "Every household will possess a widget". Vision statements are seen as developments of the Mission Statement, which says, for example, "We aim to be the largest provider of high quality widgets in the country". Vision and mission are couched in broad statements which can easily be treated as cynical expressions of a fashionable trend for the benefit of corporate presentations to groups of market analysts in the City, or to groups of institutional shareholders. Public sector organisations such as academic, learned, local government or charitable entities have such statements to provide a focus for their funders. The organisation itself will use its vision statement as the basis for all its activities, and for creating its strategy.

The strategy of the organisation is usually based on its vision and mission statements, providing details of specific activities which will deliver the mission into reality. At the turn of this century, with the end of the Cold War and the globalisation of markets, old certainties can be guaranteed no longer and the organisation's strategy can realistically look forward no more than three years. It has to work out how to fulfil its mission in a much longer term, by building up a strategy for the medium term which moves in the general direction of its mission by ensuring that all of its energies move towards the same mission, and make it easier to achieve. It is at this level that the senior managers of the organisation decide:

- What product to make, what service to supply (market definition)
- Why it should be made or supplied
- Where to make, where to supply it (market positioning)
- How it should be made or supplied (market level)
- For whom it should be made (market segmentation)
- How it should be made.

The firm has to make its decisions on this basis, bearing in mind that it has to consider the interests of shareholders, customers, staff and the community as a whole, while updating its knowledge of rival companies and of technological, political and social change which might affect its markets (political risk, technological risk, environmental risk) during the next three years. Generally, the strategy has to be looked at again every year, so it has a rolling strategy which reviews the options and opportunities open to it, changing its strategy as some targets are met and others are seen as unnecessary in the light of new developments. You must be part of the process if you are to get any resources at all, and you have to persuade your manager(s) that the resources are better spent by you than by other departments.

Information service mission and strategy – for three years

What has this to do with resourcing the information service? After all, it doesn't get mentioned in the mission statement, let alone the vision: why are we always left out? Well, no other department in the organisation is, so there is no reason why the information service should be included. Vision and mission are statements which include everybody in the organisation. Implicitly, all departments have to work towards the achievement of the mission, and are resourced accordingly.

The information service should have its own mission which clarifies this, so that it can always justify its existence during reviews and appraisal, and when budgets are set. A typical mission statement might read: "The Mission of the Information Service is to ensure that all staff and clients have full, relevant information on which to make their decisions".

You can see that this is a general, vague statement, which is often criticised as a 'motherhood' statement. But it is what the service is *for*, and any resource allocated has to pass this criterion. If something is bid for which does not lead to helping staff meet the mission of the organisation then some very hard thought has to be put into it. The strategy of the information service translates the mission statement into specific activities over the next three years, or other such timescale as laid down by the organisation. This may include such activities as:

- Raising profile with managers, so their added value to the organisation is maximised (means explaining carefully in simple English to all managers)

- Increasing the staff of the Information Centre, (will they earn their salaries plus superannuation plus service costs in income, either by direct charging or by enabling other staff or clients to earn that amount of extra income?)

- Increasing the space of the Information Centre (why, in an age of CD-ROMs and online access, do you want to fill up space with paper?)

- Re-equipping with new computers and upgrading the software (why won't the old equipment work? Is it the cables that need upgrading instead?)

None of these items specifies by how much, or how, they should be achieved. But they should all be the predicate to the argument that they contribute to the strategy of the organisation. Raising the profile with managers is a strategy for ensuring that the managers are aware of the support the information staff can supply, so they can make better quality decisions faster in order to meet the strategic aims of the organisation. It doesn't necessarily mean the information service can throw the biggest Christmas party. Though that can help. Increasing space is a strategy for housing more information which is crucial to the organisation's development and for organising the information so it is easier to find. It isn't about increasing your empire.

Getting more staff

This is not a self-evident strategy for the information service: it is necessary to prove that the current staff cannot cope with the demand, and in a culture which demands long hours and short holidays the main arguments for more staff are the need for skills and for quality in order to get the right information to the right manager in the right form at the right time. Going home at 8pm every day is not a good argument. In addition, you have to explain why you should spend more money answering more questions: wouldn't it be better to cut the number of questions asked by less marketing? Immediate recourse to the organisation's mission may be necessary here. Upgrading the equipment is probably the easiest strategy to follow: the intense media interest in the wonders of computers has made all managers, especially IT managers, worry about being left behind. But the technology has to work and has to be set up, provides training problems, and has to be staffed.

Aims and objectives – one year ahead

The strategy of the information service is to improve its contribution to the organisation's strategy for the same period. The organisation itself will have set limited aims to achieve during each of the years of its three-year strategy. The information service should itself follow the same pattern. Its aims should lock into the organisation's aims; so, for example, if the organisation is going to invest in a quality programme the information service should do so too. An application for resources to improve the quality of information to other departments will therefore be much easier to obtain since it reinforces the aims of the organisation as a whole, rather than setting up an irrelevant activity. Avoid the cynicism of old hands who 'have seen it all before' and demonstrate that you, too, believe in quality.

Objectives are not the same as aims. They are even more specific. If your aim is to improve the quality of service, your objectives will be several: log all enquiries; deal with all enquiries within x days; seek feedback y days later; act on feedback received. Sampling is a good way of cutting the costs of this: though you have to be careful to choose typical days or typical groups. These are clearly measurable and you can tick them off as achieved. They can be spread out throughout the course of the year and meeting them will be the real test of your abilities.

Tactics – one year ahead

When you have a specific objective, such as cutting down the length of time to answer an enquiry, tactics is the method of doing it. The easiest solution is to hire enough staff to meet the peak load. Staffing resource is the most difficult to increase immediately, because the costs are so obvious: if they are permanent, the organisation has to add superannuation, and insurance, and will not be able to cut the cost easily if circumstances change. Temporary staff through an agency are expensive if you intend to keep up the service permanently and you have a major training burden. Tactically, the best method is to propose disintermediation, where staff can actually look for materials themselves, and get the relevant companies offering online services to managers to demonstrate how easy it is to answer enquiries themselves. End-user access is a fashionable solution, and many managers who believe in right-sizing see information as something they can get themselves rather than pay a secretary or a librarian to do for them. If managers in your organisation believe this, then your calls for resources will attract unwelcome attention whatever you do. A presentation on end-user access is needed. It will take a little lobbying, but if corporate planners, R&D specialists, or the company lawyer attend such a presentation, they may well ask questions which a commercial service cannot fully answer. They will better appreciate what you offer. It is important to ensure that you already know such people well. It is tactics like these which help meet objectives.

BUDGET PLANNING

For a fuller explanation of the budget and its methods see Duncan McKay's *Effective financial planning for library and information services*, Aslib, 1995.

Cost centre

For most organisations an information service is a cost centre. That means that it is not expected to make money itself, but is a part of overhead expenses which are necessary for the organisation to deliver its product or service. It is important to discover the value added by the information service to its clients. This is sometimes very difficult and requires great attention to logging the enquiries you deal with and following up the information later. Particularly in law, property, or companies with a large research activity, the information you supply will lead to winning a case, clinching a sale or developing a new patent. This has some cash value and should be treasured as evidence when budgets are being constructed. In many cases the information service is funded by individual departments in a shadow market environment so that costs can be clearly attributed to the departments incurring them. In theory, this works well but in practice it can lead to inefficiency and politics, particularly where an expensive resource is essential for two departments but one refuses to pay its contribution, perhaps because it can find another source for the information. Under some management styles overhead is expressed as cost of sales, and this ratio is reduced as far as possible.

One major way of cutting cost ratios is to reduce the staffing to a minimum and outsource the activity to specialist companies. This has been undertaken frequently in the UK National Health Service and particularly in information technology services. It is also undertaken by library services companies who can provide a standard information service to a detailed contract within a fixed period. Staff who work for such companies often welcome the variety of work, and the confidence that their activity is specifically contracted for means they can be more forthright about an organisation's information needs than a pensionable employee might be. If you are in a company which is considering outsourcing your information service, stress that the company needs to write a very detailed contract with performance levels and a get-out clause, and that the company needs an inhouse expert to vet the outsourced activity. In these circumstances, the incumbent postholder can either be promoted or made redundant. There is little that can be done by this stage and, if you are in this position, you should look for more satisfying work elsewhere.

Profit centre

Where the information service is seen as a profit centre, it has to generate income. This is a very interesting environment to work in because it can lead to original alliances with commercial organisations for mutual benefit and imaginative projects. An information service can offer research services in competition with commercial providers, can sell books or research reports, can undertake consultancy on setting up information services, publish and sell journals, sell advertising space, or set up a Web page and sell its services through the Internet. Conventional wisdom is that the only service that actually generates profit, rather than just income, is a self-service photocopying service. With being a profit centre, an information service can obtain resources much more easily because it has only to say that the expenditure is necessary in order to earn a return. An information service which is part of a charity, or in the public sector, has to be very careful about its status, and it is recommended that a service conducted for profit be a separate unit which has a separate account for tax purposes. It is possible that discounts available for not-for-profit organisations are not available to profit centres, which then have to make internal payments for such resources.

The major problem for profit centres is the conflict between commercial goals and other aims, or even the organisation's mission. For example, if a membership organisation sets up its information service to charge for service, members may legitimately argue that they have already paid for the service in their fees, and question the organisation's aims. For sure, if an organisation has a mission to be the best, yet also runs a commercial arm which intends to make as much profit as possible, its strategy is likely to get into a mess. The fundamental problem for organisations running information services for profit is that in the UK, at least, most information can be got free or cheap from public sources; and indeed information services rely on such information to make their profit.

Interdepartmental transfer

The advantages of interdepartmental transfer are that it matches expenditure with use, so that users are aware of the cost of the service they receive. Unfortunately, the value of the information is not the same, and that cannot be assessed at the point of expenditure. Finding no information, for example, can be of great value (if no patent exists for an innovation, for example). Different managers have different definitions of value, and the value added by the information may not be known till the next financial year.

Income/expenditure

Different organisations approach budgeting differently, of course. Essentially, expenditure covers staff wages, National Insurance, temporary staff, overtime, telephones, utilities (electricity, heat etc), photocopying, travel, entertainment, hotels and subsistence, advertising, stationery, equipment, materials, services and miscellaneous expenditure. Revenue (money spent over the year) is different from capital (one-off projects of high value, often depreciated over several years). Materials are split, for preference within the department rather than in the organisational budget, by type or by subject; and services by type and by supplier.

Income includes headings for photocopying, fines, sales of reports, advertising and sponsorship, payphone and drinks machines. All these need to be projected over 12 months so that the end-of-year outcomes become clearer as the year progresses. Most library packages are equipped with accounts packages which can track expenditure on materials such as books, journals and standing order payments and these can be transferred into a general accounts package like Microsoft Excel which can be set up to include the other heads as well. You are advised to keep on very good terms with the organisation's accounting staff because they can ensure that you keep up-to-date on expenditure, that key payments are expedited, and towards the end of the year can switch expenditure between heads if you got your sums wrong or something unexpected happened.

Capital/revenue

In the organisation's accounts, capital projects such as new automation systems or building extensions are treated differently from the revenue accounts because they are depreciated over a number of years (usually four or five) and appear under a different heading in the annual report. Capital projects often have to be fought for at senior management level, meaning that you have to rely on your line manager to represent your arguments at a higher level, and you will not be present at the important meetings where senior managers make decisions.

Underspend/overspend

Underspend and overspend are quite usual in budgeting where you are projecting next year's monthly expenditure. They matter if your margin of error is large, or if it happens regularly on the same headings. The easiest method of budgeting is to use last year's figures and extrapolate, or even just alter the date and send it in. However, you will be budgeting before the year end so you don't know last year's outcomes yet; and the problems with using the figures from two years back are: inflation (it still exists in publishing, and does not follow the retail price index), the items you bought two years ago that you cancelled, special expenditures to cover, say, a new product or service the organisation started offering, or a different staff structure.

Staffing is probably the biggest problem in the budget because an information service is labour intensive, so an increase or decrease of one person in the course of a year will make a dramatic difference. Since the financial year and staff pay rises do not always match, it is difficult to forecast what the pay commitment is before the end of the financial year, and if bonuses are given at Christmas, that has to be built in too. The alternative arrangement, of leaving the staff part of the budget to the personnel department, is tempting but not always wise. It is easy to blame them for getting their forecasts wrong, but unless the rest of your budget is ringfenced you may be faced with an unexpected deficit if somebody gets a payrise – and you lose control, of course. The budget should be memorised, because when you are talking to senior staff informally you need to be sure of any figures you quote.

Budgeting techniques

There are several budgeting techniques that have been advocated over the years: line item budgeting, formula budgeting, program budgeting, performance budgeting, planning programming budgeting system (PPBS) and zero-based budgeting (See Duncan McKay *Effective financial planning*). But the one which works is the one your manager understands, and the performance indicators which work are the ones that your manager warms to (cost per use, cost per member of staff, cost compared to other organisations, or just total cost).

MAKING THE BUSINESS CASE

If you want to get more resources you have to show that there is a 'business case'. That means it has to be within the strategy of the organisation and has clear aims; that it will be sustainable, and that its costs will either be covered by your current budget or by income or by other criteria, depending on the current policy of the organisation and whether the information service is a cost or a profit centre.

Cost projections – for three years

Assuming the organisation's strategy is three years, and that your strategy is the same length, it is easiest to project for three years. Beyond that, it is usually guesswork anyway. You need to investigate whether anybody else has done the same thing- by putting a message out on LIS-LINK or by phoning other information managers you know, to see if anybody can give ballpark figures for your proposal, say, for CD-ROM archiving of the organisation's publications. Of course, the capital bid has to include staff costs (including national insurance and pension), space costs, equipment costs (for purchase or hire), running costs (stationery, consumables), and opportunity costs (what you would have done if you didn't do this) as well as the costs to other departments such as the IT department. What would be the cost to the organisation of not doing anything? For capital items, a read of *What to buy for business* or a consultation with CIMtech should precede a tender invitation to three companies to supply – this in itself will cost a considerable amount of time, and secretarial time too. Be prepared for managers to change their minds or their timetables, or to cease co-operation with you or the tenderers for internal reasons, (Guy St Clair's book *Entrepreneurial Librarianship* is useful).

Sales projections

From the start it is important to know whether the project is to contribute to the organisation's strategy. If this includes financial viability, then you should make a strong case for sales potential. This involves an accurate assessment of the marketplace and it would be wise to talk to the marketing department about it. It may well sell internationally, but can you support an international sales effort? Advertising it on the Web may be cheap and easy, but will your customers be looking? If you are to advertise in your organisation's journal, for example, there is the cost of space. And you have to work out at what price and at how many copies you will break even.

Profit: definition, legitimacy, related to mission

Profit is not the same as income, but is the balance after costs have been accounted for. In some organisations this is not understood. It is not in the interests of the information manager to point it out. The only information services that make a profit are those whose vision and mission statements set that as the organisation's. Examples include Reuters, Bloomberg, SVP. The view that an information service has to make a profit to be efficient is often argued, but is wrong. The information service is there to further the mission of the organisation, and to maximise the profits of the organisation as a whole, which it is unable to do if it has a confused role. This has to be argued firmly by the information manager, in a positive and helpful way, pointing out examples of effective use of information. A common reaction is to blame management for its boneheadedness and to become a victim. It may well be that the language of profit is just a cover and that in practice a contribution to covering costs is what is expected. Don't become arrogant in your professional skills and you need to remain open to the other side's reasoning – you are not there to build your own empire. But make your case in simple, non-technical language and do it from the other party's perspective.

Interdepartmental costs and benefits

The information service not only supplies information to members of the organisation who need information, but also has a uniting role between various groups within the organisation. So in making the business case for a project, the costs that have to be borne, say, by the IT department, or by the advertising department in promoting the product, have to be spelt out in your presentation, having been cleared in advance with those departments. Any benefits to other departments need to be spelt out too. If the project is to develop a Web-site selling the information department's information to a wider clientele worldwide, the publications department may be able to generate more orders, the training department could sell its courses, and sales could establish new markets in distant countries.

Benefits to users

It must be recognised that the benefits derived from the project should come in part, at least, to users of the information service. An innovation may make the service busier and leave less time for traditional users, as will be recognised in adding up the opportunity costs of a project. However, if it saves staff time, for example, by allowing remote renewal of loans or remote delivery of a list of documents electronically, the traditional user will get better service. This is no area for using the conditional tense – the service *will* deliver quality.

Benefits to the organisation

The benefits to the organisation from a project have to be rigorously related to the strategy of the organisation. A project which will improve its reputation among information managers will not impress, but one which will impress its customers will secure funding. So reforming the classification scheme or removing ancient books from the catalogue will not attract funding, but making the imperfect catalogue available to the Singapore office so they can order items electronically will succeed because it will keep Singapore in touch with the information they need to do their job better.

Lobbying process

It is vital to lobby colleagues to ensure that a project is supported at manager or director level. You need to know which colleagues are important, and which are not. This means finding out about office politics, and this is usually discovered over a few beers in the pub and taking a systematic note of staff prejudices without subscribing to them. This works best in your first month with the organisation when people will be happy to show off their superior knowledge, and an induction programme is ideal for this. The organisation chart will give some guidance, but it is important to avoid vigorous support from a department which has a poor reputation (typically IT or sales) because you will be branded either as naive or as having a secret agenda. Finance department or corporate planning are quite often good allies, finance because if you can convince them, you can convince anybody; corporate planning because they can build it into their next three-year strategy and have a direct line to the chief executive.

Implementation

The implementation plan will have been part of the original Business Plan you submitted and must start immediately, so that the money is committed and equipment, software or staffing invoiced as soon as possible. Any delay may indicate a lack of commitment or uncertainty, and once your project has been approved there are bound to be people, possibly in the sales or IT department, who will be jealous. If you are near to the end of the financial year, the money could be lost. Your best friends should be in the finance department.

GETTING RESOURCES: BUYING

Aims and objectives

In buying resources for the information service you have to know the major needs of your user departments in terms of the industries, companies, products and techniques they need to know about, how up-to-date they need to be and in what depth. These needs must be related to the organisation's strategy, and if they are not, the user department will be obliged to make a business case to you for the purchase. You have the major role in assessing the quality of the materials you are buying – you can't delegate to other people because they do not have as comprehensive a view of the organisation's needs. For a more detailed discussion of purchasing and quality assessment routines, see Jill Lambert's *Information resources selection* (1996).

Acquisitions department, scheduling purchases and allocation to heads

In the financial year, the major expenditures depend on whether all items are bought separately or through an agent. If you are buying a reasonable spread of journals or CD-ROMs or a static collection of standing orders, there is an annual invoice to cover their purchase. This will have been noted in your budget projection and it is important to ensure that the invoices get paid at the right time. This may need to be checked with the finance department which will have views on cashflow (we are short of money in January, so please reschedule payment for later in the year) or on whether invoices for next year's subscriptions should be paid next year. In case of doubt, the best time to have invoices paid is just before the year-end and you are reviewing your budget for next year. If you still have money unspent, and next year may be tight, invoices could be paid early. The alternative is cancellation of subscriptions, but since this has to be done before you have been invoiced, the decision has to be made early, ideally at the time that next year's budget is being approved. The allocation of funds between heads is either by type (books, journals, standing orders, CD-ROMs) or by subject/department, depending on the arrangements of the organisation. Unless your organisation is large and divided into subject areas, the latter is an invitation to departments to look on it as 'their' money and expect a say in how it is spent. In principle, this is fair, but in practice leads to trouble even over small purchases.

Acquisitions policy

If you delegate the purchase to others, it is important to write down the criteria for purchasing materials, not only so somebody else can choose materials efficiently but also as part of the procedures manual which most organisations now require. This should cover:

1) Core collection, for which all available materials must be bought: books, journals, standing orders, grey literature, electronic documents (including encyclopaedias, glossaries and directories) and online services. You should be able to answer any crisis in this specialist area from your own resources; for example, if the company makes lubricants for drills, you cannot expect to rely on another lubricant company's information department to help out, particularly after working hours.

2) Supporting collection, for which all major materials need to be purchased but not general or very specialist material: books, journals reviewing the subject, online services. Typically, this is an area which every entity in the industry has an information service, and should be able to sustain the study needs of staff studying for professional qualifications or undertaking continuing professional development. You may find the training department has a collection of audiovisual materials for this purpose already. (If so, depending on your other responsibilities and the ambitions of the training manager, you can send enquirers on to training, offer to record and update their collection, or take over responsibility for it).

3) Peripheral collection, for which only basic introductory material should be obtained: the latest updated textbook, online services. This collection should be supplemented where possible by your contact list of experts for emergency support when the subject arises. (For example, if the chief executive is lunching with somebody from local government and wants a quick browse through the latest policy on local government finance).

Buying books

Given a budget, you need to identify where to source books for the information service fast. The easiest source is a subscription to *The Bookseller* which lists new books weekly by subject, but is general in focus. It is very important to find a supplier which can provide books in the subject area you are specialising in, and although you can find these by talking to your trade association and other information managers, you need to keep in touch with several providers to ensure that you get the best discounts (yes, discounts are possible) and most efficient service. Contact in particular the National Acquisitions Group (NAG), Westfield House, North Road, Horsforth, Leeds LS18 5HG, 0113 259 1447, *swolf@nag.eunet.co.uk*. You need to ensure your acquisitions system can calculate the average time it takes to supply items from order to delivery. Particular difficulties arise in obtaining British government publications or items published abroad, and it may be best to use separate specialist agents to obtain these. Your users will expect you to have books on the shelf the day they read about them in the newspaper, when the earliest they are available to the general public is two weeks after the press gets them. If you work for an organisation which is influential, specialist or prestigious and runs its own journal, you may find the editor or book reviewer gets pre-publication copies.

Bookselling is more of an art than a science, and publishing is still a matter of flair, so it is still likely that however efficient your agent is in finding and delivering materials there will always be a sum of money locked up at the end of the financial year in outstanding orders which has to be carried over to the next year. Even if the organisation insists that accounts be closed on a specific date, you need to ensure the finance department is aware of your overhang, and if it is roughly the same overhang of outstanding orders as last year there should be no difficulty in arranging an accommodation. Ensure where possible, that the bulk of the book orders is arranged with an agent which operates EDI so that orders generated on your acquisitions database can be electronically sent to your supplier, cutting out a lot of the paperwork which would otherwise cause delays at all stages. Even so, the buying of books requires memory above all, because you are likely to find the most interesting tips for purchase 'on the fly', talking casually with somebody, socially, or seen in a newspaper article with very sketchy detail. Books are still very popular with users, to whom electronic sources are acceptable as reference manuals or legal encyclopaedias but not for getting to grips with a difficult subject.

Buying serials

You can either buy serials through an agent or from individual companies. The former is much to be preferred because they can save you a lot of work, for example in invoicing you annually and alerting you to price rises in good time, and in chasing unsupplied issues. Serials management is dealt with in more detail in a separate chapter.

Buying standing orders

Standing orders are important because they are likely to be the most uptodate reference sources. Increasingly, they are appearing as CD-ROMs, sometimes linked to online databases. If you are tied to hard copy you have major staffing problems. Loose-leaf publications are particularly difficult: no information manager has really had proper training without a week of updating legal manuals. If this manual labour has been left for some time, the whole subscription becomes valueless; and if the supplier has forgotten to send you the update, you may not know until the next update arrives, and that update cannot be put in until the previous one has been, leading to further delay. CD-ROM versions may have a higher cover price but save staff time which can be devoted to maintaining the CD-ROM network or explaining how to use the electronic version. Increasingly, the Internet is being used for publication of time-critical information and downloading to your own Web-site and to your intranet should allow users direct access from their terminals.

Buying CD-ROMs

As with standing orders, CD-ROMs are best bought through a specialist agent who can mediate on subscription prices and technical difficulties. It is important to remember that CD-ROMs will always exclude the latest information and have to be supplemented by online sources. This is a specially critical issue with company information. A massive bank of company accounts obtained from international sources and broker reports on CD-ROM will probably include the mass of information needed for an investment, but it has to be melded with newspaper or press agency comment in order to maximise the use of information for a trader's decision on the markets under rational expectations.

Buying online services

CD-ROM has long been considered an intermediate technology and information providers offer an online supplement to CD-ROM services, or even replacement services. Of course, the problem for the information manager is how many concurrent users to licence, and how much time to allow for access. Clearly, if the organisation is subscribing to major online suppliers it may be possible to set up special deals for a discount, and for intranet use with regular updating of the intranet's cached data to ensure that information is never more than, for example, 30 minutes old. This allows internal control of 'online' activity, preventing access to porn channels. In addition, such an arrangement improves the stability of the system, which still suffers from inadequate bandwidth and a high incidence of failed access. Paying for online services is based on annual subscription plus charges for time and/or pages downloaded. Increasingly packages combine different formats, different databases, and access to other hosts; it is simple to renew a subscription to such services but not so simple to justify one, as opposed to another, on the basis of value for money. In essence, there is a limited amount of relevant data in the market place and most companies offer the same data in a different package. The major difference is in the interface, which, for most systems, is so difficult that the information manager is assured of a job in training people. It is sometimes difficult to justify expenditure on a service which cannot be presented as a physical entity and you may need to encourage end-users to express their views. If there is a problem in providing hardware to deliver the information, it is sometimes possible to lease a customised terminal to present the new service.

Buying research reports

Research reports are produced by:

- *Brokers* who specialise in specific markets and produce regular reports on market participants, based partly on special presentations by companies and partly on desk research and industry contacts. There are useful summaries, but sometimes influenced by market sentiment and the need to keep their sources friendly.

- *Research companies* produce country reports and industry reports. Typically, a country report will be published annually, or biennially for less important trading partners. The biggest are available online on several hosts. The really useful reports come from industry specialists, and are still produced for a small number of subscribers in paper form. Your ability to get hold of these, even if they cost a lot, will enhance your value to the organisation.

- *Academic research*. Often free, and sometimes not supplied automatically to a mailing list, research reports by university academics can sometimes appear to be abstruse but they have time to think about the industry and analyse it in a different way to more commercially oriented research companies. A clue to their existence can be found in the *Current Research in British Universities and Colleges*.

Buying grey literature

If the organisation sells widgets in the Mexican market, you need to collect data about widgets (though the Production Department knows far more about them than you will ever do, but nobody would ever think of asking them) and you need to know about Mexico's socio-political environment, the value of the peso, Brady Bonds and the North American Free Trade Agreement. You will have to spend money on membership of the Widget Trade Organisation which should collect information about widgets. Journalists working for the trade journal will be sent information about the industry, press releases, unpublished reports and other items of current interest. Very rarely, an address or telephone number can be picked up and sometimes the name of the author or the title of the report. Contact with the journalist can lead to being sent a copy, and possibly being told about further information. This grey literature is often free but sometimes is extremely expensive, being produced for 'member organisations only'. Many newspaper articles can be carefully analysed to identify a whole network of contacts, which has to be committed to a database, to memory or to paper before you forget.

Freebies

If you work in a specialised firm or one with a high profile you will be deluged with glossy brochures and invitations to subscribe to services. You have to work out whether these will be of any use to the company before tackling the intray. You may want to set up a trade literature collection, a new ideas file, or simply note a contact name and address on your personal database. If your view is that if it's free they must want to sell you something, and if it's any good somebody will tell you about it again, and you've got quite enough new ideas to be going with, bin it. And you will usually be right. If, on the other hand, you want to be noticed, post it on to somebody you think may be interested; quite often they will have seen the same information and sent it to you. Some people set up files for particular users to alert them to new developments and provided you don't send too much to them they will be happy to be noticed. If you have to think hard about it, bin it.

EQUIPMENT PURCHASE

Who should pay?

The purchase of systems and equipment for the information department may be under your control, meaning you can do things now rather than wait for it to come to the top of somebody else's queue. The downside is the staff resources in investigating the right equipment which will be compatible with everybody else's, the obsession with technical detail which distracts your attention from supplying information, and additional 'hostages to fortune', exogenous risks if the suppliers fail to deliver. On the other hand, you can pass the costs to the IT department, which will probably charge them back to you. These are issues to be discussed over drinks with your opposite numbers in other organisations.

Server and client networks

The information service must have a network of computers which is part of the organisation's main network. Server machines (dedicated PCs) for internal databases and for CD-ROM access must be able to talk to all parts of the organisation. If there are remote sites, data lines may still be of low capacity and deliver databases to remote clients (computers which are linked to servers) unreasonably slowly. The cost of a second subscription to particular CD-ROM titles can be quite high, but in some cases it may pay off in putting pressure on the IT department to obtain a line with wider bandwidth.

Local systems

It is usually best to work with the IT department in deciding what sort of local system to purchase so as to ensure that not only is equipment cheaper to purchase if bought in bulk, but it may well come from the IT budget rather than the information service budget. Goodwill is needed between the two departments if the IT department is to service and maintain the equipment. If this is outsourced, the detail of any contracts signed should be examined to ensure that the call-out period is adequate and, where possible, penalties for non-compliance agreed. Internet access has major security problems, so the information department has to ensure that no hacker can obtain access to the organisation's network, and also to ensure that all external information supplied is clear of virus infection. This means that firewalls have to be bought to protect any 'bridges' between the information network and the rest of the organisation, that the latest virus detection programs are loaded on all machines in contact with files from outside the organisation, and that where possible PCs accessing the Internet are free-standing.

Remote systems

These are usually under the control of somebody else, and in particular IT departments, so your purchase of equipment will be constrained by what is compatible with the remote systems' protocols. They are usually incompatible, except through tweaking by experts.

Document delivery, fax, scanner, photocopier

Remote delivery of documents can be by post (normally highly efficient in Northern Europe) or by courier, depending on your post budget and the urgency. Faxes are efficient if the information is single-sided sheets and short, but are expensive in time (it may have to be photocopied first) and reproduction quality may be poor. Electronic transmission, if the material can be scanned in, is very efficient if your recipient has the appropriate software to read it. Expenditure on a good flatbed scanner and on a good, fast fax machine that can take multiple sheets, and has a large memory, is important. In addition, fax software on the PC should be used for composing fax messages since handwriting, though friendly, does not look professional. A good photocopier which can collate and staple, though comparatively expensive, will be useful for producing multiple copies, since unless some wonderful new technology transforms laserprinters, printing out from electronic databases is slow and expensive, subject to mechanical faults and, if shared over a network, liable to failure. Sharing with the secretaries is not possible. Remember that if you are allowing your users to copy themselves you should ensure they are complying with the 1988 Copyright, Designs and Patents Act. If your organisation works all hours and has offices in other countries your users will appreciate being able to contact you at any time of the day or night so if they are not e-mailing or faxing you, you need a simple voicemail on your telephones so that messages can be left. Sophisticated phone systems should be avoided because they still upset some callers.

Multimedia

The use of multimedia is important in the training or staff development environment, so if your organisation is undertaking 'Investors In People' or is taking appraisal seriously there will be a demand for audio-visual packs on improving people skills, self-organisation skills and technical skills. In addition, interactive computer-based packages which teach skills like wordprocessing or simulate high-pressure work situations, such as dealing room simulations, are useful ways of raising the profile. Display is important, so you should ensure an adequately specified PC (with sound card, appropriate drives and the largest possible RAM memory) is prominently placed, and operating, in the information unit. Collaboration with the training department and human resources is very valuable in sharing resources and publicity for self-learning methods. Since the equipment has to be paid for, and the packages cost a great deal, cost-sharing is worth pursuing.

STAFFING

Staffing levels

Staffing levels are right when there is a backlog of work for everybody in the information service, and sickness means everybody has to leave something undone which should be done. This means that the standards of the database are not always met and some materials do not get put away as soon as they ought. Every department in the organisation is short of staff, but the department which has time to meet all deadlines and holds staff meetings to moan about the workload is overstaffed. Comparisons with other similar organisations, benchmarking, can be used if you prove that they perform better (deal with more enquiries, open longer hours, have markedly more users). The most important argument is to relate staffing levels to the meeting of this year's objectives, and therefore to the organisation's strategy and mission.

Staff training

This is closely related to the information department's mission, aims and objectives, and each member of staff needs to know specific training objectives for the year. Since these are agreed in the appraisal process, resources should be made available from the training budget, if there is one. A lot of staff training can be done by regular weekly updating/awareness sessions and by internal seminars. Many information industry organisations will send you details of courses if you are on their mailing lists: in the UK, the Library Association, the Institute of Information Scientists, Aslib, TFPL, and informal sectoral groups. The purpose of such courses has to be spelt out in advance, and staff must feed back on what they have learnt both on return to work as well as several weeks later.

SELLING

Definition of selling and its purpose

In resourcing the information unit, any selling you can undertake gives you leverage to increase your services. Its purpose is to make money so that the information service can justify its existence 'at the bottom line'. There is no known instance of an information service actually making a real profit but there are many examples of services which sell their products: bibliographies, market research reports, photocopies, gift tokens, for money. The expression 'Sell it to me' is an invitation to say how useful the service has been to its users, and how little it costs – which is very close to marketing. The commercial attitude is appreciated by those who do not use the service as well as by users who believe it means efficiency. You may consider your objective is to be effective, but in selling you must display a positive attitude at all times.

Selling to the organisation

The service has to be sold to the organisation particularly if the organisation thinks it is commercial and only supports activities intended to make money. Both sides know, underneath, that an information service is not commercial, because there are few commercial information services. But the selling has to be done. Particularly helpful are instances of helping the chief executive or the marketing or finance departments, which need to be documented at the time they occurred and filed for future use. These should be translated where possible into specific sums of money which would have been wasted had the information not been supplied, for example in finding local suppliers of a product. The costs of information service activities have to be regularly monitored so that the worth of, say, providing a service to a department, can be realistically assessed and used carefully in preparing annual reports of activity. If you have 'sold' the service well to an internal user, then they will be happy to 'pay' for it. If not, an aggregate cost of services is more appropriate.

Selling the organisation

The information service has a range of outside contacts which should be widespread and unique, particularly if it has its own Web-site and Internet address. If it has 'sold' its service to the marketing department, collaboration will be fruitful in that the organisation's mission and aims can be made available to a far wider group of people than if they worked on their own. Differentiating the information service to the outside world may well confuse potential clients of the organisation, of which the information service is only part. This may lead to the danger of takeover by, say, marketing, but if you have sold yourself well this may lead to more opportunities, and would probably have happened anyway. Selling the organisation is usually one of its main strategic activities, and you will be valued for doing that.

Sponsorship

If your organisation is prestigious but poor, you can get resources by obtaining sponsorship, thus modernising without affecting the balance sheet. While sponsorship is usually for sporting or similar high-profile activities like fashion shows, firms may be prepared to sponsor publicity events provided their names and activities are displayed to a large number of potential users, and to provide equipment in exchange for advertising space. Clearly such firms have to be complementary to your organisation's activities so they do not compromise the organisation's mission or offend its users, and if it is a charity the sponsorship should meet charity legislative controls. The sponsors have to be 'sold' the deal actively and need special attention.

Selling research

Research produced by the information service can be sold to users who are not already paying for it. If the resources put into the research are disproportionate, the quality of the work done has to be controlled if any cash benefit is to be achieved (unless, of course, your organisation is more interested in income than in profit). A premium band of service is a good way of charging rich clients such as consultancy firms, and a discounted band of service for students, for example. Sometimes work for subscribing members can be offered at a discount, say free research time up to 30 minutes, or a 50% discount for members. There is hardly ever any pattern to research requests but the advantage of having done a good report on a subject and charged one user, are that the results of that work can be stored and charged to another at the same price, the only costs being the work involved in updating and printing. The key to success lies not in being comprehensive and providing a thick report but in giving just the right amount of data, preferably in graphic form, ideally in colour and charging a commercial price for a commercial-looking product which tells you by its price what it is worth. Always note the likelihood that people who are paying a fee expect higher than standard responses, even if they are paying at a bargain rate. The income from such activities must be clearly differentiated and set off against the costs. Here again, you can obtain resources you could not afford if you did not charge some of your users.

Document delivery

Document delivery can be priced according to urgency, so that an item can be couriered or faxed for a premium (gold) price, for next day delivery by post for a silver service, and by economy (bronze) service with a lower priority. It is safe to charge for a service beyond the levels of normal expectation, even if it may become a way of governing demand. Always be careful about the priority given to commercial clients in case there is a conflict of interest with another category of users who expect a service in exchange for funding of basic facilities.

Selling skills

Selling skills are important and are often disregarded by staff concerned more with the technical difficulty of finding, ordering and presenting of information. They form a combination of offering a service in a positive, confident way, reassuring the customer, presenting the service in a clear, direct way relevant to that user's concerns, pressing the right keys on the terminal and taking payment through a till or by credit card confidently and quickly, while preparing for answering another enquiry and wishing the customer good luck.

Management information: the marketing role

The information obtained from users or customers is invaluable and needs to be committed to a systematic file of contacts: they may have special requirements that need to be followed up, they may be alerting you to a new type of enquiry or a new field of general interest, or need adding to your group of users for regular updating, or they may be experts in an area that other users are asking about and might be able to offer direct advice. This could, possibly, be another idea for a selling opportunity. The users sometimes know more about the information available on their subject than you do, and need cosseting. It is possible that some of them might be able to help produce a report. They also add to the statistics, which can show use rising, or changing, on monthly statistical printouts from your worksheet package.

Obtaining resources from Web-sites, adhoc publishing activities

There are many ways of making small amounts of money but, from the resourcing point of view, unless they increase your ability to increase the resources available to meet the organisation's mission, they are to be avoided. In all cases, their costs and revenues must be rigorously separated from other activities in terms of hours worked, equipment and database access costs, and should be monitored regularly.

THE NEXT ROUND

Technical developments

After the first nine months of your one year plan there will have been technical developments in the information industry which alter your potential activities: this could be a faster fax, cheaper laser printing, or (most often) the launching of new computer software. This may lead to a general upgrade of organisational machines, which you can use to advantage. But it also means your plans for the next year have to be reorganised accordingly. Evaluate progress so far, using statistics as well as qualitative measures to check whether the resources you are deploying are in the right areas and are adequate to your purposes. If a plan has not come off in time (for example, a multimedia training support service) consider ruthlessly whether it will be achieved in the next year, or ditched altogether, and at what price (in political terms as well as in physical resources).

Industry changes

During the year your organisation's product range, markets, or customers may have changed and the legal environment presents new challenges. Personnel may have changed and revisions have to be made to information profiles. Firms may have amalgamated, information sources you relied on may have ceased and your Christmas card list may be totally out of date.

Redefinition of the mission

Don't start with the detail, because that prevents you dealing with change systematically. Has the organisation's mission changed? This has to be checked thoroughly because you have to be an active seeker of the truth and for many organisations changes may appear in the *Financial Times* without notice. Does the organisation intend to change the strategy it set up to achieve its mission? Will it compete successfully with its rivals or acquire other companies to increase its size, or downsize to become leaner and meaner?

Implications of restructuring the organisation

In order to meet its restated mission the organisation may want to restructure. The information service depends for its future on how it is perceived by senior management, because it may well be moved from an administrative directorate to marketing or to another area, depending on whether it is seen as a corporate resource, a way of making money, one manager's fiefdom, or to balance up the organisational chart so that a demoted director has something to occupy him/her. Your future could depend on random conversations in the corridor. But the key question is whether resources go with you. If not, this could be the hint to move on.

Changes in aims and objectives

A new manager will have a different way of looking at the organisation, and have different aims and objectives. These need to be talked about, and if your aims do not match, some adjustment is necessary. For example, a new line manager may not appreciate your use of resources to entertain outsiders because external activity is seen as a reduction in resources applied to the task in hand. The new line manager may be right, but if wrong, the usefulness of the contacts has to be proved in a straightforward way without a major application of resource. Flexibility is required.

Changes in professional needs of users, new users

Evaluate progress so far, using statistics as well as qualitative measures to check whether the resources you are deploying are in the right areas and are adequate to your purposes. If continuing professional development is to be promoted as part of the appraisal process, expect a rush of keen staff wanting to know about subjects they should have been keeping up-to-date on for years. Resources will have to be spent supporting them. Your highly relevant marketing plan may have resulted in new users asking new questions about subjects you have never supported, and resources have to be set aside for that.

IMPLICATIONS OF CHANGE:

New staff, new needs, outsourcing

If the organisation is expanding, you will need more staff. This resource argument will start with the relevant statistics and continue with appeal to the objectives, aims and strategy of the organisation and how vital these people are for continuing success, particularly if they allow time to be spent on supporting flagship projects which generate resources. If the organisation is contracting or looking at new markets, the line manager needs to know about the implications for costs, particularly if it is going to affect other departments as well, and if others have not been as astute in thinking the strategy through. Outsourcing is always worth considering, because it gives you more time at the expense of money. This can be applied to routine purchasing and processing, and maintenance support for automated systems. Outsourcing the enquiry service is unwise for commercial secrecy reasons as well as for quality control. But changes in strategy towards disintermediation of database searching and greater handholding (training) of end-users is a powerful argument for concentrating such skills on a trustworthy internal manager, however much assets are outsourced. Whichever way it goes, you should be the leader, taking a unique role in influencing and moulding the company through customer focus (to quote Guy St Clair).

Marketing resources

Any change has to be explained to users and non-users in particular (and this is a reason for resources being put into marketing). If the changes are general, try to get the marketing department's budget to bear the cost.

R&D

The implications of change in research orientation are comparatively obvious: a new subject needs a different set of standards, patents, even new subscriptions to new information providers and the setting up of new Web pages with relevant URLs for appropriate research sites abroad. A meeting with relevant researchers should establish their approach to the subject and allow you to set up electronic alerts (Selective Dissemination of Information) for their e-mail pages. This has resource implications, usually to increase your capacity, unless downsizing has been introduced. Under downsizing, it is necessary to work out which online hosts to cancel and find out who is left, if indeed any research is being continued. The organisation may decide it has made a mistake in two years' time and want to re-establish a research effort, or buy somebody else's in a merger. But do not hold your breath.

Corporate strategy

The Corporate Strategy department should have kept you informed about developments as they happened. If not, make sure they think about you next time. You still need to devote some resources to their scanning of the business environment, looking at new market opportunities, impending legislation and European Union regulations which may affect the organisation. Their interest in management techniques will also change as the organisation re-engineers itself, which it is likely to do from time to time.

Administration

The staff who implement change need to know whether similar change has taken place in other organisations and the critical success factors of new ways of doing things, project management and motivating staff to accept and implement new procedures efficiently and effectively.

Users outside these areas

If change is major, other people in the organisation will need help, not just in jobseeking (is the careers section up-to-date? Do the jobs supplements of the newspapers disappear?) but in coping with change. They may well use the information service as a friendly environment where they can escape from stress elsewhere. Some resources should be devoted to counselling, career development and coping strategies. There may also be some multimedia presentations people can take home.

Early definition of next bid for resources

Bidding for resources for the coming year should start well before the end of the current year, just as your strategy changes. While keeping the three year strategy in mind, a budget bid should be cleared with other departmental managers before being put forward so that you can support each other in budget meetings where the cross-departmental links are bound to attract the attention of the finance director. That means the IT manager will support you and you can support the IT manager, both confident that the proposed spend is part of the organisation's strategic path to meeting its objectives.

Close relations with line manager/committee

The most important person in putting a case for the next year's budget is your line manager, or if you have a committee supervising you they will expect a detailed budget rationale so that they are convinced you are on the right track. They may not be as fully aware of the strategy as you, but must be treated as if they were, and addressed in plain English so that they can understand what you are telling them. They are your allies, so they have to understand your need for resources if they are to persuade senior directors.

NEW TECHNIQUES FOR BUDGETING UNDER CHANGE

Recognising redundancy of resources

If a subject is no longer of interest through downsizing or technical obsolescence, you need to allow for resources to get rid of material no longer needed. This can take up as much time as adding materials to stock, and is usually left to clog up the shelves until the next premises move, when you can bid for extra temporary staff to help dispose of old or redundant material. Ignore the temptation to withdraw your resources list from the Web until it is clear of such materials. Nobody else will notice because they are only interested in what they want to see.

BIBLIOGRAPHY

This is a select list of materials which excludes items likely to be out of date by the time a new edition is planned. It concentrates on helpful books which discuss fundamental issues of resourcing, and titles of journals which can be used for updating purposes on a regular basis. Active scanning will alert you to new developments which you can follow up through searching databases at the time, or by using bulletin boards set up by information associations or groups.

General guides

Broadbent, M. Butler, C. and Hansell, A. Business and technology agenda for information systems executives, *International Journal of Information Management,* **14** (6) December 1994, 411-426.

Information management: a survey of current trends and practices, Touche Ross, London (1994).

Lancaster, F. W. and Loescher, J. The corporate library and issues management, *LibraryTrends,* **43**(2) Fall 1994, 159-169.

Materazzo, J. M. and Drake, M. A. *Information management: a handbook,* Special Libraries Association, Washington D.C. (1994).

Orna, E. Why you need an information policy – and how to sell it, *Aslib Information,* May, 1993, 196-200.

St Clair, G. *Entrepreneurial librarianship,* Bowker Saur, London (1996).

Webb, S. P. *Creating an information service,* Aslib, London (1996, 3rd edition).

Case studies

Regular articles on managing information in *Managing Information* (monthly, Aslib, London, ISSN:1352 0229).

Regular articles in *Information World Review* (monthly, Learned Information, Oxford, ISSN: 0950 9879) or its US equivalent, *Information Today* (monthly, Learned Information, Medford N.J., ISSN 8755 6286).

Techniques

Baker, D. Counting the cost; the future economics of libraries, *Information Europe*, **2** July 1996, 14-16.

Debachere, M. C. Problems in obtaining grey literature, *IFLA Journal*, **21** (2) 1995, 94-98.

Lambert, J. *Information resources selection,* Aslib, London (1996).

Lyon, J. The gentle art of negotiation, *Library Manager*, 15 February 1996, 8-9.

McKay, D. *Effective financial planning for library and information services*, Aslib, London (1995).

Stoker, D. *Electronic information sources: an evaluative guide*, Bowker-Saur, London (1996).

Equipment choice

Byte, Byte Publications, Peterborough, NH, ISSN 0360 5280.

What To Buy For Business? What to buy for business, London, ISSN 0265 296X.

Business Equipment Digest, Techpress Publishing, Bromley, ISSN 0007 6708.

Personal Computer World, VNU, London, ISSN 0142 0232.

PC User, EMAP, London, ISSN 0263 5720.

Digital Publishing Technologies, Learned Information, Oxford, ISSN 1365 067X.

Understanding End-users

David Nicholas

INTRODUCTION

Despite their vast numbers, the massive challenges and threats they pose for information professionals, the responsibility we have for many of them – those that do their searching on library-managed facilities, and the fact that we share a common interest – in computerised information systems, we really do not know enough about end-users. We know the systems they use well enough, but need to know more about how they use them – though the suspicion is that they use them badly. However, we cannot continue to adopt the head-in-the-sand approach for there are now millions of end-users with whom we shall have to come to terms. This chapter provides a framework for understanding end-users, pointing out what we should know about them and summarising what we actually know about them. The data is organised in such a way as to make it accessible for those involved in systems purchase, monitoring, training and design. Much of the data used in evidence comes from the author's investigation of end-users at *The Guardian* and at The House of Commons[1].These long-term investigations concerned a full-text system (FT Profile), a partial text system (TEXTLINE) and an inhouse system, POLIS, that had much in common with a library OPAC. This data is supplemented by research studies of OPACs and CD-ROMs, largely in an academic setting. Methods of collecting data on end-use are also described.

WHY TAKE AN INTEREST IN END-USERS?

Information professionals have never been very good at collecting data on their users and end-users are no exception. But things will have to change if information professionals are to embrace the new opportunities proffered to them by widespread end-use. Unless the opportunities are taken soon all that will be left are the threats.

Plainly you cannot ignore the fact that millions of users are helping themselves to machine-readable data every day of the year – many for the first time, and often on systems that were once the exclusive preserve of the information professional or dedicated academic (scientists usually). There are good and pressing reasons why information professionals should care:

- They are often responsible for the provision and management of the systems that end-users search, and monitoring their use and satisfaction must surely be part and parcel of this role; at the very minimum there is a need to understand how often they search, what they search for and whether they find anything

- The training and advisory opportunities that arise from widespread end-use are welcome to a profession always looking to enhance its portfolio and status

- With end-users searching the same systems as information professionals – and sometimes with greater frequency and familiarity, it surely makes sense to swap notes; the once very distinct dividing line between the two information communities has surely blurred

- And at the very least – to avoid duplication, there is a need to know where end-users' searches stop and those of the information professionals begin: this is fundamental to the delegation process

- They might take away the jobs of information professionals. This has been a long-running concern and rightly so, for knowing the strength of the competition is a fundamental tenet of business practice everywhere.

WHO AND WHAT ARE END-USERS?

The term end-user is used so loosely that it is necessary to define it. The term is now widely used outside the information field to denote the consumer of a product: in business, for instance, they use it irrespective of whether the person is using a computerised system or not. From an information professional's perspective however an end-user is someone who searches information systems themselves, either through choice or necessity. Invariably the term is used in a computerised setting. The dividing principle behind the information intermediary/end-user classification is degree or level of (information) professionalism, or perhaps more accurately in today's increasingly deregulated information environment, whether online searching is the person's principal job or not. In practice a line is being drawn between expert and novice searcher. There is a systems logic to this: expert searchers are more demanding (of systems) and systems in turn can be more demanding of them. In some ways it is perfectly understandable that such a distinction between online users should be made, given:

- The higher levels of training and education information professionals obtain in online searching and information retrieval in general

- Their greater opportunities for going online – after all the typical intermediary services the online needs of not just one person, but many

- The greater motivation to learn and enhance skills that might be expected from individuals working in the information profession.

But can you draw the line that confidently, for after all both groups are far from homogeneous? One might expect that even information professionals would vary in their online expertise, levels of professionalism, motivation and experience. Also the term end-user might be a convenient and popular term, but with the huge growth in the end-user population it has lost much of its meaning; bracketing together the home user, academic user, and professional user does not make a lot of sense. Most computer log studies have treated end-users as one big homogeneous group, which you can probably get away with rather more so in the case of academics than with practitioners – a far more heterogeneous group.

WHAT DO WE KNOW – AND NEED TO KNOW, ABOUT END-USERS?

Combing through the published research and computer logs we can get a pretty good idea of how end-users behave (or do not behave, as the case may be) at the terminal. However, some of the evidence is contradictory. Also much of it appears to have no other purpose than providing a testament to the poor searching skills of end-users. As a consequence, a very blinkered view of end-users can be obtained. The main things we need to know about end-users are:

- Their general characteristics – gender, occupation, position/ role in the organisation, age; what makes them search themselves, and correspondingly in what circumstances do they delegate
- The amount, frequency and duration of searches – this in particular is an area of folklore and mis-information
- The types of search statements and strategies that they use
- The range of commands and search facilities used, especially the so-called *advanced* commands
- Their use of display commands
- The files/sites they choose to search
- Their proficiency and skill – this has been the major preoccupation of information professionals
- The success and satisfaction they have with their searches
- Their training needs
- How their online searching behaviour is explained by their information needs.

General characteristics of end-users

Who are end-users, where do they work, and what subject, occupational and personal characteristics do they have? Of course, not everyone wants to be or can be an end-user. Of the journalists at *The Guardian* and research assistants at The House of Commons just 20% of them were end-users. Neither are end-users spread evenly throughout the population. In the case of some professional groups – like MPs, they are thin on the ground, yet in others (stockbroking) they are thick on the ground. Perhaps the biggest group of all are academics. But even in areas where end-use is fairly widespread you can always find organisations where no one searches, and even in institutions where people do search, you can always find individuals that do not search.

However, irrespective of their uneven distribution, end-users do now inhabit every walk of life, though it was not so long ago that they were really only a feature of academe and relatively rich commercial organisations. They are even in the home now, thanks to the spread of multimedia PCs. If you go by the users of the Internet then the global population of end-users is somewhere near the 15 million mark. Their huge and recent growth requires that they be categorised further to create more homogeneous groups. Academic, practitioner and consumer and home end-user is a useful start. Other ways of classifying end-users are discussed below.

Age, gender, seniority – and a whole range of personal factors are influential in determining whether someone becomes an end-user and how active an end-user they become. Thus we are told that Internet end-users are largely young and male. Gender, but not age difference, crops up in the searching of the traditional online hosts. At *The Guardian*, for instance, female journalists were less likely to conduct their own FT Profile searches than their male colleagues. Thus, while 21% of the staff were women, they accounted for 29% of the non-users and just 13% of heavy users. Looking at the figures in another way, half of the female journalists categorised themselves as non-users (only a third of the men regarded themselves as such). There is no single explanation for this difference, but it is possible that: women reporters were more computer-phobic than men reporters, that women were happier to delegate their searching than their male colleagues or, maybe, women rated their abilities more honestly. A number of CD-ROM studies have also found gender differences amongst online searchers too. Both Barber and Riccalton[2] and Borgman[3] found that women used more commands than men and, possibly related, they spent longer on a session.

With age usually comes seniority and with seniority comes delegation, especially in the business and legal professions. There are also less obvious differences amongst end-users. Thus it has been found that that dial-up users search very differently from inhouse users – geographical factors and telecommunication charges accounting for the difference[4,5]. Subject affiliation makes a difference too. Thus financial journalists at *The Guardian* searched very differently from most of their other newspaper colleagues. Indeed their searching characteristics were more akin to those of their library colleagues.

Reasons for end-use

There are a number of general factors which determine whether people will or will not become end-users:

- At the most basic level, whether the individual has access to a computerised information system. Obviously such systems

- with the exception of the Internet – are expensive and if an organisation is not well-off then these facilities will not be provided. It can be no coincidence that rich fields like business, law and the media have some of the biggest concentrations of end-users

- There is another aspect to access, for a system might be provided, but it might not be accessible, for reasons of distance, situated in an inconvenient place, or perhaps access is frustrated by queues, unhelpful menus or by slow response times

- It also has to do with whether appropriate databases containing quality information are provided

- The extent to which efficient information retrieval is seen to be an important part of the job and whether the particular strengths of computerised retrieval have a direct impact on job performance.

User friendliness has long been thought to be the major factor involved in whether an information system is used or not, but there are now a number of writers who are questioning this. Koblas[6], for instance, opines that, contrary to perceived wisdom, accessibility and ease of use are not prime determinants in people's use of information systems. She detects quality (of the data) considerations too and believes that it is not so much ease of use that is important but perceptions of how easy it is to use. For her, it is even more complex than that, for she would add personality, environmental and social characteristics as important determinants as to whether someone goes online or not. Oppenheim[7] is of a similar mind, for as far as he is concerned hosts too readily believe that their failure to crack the end-user market is because their product is technically lacking; their solution is user friendliness: menus, gateways, Windows, CD-ROM etc. According to Oppenheim, this emphasis is misplaced, for what really concerns the user, is whether the system offers "the answer to the person's questions – the right information at the right time at the right place". In defence he points out that spreadsheet programs sell hundreds of thousands of copies despite their well-known complexity.

A recurrent theme of much of the online literature on journalists, is that journalists would prove resistant to searching themselves because hosts, like FT Profile, supply just text and not the image – and that was not good enough for journalists for whom the image was very important. Thus Poynder[8], quotes a News International librarian as saying that, "to journalists the value of a newspaper story is as much in seeing where it appeared on the page and what it looked like, as [for] the information it contained. ... where a story appears on the page indicates how important it was".

This obviously applies more to tabloid journalists than broadsheet journalists but even so an early study of News International journalists showed that they searched FT Profile with alacrity[9]. Despite that evidence, this (misplaced) view has been the principal driving force in the move towards introducing costly optical storage systems in newspaper libraries.

In fact, journalists have proved particularly appreciative of online qualities. They seem to readily understand:

- The attractions of online as compared to the journalist's traditional information store – the cuttings collection
- Online's interactive and cross referencing facilities
- The speed with which information could be delivered online
- Online's special attraction to a new and inexperienced staff.

Indeed, journalists' passions are aroused by any possibility of its removal: "Datasolve (FT Profile) is the best thing about the place, journalistically speaking; the single most useful (information) tool we have; Datasolve has become absolutely indispensible"[10]. MPs' research assistants too were appreciative of onlines qualities. Thus, despite the fact that the House of Commons works on a highly delegated and efficient form of information provision, the vast majority (70%) of research assistants favoured doing their own searches.

Personal characteristics may be influential too in the decision to go online. Thus newspaper management have long attributed the alacrity with which journalists took to online to laziness "too lazy to walk a hundred metres to the library" and to their *spend* mentality "it's in their nature to be big spenders ... they book the best hotels, travel first class and run up big online bills"[11].

The main reasons why people choose to search themselves when facilities for delegation are provided are:

- An inability to explain their information needs to a third party or, indeed, to themselves -it is only through browsing that they see what they need. A journalist explained – "it's usually difficult to specify precisely what l want, it's only by browsing do I spot what I need; I am looking for something and in the process often find something of similar or greater use; I have the most extraordinary tastes, and I would not expect a librarian to second guess them; and I often find inspiration in information which I might not have initially, thought relevant"

- The inability of library staff to assess relevance: thus MPs' research assistants felt that library staff would not be able to "appreciate the significance of information", whereas the end-user could "assess the information and not miss anything"; the politically slanted data required by politicians often meant that research assistants were in the best position to make judgments about the political worth of the data

- A number of searches have to be undertaken or a number of lines of inquiry have to be carried out – and in these circumstances it is rather more difficult to delegate

- A need to have full control over the conduct and direction of the search. Delegation, it is felt, would cramp the creative process: this was the most frequently voiced reason for journalists conducting their own searches – "I prefer to follow my own line of thought, otherwise you are unable to make further checks on what is uncovered". Research assistants at The House of Commons thought similarly. Searching on their own offered "more control and flexibility". During the session, they could formulate their own search, broaden or narrow the search enquiry at will or, maybe, follow an interesting area of investigation

- There is insufficient time to delegate. Characteristic of the responses here are that it – "takes too long to explain what I want". End-users are forever in a hurry;

- The information required is specialist or technical in nature

- The search is of a confidential nature

- A lack of trust in the intermediary prevents delegation taking place

- Library staff are too busy or thought to be too busy to do the search.

Reasons for non-use

Certain groups are plainly not interested in searching themselves, even when provided with suitable, friendly and free systems. The usual reason is that they are too busy or self-important to search themselves and that they have very good information professionals to who they can delegate the search. Take the case of MPs. A group were given free access to FT Profile as part of a short term (12 months) experiment; 13 Members were signed up for the experiment and given training and a search allocation, but few Members took up their allocation, leading the House of Commons Library to the opinion that "most Members are content for Library staff to carry out searches on their behalf"[12]. Now other groups, like journalists for instance, would have fought tooth and nail to retain access to the facility.

Of course even end-users delegate their searching sometimes. Thus despite widespread end-use at *The Guardian* only 19% of journalists relied wholly on their own endeavours – less than the proportion (25%) who said they relied entirely on the library for their online searches. The rest, the large majority, were quite content to do both.

There are three main reasons why end-users delegate the online search:

- What encourages most to delegate is the proficiency and experience of the library staff – and by extension their own low level of expertise. They go to librarians for the difficult searches. Amongst journalists at *The Guardian* this accounted for 58% of the instances for delegation

- Access problems force them to do so – busy or fragile telephone lines or long queues at the terminal – this reason accounted for 26% of the instances of delegation at *The Guardian*. However, if the need for rapid information retrieval is there – as it patently was with journalists, end-use can flourish even in the most trying of conditions: a hundred or so journalists got by on just two passwords

- While lack of time is a reason not to delegate it is also a reason why users delegate – they think that librarians, because of their expertise, could do the search more quickly. At *The Guardian* this accounted for 17% of the instances of delegation.

Amount of use

It was once thought – and not so long ago, that levels of end-use were low and highly variable. For some groups that probably is still the case, but for others, levels of use can exceed that for information professionals; and, undoubtedly, levels of end-use are on the increase everywhere. East and Tilson[13] put the inexorable rise of the academic end-user down to such factors as increased familiarity with information technology, greater availability of databases and increased student numbers as driving the growth of end-use ever higher.

Among journalists at *The Guardian,* significant numbers did achieve volume levels normally associated with information professionals, searching five, six or even seven times a day. This was also true of MPs' research assistants. Even given the constraint of sharing one terminal with dozens of other researchers – and a terminal that was a long distance from their offices, the volume of end-use of TEXTLINE could only be regarded as phenomenal. Driven, no doubt, by an all-powerful need for current affairs information. Whatever statistic you take: the peak number of searches conducted in a day (34); the 2,340 search sessions conducted in a year; or the fact that end-use of TEXTLINE accounted for more than half of all commercial online searching done at The House of Commons – the performance was impressive.

The picture is a mixed one though. Thus Sullivan[14], surveying the use of Medline by practising scientists, found that despite nearly 150 of them having been trained in its use, the system was only accessed three times a day; and on average each of the 106 scientists who accessed the system used it once per month for about 22 minutes.

Measuring use

Use and non-use are at the very heart of most end-user discussions and investigations. There is a complicating factor though for use can be measured in a variety of ways. Use can be measured in terms of:

- Time online – the conventional measure
- The number of sessions, searches or transactions undertaken
- The number of documents retrieved or displayed
- The number of screens or lines viewed.

By their charging systems online hosts recognise that, as far as they are concerned, there are just two key components to use: the latter two – connect time and data (lines or records) displayed. Use data is best gleaned from computer logs. Surveys are too open to lapses in the users' memory and a natural inclination to overestimate the amount of their searching.

Use measures provide evidence of the value or worth of the system to the user. Plainly if a system is being used a lot then that is an indication of satisfaction with the system. Use measures may be used as indicators of other things. Thus:

- The amount of time online is used as an indicator of expertise – the better the searcher the quicker the searcher

- The number of records displayed is used as a measure of search success – zero displays indicating a 'poor' or 'bad' search, and as an indicator of whether the user requires comprehensiveness or not

- The amount of time online and the number of records displayed is said to point to searching style – browsing, for instance.

Search sessions

A search session can be defined as the online activity that occurs as a result of a particular query or line of enquiry. Practically it is identified by a log on and a log off, although it is always possible for a user to log off and return to a search later – maybe after a period of reflection. In connection with inhouse systems there is a problem of identification and demarcation, for they tend to be left on during the working day, thus users do not always mark their arrival or departure by logging in or logging out (many sessions are not formally terminated, they are just left in the air) and picked up by the next person. With commercial, connect time payment, searching is inevitably much more disciplined, and as a consequence a lot more can be read into session data – indeed, into all forms of activity data. A session may encompass more than a single search; users, especially librarians, stack queries for convenience and economy. For this reason it is important to distinguish between a search session and an individual search. In addition to containing a number of individual search statements, a session might also feature the changing of files and possibly, hosts, too.

123

Searches

An online search can be defined as that activity associated with a single query. It might, of course, involve a multitude of individual transactions – the use of various commands, displays of indexes and documents, and alternative search statements. In practice it is not always easy to distinguish between a search session and an individual search, because a user might use a variety of very different search approaches to find something. Normally, this is determined by a change in terms or strategies. The problems encountered in session identification (i.e. when one starts and finishes) are also problems here, too.

Time online

There are two calculations that can be made from the time spent online: the total amount of time spent online and the amount of time spent on individual searches. Time is probably the most obvious manifestation of use – and it is one that certainly preoccupies most investigators, but determining what can be read into the amount of time people spend online is a real problem. On the one hand someone spending a lot of time online may be regarded as a practiced, experienced and even successful end-user. On the other hand short searches are sometimes seen to be a sign of skill and proficiency. It is probably all too easy to fall in the trap and see time as a skill indicator. It is enshrined in professional folklore that end users are slow searchers – and, indeed, this is what some researchers have found[15]. Plainly, there is more to it than that for users, like journalists, might be constrained in the amount of time they have for searching; also, someone with a limited grasp of the system is unlikely to search for very long without getting frustrated or humiliated and wanting to stop searching. The one – and only – thing that can be said for certain, is that quick searches are going to be cheaper – hence the association with speed and prowess. The duration of searches can also point to the type of search being conducted (e.g. comprehensive) or searching method (e.g. browsing).

When end-user facilities were first being introduced the principal worry of librarians was that end-users would hog the terminals, soon breaking the library budget. Indeed this fear has stopped some libraries offering end-user facilities in the first place or preferring CD-ROM over online. In fact most of these fears have proven groundless. End-users are not the financial liability that many people thought. Even amongst free-spending, browsing journalists who were provided with a user-friendly full-text information system (FT Profile) searches proved to be extremely short. In fact their searches were sometimes accomplished (a little) more quickly than those undertaken by information professionals. In the case of journalists, an untrained user group, using a full-text database with a cumbersome **get** and **pick** approach, this must surely come as a surprise. Well over half the search sessions and individual searches were over in five minutes or less. Four minutes was the most common session time, with a general clustering of times around the three – six minute mark. Thirty five minutes was the longest time spent online by journalists, but generally very few sessions lasted beyond 20 minutes.

These short searching times were also found at The House of Commons, where 63% of the research assistants using POLIS accomplished their searches within 10 minutes. TEXTLINE use at The Commons also provided collaboration for end-user' short searches: more than half of their searches were accomplished in 10 minutes and an astonishing third were completed in five minutes. This was doubly surprising, as TEXTLINE was not generally noted for its speed of response at the time.

Lancaster *et al*[15] compared the times librarians and end-users took to conduct the same online searches. End-users took on average twice as long to search: librarians averaging 20-25 minutes and end-users 55. Interestingly, there was no obvious correlation between length of search and success in obtaining relevant documents.

Possible reasons for the relative brevity of end-user searches are:

* Searches are poorly formed and nothing is found – with nothing to print out, searches can be completed very quickly
* Systems are searched for material they do not have and drawing a blank, users abort the search
* Users can spare little time for the search
* End-users, knowing their limitations restrict themselves to very straightforward searches
* End-users are easily satisfied.

Records displayed

The number of records displayed as part of a search provides relatively hard evidence as to the use made of an information system. In the absence of posting counts – and these are often not supplied with transactional logs (the major source of data on records displayed) – they may also be used to measure the amount of data retrieved by end-users in relation to an individual search. Patently, the number of records displayed, is not necessarily the same thing as the number of documents found by a search, although it could be. However, it is always likely that users retrieved more documents (postings) but chose to display only a proportion, especially in the cases where large numbers of documents were found. In the case of inhouse open access OPACS, where it is difficult to distinguish between individual users the 'records displayed figure' gives the best evidence of system use. The display of documents is a conscious, demonstrable and quantifiable act.

Whether the number of items displayed provides, additionally, a measure of satisfaction or success of a search – as is claimed by some researchers[16] – is open to dispute. Because the display command is used to screen for relevancy, items displayed might be a better indicator (than postings) of how many items a user wants in regard to a query. Furthermore, successful searching – especially in the case of full-text systems – requires that documents be retrieved and then displayed; although a 'no display' might indicate that no material was available on a topic – possibly a positive result in the case of a journalist checking to see whether anybody had covered the topic that they were interested in writing a story on. Also, if a search finds nothing, then nothing can be displayed. Even if zero displays are taken to be an indicator of failure at the terminal then it is not necessarily always the user's fault. Failure may also be attributed to inadequacies in database coverage, failure to add new material to the system in time, inadequate training or poor system design.

There is a strong presumption in the published literature that more documents viewed (or found) means higher degrees of success. But does it? Take the case of a user who typically displays, say, 50 records and another who averages 10. Is the first a better searcher because they find more, or are they in fact the poorer searcher because their broad and ill-defined searching results in more documents and noise? Perhaps, they were just doing different kinds of searches – the fact that one was doing an idea-generation one and the other a fact-finding one could account for the difference. Large displays of documents can then be a sign of other things: searching style (browsing), retrospective searching (with the reverse chronological displays most systems default to the display of lots of documents inevitably means going back further in time), and the need for thoroughness or comprehensives in searching. The last association is the one that has captivated most researchers. Barbuto and Cellavos[16], for instance, defined a comprehensive search as one that retrieved more than 50 records – a definition very much grounded in academia, and why 50 you might ask and not 30? Indeed, the validity of this number was called into doubt when the author observed that the number of records needed by users saying that they required a comprehensive search was scrutinised – a third of them were looking for just 1-10 records. Comprehensiveness is of course a relative term and the attempt to measure it by document numbers alone can result in some not so convincing observations. Dividing the number of records displayed by connect time possibly provides a rough measure of productivity or search efficiency.

Number of screens viewed

A variation on the number of records displayed is the number of screens the user views as a result of a search. While an interesting measure in its own right, it is another rough and ready activity measure. You cannot equate screens viewed with the number of records displayed, because the number of records displayed per screen is variable, being dependent on a number of factors:

- The format chosen – the briefer the format the more records contained on a screen
- The length of the record – the longer the record the more screens needed to view it
- Because it is often a carriage return that signals a new screen, if users choose to override the automatic break then there is no knowing how many screens they viewed.

Number of online interactions

It is possible to make a distinction between a search and the component parts of the search: individual interactions or transactions. Thus a single search session might involve a large number of individual interactions with the system: terms may be input, added to or changed or, perhaps, the index is examined to check on term availability. The attraction of using the number of operations as a measure of activity is that it provides a measure of busyness when online. As Peters *et al*[17] point out "two search sessions may last the same amount of real time, but one may feature a lot more commands than the other ... two searches may contain the same number of commands yet one could last substantially longer than the other ... "

Search formulations, strategies and approaches

Anecdote has it that end-users search very simply indeed, and, if true, no doubt this is a function of the very limited amount of training most of them receive. Specifically we need to examine end-users' searches in the light of: access points adopted; term use; the development of the search during an online session; type of search conducted.

Access points

There are two questions here: what access point(s)/field(s) are used to search the system; and whether the search is a simple or hybrid one – one involving more than one access point. Akeroyd[18] provides us with evidence that, when given a choice of approaches, end-users opt for the simplest search key – the one they could grasp most easily. Invariably this key is the subject one[19]. Even when the initial search was not a subject one, as the search progressed, it soon turned into one. Thus Hancock-Beaulieu[19] found that one third of all specific (known) item searches turned into subject searches during the search process. We can expect more known item searches in the case of OPACs – and this is what Akeroyd largely found, but then OPAC users are typically chasing references and not information – as would be the case with practitioners, who are searching full-text databases from their desks. In fact all the evidence points to practitioners being exclusively subject searchers. Thus *Guardian* journalists hardly ever conducted non-subject searching: title and author were on average employed, respectively, in four per cent and one per cent of searches.

Of the forms of subject searching title keyword searching has proved popular. In one study it was found that these searches accounted for 44% of all searches, whereas subject heading searches only accounted for 16% of all searches[5]. The use of controlled terms or subject headings has interested researchers because of the added complexity involved (and the large investment made by librarians in controlled languages). In an extensive study Ensor[20] discovered that keyword (controlled terms in this case) knowledge was woeful, and that a knowledge of keywords made users more satisfied with their searches. Unfortunately, this was not everybody's experience, for Barbuto and Cellavos[17] declared that thesaurus use – something quite important to controlled language searching – did not lead to higher levels of user satisfaction, non-thesaurus users retrieved more documents; and that users commonly failed to distinguish between descriptors and keywords (natural language terms). Larsen's[21] earlier work had already pointed to end users moving the way of natural language searching.

Subject searching of whatever kind is problematic because of the difficulties of clothing concepts with terms – synonyms, related terms, broader and narrower terms and word forms all have to be taken into account. And that takes its toll. However *Guardian* journalists (obviously a canny group of end-user) had overcome some of these pitfalls by searching on name as a subject: the vast majority of their searches were of this kind.

Term use

There are a number of quite interesting points to consider here: choice of terms – are they broad or narrow, are they appropriate, how many are employed, do they match the systems' vocabulary?

It appears that end-users' information needs are more nebulous than indicated by search terms[19]. Users also exhibit a tendency to put all the information they had into the first search, rather than hold some back in the case of a poor return[5]. Stanbridge[22] was of the opinion that journalists choose terms almost randomly: "reporters working under pressure usually bait their hook with a random keyword or two and are quite happy with anything they catch that adds some colour or gives a slant to what they are writing". Rigglesford[23] in a study of a financial CD-ROM found that end-users searched along fairly broad topical categories, whereas the searches of information professionals were typically more precise and sophisticated.

Guardian journalists showed a soundness and directness in their choice of terms but the use of alternative words or word forms were very much on the low side. The absence of truncation and the Boolean **or** suggested that journalists hardly ever present the system with a choice of related or synonymous terms. A number of researchers have found that end-users have an inadequate and limited search vocabulary: in the words of one author: "they search too literally"[24].

There is enough evidence to confirm that end-users only employ a relatively small number of terms in their searching. Thus Sullivan[14] found that searching was done at a 'simple' level with over half the end-users' search strategies containing between two to five words (a wide margin admittedly); just 15% contained more than five words. The study of *Guardian* journalists largely provides corroboration for these findings, with two-thirds of all searches containing one or two terms and just 16% of searches containing four words or more.

Matching initial search expressions with information system access points is one thing, but finding them satisfactory when used is another. Thus Hancock-Beaulieu[25] found that 81% of the terms chosen to interrogate the OPAC coincided with access points – another 15% partly matched, however when online only 29% proved satisfactory with 52% of students narrowing their terms as a consequence.

Behaviour during a session

Whether end-users persevere in the face of the difficulties experienced when they go online is open to doubt. On the one hand Akeroyd[18] found that his OPAC users had a lot of perseverance when searching: they tried to ratify a nil response by using alternative approaches to the same document. But then he did set them a test so maybe that accounts for this finding. On the other hand practitioners are probably unlikely to have the time or motivation to do this; indeed, in the study of *Guardian* journalists there was no evidence of this having taken place, it was the *Guardian* librarians that did this.

On the whole journalists end users did not appear to change their search strategies on the basis of what was found. Their searches only occasionally developed, in the sense that search strategies were adjusted and developed in the light of what was found. Online search strategies were largely direct and straightforward with 40% expressed in a single line, and over 70% expressed in two lines. A number of searches were quite complex – or long-winded, involving six, seven or eight steps but these were by far the exception. Generally speaking, journalists' searches contained more steps than those of the librarians. Sullivan[14] found that 30% of end-user searches contained three or more steps – and this was exactly the same case with journalists. The difficulty comes in knowing exactly what to read into this data. On the one hand, searches involving a number of stages can be a sign of online maturity – the searcher interacting with the data and fine-tuning the search as a result. However, on the other hand, it could say something about the quality of the initial search expression. i.e. it was poorly constructed and thus had to be changed.

Types of search

The question whether end-users require everything on a topic or just a few items has pre-occupied information researchers. Academics, when asked, said they required a comprehensive search, but when prompted to quantify this the responses were very variable – a third believing that 1-10 items would constitute such a search, while a quarter thought this to be more than 50. Other academic studies however have indicated that users were in fact satisfied with a small number of pertinent documents – perhaps using these as keys to unlock more material at the shelves[18].

Akeroyd[18] has pointed to the large amount of browsing that goes on, but didn't really quantify it, though he identified two types:

- Compensatory browsing where because of some error or problem at the input stage the user tries to rectify the position by scanning large numbers of documents
- Meaningful browsing – structured, directed and purposive searching.

Guardian journalists did browse a lot, but in this they were no different to their information professionals. The idea, that end-users, forced by poor searching skills to scroll through screen after screen to unearth something relevant, appears to be a nonsense. Indeed, it was the librarians that did this, partly because of their professional tenacity; partly because of an obligation to give users more data, so that they could fine tune it; partly because they were not so well placed to make immediate value judgments and partly to do with the fact that the librarians got the more difficult searches delegated to them.

Commands used

End-users are said to use a limited range of commands and few, if any, of the so-called advanced searching features, like Boolean operators and truncation. This was very much true at *The Guardian*, where even Profile's limited range was not fully utilised, 40% of Profile's commands were not used. The main uncertainty in explaining away the low use of commands is whether to attribute it largely to the broad brush information seeking styles of end-users, to inadequate training or to the fact that end-users cannot grasp how databases are constructed. Perhaps though it has something to do with practice for it seems that frequent users employed more search commands (twice as many) as infrequent users[26].

End-users get by with very few commands and ignore or evade such advanced facilities as Boolean searching and truncation. Peters[5] found that 97% of searches were simple author, title or subject searches, with virtually no truncation being employed at all. Newkirk and Jacobson[27] discovered that a quarter of all end-user searches contained no Boolean operators. Where Boolean operators were employed it tended to be the **and** that was used. The **or** was generally wholly neglected. Kirby and Miller[28] found that 58% of search statements employed the **and**, but only 2% the **or**. Tenopir *et al*[17] in an examination of the use of full text files also noted that **or** was used infrequently.

In the case of *The Guardian* study the Boolean **or** and **not** were not used at all. In the light of this it is not surprising that the bracket – the means by which **or** and **and** logic can be combined in a single search statement, was never used. The concept of brackets altering the priority of processing the search statement is not an easy one to grasp. Indeed, if you had to choose one feature that really differentiated end-user searching from that of professional librarians, the use of brackets would surely be it.

The use or non-use of truncation has particularly fascinated researchers. Truncation is, of course, a convenient and camouflaged form of the Boolean **or,** though a concept with which few end-users appear to be familiar with. Akeroyd[18] and Peters[5] both found low or non-existent levels of truncation in their studies. The interesting thing about truncation is that, unlike Boolean operators, it is not a difficult concept to understand. It is often the information systems themselves that are responsible for its low use for they give the command very little prominence or publicity. Illustrating the contradictions inherent in log studies or, perhaps, the differences between online systems, Tenopir *et al*[17] however, produced figures to show that truncation was used quite frequently by full text users – the full text and natural language nature of the database explaining the discordance. However *The Guardian* study involved just such a database and truncation was only used by one person in one search over the two day survey period.

Display commands used

It has already been noted that end-users use the display command as a continuation of the search process – and not simply as a method of document delivery. To get an idea of how they do this, consider *Guardian* journalists' use of FT Profile. Profile is a full-text host and as a result it functions both as a library catalogue and as the library's shelves. And, to take the analogy further, all the walking and browsing is done at the terminal through a range of display commands. In common with most systems Profile has a number of display commands. Firstly, there are the commands that determine the amount and nature of detail displayed: **h** provides the title and, in some cases, the section heading; **ctx** provides the title and paragraphs containing the highlighted search terms; and **tx** provides the full text of the document.

Despite their very short searches journalists managed over four display commands per search. A visual scan of the computer logs confirmed that journalists carefully go through records online to establish relevance. The approach preferred was the two-prong **headline** and **text** display. The **context** display was quite often by-passed. There are three possible explanations. Firstly, journalists were simply not aware of it. Secondly, they felt that they just did not need it – the number of records retrieved were sufficiently manageable not to warrant its use. But in all probability it was the fact that so much journalism is looking for small detail – and that can only be obtained through an examination of the full text. Thirdly, and most likely, journalists were deeply suspicious of partial data. This suspicion is based, in part at least, on what appears to be a complete misunderstanding of databases in general and Profile in particular. A *Guardian* librarian provided this example in illustration. "Say you are looking for something on Arizona and you find a story whose headline clearly indicates that it is an article on Lancashire. In this circumstance we would give the journalist a **ctx.** But I have had people *insist*, despite my explanations and protestations, that I print out the full text. On having done so, they say, in disappointed tones ' oh but that's the **only** mention of Arizona in the article".

File selection

End-users are thought to be limited in their knowledge and use of hosts and databases. Thus Peters[5] found that one of the major reasons users failed to find what they wanted was because they were searching inappropriate databases – this was attributed to 39% of their failed searches. However, often end-users are only provided with access to one system and even in the case of the system they are provided with, they are furnished with very little information on file coverage. In such circumstances what else could you expect? Even so, *The Guardian* study found that end-users were not noticeably single-source oriented. Thus on average, each journalist searched two files and changed files once in 10 searches. They were really not significantly more single-source oriented than the librarians, and, indeed, their searches actually ranged over a larger number of files – 10 of which were not used by the librarians. Research assistants at The House of Commons had no problems searching two very different systems – FT Profile and POLIS – both were very heavily used.

Proficiency

Proficiency judgments are made on the basis of assumptions concerning many of the previous searching traits. Thus heavier users are supposed to be skilled users; searching a wide range of database and files is seen to be a sign of expertise, utilising a wide range of commands and facilities is a hallmark of a good searcher; fast searchers likewise, but the use of advanced system commands in particular has been used as the main indicator of expertise. Librarians frequently disparage the online searching skills of their end-users. For many professionals the moment you let users do their own searching, quality goes out of the window. No hard evidence is provided in support, but many anecdotes are recounted. There is always the slight suspicion that librarians say this because they are never really at home with the whole idea of end-use; for they feel threatened that their (alleged) superior searching skills are being put to the test.

End-users do search simply, but whether you can call this type of searching lacking in proficiency is something else. Certainly end-user searches have proved to be straightforward and simple, in that they contain few terms and commands and that truncation, Boolean **or**, field and word proximity are rarely practised. The hallmark search does tend to be a bare essentials one, which gives very early contact with the data, and then maximum time online to browse and display records. Some of the problems end-users encounter when entering compound statements are circumvented by entering search statements in phrase form. They do not disassemble their queries into keywords, and then shepherd these terms, into facets and keywords, as librarians frequently do.

However when asked about the problems they encounter, end-users rarely mention systems commands and search strategies. Instead they highlight the practical problems associated with searching – logging on, scrolling and downloading data. There is evidence to indicate that it is every-day problems, like typing and spelling errors, that cause them much grief; Peters *et al*[5] found that such errors accounted for 21% of the problems her users experienced. At *The Guardian* too, journalists' searches were not so much characterised by misuse of the search and display commands as by typographical and spelling errors – 44% of their searches contained such errors.

Despite the fact that many end-user groups have now been active for a good number of years, the indications are that there has not been much of an improvement in searching skill[29]. Miles[30], reviewing the searching of News International journalists also provides support for the view that little has changed; indeed, in her case things might well have regressed.

Success and satisfaction

Whether success and satisfaction can be bracketed together is a controversial point. Plainly if end-users feel satisfied with their searches then their searches must have been reasonably successful. What is disputed is whether the user is in the best position to judge this. Say you had presented the results of the end-user's search to an information professional or measured it by some precision/recall notion it might not seem to be as successful as thought. Success, like beauty, is often in the mind of the beholder. Of course, there must be some relationship between skill and search success – otherwise no one would ever bother to train. But the relationship is not a simple one. It all depends on how you measure success and who does the measuring. Thus end-users are frequently found to be highly satisfied with their searches, when perhaps an information professional producing the same results would not be. Also, what of the parameters of success – if only one document is found, but provides an acceptable answer, why should a search producing lots of documents prove any better?

It would be true to say that the prevailing view amongst information professionals is that end-users meet with very little success when they go online, which is an interesting view when you consider the vast and increasing numbers who choose to search themselves. But many of their criticisms are made on the back of anecdotes – personal observation at best. The following is par for the course: "I have frequently found people searching [Medline CD-ROM] in the most peculiar, inefficient and totally illogical fashion. It is a slightly hair-raising prospect when the searcher is a junior doctor sent by his chief to do the spade work for an article to be submitted for publication, let alone searches relating to treatment of actual patients[31]. It is not just hospital doctors that come in for criticism. Barker[32] singled out top research scientists as well: "Once you let inexperienced users do their own searching, quality can no longer be guaranteed".

A lot of the earlier criticisms of end-users must be regarded as highly suspect for until quite recently end-users simply did not have sufficient exposure to online systems to be able to establish patterns of online searching.

How then can end-user success and satisfaction be measured:

- The traditional measure has been to use recall/precision measures
- You can also ask people whether they were satisfied
- By the number of documents retrieved; especially the failure to find anything – the no-hits search
- You can use the number of fulltext displays as a measure on full text systems
- By comparison with information professionals.

Recall / precision measures

Such tests have a long history in measuring the success of searches and are largely associated with the evaluation of systems. But the presumptions behind them are rather shaky, particularly when considered in the practitioner environment. Because of the inverse relationship between the two measures, there is often a need to plump for one or the other, and recall has proved the librarian-favoured measure. But this is a measure of success more likely to be accepted by a researching academic, determined on completeness (pinning down all the potentially relevant literature). Fraught and busy practitioners, with deadlines of minutes, using the facility as a supplement to their other methods of information acquisition are unlikely to see it that way. Given the aforementioned, it might be expected that practitioner end-users would score more highly in precision terms and look more favourably at precision as a measure of success, but the way that many journalists and politicians generally seek information – by browsing around – means precision scores are not going to be all that significant either. Recall/precision methods assume that you know what you are looking for in the first place and that others can identify and establish exactly what you should be finding, but the serendipitous route to end-user success and the difficulties of establishing target populations in full-text natural language databases means there are going to be problems in the computation of the scores. Lancaster *et al*[24] overcame some of these objections by allowing the users to determine the relevance of their searches and those of the librarians, but this is much easier to do in the context of a bibliographic database, where populations of relevant documents are much more easily assembled, and in the light of the much more focused needs of academics.

Asking end-users whether they were successful

If success can be measured by satisfaction, then much end-user searching is successful, because many studies show high levels of satisfaction amongst end-users. This was very much the case in the author's own researches. Thus at *The Guardian* well over a third of journalists said they were almost always wholly satisfied with their searching and more than half were sometimes satisfied – high praise indeed in the case of a system (Profile) that was not easy to log into, and, when connected, not always easy to get relevant data out of. At The House of Commons, where the question was phrased a little differently, politicians also showed their satisfaction – 84% said they were usually satisfied with their POLIS searches and 72% with their TEXTLINE searches. The lower level of satisfaction with TEXTLINE was probably due to the hit and miss nature of searching natural language, full text databases. Also, the very fact that so much end-use was taking place would suggest that a good deal of searching was successful.

Both groups of end-users did not have time on their hands and they did have alternative sources to turn to, so they would not prevail with online unless they felt it gave them what they wanted.

The number of records retrieved or displayed

Larsen[21] is one of a number of authors that have taken no-hits as a mark of an unsuccessful search and believes that no hits are indeed characteristic of end-user searches, "We can assume that ... 35-50% of the searches [of end-users] will result in nothing, and that even when material is found it is not always relevant". He seems to have some support for this view from Peters et al[5], who found in a transactional log study of American academics, that as many as 40% of the searches produced no apparent result. They also measured satisfaction by comparing the number of documents the users said they wanted, with what they actually found. To probably nobody's surprise only those requiring 1-10 documents were most satisfied.

In regard to The House of the Commons and *The Guardian*, end-users did perform less well than the librarians. In regard to the former: 24% of the searches of MPs' Research Assistants ended up with no displays of records, whereas the figure for House of Commons librarians was 18%; in the case of *The Guardian* it was much closer than that − 18% (journalists) and 17% (librarians). However, in the politician's study, where library searching groups could be identified, there were a number of groups who recorded an even greater zero display score.

The fact that no-hits are not necessarily a sign of failure would seem to be supported by Akeroyd[18] for he found that the more experienced users accepted zero results more readily.

Comparisons with information professionals

End-user search proficiency has often been determined by comparing it with that of information professionals, but these comparisons have not always been conducted on a level playing field. Typically end-users have had poorer access to online systems than the intermediaries and few, if any, of them received any training. Rubbishing the abilities of end-users on the basis of restricted (and formative) searching is plainly wrong.

However, very much part of the professional folklore is that information professionals have a lot more success with their searches.

It is argued that their success arises out of their professional training, the greater opportunities that they have to practise their online skills, and their professional commitment to improve and update their skills. The professional literature – no doubt with a little self-interest and self-preservation in mind – is rich in studies parading the professional searchers' virtues. Salovaara[33] examined the differences in a technical research and development environment. On the basis of a limited amount of searching it was concluded that: professional searchers found more relevant references per topic than end-users and this was largely achieved by the professionals searching more databases, though a half-professional searcher had as good a result as the professional and yet looked at fewer databases.

Lancaster et al[24], looked specifically at the issue of end-user versus information professional searching. The main aims of the research project were to establish whether the searching of academic librarians produced better results than their users, and to compare their search approaches. The hypothesis being tested was, that experienced and trained searchers (the librarians) would get better results than novices (end-users) – despite the fact the end-users were best placed to determine what they wanted. Thirty five test searches were undertaken and, indeed, the librarians proved more successful in retrieving items that the end-users thought were useful. But the authors did point out that this has to be qualified by the fact that, even in the cases of the best professional searches, only half the items retrieved proved useful – in the end-users' case this was nearer one-third. This was attributed to the limited information the librarians had to work with (i.e. the request forms). A weak argument this, for many librarians, like those offering essentially phone-based information services, have less than that to work on.

However, even if all this follows, does it necessarily mean that intermediaries provide the better search results: does a detailed knowledge of system commands and long hours online necessarily mean that the product of the search is actually superior? Surely, what makes a good search, is crucial to the whole debate (and at the end of the day the only opinion really worth hearing is that of the consumer) and when asked about their searches they say that they are generally well satisfied with what they get from their online labours[34].

Training

Perhaps the question is not so much whether end-users have the skills they need, rather have they got the skills they want. It is all a question of balance and competing demands. It is very doubtful whether training programmes are really worth it, with perhaps an exception being introductory courses for newcomers. Apart from students and some regimented groups like scientists, it is unlikely that end-users will turn-up or stay the course. Journalists never did. Journalists are not only untrained but they seldom have quick-reference sheets to assist them. They also show a marked reluctance to read and apply the help and guidance provided on the screens. They generally get by asking colleagues and not the library for help/guidance. There is evidence that this is true of other end-user groups too.

Therefore searching behaviour was as much a function of untutored use as end-use. In the circumstances could anything other than simple, error-ridden searching be expected? The fact that this was not always the case is the real surprise. Librarians seemed quite quick to denigrate searching behaviour but did not seem so quick to provide the most obvious solution to the problem – training. This lack of concern or support could not be simply fobbed off with the excuse that the systems were user-friendly and, as such, required no training or support.

Information needs

No analysis of online information seeking behaviour (after all that is what end-use is) is complete without a consideration of the information needs and general information seeking behaviour of the subjects studied. Without such an understanding it is very difficult to interpret the raw data, that transactional log analysis in particular, generates in vast quantities. End-use is not conducted in a vacuum. It is not just a case of discovering, say, that journalists take four minutes to conduct a search – for that is the easy bit, but also determining *why* that should be so. Searching behaviour of end-users should be viewed, wherever possible, in the light of what is known about their information needs and information seeking behaviour.

REFERENCES

1. Nicholas, D. *Stereotypical online searching behaviour: end users,* PhD dissertation, City University (1995).

2. Barber, A. and Riccalton, C. *The use of LS2000 Online public access catalogue at Newcastle University Library,* British Library Research and Development Department, London (1988).

3. Borgman, C. *et al.* Children's use of an interactive catalog of science materials, In: *ASIS '90: Proceedings of the 53rd ASIS annual meeting,* Learned Information, Medford, N.J. (1991).

4. Sloan, R. Hightech/Low profile: automation and the invisible patron, *Library Journal,* **111**, November 1986, 4-6.

5. Peters, T., Kurth, M., Flaherty, P., Sandore, B. and Kaske, N. Transaction log analysis, *Library High Tech,* **11** (2) 1993, 37-106.

6. Koblas, J. So why do people use online? An investigation into the discretionary use of electronic information resources, In: *Online Information 93: 17th International Online Information Meeting Proceedings, London 7-9 December 1993,* Learned Information, London, 219-226.

7. Oppenheim, C. Designing for the end-user marketplace, In: *Information systems for end-users: research and development issues,* edited by M. Hancock-Beaulieu, Taylor Graham, London, (1992, 25-34).

8. Poynder, R. Meeting the needs of journalists, *Information World Review,* June 1993, 8.

9. Nicholas, D, Erbach, G., Pang, Y. and Paalman, K. *End-users of online information systems: an analysis,* Mansell, London (1988).

10. Nicholas, D, Erbach, G., Pang, Y. and Paalman, K. *End-users of online information systems: an analysis.* Mansell, London (1988, 24-25).

11. Nicholas, D, Erbach, G., Pang, Y. and Paalman, K. *End-users of online information systems: an analysis,* Mansell, London (1988, 23)

12. House of Commons, Information Committee, *The provision of a Parliamentary Data and Video Network,* HMSO, London (1994, 99).

13. East, H. and Tilson, Y. The liberated end-user: developments in practice and policy for database provision to the academic community, British Library Board, London (1993).

14. Sullivan, M. Training for Medline on CD-ROM: a case study in an industrial environment, In: *Information Systems for End-User,*. edited by M. Hancock-Beaulieu, Taylor Graham, London (1992, 71-78).

15. Lancaster, F., Elzy, C., Zeter, M., Metzler, L., and Low, Y-W. Searching databases on CD-ROM: comparison of the results of end-user searching with results from two modes of searching by skilled intermediaries, *RQ,* **33** Spring 1994, 370-386

16. Barbuto, D. *and* Cellavos, E. End-user searching: program review and future prospects, *RQ,* **31** (2) Winter 1991, 214-227.

17. Tenopir, C., Nahl-Jakobovits, D., and Howard, D. Full-text search strategies and modifications: the role of the searcher and the role of the system, In: *Beginning our second decade: proceedings of the Eleventh National Online Meeting,* Learned Information, Medford, N.J. (1990, 383-399).

18. Akeroyd, J. Information seeking in online catalogues, *Journal of Documentation,* **46** (1) March 1990, 33-52.

19. Hancock-Beaulieu, M. *et al. Evaluation of online catalogues: an assessment of methods,* British Library Research and Development Department, London (1990, B).

20. Ensor, P. and Curtis, R. Search helper: low cost online searching in an academic library, *Reference Quarterly,* **23** 1984, 327-331.

21. Larsen, G. End-user searching and the human aspect, In: *Online Information 88: 12th International Online Information Meeting, London 6-8 December 1988,* Learned Information, London (1988. vol, 2, 467-474).

22. Stanbridge, R. Journalists begin to embrace online databases themselves, *Information World Review,* **76** December 1992, 46-48.

23. Rigglesford, D. CD-ROM: the answer for end-users? In: *Information systems for end-users.* edited by M. Hancock-Beaulieu, Taylor Graham, London (1992, 35-44).

24. Lancaster, F., Elzy, C., Zeter, M., Metzler, L., and Low, Y-W. Searching databases on CD-ROM: comparison of the results

of end-user searching with results from two modes of searching by skilled intermediaries, *RQ,* **33**, Spring 1994, 375.

25. Hancock-Beaulieu, M. Evaluating the impact of an online catalogue on subject searching behaviour at the catalogue and at the shelves, *Journal of Documentation,* **46** (4) December 1990(A), 318-338.

26. Penniman, W. Modelling and evaluation of online user behaviour, In: *Information Interaction: Proceedings of the 45th ASIS Annual Meeting,* Knowledge Industry Publications, White Plains, N.Y. (1982).

27. Newkirk, J. and Jacobson, T. CD-ROM search strategy analysis: a pilot study, *Computers in Libraries Conference,* Meckler, London (1993).

28. Kirby, M. and Miller, N. Medline searching on Colleague: reasons for failure or success of untrained end-users, *Medical Reference Services Quarterly,* **5** (3) Fall 1986, 17-34.

29. Fisher, J. and Bjorner, S. Enabling online end-user searching: an expanding role for librarians, *Special Libraries,* **85** Fall 1994, 281-282.

30. Miles, E. *I.T. and the editorial production at The Times,* MSc Dissertation, City University, London (1993).

31. Brewster, P. Letter, *Information World Review CD-ROM,* May 1995, np.

32. Barker, C. [Quoted in] Pros and cons of end-users' direct access to electronic data, *Information World Review CD-ROM,* March 1993.

33. Salovaara, I. Experiences in end-user and intermediary searching at the technical research centre of Finland (VTT), In: *Online Information 88: 12th International Online Information Meeting, London 6 – 8 December 1988. Vol. 1,* Learned Information, Londond (1988, 103-110).

34. Jacobson, T. and Ullman, J. Commercial databases and reporting: opinions of newspaper journalists and librarians, *Newspaper Research Journal,* **10** (2) Winter 1989, 15-25.

Knowledge Management

Marcus Speh

INTRODUCTION

Knowledge management (KM) describes the way in which organisations are attempting to capture, enhance, and utilise the knowledge necessary for their survival. There is a fair overlap between knowledge management and information management as a way of dealing with the information needed and produced by an organisation. Hence, KM has professional implications for information managers and librarians who work as specialists in organisations.

Technology is rapidly making external information easily available world-wide. As companies move more and more towards knowledge-based activities as their primary product, knowledge of and access to these sources becomes vital to competitive advantage and business performance. Even more vital is knowledge of, and access to, information residing in the heads of an organisation's employees. In most companies this knowledge has never been identified or recorded, and is of course lost if the employee leaves. Even if the knowledge were known and available, few mechanisms exist to ensure that it is shared where needed and utilised creatively. Yet it is widely believed that managing this knowledge is likely to become the key to future wealth creation, and that it is, in fact, already at the core of present industrial performance.

In his seminal book on KM[1], Karl Wiig writes about the paradigmatic shift from *factual* to *reasoning* and *methodological* knowledge, linking it to the traditional way in which information professionals work:

"When analysing the work of novice, and even some seasoned, knowledge professionals, for example, it is remarkable to observe that they often focus only on 'factual' aspects of knowledge, such as: "What do you know about market conditions? Products? Who do you go to for help?" Only the more experienced knowledge professionals who are given deeper understanding of how knowledge is used by people and organisations have the additional insights to focus on the knowledge needed to use factual knowledge – i.e. knowing *what to do* and *how to do it*. In addition to factual knowledge they also understand to focus on knowledge required to reason and perform knowledge-intensive activities proficiently. Even though factual knowledge is very important, it is reasoning and methodological knowledge that creates value for the organisation by making it possible to build quality products and deliver quality services."

The public discourse is also reacting to the interest in KM. Typical titles of talks at conferences featuring KM read:

- Leveraging knowledge for performance and competitive advantage
- Who in your company should drive knowledge management?
- Effectively communicating to employees the value of knowledge sharing
- How to retain knowledge within the organisation which would otherwise be lost.

Information centres are the logical place for managers to look when trying to leverage their corporate knowledge, but the tasks required are not tasks fulfilled by most information professionals today. Nor do most people understand what the activity of KM requires. Nevertheless information professionals are increasingly being asked to act as knowledge managers. A new profession is forming here. The actual role is still not totally clear, but we are beginning to see the outline.

This chapter will attempt to explain what KM involves, and thus what the extended roles and responsibilities of knowledge managers are likely to be.

THE KNOWLEDGE MANAGER'S ROLE

The primary role of a knowledge manager is to provide continuity and integration across management and content/relevance changes. Changes of management occur when the organisational structure is changing or when employees are moving into or out of their positions. Changes of content/relevance occur, for example, when a company is changing its products, its market or its position in the market.

But how does an information manager go about making this move, and what are the activities of a knowledge manager? To answer this question, I will discuss four activities of a knowledge manager in some detail and link them to the needs of a business organisation which is modelling itself into a knowledge managing organisation:

- Catalogue, i.e. define the organisation's knowledge assets
- Capture, i.e. decide how the knowledge will be structured and made available
- Retrieve, i.e. assist users in the proper use of IT tools to access the knowledge
- Utilise, i.e. assist managers to use the available knowledge creatively.

As activities to collect and provide factual knowledge and information to customers, these areas are already part of the task package of today's information manager. I have chosen the categories deliberately with this fact in mind. As you will see, KM is to some extent about doing things you either already are doing, or know how to do, in a different way, with a different perspective and within a different culture. There is no need to re-invent existing information services. Rather, the role of the knowledge manager is, for the most part, an extension and re-definition of the role of the conscientious, dedicated and creative information manager.

Catalogue knowledge capital

Cataloguing knowledge capital means supporting the definition of the knowledge assets of your organisation. This task area includes the following responsibilities of a knowledge manager:

- Help determine what knowledge is important
- Conduct internal audit of resources
- Identify external resources.

There would not be an incentive to think about managing knowledge, or even improving on the acquisition of information, if organisations were not interested in improving the quality of information, the applicability and accuracy of the knowledge employed to provide business solutions. It is *best knowledge* that we want to collect, store, and disseminate, not just any information or *factual knowledge*. This knowledge is what is then called *knowledge capital*.

The very first step of every KM programme must therefore be to determine what the knowledge capital of the organisation is. Based on this assessment, the next step is an audit of the existing knowledge assets of the organisation – the best knowledge. This includes physical as well as non-physical collections of knowledge, explicit as well as tacit knowledge. There is a great variety of forms of tacit knowledge such as ideas, experience, intuition, expertise, learnt behaviour, understanding and skills.

The knowledge audit will need to be led by the most experienced executives in the organisation. Information professionals can provide valuable insights into both the nature of the knowledge to be audited, and into ways of performing the audit. At a later stage, knowledge managers will also be the guardians of the knowledge to ensure that it is continuously weeded and that obsolete knowledge is replaced by new state-of-the-art knowledge.

Example 1

The board of a middle-sized manufacturing company established a multidisciplinary task force to perform a complete audit of the company's knowledge assets. The main objective of the task force was to find those business functions which most critically depended on knowledge sharing between the employees and the quality of knowledge employed. The task force had two information professionals on board – a specialist industry information officer and the firm's head of information services. The head of information contributed to the task force's final report by producing research enquiry statistics of the firm's departments and by marketing the knowledge management to several senior executives. Her detailed knowledge of running a whole service allowed her to present the complexity of the information needs and the effort required to satisfy these needs in a value adding way. The industry information officer contributed a detailed account of the information required by industry specialist managers during a period of expansion into a new market, and how this information was relevant to the successful market penetration. Using her industry information experience, she also compiled a list of keywords which allowed her to reorganise the internal reports produced by managers. One executive later said: "Before I saw this list, I had no idea that we had knowledge in several areas. This repre-

> sents a great amount of experience extremely relevant to our competitive position!" After the initial knowledge audit had been finished, it became clear how important it had been to have the two information professionals on board. Their involvement in subsequent steps of the knowledge management programme, planned as a result of the audit, provided an important element of continuity.

The audit of internal knowledge resources can be arbitrarily complicated. It can, and should, go well beyond merely cataloguing available internal information. It should include the recategorisation, in terms of the organisation's knowledge capital, all areas in which the company performs. Examples which would not usually be contained in an ordinary audit (focused only on document management) are: to what degree are recently recruited and departing employees debriefed about their experiences on the job? What did the company learn about the new market which it penetrated last year? Why did the organisation fail to impress a particular client?

Many companies who are interested in KM are realising that they are sitting on a gold mine of *internal* knowledge of which they are making only very limited use. This positive view for the nurture and development of internal knowledge capital can lead to underestimating the benefits of *external* knowledge capital. Internal knowledge capital is valuable knowledge which has originated in the organisation. External knowledge capital is everything else – outside experts, online databases, the Internet, etc. From the finance director's point of view, the difference between internal and external resources is clearly that the organisation does not have to pay for internal knowledge while every byte of external information costs extra, in one way or another. In this situation, a very important responsibility of the knowledge manager is to create awareness of the role of external information, help identify relevant sources of external information for the organisation and make it available.

Example 2

> The R&D department of a company had recently acquired Internet access for all its members, the first department to do so. Management realised that the fast-growing knowledge management team of the firm (rather than the IT department) ought to market the Net as an important channel

> of external information to the employees. Instead of exclud-
> ing the non-technical members of staff, the knowledge man-
> agers did an excellent marketing job for this new service by
> emphasising the human side of the Internet, the communi-
> ties of interest, as well as the importance of the Net as a
> cheap self-service information resource.

The situation is further complicated by the fact that the customer
is usually not concerned with whether information is of internal
or external nature (a distinction which is more important to the
information professional). He/she often comes to the knowledge
manager with a *problem*, not with a request for any particular
information resource. Anything that brings the user closer to resolving that problem is welcome.

Capture knowledge capital

Capturing means increasing the amount of knowledge capital contributed by members of the organisation. Decide how the knowledge of your organisation will be structured and made available
to all. This task area includes:

*   Contributing to the creation of a managed vocabulary
*   Collecting knowledge capital and acting as experts in the
    structuring of stored knowledge
*   Creating new applications to capture and access knowledge.

Capturing means designing processes in which the users themselves stop being mere information consumers and become
proactive creators of knowledge capital. Especially in the startup
phase of a knowledge management programme, capturing knowledge capital may involve going out there and working side by side
with the user: the information service as the cradle of knowledge
creation, so to speak.

The development of a controlled knowledge vocabulary is an important prerequisite to capturing knowledge capital. The vocabulary is a set of well-defined keywords which reflect the business
of the organisation. Its content must flow from the completion of
determining the relevant knowledge capital of the organisation
(see above). The terminology hitherto used by the organisation to
store relevant information may not fit the new categories which
have emerged in the knowledge audit. To be effective during capture and later, during dissemination, the knowledge vocabulary
must fit the business like a well-made glove.

Example 3

After one year of an intense knowledge management programme, the employees of an advertising company, operating in several European countries, are now sharing their knowledge across the board. Besides the informal knowledge exchange on an internal network, they are used to having frequent access to a team of highly skilled knowledge managers who make contributing to the knowledge pool easy. These knowledge managers accompany new recruits from their very first days through a dedicated KM module in the induction programme; they contact project teams at regular intervals; through frequent contact with the schedulers, the knowledge managers know when project teams are starting their work and need research support, and when they are about to close a project. After a project has been closed, the project manager is obliged to get in touch with the knowledge manager who will help him to summarise lessons learnt on the project. The company's knowledge management dictionary, developed by knowledge managers, is used by the project manager to prepare the material from the project for the meeting with the dedicated knowledge manager. Project team members can use the dictionary later to look their work up on the knowledge sharing and storing network. Since the knowledge capturing process takes chargeable time, the company makes participation in the programme more attractive with a series of Knowledge Management Awards which are given to managers at different levels. The awards are used as direct input for the manager's annual performance assessment and bonus calculation.

Knowledge managers are experts in how best to structure knowledge so that it can later be accessed easily by the user. When capture processes are designed, they need to bring this expertise to fruition and work with business experts on these processes to make them efficient and user-friendly. This means that the knowledge ought to be comprehensive and of the highest quality, and that it is easy for the user to serve him/herself, with minimal guidance by the knowledge manager.

Especially when working with a knowledge sharing system, an intranet or some groupware-based vendor-net, there is a niche for knowledge managers to develop new applications which improve access, overview and data structure. Examples of this kind of application are community home pages as part of an intranet, knowledge maps (see below) or agent technology applications. These applets require varying degrees of technical expertise.

Example 4

> In a company with an internal knowledge sharing network using moderately sophisticated groupware, the knowledge management team changed the day of every single member of this firm through the rollout of knowledge maps. These maps are an extensible collection of bookmarks to memorable places on the internal web. Upon joining the firm, employees are handed a rudimentary knowledge map which contains links to the central yellow pages on the web, as well as a collection of community pages. As they grow into their professional roles, these knowledge maps are added to, both by the knowledge management professionals, and by the employees themselves. Over time, the knowledge map becomes a personalised agent tool which reflects the knowledge of its owner and the company's knowledge management.

Retrieve knowledge capital

Retrieval support means assisting users in the proper use of information technology to access the available knowledge. Examples of tasks covered in this area of responsibility are:

- Become an expert on your internal knowledge sharing network
- Train users to navigate the knowledge base more skilfully
- Provide knowledge as information researchers.

Capture is the key to populating the knowledge base with internal knowledge capital as well as pointers to external knowledge capital. Once the knowledge base contains useful knowledge, the organisation is ready for the next step, which is focusing on retrieval. Here, the knowledge manager primarily assists users in the use of enabling information technology.

The question of which information technology to use is often asked far too early in the KM planning process. At later stages however (after, or in parallel with, crucial cultural and habitual changes required from employees) important decisions have to be made on which technology to use. Here, the knowledge manager ought to advise the IT department on these decisions from a usability point of view.

The introduction of a network structure for knowledge sharing is a step which profoundly changes the corporate culture. Many IT systems, especially intranet technology and groupware products, have the scope to be used as system tools to help integrate KM in the workflow process. In most cases, however, the system merely acts as a knowledge carrier. Content and content-rich interfaces, which are attractive to the user, still have to be added. They are important for that part of the user community (often a majority) which needs to be convinced to spend time sharing and contributing knowledge routinely. Even the smallest of these networks requires not only IT experts for maintenance, but also knowledge managers to develop policies and guide users who are discovering the new medium.

How many technological skills a knowledge manager should possess cannot be said with certainty. What can be said is that you can never know enough about how technology works and which technology works best. Beyond that, the knowledge manager should be conscious that he/she is not an IT expert. The extent of the technological skill you will need depends on the way the knowledge is managed in your organisation. What people who complain about a lack of technology and equipment often really mean, is that they do not know how to use available technology creatively in order to achieve the greatest benefit and pleasure from their work. The knowledge manager's mission is the creative use of knowledge that mostly already exists.

Navigation on the internal network requires skills which most users do not possess, at least initially. They can often be learned by playing with the new medium which is, however, not very cost-effective. The fewer the navigational skills users possess, the longer the time they must spend searching for information. Frustrating search experiences are a backlash for capturing, since users turn away from a medium in which they cannot find anything worthwhile in a reasonable amount of time. The same is true for other end-user services (e.g. CD-ROM), not only the ones introduced for internal knowledge sharing. The knowledge manager who has trained the users to navigate the system competently themselves, will not need to spend time merely finding and delivering documents, but can use his/her time to add value in different, and more interesting, ways. Navigation skills training ought to transcend the knowledge required to know which button of a system causes the desired effect – it should teach solid knowledge of the knowledge vocabulary/keywords used for knowledge management, and of the content and organisation of the knowledge bases.

Example 5

> The information service of a big pharmaceutical company pioneered the new relationship between knowledge management and user by piloting a 'Knowledge Broker' programme. In the course of this programme, selected users spend up to three months in the information centre to get more comfortable with the resources available and to initiate knowledge management programmes for their communities. After they have gone back into the field, these individuals are true knowledge champions who not only know their industry, but also have a firm grasp of how best to capture, organise and disseminate the knowledge of their peers. Originally fed by more experienced volunteers, the programme has considerably raised the profile of being a knowledge broker, and junior team members are now queuing to get on the list of candidates for this job, which has a very high visibility to senior management.

No matter how good the internal knowledge base and how skilful the users, the traditional role of responding to research requests efficiently and accurately remains equally important to the knowledge manager. In principle, however, more value can be added in an organisation whose employees manage their knowledge better since some of the job of researching has been given back to them.

Utilise knowledge capital

Utilisation support means assisting managers in using the available knowledge creatively. This is a major cultural change. In its course, the knowledge manager needs to:

- Act as a catalyst for the necessary culture change
- Train people to manage their own knowledge better
- Facilitate knowledge champion networking.

In actual fact, few organisations today support knowledge sharing or knowledge management *through their culture*. In a culture where individual knowledge ownership is held in higher esteem than collective knowledge ownership, unproductive, unmanaged pockets of owned knowledge can 'survive' the introduction of knowledge sharing systems and habits. This climate is not conducive to knowledge management. Consulting firms are positive examples of knowledge sharing companies – knowledge capital for their clients is their main product and to turn knowledge around more quickly and make it usable across the globe is a goal directly linked to their growth. Equally good at sharing are the R&D departments of most companies – here, knowledge sharing is the heritage of the academic culture of their peers.

The issue of the cultural changes which are necessary to create a knowledge managing culture is far-reaching and we cannot even begin to explore it properly in this chapter. However, *at the end* of this change we see a user of the information service who has a responsibility for his/her own knowledge management. While this change is being made, the knowledge manager acts as a catalyst. To do that he must be much more part of, and *understand*, a business which, as an information manager, he used only to serve from the back office.

The ultimate goal of knowledge management is not to create an impermeable, infallible central knowledge service, but to give the working individual the capability, and the will, to develop his or her professional knowledge on an ongoing basis. The practice of KM focuses on the individual, not on the organisation. The benefits of good KM are shared between the individual and the organisation. A useful parallel, which everybody understands, is time management: the individual gets to be a more organised, generally happier person who feels more in control of his/her workload, while the organisation gets more value from the more effective worker. Likewise knowledge management, where both the individual and the organisation maximise their return on what tends to take the longest and is the most difficult part of every job: learning and skill development.

Thus, to get people in the organisation to manage their knowledge better is a prime responsibility of every organisation which wants to be a learning organisation, keep its competitive advantage and improve business performance. The knowledge manager can contribute a lot to this mission as a KM coach. The coaching should be planned as a cascading process by which best KM practice is communicated throughout the organisation, from the leaders downward as well as upward from the individual user.

Example 6

Information professionals are frequently exposed to the knowledge that counts. At a global consulting firm, knowledge managers routinely assist junior consultants in structuring their proposals – as a result of having been exposed to, and seen, many more proposals, in many more different subjects, than even many senior consultants themselves. In some divisions of this consulting firm, this assistance has been formalised and consultants and managers are now obliged to call information professionals into initial meetings where the client job is shaped, necessary resources are screened etc. The role of the knowledge manager includes different kinds of 'knowledge allocations': dedicated research support during the project, a brief on relevant credentials which are available on the firm's internal knowledge sharing network, etc. The knowledge manager is included at this early stage of the project because 'knowledge allocations' are appreciated as vital, integrated components of business success. The impact on the quality of the work delivered by the knowledge managers is impressive. The knowledge management team has repeatedly been awarded quality awards and career and remuneration prospects within the team are excellent.

Coaching to cascade knowledge management up and down the organisational hierarchy creates a new brand of manager: the knowledge champion. This role is usually assumed de facto by more experienced personnel – in fact, no organisation could survive without its knowledge champions. Without a knowledge management programme, their role and importance, however, may remain obscured. It is the knowledge manager's task to nurture and support a network of knowledge champions. As the organisation reorganises itself according to knowledge management principles, the knowledge champions become the leaders of dynamic communities of knowledge across the organisation. These communities, too, become customers of the knowledge manager. Their success catalyses the formation of other knowledge-based communities.

SUMMARY

I have described the few big task areas in which the knowledge manager can support the journey of his/her organisation towards a knowledge-based and knowledge managing organisation. These areas will initially have to be carried out in sequence – first audit, then populate, then retrieve, then use. As the organisation's culture changes, more of these tasks will have to be executed simultaneously. The tasks will change in character and level of demand, too. As an example, the audit of knowledge assets will need to be repeated regularly as a knowledge quality assurance procedure. Its course will be defined and checked by the knowledge management team.

An often asked question in this context is "how do we get started if senior management has not seen the importance of KM yet?" The answer to this question is a step which was implied here all along: *knowledge managers must continually successfully market their own services in very close alignment with the demands and changes of the business around them*. The single most important key to the success of this journey as far as knowledge management, as we understand it today, is concerned, is to proactively seek involvement in the business process, and make knowledge creation and management an integrated part of the business process. In this way, yesterday's successful information manager will become tomorrow's most wanted knowledge manager.

REFERENCES

1. Wiig, Karl, *Knowledge management foundations: thinking about thinking*, Schema Press, Arlington, Texas (1993, ISBN 0-9638925-0-9).

2. Barton, D. Leonard, *Wellsprings of knowledge*, Harvard Business School Press (1995, ISBN 0-87584-612-2).

3. Nonaka/Takeuchi, *The knowledge-creating company*, Oxford University Press (1995, ISBN 0-19-509269-4).

4. Van der Spek, R. and Spijkervet, A. *Knowledge management*, CIBIT (1996, ISBN 90-75709-02-1).

5. Marshall, J. *et al. Competencies for special librarians of the 21st century* (Document submitted to the Board of the Special Libraries Association, USA).

5. Amidon, D. and Skyrme, D. Creating the knowledge-based business, in *Business Intelligence* (1997, ISBN 1 898085 27 7).

The Internet

George McMurdo

INTRODUCTION

The Internet, the global network of networks based on the TCP/
IP suite of protocols, is sometimes called Cyberspace, a borrowing
from sci-fi author William Gibson[1]. This carries a connotation of
being something new and futuristic, offering radically different
ways of interacting with other people, both at work and socially,
within new Utopian models of virtual representative democracy[2],
and it may be that concomitant reflections on the effects of information and communication processes will enable new perceptions
of reality[3]. However, others [4,5] have noted that from early human
history there have been recurring cycles of social and political
change which have been enabled – if not determined – by techno-
logically-assisted media for information storage and communication. It has also been noted that down the centuries military
imperatives have often been the driving force in the development
and exploitation of such technologies, from the pen and the papy-
rus to the computer.

HISTORY

The Internet had its origins in the paranoia of the Cold War era.
In 1969 the US Department of Defense's Advanced Research
Projects Agency (ARPA) funded a project to develop a fault-toler-
ant computer communications network, capable of having some
of its links disrupted by enemy attack, but maintaining its functionality by automatically re-routing data via surviving links[6].
The result was the ARPANET. The ARPANET, and the networks
that grew from it, move information by packet-switching rather
than circuit-switching. Circuit-switching depends on a continuous fixed connection between two computers, during which data
is transmitted or exchanged. With packet-switching protocols,
however, there is no fixed connection. Instead the information to
be communicated is broken down into a number of individual packets, to each of which is attached a header containing its sequence

number and the address of the destination computer. The packets are released into the network and routed between intermediary computer – and not necessarily all travelling by the same route – until they reach their destination, where they are reassembled in sequence.

The TCP/IP protocols and Internet addressing

This system of packet-switching protocols developed for the ARPANET was called TCP/IP, for Transmission Control Protocol/ Internet Protocol. The TCP part provides error-free logical channels between connected computers. The IP part takes care of addressing the TCP packets, analogous to an envelope in the postal system. The IP addresses of computers connected to the Internet are four-part numbers, for example `193.62.47.2`, in which the right-most number identifies the actual computer. However, while human users can utilise such numeric IP addresses directly for some purposes, it is usually more convenient to work with address names in an alphabetical format, such as `cis.qmced.ac.uk`, known as a Fully Qualified Domain Name (FQDN). The hierarchy of domain names is the reverse of IP addresses, so that the left-most part identifies a specific computer. The scheme for converting to and from numeric IP addresses and alphabetic FQDNs is a distributed database known as the Domain Name System (DNS). Whenever an Internet user keys in or clicks on a FQDN as part of some operation, an automatic DNS look-up is performed to translate to the corresponding IP number to obtain the physical address of the specified computer.

The Internet and human computer-mediated communication

In the 1970s, the Internet did not exist as such, still being officially the US defence application called ARPANET, and for which an electronic messaging function had not originally been intended or anticipated. Murray Turoff, one of the pioneers of computer-mediated communication system development[7], recounted a visit to ARPA in 1971, when he asked for data on the use of the ARPANET for messaging.

"In a rather frank discussion it was pointed out to me that they were very embarrassed that the single biggest application of the network at that time was message traffic. This sort of application was completely unintended and had no justification under their formal requests for funds to support ARPANET. As a result they were not releasing any measurement data on applications of the network."[8]

Turoff goes on to relate that a few years later the ARPA staff rewrote the objectives of their research effort to include messaging as part of a new mission to examine management applications. The ARPA office subsequently began to publicise message systems as a great innovation resulting from their R&D effort.

First generation Internet tools – e-mail, telnet, ftp

Electronic mail depends on the concept of an address to enable the delivery and exchange of messages. Such an address will typically be for an individual person, but need not necessarily be so. An e-mail address may be for a list of people, or for a server which processes messages as commands. E-mail addresses are usually in two parts separated by the 'at' character `@`, for example: `g.mcmurdo@cis.qmced.ac.uk`. The first part usually identifies an individual. The second part is the domain name which identifies the computer which hosts the individual's mailbox. While other Internet tools have evolved (and in some cases neared extinction) very rapidly, e-mail has remained fundamentally the same. However, its user-interface has developed, from basic command-line 80 column x 24 line text screens, to more modern graphical interfaces and integration with other contemporary Internet tools.

Telnet is used to log onto other computers elsewhere on the Internet. This may be for a login to a private account, where a password is required to authorise access. However, telnet is also used for access to public services, such as online library catalogues (OPACs) and bulletin board systems. The address for making a telnet connection to a remote computer is its FQDN, for example: `opac.qmced.ac.uk`. Although many library OPACs are still only accessible via telnet, the use of this protocol for access to online information systems has been widely overtaken by client/server protocols, such as Gopher and the World Wide Web.

File transfer protocol (ftp) is used to move and copy files between remote computers on the Internet. Although ftp is still in very common use, and can still be used effectively with its original, basic, command-line interface, it is now more often operated either via a graphical client, or via a World Wide Web browser which also supports the ftp protocol.

Second generation tools – WAIS and Gopher

Gopher was developed by McCahill and others at the University of Minnesota (UMN)[9]. Initially designing a local CWIS (Campus Wide Information Service) for UMN, to provide a single menu system to information physically located on multiple servers throughout the campus, they realised this menu system could work across the whole Internet, since the same TCP/IP protocols were used. Thus was Gopherspace created, and the Internet Gopher was announced in late 1991.

WAIS – Wide Area Information Server, pronounced 'ways' is a distributed database of databases, based on the Z39.50 standard familiar to librarians and information scientists, and was developed primarily by Brewster Kahle[10], of Thinking Machines Corp. Databases within WAIS are called sources. Hits from WAIS searches are ranked on relevance, with best fit scoring 1,000. A technique called relevance-feedback allows words or sections of search-results to be used in future searches. At one time tipped by many to take over from Gophers, WAIS lost out to the World Wide Web. However, several important concepts from its development have transferred into current Internet systems.

Third generation – the World Wide Web

The World Wide Web is a global hypertext information system, and also increasingly a multimedia information system. It was mainly developed by Tim Berners-Lee[11] and a group at CERN, the European Particle Physics Lab in Geneva, originally for the High Energy Physics community there and worldwide. Development began in 1989 and the WWW was installed at CERN in 1991. The early client or browser software ran on the relatively obscure NextStep platform. However, in 1993, Marc Andreessen and a team at the National Center for Supercomputing Applications (NCSA) and the University of Illinois, announced plans to release a new browser called Mosaic. Although there are alternative browsers, the combination of the NCSA Mosaic client and Web servers will probably be remembered as the 'killer' application that drove the explosive growth of information on the Internet in the early 1990s. In 1994, Andreessen left NCSA to co-found Netscape Communications Corporation, and develop Netscape, currently the rated client, for speed and other extended features. The basis of retrieval from WWW servers is the Uniform Resource Locator (URL), for example: *http://bubl.ac.uk/index.html*

A URL is composed of three components: Firstly the transport method (e.g.: *http* for HyperText Transfer Protocol); secondly, the fully qualified domain name of the host machine (e.g.:*bubl.bath.ac.uk*); thirdly, the pathname of the sought file itself (e.g.:/*index.html*). In fact, users rarely need to be aware of, or type in, URLs, because they can be embedded invisibly in Web documents as hyperlinks, by default indicated as text underlined in blue which can be clicked on to jump automatically to the new document. Any document can be linked to any other document this way, thus creating the 'Web' of hypertext information.

THE INTERNET AND SPECIAL INFORMATION UNITS

In the introductory chapter to an earlier *Aslib Handbook,* Anthony[12] summarised the activities the staff of the information unit would need to attend to, in order to be closely integrated with the total objectives of the parent organisation as:

1. Study continuously and monitor the current and long-term objectives of the organisation

2. Study the communication pattern of the organisation and identify the prime movers, the technological gatekeepers and organisational entrepreneurs who act as catalysts in the innovation process

3. Provide information sub-systems to meet particular and often temporary needs, e.g. the attachment of information specialists to study groups and decision-making teams

4. Be capable of tapping a wide range of external information sources and ensure that information provided is as accurate and reliable as possible

5. Adapt information by repackaging and reformatting to the various functional needs of the different levels of users

6. Provide a corporate memory

7. Monitor the performance of the information function itself to ensure that it is constantly in tune with the objectives and needs of the organisation.

That author also advocated a willingness to seize opportunities to become involved in any aspects of the organisation's activity which might benefit from the specialised knowledge and experience of information management staff. It was doubtless intentional that the above activities were worded to be applicable to conventional media, electronic media, or a mix. Fifteen years later, they can also clearly be seen as applicable to the evolving information and communication options offered to information professionals by the Internet. This could include both access to, or provision of, information globally available on the public Internet, or information accessible only within a private organisational intranet.

On a personal level, access to the Internet offers the information professional additional means for keeping up to date with ongoing developments which may not have reached the print media, via electronic discussion lists and other sources[13], including professional organisations (see appendix 2.1). This is not to say that the Internet is a replacement medium. One of the most insightful commentators on the using of networking for professional objectives offers regular reminders that electronic interaction should be seen as part of a larger ecology of communication media, each with its own role to play[14]. Similarly, the Internet extends the information professional's options for searching online sources of information, yet obviously doesn't replace the use of either the 'conventional' online database hosts, or print sources when they are appropriate. There may, however, be some convergence in the means of access to such sources.

The Internet may offer information professionals some new options for the production and dissemination of information, now that there is such an imperative for organisations of widely varying scales to have an 'Internet presence'. It is true that there is an element of hype in this at the present time. But – particularly for organisations seeking to operate at the core of the information sector – there are also genuine opportunities (or threats) from being visible and accessible (or not) via this medium. Historically, of course, one of the earliest information sources made available via the Internet was provided by librarians offering telnet connections to the OPACs of academic libraries.

Finally, beyond the options information professionals may have for exploiting the Internet for personal and organisational development, there is a range of clear indications that they also have an important contribution to make in shaping the development and use of such resources[15]. What may seem a suddenly-arrived information revolution to laypersons, may seem to information professionals more like the latest incremental shift in a more historical process in which existing professional principles and practices have an ongoing application. For example, the citation and evaluation of information provided via the new publishing dynamics of the Internet and the World Wide Web is often perceived as requiring entirely new approaches. Yet the emerging conventions for citation are basically based on the principles of authorship, plus the use of the URL format as the electronic address[16]. The methods generally proposed for evaluating Internet information are essentially as derived from the professionally recognised methods for evaluating print information sources (see appendix 2.2).

ACCESSING THE INTERNET

A survey of Internet usage in UK business libraries[17] found that less than a third of the information professionals working in the banking and finance sector had Internet access at the time of the study. The authors concluded that the Internet was still primarily a complementary information source, but might later become an entry-point to other information sources. One way in which this prediction has been realised has been in a shift to accessing online hosts via telnet over the Internet, rather than via PSTN dailup. Traditional online information services have also been establishing their own Web pages[18].

Internet Service Providers (ISPs)

Although in principle 'offline' use of Internet services is feasible via e-mail through Internet gateways, in practice either a dedicated or dial-up TCP/IP connection is required, for example, in order to make use of a graphical Web browser. Users in the academic sector or in large organisations may already have connections. For others, however, the growing marketplace of commercial Internet service providers (ISPs) provides a good range of choices[19, 20] at this time. (see appendix 3.1). There are predictions both of a 'shakeout' of the smaller ISPs, and of government intentions to tax ISPs. However, costs to users will remain partly dependent on technological costs, which will continue to decrease even though some other cost factors increase. For as little as a few hundred pounds per year, a user with a standard PC can not only obtain access to Internet services, but also has the option of providing a Web site, since many ISPs are currently offering 5-10 megabytes of free Web space to subscribers.

Offline access via e-mail

Users who are either unable to make either a temporary dial-up connection to an Internet service provider, or do not have access to a dedicated connection to the Internet are in principle denied access to a range of information tools and services which have an increasingly high contemporary profile, both in the information profession and popularly. The list of Internet tools and services below[21] would also serve as a fair checklist of the key Internet services generally. However, this is also a list of Internet services which can be accessed without any direct TCP/IP connection, through a system of mail gateways and mailservers which will receive batch commands by e-mail, submit corresponding requests to the appropriate Internet services, and return the results by e-mail[22].

- BITNET LISTSERV e-mail discussion lists, with information retrieval from archives
- Archie index searches of Anonymous ftp archives
- Anonymous ftp for file transfer from Anonymous ftp servers
- Gopher menu interface to Internet information
- Veronica for indexed information retrieval from Gopherspace
- World Wide Web for hypertext information browsing and retrieval
- WAIS – Wide Area Information Server sources information retrieval
- Usenet Newsgroups electronic discussion groups
- Whois, Finger – directory services for people and e-mail addresses.

The authoritative source for keeping up-to-date with developments in Internet services accessible by e-mail is a freely available electronic document *Accessing the Internet by E-mail* published by Bob Rankin (see appendix 3.2). In addition to documenting the standard utilities addressed above, it provides information on other miscellaneous e-mail accessible options.

ELECTRONIC DISCUSSION FORUMS

E-mail discussion lists are sometimes generically called 'listservs' after the original LISTSERV programs (named from 'list server') implemented for the Bitnet[23] network by Dr Eric Thomas. These programs enabled users to join (or 'subscribe to') e-mail discussion lists, leave them, and perform other functions without human intervention. There are also now various other such list-serving systems operated on similar principles. All such automatically maintained electronic discussion lists have two e-mail addresses. One is the address to which informational discussion messages are sent, to be read by other list-members. The other address is for specially-formatted command messages, which are received and processed automatically by software, without human intervention, for purposes such as subscribing to or signing off a list and other possible list management options (see appendix 4.1).

For information professionals for whom 'subscribing' to receive information is likely to have budgetary connotations, the good news is that in the context of Internet discussion lists such subscriptions are free, beyond the costs of equipment and access. Conversely, compared to the content of subscribed-to print journals, which tends to be densely-packed with information, information from e-mail discussion lists is often described as having a low 'signal-to-noise ratio'.

Managing subscriptions to e-lists

In the UK, the major group of over 1,000 e-mail discussion lists is provided by the Mailbase system, primarily for the UK academic teaching and research community, but not excluding membership from other countries or sectors. For all Mailbase lists command messages are sent to the address: **mailbase@mailbase.ac.uk**. Informational discussion messages, to be delivered to members of a particular Mailbase list are sent to an address of the format **listname@mailbase.ac.uk**. For example, there is a Mailbase list named LIS-IIS for discussion of information science. Messages to be read by members of the LIS-IIS list would be sent to the address: **lis-iis@mailbase.ac.uk**.

The most useful Mailbase e-mail commands, using the list LIS-IIS as an example, include:

help
> *get information on using Mailbase lists*

join lis-iis *Firstname Surname*
> *join the LIS-IIS list*

leave lis-iis
> *quit from LIS-IIS*

`review lis-iis`
> *get list of LIS-IIS members' names and e-mail addresses*

`suspend mail lis-iis`
> *temporarily stop receiving mail, but remain a member*

`resume mail lis-iis`
> *resume receiving LIS-IIS mail*

`index lis-iis`
> *get descriptive list of files stored with LIS-IIS*

`send lis-iis` *filename*
> *get the file* filename *from LIS-IIS filelist*

For compatibility with usage on other list-processing systems Mailbase's (perhaps more meaningful) commands **join** and **leave** are synonymed to **subscribe** and **unsubscribe** respectively, and can be used interchangeably.

Finding relevant discussion groups

Within the Mailbase system, finding relevant lists to join is facilitated by a Web site (see appendix 4.1) at which descriptions of the lists can be keyword-searched. In addition, monthly archives of discussion messages to most of the Mailbase lists are maintained for a retrospective period of 12-14 months. These can also be keyword searched, or browsed, either to evaluate the relevance of their content, or for some particular information. The Library and Information Science community has been a particularly active participant in the Mailbase project, and there is a substantial group of lists with a LIS- prefix, covering a wide range of specialised interest groups.

For e-mail lists within other systems, searching for relevant lists is less systematic. However, a number of web sites offer lists-of-lists and searchable directories of discussion lists (appendix 4.1).

Usenet FAQs

Usenet newsgroups, of which there are now upwards of 10,000, constitute another forum for electronic discussion, but with different methods of transport and access from e-mail lists[24]. Depending on a user's method of Internet provision, getting access to a news server may be very easy, or else problematical. The messaging on some newsgroups is mirrored to corresponding e-mail discussion lists, and vice versa. Although some newsgroups have very erudite content, reflecting the best knowledge on the Internet, generally their content can be more trivial than is typical of e-mail lists. (Some would strongly dispute the previous assertion).

Most providers of news servers expire articles after a period of around a week to 10 days, to free up new diskspace. This transience has led to the development of an interesting genre of publication – the Frequently Asked Questions document, or FAQ[25]. As the name suggests, they are compilations of the core knowledge of the newsgroups to which they belong, usually literally in a question and answer format. Their intended purpose is to provide new newsgroup members with a starting-point to familiarise themselves with the culture and knowledge-base of the group, before they post questions which may have been asked and answered previously. The sum total of the Usenet FAQs is therefore a substantial resource, archived at a number of locations (see appendix 4.2).

Networking etiquette

Some of the first studies into social psychological aspects of computer-mediated communication also took place in the pre-Internet era, as a series of experiments at Carnegie-Mellon University (CMU) in the USA[26]. Some of the features the CMU researchers noted include, for example, that sometimes users lose sight of the fact that they are really addressing people, not a computer, and that the absence of nonverbal regulating feedback could lead to uninhibited, overly-expressive verbal behaviour, known as 'flaming'. They concluded that there was, as yet, no strong etiquette or widely shared norms.

A decade later, however, while it remains to be seen whether the influx of new users to the Internet adopt it, there does exist a fairly strong etiquette for at least the superficial, prescribable aspects of CMC, and one that is widely shared, at least in terms of its documentation and dissemination from print [27,28,29,30,31,32] and electronic sources (see appendix 4.3). There are conventions for aspects such as message formatting, care with addressing, typographical usage and acronyms, and issues of courtesy and ethics. One of the typographical conventions is the 'smiley', of which hundreds have been catalogued [33,34]. However, the ones below – perceivable as faces if viewed sideways – are the most common.

| : –) | : | the basic smiley, happy |
| : – (| : | a sad smiley, unhappy, angry even |

; -)	:	a winking, knowing smiley
: - >	:	an ironic, sarcastic smiley
(- :	:	a left-handed smiley
: - |	:	apathetic, neutral smiley
: - o	:	shocked smiley
: - D	:	laughing out loud smiley.

Use of such typographic 'emoticons' is of course a matter of choice, but it is useful to at least be able to recognise them, since others use them. Similarly, there are some commonly encountered networking acronyms, such as:

BTW	:	by the way
F2F	:	face-to-face
FAQ	:	frequently asked questions
FOAF	:	friend of a friend
FYI	:	for your information
FWIW	:	for what it's worth
IMHO	:	in my humble opinion
LOL	:	laughing out loud
PMJI	:	pardon my jumping in
ROTFL	:	rolling on the floor laughing
TIA	:	thanks in advance
TPTB	:	the powers that be
WRT	:	with respect to.

The art of networking

Beyond the level of netiquette, however, there is surprisingly little prescription for effective use of networking, in its less technical sense[35].

"The Internet and other digital networks are currently undergoing explosive growth. Several million people employ electronic mail for some significant portion of their professional communications. Yet in my experience few people have figured out how to use the net productively. A great deal of effort is going into technical means for finding information on the net, but hardly anybody has been helping newcomers figure out where the net fits in the larger picture of their own careers."[14]

Agre, the author of this quote has formulated useful advice for the use of networking at the professional level. Note that in his checklist[36] for getting help via networks he starts by advocating an enquiry-formulating process and liaison with librarians.

- Be able to explain your project
- Know what your question is
- Try the obvious sources first
- Make friends with a librarian
- Ask the right person
- Provide some context
- Don't get hung up on the Internet
- Do some homework
- Take some care
- Make yourself useful
- Ask who to ask
- Use the Reply-To: field
- Sign the message
- Say thank you
- Let it take time.

In some of the above points, and others Agre enumerates about the networking process below[14]. It is also advocated that the Internet and networking be regarded as just one of a range of communication media, in each of which a variety of skills must be developed.

- It takes time – you have to be patient and let it happen
- It focuses on particular individuals and particular relationships
- It produces bonds of reciprocal obligation through the exchange of favours
- It calls for significant but manageable up-front investment
- It requires you to cultivate a realistic awareness of power
- It involves a variety of communication media
- It forces you to develop communication skills in each of these media.

SEARCHING FOR INFORMATION

Searching for information on the Internet currently means searching the Web. Previously, it involved a range of techniques, ranging from word-of-mouth, to browsing manually-compiled lists, to using particular search tools for particular forms of information. Two important early tools were the apparently anthropomorphic Archie and Veronica.

Archie and Veronica: the first two generations of Internet searching

Archie allows keyword searching of pathnames of public anonymous ftp archives. It was developed by Emtage, Heelan, and Deutsch, while students at McGill University, Montreal, Canada[37,38]. Their technique for building the Archie dataset was simple but innovatively effective, using the standard UNIX recursive directory listing to collect each known anonymous ftp site's file list, at least monthly. In 1994 it was tracking over 2,000,000 file names from over a thousand anonymous ftp sites. Archie searches use a single term only, and do not support compound Boolean enquiries. Some Archie client software is pairable with compatible ftp clients so that, on a single screen, files identified by the Archie search can be flagged for retrieval by the ftp client. However, there are also a number of World Wide Web gateways to Archie indexes, which allow the user to use their single web client interface to both search for and retrieve files (see appendix 5.1). ArchiPlex returns the references it finds as full hypertext links. Thus, since the ftp protocol is built into web clients, this allows retrieval of files to be saved to disk, or browsing of ftp subdirectories. The intended etymology of Archie was that it sounded like 'archive'. However, retrospectively, and to some irritation on the part of the Archie group, a retrospective etymology emerged, associated with Archie Andrews of Archie Comic Publications, Inc.[39] The declared etymology of a subsequent tool, Veronica[40], was that it is an acronym for Very Easy Rodent-Oriented Netwide Index to Computerised Archives, widely perceived as a contrivance playing on the parallel Archie service, and after Archie Andrews' friend Veronica.

A year after the release of the Internet Gopher, in November 1992, Foster and Barrie, of the University of Nevada at Reno (UNR), announced the Veronica service offering a keyword search of most of the Gopher-server menus on the Internet, returning the results as another Gopher menu. Veronica is thus to Gopher as Archie is to ftp, and also like Archie, does not index document content in any way. At the time Veronica was anounced, 258 Gophers were indexed by it. By January 1995 5,057 servers were indexed[41] and the index included approximately 15 million items. Veronica searching is case-insensitive, supports nestable Boolean AND, OR, NOT combinations, and term-truncation; AND is the implicit operator for adjacent keywords. Because `gopher://` is a standard URL type for World Wide Web clients, they are also inherently capable of acting as Gopher clients.

World Wide Web worms, search engines and robots

In the early days of the World Wide Web – much as for information via ftp before Archie and by Gopher before Veronica – a user had to either:

- Know where something was to begin with
- Use a manually compiled resource list
- 'Surf the Web' discovering information rather than searching for it.

The nature of interconnections between its hyperlinked documents meant that it was problematical to compile and maintain searchable datasets in the comparatively straightforward methods used by Archie and Veronica. However, over the past year or so, a number of Web resources have become very popular for their provision of keyword index searches. These include Lycos, AltaVista, HotBot and others[42].

These searchable datasets are primarily compiled by software variously known as crawlers, wanderers, worms, search engines, and robots, which traverse the web via links within documents, recording retrieval information about these documents in the process. Koster[43] has noted that web robots can have serious downsides, both for themselves and the servers they visit, and that there are ethical problems about the bandwidth consumed by robots, if the results are not to be publicly shared.

Although the increasingly large datasets assembled by such robot-based services understandably attract attention, an alternative, or at least complementary, model is provided by a number of search services which have policies of greater human involvement in cataloguing resources. For example, the popular Yahoo! search service developed by Filo and Yang employs librarians as cataloguers and uses a system of subject-headings. Likewise, the Argus Clearinghouse of subject-oriented guides was developed by librarians at the University of Michigan in the belief that in order to make the Internet a more useful information environment, human effort should be combined with searching and browsing technologies. It is suggested[44] that while such services will tend to return fewer hits, they will offer greater precision.

Searching the Web using AltaVista

Although there is no vocabulary control, the search options of the AltaVista service[45] are otherwise comparable to what information professionals might expect from CD-ROM or online databases. Figure 1 shows the use of its advanced search for documents whose title field contains both truncations of java and also microsoft, but not sun with the query: title:

```
(java* and microsoft) and not sun
```

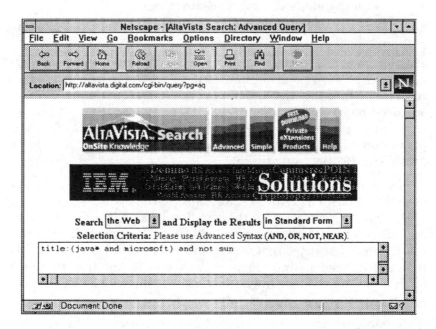

Figure 1 – Advanced search submission form for Altavista

Figure 2 shows the first screenful of the 22 documents found. Searching is case-insensitive if all lower-case is used. Any upper-cases will be matched exactly. The fields within a Web document which can be addressed in an AltaVista search query are:

anchor : matches text in the anchor of a hyperlink

applet	:	matches the name of Java applet class found in an applet tag
host	:	matches text in the host name of the source web server
image	:	matches text in an image tag
link	:	matches text in the URL of a hyperlink
object	:	matches the name of an ActiveX object in an object tag
text	:	matches visible text of a page (e.g. not in a URL or an image)
title	:	matches text in the title tag of a page
url	:	matches text in a page's own URL.

Figure 2 – Example results returned by Altavista

AltaVista also has an option to search Usenet news articles, and can match text in fields such as the 'From' and 'Subject' lines, the keyword list and the summary, and the newsgroup name.

PRODUCING INTERNET INFORMATION

HyperText Markup Language (HTML) is the main method of providing information on the World Wide Web, in pages like the illustration in Figure 3, viewed in the Windows Netscape browser. A basic text editor is all that is required, as HTML documents are just ASCII files, like the source example in Fig. 4. However, special formatting tags are used to control display, as listed in Figure 5[46]. HTML tags are enclosed in angle-brackets (< >), often paired in a *<tag>* ... *</tag>* format.

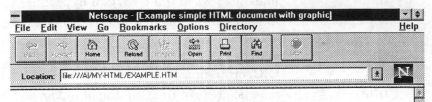

Example HTML document

This document starts with a heading, then an inline image. Its text can be in *italics* or in **bold**, or **both** indeed. It can have clickable links - shown in underlined text - to other external WWW documents or remote sites, such as BUBL the Bulletin Board for Libraries, or to related local documents provided by the same person.

You can e-mail the author of this document at cinmu@cis.qmced.ac.uk

file:///A|/MY-HTML/list-uo.html

Figure 3 – Web document with inline GIF image graphic

```
<html>
<!- example.htm - G McMurdo 20 Dec 95 ->

<head>
<title>Example simple HTML document with graphic</
title>
</head>

<body bgcolor="#ffffff">

<h1>Example HTML document</h1>
<img src="htmllogo.gif" alt="Example HTML logo
graphic">

<p>This document starts with a heading, then an inline
image. Its text can be in <i>italics</i> or in
<b>bold</b>, or <i><b>both</b></i> indeed. It can have
```

```
clickable links - shown in underlined text - to other
external WWW documents or remote sites, such as <a
href="http://www.bubl.bath.ac.uk/BUBL/
home.html">BUBL</a> the Bulletin Board for Libraries,
or to related local <a href="lists-
uo.html">documents</a> provided by the same person.</
p>
<hr>
<p>You can e-mail the author of this document at <a
href="mailto:cimmu@cis.qmced.ac.uk">cimmu@cis.qmced.ac.uk</
a></p>

</body>
</html>
```

Figure 4 – HTML code which generates Figure 3 display

The hypertext reference tag `<a href="`*URL*`">` can be absolute –
and cite URLs in full – or relative, since a browser assumes that a
partially referenced item has the same transport and pathname
as the current document. So, in Figure 4, the URL *http://
www.bubl.bath.ac.uk/BUBL/home.html* is referenced in full, but
the relative URL reference `lists-uo.html` would work both if
that file was being tested from a local floppy disk as `a:\my-`
`html\lists-uo.htm` or later, when the file is loaded onto a Web
server. Relative addressing, as in the examples below, is therefore
more flexible for Web page development.

`href="cv.html"`
`cv.html` is in the current directory

`href="personal/cv.html"`
`cv.html` is in the `personal` subdirectory of the current
directory

`href="personal/work/cv.html"`
`cv.html` is in the `work` subdirectory of the `personal`
subdirectory of the current directory

`href="../cv.html"`
`cv.html` is in the directory above the current directory

`href="../work/cv.html"`
`cv.html` is in a subdirectory `work` of the directory above
the current directory

`href="../../work/cv.html"`
`cv.html` is in a subdirectory `work` two levels above the
current directory.

There are helper utilities and software for composing HTML in a WYSIWYG environment, or for converting from various word-processing formats to HTML[47]. These can be very handy, especially for the conversion of documents originated in word-processing packages, to save the chore of marking up the basic text and character formatting tags. However, anybody doing serious web page design is probably still going to want to check the output of such HTML editors and converters at the ASCII level. Previous knowledge derived from the area of hypertext design and human-computer interaction (HCI) is applicable to Web page design and navigation[48] (see also appendix 6 for sources on good Web page design practices).

Software is available for checking the conformance of HTML source to the strict, in progress, and evolving de facto standards. Some Web sites also provide this service, to which the URLs of documents can be submitted, for HTML syntax checking to either 'strict', HTML 2.0, HTML 3.0, Netscape extended, or HotJava levels.

<!- *comment text* ->
> Optional non-displaying information can be included.

<a href="*URL*">*link text*</a>
> Creates an **Anchor** for a **Hypertext REFerence**, so that clicking on the *link text* retrieves the specified *URL*.

<a name="*label*">*target text*</a>
> Creates a target for an internal **hypertext reference**, where **href="#*label*"** instead of an external **href="*URL*"**, as above.

<address> ... </address>
> Encloses "signature" **Address** block, typically at document end, giving contact, copyright, disclaimer, etc, information.

<b> ... </b>
> Text enclosed by tags displays in **Bold**.

<blockquote> ... </blockquote>
> Quoted text, usually displayed indented from margins.

<body [background="*image filename*"]
[bgcolor="#*rrggbb*"] [text="#*rrggbb*"] [link="#*rrggbb*"]
[vlink="#*rrggbb*"] [alink="#*rrggbb*"] > ... </body>
> Encloses the second, **Body** part of an HTML document. Newer browsers recognise options to

specify a **.gif** or **.jpg** image file to give a "tiled" **background**; colour numbers can be specified for a self-coloured background (**bgcolor**), text (**text**), link text (**link**), visited links (**vlink**), and activating links (**alink**). These *rrggbb* are six-digit hexadecimal RGB values.

**
**

At the end of some text, ***Break*** tag forces a new line.

<center> ... </center>

Elements enclosed by tags display ***Centred***.

<dd>

Definition of a term – see the **<dl> ... </dl>** tags below.

<dl>

> **<dt>** *a Term, to be defined*
> **<dd>** *the Definition of that term*
> **<dt>** *another Term, to be defined*
> **<dd>** *the Definition of another term*
> **<dt>** *yet another Term, to be defined*
> **<dd>** *the Definition of yet another term*

</dl>

Definition Lists can include both definition ***Terms*** and their ***Definitions***, for an indented "glossary" format.

<dt>

Definition Term – see the **<dl> ... </dl>** tags above.

<em> ... </em>

Emphasis – usually giving *italics* like **<i> ... </i>** tags.

<font [color="#*rrggbb***"] [size=***n***] >** *text* **</font>**

Newer browsers recognise a **<font>** tag which enables enclosed sections of text to be coloured by hexadecimal RGB number and set to sizes where *n* is **1** to **7** (and 1 is smallest).

<h*n*> ... </h*n*>

Where *n* is **1** to **6**, text enclosed by tags display in ***Heading*** sizes 1 to 6 (where 1 is largest and 6 smallest).

<head> ... </head>

Encloses the first, ***Heading*** part of an HTML document.

<hr [size=*n***] [width=***n***] [align=***position***]>**

Simple **<hr>** inserts a ***Horizontal Ruler*** line. Newer

browsers use **size** and **width** options for vertical
thickness and horizontal width, in pixels. The
width value can also be *n%* for proportion of full
width. For **align** (where **width** is less than full)
position values are **left**, **right** and **center**.

<html> ... </html>
These tags enclose the entire HTML document.

<i> ... </i>
Text enclosed by tags displays in *Italics*.

<img src="*image filename***" [align=***position***]**
[alt="*description text***"] [border=***n***] >**
Loads an *inline Image* of the source filename. A
more "magazine" approach to page-layout is
possible from new **align** *position* options **top**,
bottom, **middle**, **left**, and **right** to define image
position and how text flows round them. The
optional **alt** text displays in text-only browsers.
For **border** the *n* number sets the thickness of an
image border, and defaults to **0** unless an image is
used as a clickable link.

<li> *List Item* – see the **<ol>** and **<ul>** tags below.

<ol>
    <li> *first List Item*
    <li> *second List Item*
    <li> *third List Item*
</ol>
List Items between *Ordered List* tags display
prefixed by sequential numbering.

<p>
Paragraph tag, causing a line-break and blank
line.

<pre> ... </pre>
Preformatted text – displays enclosed ASCII text
as-is, proportionately, preserving all spaces and
line-breaks.

<strong> ... </strong>
Strong emphasis usually in **bold** like the **<b> ...**
</b> tags.

<title> ... </title>
Enclosed text appears in browser's *Title* bar at
top of screen.

<tt> ... </tt>
Enclosed text displays in monospaced *Typewriter*
font (such as Courier).

<ul>

```
<li> a List Item
<li> another List Item
<li> yet another List Item
</ul>
```
List Items between ***Unordered List*** tags display prefixed with bullets.

Figure 5 – A quick-reference to the main HTML tags and their syntax

Web graphics – GIF and JPG picture file formats

While the production of computer graphic images can require specialised skills and equipment, much can be achieved with basic computer literacy and standard hardware[49]. Figure 6 illustrates the method of producing the inline graphic displayed in Figure 3, using the Microsoft Paintbrush paint package found in the Windows Accessories program group, and hence available on most PCs.

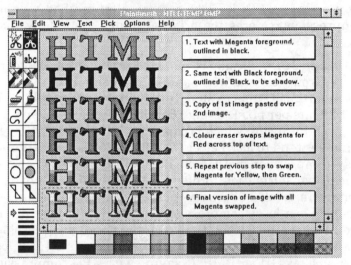

Figure 6 – The Figure 3 graphic as produced in MS Paintbrush

Web browsers can be configured to deal with any known filetype[50,51], including Windows BMP by spawning an external 'helper' application. However, in order to display as inline images, positioned within documents, they have to be in either the GIF (pronounced 'jiff') or the JPG (pronounced 'jay-peg') format. Broadly speaking, JPGs are used for photographic images of the real world or naturalistic artwork, whereas GIFs are used for graphical images with relatively few distinct colours, such as line

181

drawings, lettered artwork, cartoons, etc. So, the final step in the development of the **htmllogo.bmp** file in Figure 6 would be to convert it to be GIF or JPG. MS Paintbrush's Save As options are limited, and don't include either of these formats. However, a widely-available public-domain graphics package called LView is one means of achieving this conversion. Any good commercial graphics package will be able to convert to and from these formats, and many others.

GIF is an acronym for Graphics Interchange Format. It was created by CompuServe in 1987 for the storage and online retrieval of bitmapped graphical data, and uses a lossless method of compression. The effectiveness of compression in GIF files depends on the amount of repetition in an image. A 'flat' area with contiguous pixels of the same colour will compress well, often down to one tenth of the original filesize. Complex, non-repetitive images will compress much less. GIFs are limited to a palette of 256 colours or less. GIF's lossless compression method means that decompression restores the original image identically, pixel for pixel.

The JPG or JPEG format is named for the Joint Photographic Experts Group, the original name of the committee which wrote the standard. JPG images store full colour, or grey-scale, information at 24 bits per pixel, giving 16 million possible colours. Consequently, on hardware which is capable of displaying 24-bit colour, JPG images tend to look better than 8 bit, 256 colour GIFs. JPG is a 'lossy' compression method. Its algorithms are based on a mathematical transformation to discard the less significant parts of the image in terms of how it is perceived by the human eye. Because JPG is a lossy compression it should not be used until an image has been developed to its final version using lossless formats. Likewise, an original copy should be retained in a lossless format such as GIF or BMP, as saving with JPG compression entails an irretrievable loss of data.

Registering URLs with search services and indexing web sites

In theory, a Web site that is linked to by another site that has been indexed by a robot-based search service such as AltaVista, will in turn be visited by a robot and have its URLs indexed. However, most such search services provide a form to which URLs can be manually submitted to invite a visit. In a document's HTML, use of the <meta> tag can give some control over how it gets indexed. The tags below would cause AltaVista to index on both the description and keywords fields, and if hit in a search, to return the description text along with the URL, instead of just the first couple of lines of the page.

<meta name="description" content="We'll teach you HTML and Web design.">

<meta name="keywords" content="HTML, web graphics, java">

Conversely, it is possible to ensure that indexing robots are excluded from all or part of a Web site. This can be achieved via the Standard for Robot Exclusion[52]. A /robots.txt file can contain fairly simple entries to allow or disallow access to visiting robots either globally or selectively for specified robots.

For generating local Web site indexes, search engine software sometimes comes bundled with Web server software, or may be available free. For example, see appendix 6.3 for Excite Inc's downloadable search engine.

TRENDS AND FORECASTS

The growth of the Internet in recent years has been a subject of some fascination. It is often described as doubling each year. The growth of the part of the Internet represented by Web servers has been particularly dramatic, as also has the component which is the commercial Web. Hand in hand with the commercialisation of the Internet has come demand for new methods of estimating its size and market segments.

Counting the hosts and their domains

One of the longest standing indicators of Internet growth have been the surveys of Internet hosts and domains carried out by Mark Lottor (see appendix 7). A 'host' is any computer system connected to the Internet which has an IP address associated with it. Lottor's ZONE program cycles through the Domain Name System (DNS), requesting and retrieving statistics of hosts within domains. In principle, traversal of the full DNS tree enables a count of all computer systems connected to the Internet. From August 1981 to October 1991 the total rose from 213 to 617,000. Figure 7 shows the comparable results for the subsequent period from July 1992 to July 1996. Note that the vertical axis is scaled by a factor of one thousand, so that the range of totals is from 992,000 to 12,881,000 for this period. The host growth illustrates the often quoted statistic that the Internet has been doubling in size every year.

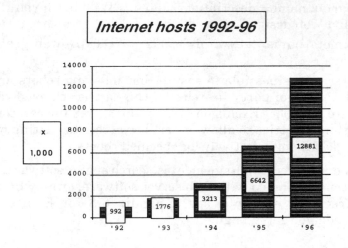

Figure 7 – Lottor's Internet host counts 1992-1996

Measuring the growth of the Web

In Spring of 1993 Matthew Gray wrote a program called the Wanderer to systematically traverse the Web and collect sites. His program covered 100 Web servers containing over 200,000 hypertext documents in June 1993. The Wanderer performed regular traversals of the Web and was the first automated agent, or spider, or robot – a predecessor of the software robots which were later to build the current indexes to the World Wide Web. The focus of Gray's activities switched to charting the growth of the Web and by January 1996 he had located 100,000 Web servers. Figure 8 illustrates the change in the ratio of hosts which are Web servers to hosts overall. Thus, in June 1993 only one in every 13,000 Internet hosts was a Web server. By January 1996, the rate of growth of Web servers relative to other kinds of hosts was such that one in every 94 was a Web server. Gray's report also confirmed the growth of the commercial Web. Whereas in June 1993 only 1.5% of Web sites were in the .com domain, by January 1996 this share had risen to 50% (see appendix 7).

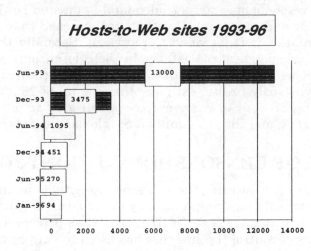

Figure 8 – Gray's ratios of hosts to Website ratios 1993 to 1996

How many Internet users are there?

Now, with the commercialisation of the Net, this question has a new basis in the identification of the market potential of the Internet. Internet demographers Hoffman and Novak, of Vanderbilt University, have argued that the original methods of estimating Internet user populations by counting the computers connected to the Internet is inadequate in the new commercial context, and akin to estimating the number of people in the US by sampling the number of buildings, without regard to their function or contents[53]. They proposed a different approach, so that – rather than inferring the number of users by counting and sampling machines – the users themselves should be sampled.

Towards the end of 1995, such a survey was provided by the Nielsen ratings organisation, and was enthusiastically received by a Wall Street which had been investing heavily in Internet-related stocks[54]. It was reported that 37 million people in the US and Canada had Internet access – a higher number than estimated by other surveys[55]. At the same time, the methodology and findings of Nielsen's Internet survey was also receiving criticism from Hoffman and Novak, who had helped design the general parameters and approach of the study, and had sat on the committee that selected Nielsen from the bidders for the project. They noticed two apparent flaws in the survey. Firstly, that the weighted

185

sample of respondents was not adequately adjusted so that its demographic and socioeconomic attributes matched those of the wider population it is intended to represent. Secondly, that the estimates lacked logical consistency in their definitions of what an Internet user is. After re-working of the data, they came up with a downwardly-revised estimate that a total of 28.8 million people in the US aged 16 and over have potential or actual access to the Internet, and that 16.4 million people use the Internet[56].

ISSUES OF CENSORSHIP AND CONTROL

Given its military ancestry, there is some irony that the Internet is often described as defying control by the government that gave it life and spawning battles over free speech and privacy. The two major crises of control the Internet has faced to date have been over the US Clipper encryption chip, and threats of censorship under the US Communications Decency Act.

Encryption and the US Clipper chip

In April 1993, the White House announced a new encryption standard, to replace the Data Encryption Standard (DES), which became known as the 'Clipper chip'. Clipper is a public-key[57] encryption/decryption chip intended to encode voice communications on digital telephones and fax machines, with a corresponding device handling encryption of data and e-mail. The DES had been released in 1987 with a 56-bit key which even then was thought short and susceptible to a brute force attack. Clipper contains a classified 80-bit encryption algorithm which is supposedly 16 million times harder to crack than the DES. However, that security has one exception – the US government can read any message encrypted on any Clipper chip, because it has a copy of the keys, giving it a 'back door' to eavesdrop on any communications[58]. The government view is that wiretaps have been essential for preventing and solving many serious crimes and terrorist activities. Civil liberties groups feared misuses and campaigned against it. The US administration has never spoken of outlawing alternative methods of encryption, and have sought compliance with Clipper mainly through market forces. However, many liberty groups advance a convincing logic that a public key encryption system can only be made effective if alternative encryption systems are outlawed.

Phil Zimmermann's Pretty Good Encryption (PGP) public-domain software is such an alternative encryption system. The first version of PGP appeared in 1991, its release precipitated by Zimmermann's concerns over earlier proposed legislation which required providers of communication systems to ensure that they permitted the government to obtain the plain text contents of voice, data, and other communications. Although Zimmermann claims he only gave a floppy disk copy of PGP to a friend, it was quickly available on the Internet, and distributed around the world[59,60]. Based on PGP's 128-bit key-length, and present rates of increase in computing power, it is reckoned resistant to brute force attack for the next hundred years. Zimmermann has also developed PGPfone, a software package which enables computers with soundcards and modems to function as secure telephones. The release of PGP precipitated legal problems for Zimmerman, with national security and customs officials who investigated him for illegally exporting munitions, which is how encryption is classified in the US[61].

The US government is not currently pursuing its Clipper initiative, possibly due to technical flaws. In Britain, the United Kingdom Education and Research Networking Association (UKERNA) which runs the Joint Academic Network (JANET) has seen the current solution to the privacy of documents, and the authentication of information, to be PGP. At this time, civil liberties groups are expressing concern both about a possible Euro-Clipper chip and also a Clipper II in the US. For further information on the Clipper chip, see appendix 8.1.

While for some PGP is a symbol of civil liberties, for information professionals it is a valuable practical tool. It is widely recognised that security is the primary concern of managers considering the use of the Internet to transport strategic organisational information. The use of strong encryption, such as PGP, sees the solution in accepting the security weaknesses of the carrier, and instead ensuring the security of the content and obtaining confidential, authenticated communication via cryptography[62,63]. PGP, which is available for all common platforms, has a simple command-line usage[64,65,66], has been provided with some graphical interfaces, and can be configured with many contemporary e-mail systems. Conversely, the encryption utilities supplied with some proprietary e-mail software may be inneffectual against serious attack due to limited key-lengths.

Censorship and the US Communications Decency Act

On 1st February 1996, the US Congress passed the Communications Decency Act (CDA) by 414 – 16. Minutes after it was signed into law, coalitions led by the American Civil Liberties Union (ACLU) and the American Library Association (ALA) filed lawsuits in the federal court in Philadelphia challenging the constitutionality of the CDA. The original sponsors of CDA promoted their bill as an effort to save cyberspace from becoming a debaucherous haven for perverts and paedophiles. It criminalised any 'obscene, lewd, lascivious, filthy, or indecent' material sent through an electronic network of any kind, with a penalty of up to US $100,000 in fines and two years in jail. Opponents of the CDA argued that it would be unconstitutional under First Amendment protection of free speech. The CDA proposals were also widely criticised as reducing the level of Internet content to that suitable for children, and it was noted that works such as James Joyce's *Ulysses* could be found 'indecent' if placed online.

In June 1995 a now somewhat notorious 'cyberporn' issue of *Time* magazine played an influential role both in initially providing support to the advocates of the CDA, and subsequently as a catalyst and focus for those arguing against it. The cover story's primary finding was that:

"There's an awful lot of porn online. In an 18-month study, the team surveyed 914,410 sexually explicit pictures, descriptions, short stories and film clips. On those Usenet newsgroups where digitised images are stored, 83.5% of the pictures were pornographic."[67]

The article would shortly transpire to be a curious mix of undergraduate hoax, poor journalistic research, and competition in the newsweeklies publishing market[68,69]. However, the afternoon it went on sale, a Republican senator held the magazine aloft during his floor speech against cyberporn, and told Congress that 83.5% of all computerised photographs available on the Internet were pornographic.

Within days the *Time* story was receiving a damning review on the Internet, notably with *Wired* magazine's HotWired Website creating a special *JournoPorn* section (see appendix 8.2). An interview with the author suggested that the editors of *Time* knew there were serious doubts about the study but decided to run the story anyway. Hoffman and Novak's *The Cyberporn Debate* Webpage[70] provided brief background information, plus a detailed guide to related documents. In fact, the 917,410 files did not come from the public Internet at all, but from private adult-oriented BBSs, whereas the wording used by *Time* conflated this source with Usenet newsgroups. From *Time*'s own wording that pornographic images represent 'only about 3% of all the messages on the Usenet newsgroups, while Usenet itself represents only 11.5% of the traffic on the Internet', the logical conclusion which would be that less than half of 1% of traffic on the Internet contains pornographic imagery.

On 11 June 1996, three federal judges convened in Philadelphia to review the CDA, pronounced the government's attempt to regulate online content more closely than print or broadcast media 'unconstitutional on its face' and 'profoundly repugnant'. They extended over the Internet the umbrella of the US Constitution's First Amendment, which protects free speech. Godwin [71] expressed particular vindication from this passage from Judge Dalzell's opinion:

"It is no exaggeration to conclude that the Internet has achieved, and continues to achieve, the most participatory marketplace of mass speech that this country – and indeed the world – has yet seen. The plaintiffs in these actions correctly describe the 'democratising' effects of Internet communication: Individual citizens of limited means can speak to a worldwide audience on issues of concern to them."

While there is an optimistic view[71] that the scope and force of the judges' written opinions would make it hard for the Supreme Court to do other than affirm the federal judges' basic finding that the CDA was unconstitutional, there is a view[72] that even if the Justice Department decided to forego a Supreme Court appeal, various family values groups would keep up pressure on politicians. At the time of writing, the Supreme Court is due to hear the case in March 1997, with a ruling expected in July.

CONCLUSION

Who can say what the Internet will be like in five or so years, given the last five? A couple of things are likely. Firstly, Web browsers will feature, but probably doing quite a lot more than they do now, in some respects like operating systems. To some extent this is already apparent in the way browsers are being used for the remote administration of some systems software. Secondly, to reiterate some of Anthony's introduction[12], there will still be opportunities for information professionals to seize to become involved in aspects of their organisation's activity which might benefit from their specialized knowledge and experience.

REFERENCES

1. Gibson, W. *Neuromancer*, Ace, New York (1984).

2. McMurdo, G. Getting *Wired* for McLuhan's cyberculture, *Journal of Information Science*, **21** (5) 1995, 371-381.

3. McMurdo, G. Stone Age babies in cyberspace, *Journal of Information Science*, **22** (1) 1996, 63-77.

4. McGarry, K. *The changing context of information*, Bingley, London (1981).

5. McMurdo, G. Changing contexts of communication, *Journal of Information Science*, **21** (2) 1995, 140-146.

6. Salus, P. Casting the Net: from ARPANet to Internet and beyond, Addison-Wesley, Reading MA (1995).

7. Hiltz,, S. R. and Turoff, M. *The Network Nation: human communication via computer*, MIT Press, Cambridge MA (1993, 2nd edition).

8. Turoff, M. The anatomy of a computer application innovation: computer mediated communication (CMC), *Technological Forecasting and Social Change*, **36** 1989, 107-122.

9. McCahill, M. The Internet Gopher: a distributed server information system, *ConneXions – The Interoperability Report*, **6**(7) 1992, 10-14.

10. Kahle, B. WAIS: Wide Area Information Servers, *NSF Network News*, **11,** March 1992, 1-2.

11. Berners-Lee, T. A summary of the World Wide Web system, *ConneXions: The Interoperability Report*, **6**(7) 1992, 26-27.

12. Anthony, L. J. Information management, In: *Handbook of special librarianship and information work*, edited by L.J. Anthony, Aslib, London (1982).

13. Clausen, H. Electronic mail as a tool for the information professional, *The Electronic Library*, **9** (2) 1991, 73-83.

14. Agre, P. Networking on the Network, University of California, San Diego, La Jolla CA (1994)
    http://communication.ucsd.edu/pagre/network.html

15. Schneiderman, R. A. Why librarians should rule the Net, *E-NODE*, **1** (4) 1996, 1-3
    http://www.mailbase.ac.uk/lists/lis-iis/files/lib-rule-net.txt

16. Fletcher, G. and Greenhill, A. Academic referencing of Internet-based resources, *Aslib Proceedings*, **47**(11/12) 1995, 245-252.

17. Kelly, S. and Nicholas, D. Is the business cybrarian a reality? Internet in business libraries, *Aslib Proceedings*, **48**(5) 1996, 136-144.

18. Green, T. Online information services: caught in the Web? *Online*, **19**(4) 1995, 23-31.

19. Perry, J. Why it matters which ISP you choose for your corporate site, *New Media Age*, **4** (July) 1996, 10-11.

20. Schuyler, M. Hooking up to the Big-I Internet, *Computers in Libraries*, **16** (8) 1996, 26-30.

21. McMurdo, G. Mailing to the machine, *Journal of Information Science*, **21** (3) 1995, 217-227.

22. Bauwens, M. The poor man's Internet: reaching the Internet with e-mail only, *Aslib Proceedings*, **45** (7/8) 1993, 201-207.

23. Fuchs, I. H. BITNET: because it's time, *Perspectives in Computing*, **3**(1) 1983, 16-27.

24. Emerson, S. L. USENET: a bulletin board for UNIX users, *Byte*, **8** (10) 1983, 219-236.

25. Shaw, R. *The FAQ Manual of Style*, MIS Press, New York (1996).

26. Kiesler, S., Siegel, J. and McGuire, T. W. Social psychological aspects of computer-mediated communication, *American Psychologist*, **39** (10) 1984, 1123-1133.

27. Feinberg, A. Netiquette, *Lotus*, **6** (9) 1990, 66-69.

28. Goode, J. and Johnson, M. Putting out the flames: the etiquette and law of e-mail, *Online*, **15** (6) 1991, 61-65.

29. Kantor, A. Learning the ropes: a usenet style guide, *Internet World*, **5**(8) 1994, 24-25.

30. McMurdo, G. Netiquettes for networkers, *Journal of Information Science*, **21** (4) 1995, 305-318.

31. Rose, D. *Minding your cyber-manners on the Internet*, Alpha Books, Indianapolis PA (1994.)

32. Shea, V. *Netiquette*, Albion Books, San Francisco (1994).

33. Godin, S. *The Smiley dictionary*, Peachpit Press, Berkeley CA (1993).

34. Sanderson, D. *Smileys*, O'Reilly, Sebastopol CA (1993).

35. McMurdo, G. Networking for trust in tribal organisations, *Journal of Information Science*, **22** (4) 1996, 299-314.

36. Agre, P. The art of getting help, University of California, San Diego, La Jolla CA (1994), *http://communication.ucsd.edu /pagre/getting-help.html*

37. Emtage, A. and Deutsch, P. Archie – an electronic directory service for the Internet, Proceedings of the 1992 Winter USENIX Conference, San Francisco, January 1992, USENIX Association, Berkeley CA (1992. pp. 93-110).

38. Deutsch, P. Resource discovery in an Internet environment – the Archie approach, *Electronic Networking: Research, Applications, and Policy*, **2** (1) 1992, 50-51.

39. McMurdo, G. How the Internet was indexed. *Journal of Information Science*, **21** (6) 1995, 479-489.

40. Foster, S. *Common questions and answers about Veronica, a title search and retrieval system for use with the Internet Gopher*, 1995 *gopher://Veronica.scs.unr.edu/00/Veronica/Veronica-faq*

41. Foster, S. *How to compose Veronica queries*, 1994 *gopher://Veronica.scs.unr.edu/00/Veronica/how-to-query-Veronica*

42. Winship. I. World Wide Web searching tools – an evaluation, *Vine*, **99** 1995, 49-54.

43. Koster, M. Robots in the Web: threat or treat, *ConneXions – The Interoperability Report*, **9** (4) 1995, 2-12.

44. Brandt, D. S. Relevancy and searching the Internet, *Computers in Libraries*, **16** (8) 1996, 35-39.

45. Seltzer, R., Ray, E. J. and Ray, D. S. *The AltaVista search revolution*, Digital Press and McGraw-Hill, Maynard MA and Berkeley CA (1996).

46. McMurdo, G. HTML for the lazy, *Journal of Information Science*, **22** (3) 1996, 198-212.

47. Carl, J. HTML helpers, *Internet World*, **6** (9) 1995, 63-66.

48. Strain, H. C. and Berry, P. M. Better page design for the World Wide Web, *Online and CD-ROM Review*, **20** (5) 1996, 227-238.

49. McMurdo, G. Web graphics for the lazy, *Journal of Information Science*, **23** (2) 1997, pp149-162.

50. Murray, J. D. and Van Ryper, W. *Encyclopedia of graphics file formats*, O'Reilly, Sebastopol CA (1996).

51. Kientzle, T. *Internet file formats*, Coriolis Group, Scottsdale AZ (1995).

52. Koster, M. *A standard for robot exclusion*, 1994 *http://info.webcrawler.com/mak/projects/robots/norobots.html*

53. Hoffman, D. L. and Novak, T. P. Wanted: net.census, *Wired (US)*, **2** (11) 1994, 93-94.

54. Dibbell, J. Nielsen rates the Net, *Time (International)*, **146**(24) 1995, p.68.

55. McMurdo, G. The Net by numbers, *Journal of Information Science*, **22** (5) 1996, 381-390.

56. Hoffman, D. L., Kalsbeek, W. D. and Novak, T. P. *Internet use in the United States: 1995 baseline estimates and preliminary market segment*, Owen Graduate School of Management, Vanderbilt University, Nashville TN (1996, Project 2000 Working Paper), *http://www2000.ogsm.vanderbilt.edu/baseline/1995.Internet.estimates.html*

57. Diffie, W. The first 10 years of public-key cryptography, *Proceedings of the IEEE*, 1988, 560-576.

58. Elmer-Dewitt, P. Who should keep the keys? *Time (International)*, **143** (10) 1994, 50-51.

59. Levy, S. Crypto rebels, *Wired (US)*, **1** (2) 1993, p.54.

60. Stallings, W. Pretty good privacy, *Byte*, **19** (7) 1994. 193-196.

61. Zajac, B. P. US encryption policy. II. Pretty Good Privacy (PGP), *Computer Law and Security Report*, **10** (4) 1994, 201-202.

62. Thomas, B. Confidential communication on the Internet, *Scientific American*, **273** (6) 1995, 70-73.

63. Forcht, K. A. and Wex, R. A. Doing business on the Internet: marketing and security aspects, *Information Management and Computer Security*, **4** (4) 1996, 3-9.

64. Zimmerman, P. *PGP user's guide*, MIT Press, Cambridge MA (1995).

65. Garfinkel, S. *PGP: Pretty good privacy*, O'Reilly, Sebastopol CA (1995).

66. McMurdo, G. Pretty good encryption, *Journal of Information Science*, **22** (2) 1996, 133-146.

67. Elmer-Dewitt, P. On a screen near you: cyberporn, *Time (International)*, **146** (1) 1995, 34-41.

68. Godwin, M. Philip's folly, *Internet World*, **6** (10) 1995, 102-104.

69. McMurdo, G. Cyberporn and communication decency, *Journal of Information Science*, **23** (1) 1997, pp81-90.

70. Hoffman, D. L. and Novak, T. P. *A detailed critique of the Time article: 'On a screen near you: Cyberporn'*, Owen Graduate School of Management, Vanderbilt University,Nashville TN (1995) *http://www.hotwired.com/special/pornscare/hoffman.html*

71. Godwin, M. Sinking the CDA, *Internet World*, **7**(10) 1996, 108-112.

72. Quittner, J. Free speech for the net, *Time (International)*, **14** **7**(26) 1996, 52-53.

APPENDIX: SELECTED INTERNET RESOURCES

1. History

A Brief History of the Internet
  http://www.isoc.org/internet-history/
Hobbes' Internet Timeline
  http://info.isoc.org/guest/zakon/Internet/History/HIT.html

2. The Internet and Special Information Units

2.1 Library and Information Professional Resources on the Internet

American Library Association (ALA)
  http://www.ala.org/
American Society for Information Science (ASIS)
  http://www.asis.org/
Aslib – the Association for Information Management
  http://www.aslib.co.uk/
BUBL – the Bulletin Board for Libraries

http://bubl.ac.uk/
Institute of Information Scientists
http://carduus.imi.gla.ac.uk/
Library Association
http://www.la-hq.org.uk

2.2 Evaluating Internet Information

Evaluation of information sources, Information Quality WWW Virtual Library
http://www.vuw.ac.nz/~agsmith/evaln/evaln.htm
Thinking Critically about World Wide Web Resources
http://www.library.ucla.edu/libraries/college/instruct/critical.htm

3. Accessing the Internet

3.1 Internet Service Providers (ISPs)

List of UK and Irish Internet service providers
http://www.limitless.co.uk/inetuk/
Worldwide Internet service providers
http://thelist.internet.com/

3.2 Accessing the Internet by E-mail

Accessing the Internet By E-mail
http://www.mailbase.ac.uk/lists/lis-iis/files/e-access-inet.txt
Or, send a message to **mailbase@mailbase.ac.uk** with the message body send **lis-iis e-access-inet.txt**

4. Electronic Discussion Forums

4.1 E-mail Discussion Lists

Mailbase UK e-mail discussion lists service and archives
http://www.mailbase.ac.uk/
Comparative mailing list manager commands
http://lawwww.cwru.edu/cwrulaw/faculty/milles/mailser.html
Publicly accessible mailing lists

http://www.NeoSoft.com:80/internet/paml/
Searchable directory of e-mail discussion groups
http://www.liszt.com/

4.2 Usenet FAQs

Usenet FAQs archive, Europe
ftp://ftp.sunet.se/pub/usenet/
Usenet FAQs archive, US
ftp://rtfm.mit.edu/pub/usenet/

4.3 Netiquette

Emily Postnews Answers Your Questions on Netiquette
http://www.cis.ohio-state.edu/hypertext/faq/usenet/emily-postnews/part1/faq.html
The Net: User Guidelines and Netiquette
http://rs6000.adm.fau.edu/faahr/netiquette.html
Rules for Posting to Usenet
http://www.cis.ohio-state.edu/hypertext/faq/usenet/usenet/posting-rules/part1/faq.html

4.4 The Art of Networking

The art of getting help, by Phil Agre
http://communication.ucsd.edu/pagre/getting-help.html
Networking on the network, by Phil Agre
http://communication.ucsd.edu/pagre/network.html

5. Searching for information

5.1 Archie and Veronica Searches

Archie searches via the Web
http://sunsite.doc.ic.ac.uk/archieplexform.html
Veronica searches of Gopherspace via BUBL
gopher://ukoln.bath.ac.uk:7070/11/Index/Veronica

5.2 Indexed Web Searches

Lycos search service
http://www.lycos.com/
Altavista Web and Usenet searches

http://altavista.digital.com/

HotBot Web and Usenet searches
http://www.hotbot.com/

5.3 Subject Web Searches

Argus Clearinghouse
http://www.clearinghouse.net/

Yahoo! search service
http://www.yahoo.com/
and *http://www.yahoo.co.uk/*

5.4 Finding People and E-mail Addresess

Bigfoot – e-mail address searches
http://www.bigfoot.com/

WhoWhere? E-mail addresses
http://whowhere.com/

6. Producing Internet Information

6.1 HTML Writers' Information Resources

Beginner's guide to HTML
*http://www.ncsa.uiuc.edu/General/Internet/WWW/
HTMLPrimer.html*

HENSA HTML validation service
http://www.hensa.ac.uk/html-val-svc/

The HTML Station, by John December
http://www.december.com/html/

Style Guide for online hypertext, by Tim Berners-Lee
http://www.w3.org/Provider/Style/Overview.html

6.2 Web Graphics Information and Sources

Multimedia file formats on the Internet
http://rodent.lib.rochester.edu/multimed/contents.htm

Yahoo! links to public-domain icon sites
*http://www.yahoo.com/Computers/World_Wide_Web/
Programming/Icons/*

6.3 *Operating a Web Server*

Running A WWW Service
> *http://info.man.ac.uk/MVC/SIMA/handbook/ handbook.html*

Excite for Web Servers 1.1 downloadable search engine
> *http://www.excite.com/navigate/download.cgi*

7. Trends and Forecasts

Internet Domain Surveys
> *http://www.nw.com/zone/WWW/Top.html*

Growth of the World Wide Web report
> *http://www.mit.edu:8001/people/mkgray/net/*

Index of Internet surveys
> *http://www.nua.ie/surveys/*

8. Issues of Censorship and Control

8.1 *Encryption and Cryptography*

Computer Professionals for Social Responsibility Clipper chip archives
> *http://www.cpsr.org/dox/program/clipper/clipper.html*

Electronic Frontier Foundation cryptography information
> *http://www.eff.org/pub/Crypto/*

Electronic Privacy Information Center cryptography information
> *http://www.epic.org/crypto/*

International PGP home-page (other than US and Canada)
> *http://www.ifi.uio.no/pgp/*

MIT distribution site for PGP (US and Canada)
> *http://web.mit.edu/network/pgp.html*

8.2 *The US Communication Decency Act*

HotWired critiques of *Time* cyberporn article
> *http://wwww.hotwired.com/special/pornscare/*

Hoffman and Novak's *The Cyberporn Debate*
> *http://www2000.ogsm.vanderbilt.edu/cyberporn.debate.cgi*

Information Technology in the Information Centre

Phil Bradley

INTRODUCTION

In the last decade, the amount of hardware and software that can be found in an information centre has increased remarkably. However, for many of us who obtained a library qualification before this period, all this technology can seem to be so many grey boxes full of magic, particularly if the technical support department in the organisation exerts control over what is to be found in the library, and how it is to be looked after. This chapter will address some of the major technical developments in information technology (IT); what you can expect to find, how best to make use of and evaluate different products, how best to manage IT, and the skillset and the knowledge that you require to do this effectively and efficiently.

LIBRARY HOUSEKEEPING SOFTWARE

This is a subject about which I am sure it is possible to write for a very long time in order to properly cover all of the areas which are pertinent, but I will simply cover some of the major aspects, and the sort of things that you will need to consider from a predominantly IT viewpoint.

First of all, what exactly is covered under such a generic heading? As well as general housekeeping/management software, there are also text retrieval packages, acquisitions software, cataloguing packages and serials control software. Rather than attempt to cover each of these individually, I will try and highlight some of the common questions and problems you will encounter when dealing with these various packages.

A great many solutions present themselves such as tailored packages, modular, fully integrated and off-the-shelf. You only need to attend an exhibition such as the Library Resources Exhibition to see the variety which is available. So how do you choose the package (or packages) which is best for you?

- A tailored package, produced by a company, may well be the ideal solution, in that they can work with you to discover exactly what you need, and may well come up with some things that you had not thought of. The major disadvantage of this approach, however, is that it is going to cost your organisation many thousands of pounds to obtain exactly what you want, you're tied to that one supplier in future, and to a large extent, you are at the mercy of the programming skills and abilities of the team assigned to you and your project.

- Modular packages give you greater flexibility in your approach and will allow you to prioritise your needs. It is therefore a lot easier to work within a fixed or limited budget, and to provide yourself, staff and users with training in digestible amounts rather than having to teach a large, new system. However, a problem with this approach is that once again, you are limited to future purchasing from that one supplier, other products may well not fit into the modular approach you have decided upon, and when it is time to add in a new module you may have to purchase upgrades to existing modules to ensure that everything works correctly together.

- Fully integrated packages may cost more than the modular approach initially, but they will usually provide you with a complete or turnkey solution to all your housekeeping needs. The elements of the package will work correctly, and in conjunction with each other. There will be a large user base for the package, and the producer will supply upgrades which complement existing features, and will be understanding to the needs of the user base. The disadvantage of this approach can be summed up in the phrase 'Jack of all trades, master of none' in that if you have a particular need for some very in-depth software, the integrated approach may not be as comprehensive as you require. On the other hand, you may also find that you are paying for software elements that you never need, or which are too detailed for your requirements.

- Piecemeal approach, the advantages of this are that you can buy what you need, when you need it, from whichever company offers the best solution. It is therefore easier to budget for this, and to introduce elements of the system at appropriate times. The major disadvantage of this approach, however, is that it is much more difficult to ensure that all the elements will work well with each other, and suppliers have an unhappy knack of putting the blame onto another element of software, leaving you caught between suppliers, each blaming the other and neither providing a solution to your technical problem.

Needs analysis

Consequently, before you take the leap to a purchasing decision you will need to evaluate very carefully the different solutions to see which one is best for you and your situation. However, before you can do this, you will need to get a clear idea of exactly what you want to achieve, and what is possible; in other words, to undertake a needs analysis. For example, if you wish to purchase a serials control package you should look at your existing serials to answer questions such as "How many titles will the software need to deal with?" "Which frequencies and regularities must it offer?" "user types?" "item types?" "integration with other systems?" "software platforms?" and so on. An easy way of undertaking this sort of analysis is to obtain the literature produced by the different suppliers, ignore all the hype and just make a note of all the different things each package can do, incorporate it into one large list and then go through it, prioritising as you go. By the time you have finished, you should have a reasonably good indication of exactly what you are after.

Selecting the system

You are then going to be in a better position to undertake the next stage of exploration. Any producer worth their salt will be able to give you a list of reference sites that you can contact, and you may well find that it is worth sending a message to an appropriate Internet Listserv or mailing list (a list of these can be obtained by going to the Mailbase home page on the Internet at *http://www.mailbase.ac.uk* to identify a list that covers your subject interest) asking for comments and opinions on various solutions. Spend some time on the Internet; visit the home pages of the providers, and also visit some sites which provide general advice and guidance. Some examples of the latter are:

- *http://www.ewos.be/goss/top.htm* which is a guide to open systems specifications

- *http://www.nlc-bnc.ca/ifla/VII/s21/sit.htm* which is the IFLA section on information technology and is a useful launchpad site into some of the specifications available for library housekeeping systems

- *http://www.auburn.edu/~fostecd/docs/accessories.html* is a useful site in that it provides links to a large number of library suppliers who offer solutions to a whole range of housekeeping systems

- *http://www.ukoln.ac.uk/papers/ukoln/ams5.html* providers the reader with standards pertaining to a variety of networked library services, such as comms, applications, data interchange, authentication, charging and so on

- *http://www.sbu.ac.uk/~litc/publications/intropacks.html* provides details and a list of packages to guide the beginner through choosing library housekeeping software.

Procurement

Once you have visited reference sites, read postings from appropriate newsgroups and visited Web pages you should be in a position to decide exactly what you want to buy. You may well decide to tender for the work, in which case you will need to write a tender document, make it available on your Web site, post it to suppliers and so on. This document needs to be very carefully produced, since you need to be quite clear on what you want, what the software should achieve, possible future expansion, support expected, time periods for installation and your criteria for success. You should also make it clear to suppliers as to exactly when they get paid. These last two points are very important; one definition for a working serials acquisition package, for example, is that it should be possible to enter a title and obtain a full audit trail. Another definition is that the package should be able to do this for two, or 20 or even 2,000 titles with members of staff all busily using the system in the middle of the day. Both are quite acceptable definitions for 'working' systems, but if your definition does not match that of your supplier, you may be storing up trouble for yourself in the future. You need to be clear on what is expected of the software. While most of us are also reticent about money, you should also make it clear to any potential supplier what you will pay and when you will pay it. You should also write into the tender document that you will retain a certain percentage of the fee until you are satisfied that the system works properly (and also define exactly what you mean by that). As a result, you will have a certain amount of leverage if the supplier does not keep up their end of the installation.

Implementation

Once you have chosen your supplier and solution(s) you can move on to the implementation stage. This of course is where it starts to get a little bit tricky. Depending on exactly what software solution you are implementing, it may take anywhere from half a day's work to a week or longer to install all the components and make sure that they are up and running. I would strongly advise that you get involved up to the very top level of your IT competence. Make use of the technicians your vendor will bring in, and certainly get your own technical support team involved at a very early stage in the planning, but make sure you are clear what each step in the implementation is going to be, ask as many questions as you feel necessary and don't accept an answer you don't understand. Don't forget – it is you and your staff who are going to have to get this software running, and keep it running, so you need to know as much as possible. Ensure that the supplier includes training in the price of the package (or stipulate it yourself in the tender document), and make sure that it is a proper training session, not a quick 10 minutes before the technician leaves, which has been known to happen.

The technicians (both yours and theirs) should backup your existing systems for you, and you should plan to run both in tandem for a few weeks before going live with the system. That will give the system time to work itself in, for any bugs to develop, be identified and solved, train yourself and your staff in more detail, yet ensure that the normal routines are not disturbed for your users. If you are implementing a complete solution, you may wish to do this stage by stage, rather than have a 'D-Day' situation. While this means that the implementation is going to last longer, and will be a little more extended than you might perhaps like, it will give further time for the systems to bed down properly. If you introduce everything overnight, you may find that your users' expectations have been increased, causing an unexpected strain on the system which is, of course, the time when the whole thing will go down on you. A slower implementation is just that – slow, and without any great fanfares, but likely to be more efficient in the long run.

However carefully you implement systems, they will go down on you. Simply accept at the outset that the thing is going to crash; it is one of the few things that you can rely on computers to do, and that this will happen at just the wrong moment entirely. Have a back-up plan in place for how to cope if the network goes down, or there is a power cut. Ensure that you keep more backups of your system than you think is necessary – certainly keep an appropriate backup of files for once a week for a month, then monthly backups for six months, and then a six monthly and finally an annual backup. If it is a large system you might also want to have daily backups as well. There are lots of ways of doing this – backing up onto a networked server, tape streamer and so on, and your technicians can advise you of the best way of doing this.

Ensure that you have a 24 hour maintenance agreement with your provider. If something goes down you will want a technician on site as close to 'immediately' as is humanly possible. One or two of your staff should be responsible for keeping the system up and running, understanding error messages and so on, and for being the initial contact with technical support. There are further references to the whole issue of support later in this chapter, and this cannot be taken seriously enough.

CD-ROM

Compact Disc, Read Only Memory has played an astonishingly important role, both in bringing information within the reach of the end-user, and introducing the information professional to day-to-day use of computer systems. We did, of course, have limited access to technology before the introduction of CD-ROM, in the form of online searching, dumb terminals, acoustic couplers and the like, but it was really only when CD-ROM was introduced that we had the opportunity to 'get our hands dirty' and actually start opening machines up, installing interface cards and loading the appropriate software.

However for those of you who have not used CD-ROM technology, or who are at the mercy of your organisation's technical specialists, I shall provide you with a little background, and begin to highlight some of the skills that today's information professional requires in order to make use of it correctly.

CD-ROM discs use exactly the same type of technology as CD Audio discs, only instead of containing music, they can (and generally do) contain text, and with multimedia products, sound, graphics and moving image clips. Each disc can hold up to about 660 megabytes of textual data, which roughly corresponds to 1,500 floppy disks, 400 full length paperback novels, or a stack of paper about 18 feet high. Data is stored on a CD-ROM digitally (that is to say, a hole will be burnt into the single track of data, or it will not, giving us a 0 or 1) and read optically by the use of a laser tracking backwards and forwards over the disc. This data is then fed back to the computer via the cable and interface card, and interpreted by the retrieval engine being used to search the disc, then displayed on the monitor. The actual information itself is generally leased to a CD-ROM publisher, or a number of publishers, by an Information Provider which actually owns the data. Publishers then take this information, place it onto disc, ensure that it runs correctly with their own software and then market this as a product.

Although CD-ROM was very slow to take off in the beginning it has become an integral part of any information centre. According to TFPL, there are currently over 13,000 different CD-ROM titles available on the market, and it appears likely that this figure will simply continue to increase[1]. More and more companies are releasing, not only databases, but their software on CD-ROM, so having a least one CD-ROM drive (the piece of equipment required to read a CD-ROM) in the library is now virtually a necessity, rather than a luxury. Indeed, four out of every five personal computers which are sold in the UK now contain an in-built CD-ROM drive.

One should therefore ask the question – why has this technology become so popular? I have already indicated one of the reasons for this; it is because CD-ROM brings the end-user into direct contact with the information that they require, rather than having to go through the information professional acting as a 'gate-keeper' who obtains the information on their behalf. The information professional becomes much more of a 'facilitator' helping the end-user obtain the information without actually doing the searches on their behalf. This highlights one particular skill that the information professional needs to be competent in, which is in the area of training, but it is one that I will return to later.

Now, because CD-ROM is such a powerful tool, and one increasingly beloved of the end-user it continued to develop, until it became easier to network products and make them available throughout an entire organisation, not just from within the information centre. This is further emphasised by the ability to 'precache' data from CD-ROM onto hard disk. It then becomes much easier to search data, and therefore have more users searching data simultaneously than previously.

WHAT SKILLS DOES THE INFORMATION PROFESSIONAL NEED?

Today's information professional requires a number of new skills in order to deal properly with the influx of new technology. A reasonable general level of computer literacy is needed in order to have an informed discussion with a salesperson or supplier regarding exactly what equipment is required, and what it can do for the information centre. Practical skills are also necessary. Software and hardware will need to be installed, and simple problem solving undertaken. While this may be seen as really belonging within the province of the technical support department, the computer literate information professional will be able to install and keep systems up and running much more effectively than their counterpart who has to wait until the support department can find time to come and deal with general problems.

Another attendant skill is that of being able to properly manage and advertise your information centre in the face of increasing diversity and networking. In the future there will be less and less reason for the end-user to actually visit the information centre, so the forward thinking information professional will be looking for ways in which to keep the remote user aware of exactly what the information centre is doing, and why the professionals employed there are still vital to the smooth running of the organisation. Training, and effective training at that, must also come much higher on the list of priorities. It used to be very simple to provide training; the librarian could see if a user was having problems, and provide on the spot assistance as necessary. However, once information sources can be accessed remotely the information centre staff will not be seeing what the user is doing, or what mistakes they are making, so they must ensure that end-users are much more confident and happy with the information resources they have available at their disposal. An unhappy, or inept user will not continue to use these resources, thus putting them in jeopardy.

So let us now have a look at these skills in a little more detail. In order to talk to suppliers, and to find out what exactly is possible, the information professional will need to do several things. Firstly, increase their reading in these areas. Most of the computer magazines which are available will have beginners' guides, question and answer pages and so on, and these can be a useful fund of information. A wealth of other information is also available. Although I dislike the series name, the 'Dummies' [2] guides can be a good starting point in understanding computer issues. They are easy to read, clearly laid out, and do not presume much initial understanding, if any, of the subject matter.

Training organisations such as TFPL and Aslib run introductory courses in many subject areas related to computing, and although they are not cheap, they do give participants a good opportunity to talk to other delegates and course tutors in a friendly and welcoming environment. Finally, take advantage of any visits to IT-aware information centres; visits are run by many different organisations, such as UKOLUG [3] and can be used for networking and to increase the number of friendly professionals who will be happy to point you in the right direction. The kind of subjects that are important here are basic introductions to computing generally, all aspects of CD-ROM (particularly networking), an overall understanding of networking – what it is, how it can assist you, how you can put your resources onto an internal network and so on.

Practical skills are also very important. If the librarian does not have these skills, it is going to be necessary to call in technical support every single time something does not work as it should, or a new piece of hardware or software requires installation. This does not of course mean that information professionals should spend all their time providing technical support, far from it, but if the basics are understood it will increase the effectiveness and efficiency of the information centre. The clued-up librarian will be able to do simple tasks, such as installing a CD-ROM drive. Some people may be horrified at my description of this as 'simple', but it really is. It requires the ability to backup a system (and this is something that I will return to shortly), open the computer up and place an interface card inside. Once this has been completed, the machine can be put back together again, and the appropriate software installed to ensure that the computer recognises the existence of the newly installed CD-ROM drive. This is in itself a simple process, and rarely requires anything more than answering a few simple questions (such as the number of drives being installed), and accepting factory set defaults. I accept, however, that this can be a nerve-racking experience the first time it is undertaken; I would defy anyone to open up their computer for the first time without a few qualms. However, if you have a friendly technician on hand, get them to baby-sit you while you do it, and while the machine is open, get them to point out things such as the position of the hard drive(s), motherboard, controller cards and so on. Ideally, it is worth practising on an old machine first, just to get the hang of it; while this may seem to waste an hour or so of your time, it is a perfect way to get experience in a stress free environment.

OPERATING SYSTEMS

Having got used to the hardware side of things, you should also take some time out to learn about the operating system under which your computer works. Normally of course this will be MicroSoft DOS (Disk Operating System), although you may decide as much as possible to ignore this, and spend your time working with Windows instead. There are two versions of Windows currently in use; Windows 3.1 and Windows '95, and while the two systems are compatible (in that most products will work under either of them) Windows 95 looks very different to users, but is generally becoming the operating system of choice for developers and users alike. Learn how to add programs and icons into the system, how to delete obsolete programs, and how to customise Windows 95 for optimum performance in your organisation. Once again, there are plenty of books available, Internet newsgroups you can join, courses to go on, or hopefully a friendly technician in your organisation who can point you in the right direction. At the very least, you should be able to use the mouse without any problems (it is suprising what a large number of librarians have problems with this simple device). If you (or a junior member of staff you are training) have problems with the mouse, I would recommend playing a few games of the Solitaire game which comes with Windows. It is not terribly addictive, but is straightforward and will teach you how to use the mouse quickly and effectively.

SYSTEM BACKUPS

To return to a subject previously mentioned, you *must* know how to backup your system. At some point, probably as a result of nothing you personally have done, your computer will fail. It might be something very simple and straightforward, or someone may have introduced a virus onto the machine, but you can guarantee that it will fail. Work out how to backup your system (either by copying important files onto floppy disks or onto a network drive that your technical people have), and back it up weekly, at the very least. Keep each week's backups somewhere secure; don't backup onto your only set of backup disks – only re-use these once you are sure that you have backups for the last three weeks or a month. Keep one set of backup discs for a couple of months as well, which, although it sounds like overkill is the best way of ensuring that, when (note that it is 'when' rather than 'if') the system goes down you will have lost the bare minimum of work. There is no need to backup an entire hard disk (although with the falling prices of tape drives and recordable CD-ROM drives it is easier to do this now than it has ever been), but be selective in the files you decide are most important. Certainly I would suggest copies of the autoexec.bat and config.sys files and Windows files such as win.ini. While you can of course re-install software such as retrieval engines, you'll save yourself a lot of time in the long run if you back them up as well, since it is going to be quicker to restore a backup than it is to reinstall software from scratch. It need not be a difficult process – it is very easy to write a batch file to do a simple copy of specific files onto floppy or a networked drive. If in doubt, get your technical support department to write one for you (as it is going to save them time in the long run they should be quite happy to help out on this). Get into the habit of doing this on a regular basis – late Friday afternoon for example; ensure that if you are not the person directly responsible for it, that someone is, and that they know they are. Finally, make sure that this individual has a 'shadow' who knows exactly what to do in the event of leave or sickness.

Log books

Keep little 'log books' for each of your machines. This will again make life easier for you or anyone else who has to solve problems which occur now and then. In the log book you should list information such as the make and model of the computer, any additional devices such as CD-ROM drives which are attached to it, printed copies of the autoexec.bat and config.sys files, a directory listing, and a printout of the setup screen. When your computer boots first thing you should see a brief message saying something like 'Press F1 to enter setup'. Do that, and take notes on how much RAM the machine has, the type of hard disk and so on. Keep notes of which software is loaded onto the machine and what the version numbers are. You should also make a note of anything which happens to the machine. If it is moved, if new software is installed, any problems and their solutions. Once you have established a system like this it will become second nature to keep it up to date, or you can delegate the task to a junior member of staff.

TRAINING

I mentioned earlier that the IT-aware information professional is going to be spending more of his or her time in training and promotion as a direct result of more users accessing the resources remotely. Not only will you and your staff need to know how all of your systems work (from sorting out printer jams to isolating network problems to how to truncate in any number of retrieval engines), but you will need to be able to train your users in the parts of the system(s) that they use. This may take the form of quick reference cards available at each terminal (or copied and given to them to use at their desks).It is also worth contacting your publishers to see if they have either generic or product specific crib sheets available that you can use. These are either free or you can obtain permission to reproduce them as often as required. You may however prefer to run training sessions for your users and I have heard of situations where users are not allowed onto a particular database until they have been trained. If you are not used to training, I would suggest that you attend an appropriate course (Aslib, TFPL and UKOLUG all run courses of this nature) in order to do it competently and confidently.

You will also need to train your users in the basics of either trouble-shooting or failing that, in how to report a fault somewhere in the system. The use of fault reporting sheets kept by each machine to guide a user through this process will be invaluable when you are called in to sort out the problem.

THE FUTURE OF IT IN THE INFORMATION SERVICE

Despite the difficulties of forecasting future trends in IT, there are some clear indications of likely changes which may assist professional planning for the next few years. There have been, over the last few years, a number of common themes emerging. The three most important are the dramatic increase in the technology which is available, the desire by the end-user to have direct access to information quicker and more easily, and finally the role of the information professional, changing from that of the gatekeeper (who goes and finds information and provides it to his or her client) to the facilitator (who assists the client in finding the information for themselves).

CD-ROM drives have been getting faster, and have also come down in price. Seven or eight years ago a single speed CD-ROM drive would cost anywhere from £500-£700 each, yet today drives are on sale for under £100. Since that date, drives have also got much faster; instead of having an access time of 400 milliseconds, their speed has increased to about 150 milliseconds or better. Transfer rates have increased, and it is now possible to buy 8x, 10x or even 12x drives. Four out of five new computers sold today have an internal CD-ROM drive as standard, and more and more products are being produced using optical technology as the cost of doing so has dropped. However, I think we have now gone just about as far as it is possible to go using the standard technology; it is simply not possible to get drives to work faster, or to put more data onto them.

This leads therefore to two slightly different approaches to making data available; the first of these is to 'pre-cache' data, the second to move to a different optical technology. Pre-caching, or copying data from the CD-ROM disc to a hard disk started about three years ago, in response to the requirements of the users to get faster and more effective access to the data. Technically, it is not difficult to do this, and it does not require a great deal of work on behalf of software developers to 'tell' their retrieval engines to look at a hard disk as well as an optical disc. However, many publishers have still not made such changes to their software, often because the original owner, or information provider (IP) chooses not to allow their data to be made available in that particular manner. This is not suprising, since they have a large investment to protect. The same reluctance could be seen when the possibility of networking CD-ROM drives became possible. Their concern is, of course, obvious – the more that a product can be networked, the less control they have over it, with the potential to lose revenue. However, they came around to the idea of networking products over the course of a couple of years, and they will do so again.

We are now beginning to see a change in the way in which optical technology is being used; rather than the mechanism for the distribution and the searching of data, it is increasingly being used to simply distribute, and provide a perfect backup for data copied onto hard disk. I was involved in some of the early testing of this approach, and the speed of access to the data, and the transfer rates back to the client computer were quite astonishing.

The information professional is now in a position to decide how best to make information available; on stand-alone machines, networked CD-ROM drives, or in pre-cached format. However, onto this list we must now add access to the data over the Internet. Since it is possible to copy the data onto hard disk, it is also possible to make that information available on a server connected to the Internet, and a number of companies, such as SilverPlatter Information and Ovid Technologies, have made great strides in this area. It is possible to access an entire database across the Internet, together with appropriate software found on the Internet, or to take a hybrid approach, by offering some data on a local system and telling the retrieval software that it must also go out across the Internet to interrogate a remote database.

This is a very attractive position for the information provider, the publisher and the information professional. Rather than have to wait for a month to have information updated with the arrival of a new disc, there is no reason why the retrieval engine cannot get the latest information direct from an Internet server. It is attractive to the publisher since it simplifies the provision of data to customers, and it also means that they can consider different approaches to charging for the information. Rather than have a single annual subscription for a product they could, for example, sell credits to customers, who would be able to use any appropriate database to obtain the information they need, and pay for the downloading or printing of the records they feel are appropriate. Incidentally, there is, intrinsically no difference here between a CD-ROM publisher and a more traditional online host, with perhaps the exception that CD-ROM retrieval software is often much easier to use, since it was originally designed for the end-user in mind, rather than the information professional. The information provider is keen on this idea since their data can get used much more than on CD-ROM, password access limits the use of the data, and they have another form of obtaining revenue. Furthermore, there is again no reason why the end-user should not identify the records that they are interested in and using appropriate Internet software, contact a document delivery service, order the article they want, and have it sent straight to their own e-mail account.

DVD-ROM

There is though, still a problem. Fast as the newest CD-ROM drives are, as fast as information can be made available across the Internet, the end-user has now recognised that they can obtain data for themselves, quickly and effectively. Allied to this, in the entertainment industry, there is a commercial requirement to ensure that movies, for example, can be viewed more quickly and more effectively than at present. The two areas, which initially appear so different are converging with the emergence of a new technology, called DVD. This new technology can be used to store full-length movies, but also of course, data. DVD stands for Digital Versatile Disc or Digital Video Disc (there is some controversy over exactly what the V stands for). DVD comes in a variety of formats (for video, audio, recording), and our interest lies in DVD-ROM, for data storage.

DVD-ROM looks very much like an ordinary optical disc, but it has two major differences. The first of these is that both sides of the disc can be used to store data, and the second is that a disc can be either single layer or dual layered. As a result, the amount of storage available is quite phenomenal, as can be seen by the following chart:

Single layer, Single Side	4.7Gbytes
Dual layer, Single Side	8.5Gbytes
Single layer, Double Sides	9.4Gbytes
Dual layer, Double Sides	17Gbytes

While the last of these options is not currently available, databases on the smaller discs are slowly becoming available and it is already possible to buy the drives now. Distribution of products in this new format is slow, however, since we are in a 'chicken and egg' situation at the moment. Matters are not helped due to the fact that there are two different standards emerging at the moment which will delay the uptake of DVD by anything up to five years.

However, in theory at least, we should have access to, say, the whole of the Medline database on a single optical disc by the turn of the century. Other advantages are that you will be able to play CD-ROM discs on DVD drives, and that the transfer rate is initially going to be faster than 8x, and potentially faster than that. There are, of course, disadvantages with the technology, principal among them being that you will need to buy new drives in order to take advantage of the discs, and the computers on which they are used will need to be of a much higher specification (using for example 16Mbytes DRAM) than many that are currently doing sterling service in the information centre. However, because of their value to the entertainment industry, it has been estimated that by the year 2000, 1.6 billion DVD and DVD-ROMs will be sold annually [4].

This of course begs the question as to exactly what this will all mean for the information industry. It will certainly provide the publishers with another avenue in which to publish data, and the information professionals another format in which to obtain their information. Initially of course, there may well be a resistance to purchasing these new drives, but I suspect that the lure of so much data on one disc is going to be difficult for people to resist. It certainly will not mean that existing drives are going to become obsolete overnight, far from it, but I suspect that the market for traditional CD-ROM drives will fall as DVD-ROM purchases increase.

Upgrade paths

This brings me onto the very thorny subject of the equipment that you should be considering for purchase in the near future. Once again, this is a thankless task, since it is difficult to talk with any certainty about where computing power will be within the next couple of years. However, it is possible to make some well informed guesses, by looking at what is available now, and what one can expect in the future, but here I am not talking specifically about hardware, but am looking at software enhancements. Most products which are available now are designed to run under at least Windows 3.1, and increasingly with Windows 95. Consequently, in order to answer this question for yourself, I would suggest contacting your publishers, getting onto their mailing lists and talk to their staff. By combining this with a look at the market generally, and the types of products available that you may want to use, you should come up with a reasonably accurate 'shopping list'. I would certainly suggest, when possible, that you purchase Pentium based machines; a medium priced machine incorporating sound card, speakers, 500Mbyte hard disk is going to cost less than £1,000. Of course, if you do not intend to purchase multimedia products, you can shave a little off the price by doing without the speakers and sound card. Any CD-ROM drive that you buy these days, or which comes with a machine, is going to be at least 4x, if not 10x or 12x. It is worth while spending more money on RAM rather than hard disk space; in any case Windows '95 is going to require a lot of memory, at least 8Mbytes of RAM will be needed, and preferably 16Mbytes.

If you do not have the budget to buy a whole new suite of computers (and who does?) you will be looking to upgrade existing machines. Once again, spend your money on the RAM rather than a larger than standard hard drive. More RAM will help to speed things up, and will hopefully allow you to upgrade to the next version of Windows. If possible, upgrade to a Pentium chip in the machine which will also speed things up. Talk to your technical support department and find out what the plans are to put a network into place, or to increase the network. Linking a computer up to a network means that you have to have space in the machine for a new interface card, room for the appropriate parts of the Network Operating System (NOS), and enough memory to load the network drivers.

Internet access

If you are going to be providing access to the Internet you will have to choose how you provide this access, and there are a number of ways of doing it. Firstly, you could equip each machine with its own modem and telephone line. This is a quick and simple solution, but is not very cost effective. Each new telephone line could cost anything up to £100 to install if you go via BT, and you will need to invest in modems running at 28,800 baud, or up to 56K (though you should check the latter, since not all ISPs support 56K modems). If your network is connected to external modems use them, as it will be a cheaper option, or for faster access discuss the possibility of using an ISDN link, which will give 64K access out to the Internet, with the attendant increase in speed.

The Internet and intranets

I do not wish to repeat what is already being dealt with in a separate chapter, but there are a few points that need to be made about the role of the Internet in the library when considering IT requirements and skill sets.

There is no doubt that the Internet is going to play an increasingly important role in the information centre in the future, so this should be planned as part of your overall ability to make data available in a variety of forms. It will be a long time, if ever, before the Internet is able to fully replace any reference sources, journals and so on, but it can form a very useful adjunct to your existing services. Having said that, it is going to be the place that the end-user looks first, if only because of the media hype about the subject. The computers that give users access will need to be 'top of the range' machines if you want to get the most out of the Internet, so this means that you will want machines with a lot of memory, a lot of hard disk space, a good video card, sound card and speakers. Access to the Internet also needs to be fast and efficient.

Initially it appears to be very easy to use the Internet, since with the majority of search engines you can simply type in a few words and let them do the rest. However, once you begin to look in detail at the results you are presented with it becomes clear that they often bear very little resemblance to the information you actually want! Certainly, in comparison to existing CD-ROM interfaces, search engines on the Internet are very poor indeed. Consequently you will need to spend a reasonable amount of time learning how to use the Internet, become familiar with a variety of different search engines, newsgroups and mailing lists, so that you can pass this information onto your users. There are many introductory sites that you can point your users towards, but I would suggest that you put a proper training course into place in order to teach new users how best to access the available Internet resources. Point them towards these introductory sites, the search engines which you feel are most appropriate, and the sites which provide information which complements the materials that you have in your library.

Creating Web pages

You may well also wish to create your own home page on the Internet; this could be loaded as the default page when starting your browser, and could include some of the information mentioned in the previous paragraph. Of course, in order to do this, you will require yet another new skill, which is in the production of such home pages. The creation of a simple home page is actually very simple, although the results can look quite impressive. Pages are written in an HTML (HyperText Markup Language) using tags either side of text that you wish to look different, or which do something, such as act as a link. Once you know what these tags are it becomes a simple matter to create the page; you could even produce them using a simple text editor such as the Windows Notepad facility. However, you will find it easier in the long run to invest in one of the many authoring tools which are available, either free or for minimum cost – even the tools used by professional page designers only cost at the most £100.

What is rather more difficult than the actual writing of a home page is the design of it. It must be simple and quick to load, provide the reader with the information that they require quickly, guide them to other pages you have written clearly, and links to other sites should be arranged in a sensible order. Graphics should be used sparingly, and only when they provide an extra value. There are now literally hundreds of books available on writing home pages, and sites galore on the Internet which give practical advice, and you will need to study these. The best advice that I can give however, is to spend time exploring the Internet looking at home pages from a design perspective rather than an information one, work out what works well and what does not and incorporate good design elements into your own pages.

I feel that this is going to become an increasingly important area for the information professional to become involved in, since one of our strengths is that we know what information is all about, and how best to arrange and present that information clearly and concisely. It is very easy to tell if a page has been written by a graphic design company for example – all too often they look very pretty indeed, take far to long to load and present information badly. While we may not be able to make the pages as attractive as some others can, your viewers will thank you if the page loads quickly and they can get to the information they need in a short space of time.

Once you have developed this skill, you can then start to think about becoming involved in your organisation's intranet. An intranet is best described as your own internal version of the Internet, using the same protocols and browsers as used by the net. Intranets are going to become increasingly popular in the future as companies realise how effective they can be. For example, take a look around your office and note how many internal memos you need to keep, opening hours, internal telephone numbers, important external numbers, Web sites which you visit regularly and important company dates. All of this information can be placed onto your intranet, and accessed by a couple of mouse clicks via your browser software. If you have any training manuals that you have created, or indeed almost any other internal documentation that people need to be able to see, these can be placed on your intranet. Importantly, all of this information can be updated once and written to the server, rather than having to type it all out again, get it photocopied and sent around the organisation. Once you start to consider how much time and paper is used to communicate important information to your colleagues and clients, the value of an intranet becomes glaringly obvious.

I would not suggest that the actual design and construction of an intranet falls within the domain of the information professional; it is the role of your technical department to decide on the best server to use, how to link it into your existing network, how to establish the correct protocols and so on. That is their strength, but I believe that it is important that a distinction is made early on as to where the boundaries lie. Your technicians can set the system up (in the same way that they can come and install CD-ROM drives for you), but you are in the best position to decide how to make the information that goes onto the intranet available. How to design the pages, how to link them together and what to put onto them. That, after all, is where our strengths lie, and we let other people take this role on at our peril. So, once again the information professional should be able to act as the facilitator – making the data quickly and easily available to our users, while allowing them to access the information for themselves. The intranet manager is going to become as important to the organisation as say, the office manager, if not more so. You will need to be able to liase with other departments, co-ordinate the provision of data, teach other people how to design and write pages to your company's specifications (which you should be involved in drawing up) and so on. Perhaps the best way of viewing this role is to see it as akin to the editor of a magazine. The editor has overall control of what goes into the magazine, what the feature articles are going to be, what regular articles cover and to keep everyone to their deadlines. The intranet manager is going to be doing exactly the same thing; they manage, but they don't necessarily have to write everything that goes onto the web pages, though they do have overall control.

The intranet is perhaps your best opportunity to talk to the rest of your organisation, and provides the information centre with a valuable and effective tool for the dissemination of information.

SOFTWARE

Having talked about hardware, I should also mention software in a little more detail. At the time of writing Windows 95 is the de facto standard operating system and will be included with all new machines. Existing machines can be upgraded as soon as possible. Installation should be a straightforward matter, with the emphasis on the word 'should', but inevitably you will encounter problems, and some software may not work with the newer version. I would suggest therefore that you should use one machine as a 'test bed' and put as many different programs on it as possible, link it to a couple of CD-ROM drives and then try installing Windows 95 on that machine. Undertake rigorous testing to make sure that all your programs run as they should, contacting the technical support department(s) of those which cause problems, and sort out as much as possible. You will then be able to confidently install Windows 95 on the rest of your machines, secure in the knowledge that you are aware of any potential difficulties, and have the solutions to hand.

You will notice that I talk quite happily about 'you' doing it; you may understandably respond that it is the job of your technical support people to do it, and of course you are quite right. However, once your organisation makes the decision to switch to Windows 95 they will probably be hard pressed to keep up, given the number of upgrades they are going to have to do. If you are not able to argue your case successfully to ensure that the information centre is top of the priority list it is going to mean that you have to wait that much longer. If possible, book a technical support person for a couple of hours, and get him or her to run through the upgrade process with you and a couple of colleagues, preferably on your testbed machine. At least that way you will not be at the mercy of the whims of technical support, or an arbitrary time scale imposed upon you by senior management. I also accept that it might not necessarily be regarded as a traditional role for an information professional to undertake this kind of work; you do not go around fixing telephones if they are out of order for example! However, the more knowledge and understanding that we have about the tools that we use, the more independent we can be, the more knowledgeable we will be, and the more we can contribute to our organisations.

Retrieval software will continue to evolve, to become more sophisticated and more user-friendly. Internet software, particularly the search engines will also evolve as well; so called 'agents' are already starting to appear, to enable the end-user to decide what their exact interests are, whereupon the agents will go off and find the appropriate information to present back. As the expert in the retrieval and delivery of information, it is going to be your responsibility to locate, retrieve and analyse these agents. Once you have decided on their benefits, advantages and disadvantages, methods of use and so on you will then be able to present them to your end-users and train them on how best to use them.

We are beginning to see the start of a trend towards convergence of software, particularly when it comes to searching databases across the Internet. Although there are only a few retrieval engines which are currently able to do this (offerings from SilverPlatter and Ovid Technologies spring to mind), this situation will not last for much longer. Retrieval engines will be able to take advantage of protocols such as Z39.50, and by the turn of the century we should be seeing a situation where the user will be able to decide on their retrieval software of choice and will be able to use it to access all the databases that they are interested in, regardless of the original publisher. This platform and product independence will result in software houses producing retrieval engines and interfaces which are compatible with protocols like Z39.50, but they will not actually produce databases themselves. Other organisations will produce databases, but will not go to the time and expense of writing retrieval engines and interfaces, but will simply ensure that the data is available in a format which can be read by any interface conforming to the standard protocols. We have seen the beginnings of this with, for example, some of the partnerships SilverPlatter has entered into with their Partner Publishing programme[5]. The information professional will therefore again be put in the position of acting as facilitator, rather than a gatekeeper – choosing the most appropriate retrieval software for their users, ensuring that it works across platforms and varied databases effectively, then teaching end-users how to use the software to interrogate databases, rather than doing it for them.

REFERENCES

1. *TFPL facts and figures,* TFPL Multimedia (1996, ISBN 0-333-673-76-X).

2. There are a large number of 'Dummies' books; one example being: Levine, John R. and Baroudi, Carol, *The Internet for dummies,* 4th Revised Edition, IDG Books Worldwide Inc. (1997, ISBN 0 764501062).

3. UKOLUG (The UK Online User Group)
   http://www.ukolug.demon.co.uk

4. *http://www.grimes.com/bnews/bnewsdvd.html*

5. *SilverPlatter directory 1997,* SilverPlatter Inc. (1996).

The Enquiry Service

Tracy Griffin

INTRODUCTION

Dealing with enquiries offers the information professional an opportunity to gain experience of some of the most interesting and challenging work in the information unit. The success and reputation of the information service is often judged on the quality of its enquiry service and so it is crucial that a professional image is projected and a quality service approach is maintained. In this chapter I shall look at the initial groundwork necessary before establishing an enquiry service, the different stages of the enquiry handling procedure, typical questions asked, monitoring the service and the value of building on the knowledge and experience gained from answering enquiries. I have drawn on my personal experience of offering a specialist business research service in a corporate environment.

EASE OF ACCESS

The enquiry service needs to be easily accessible to users and publicised throughout the organisation. There is little point in maintaining excellent resources and offering first class research skills if users have difficulty in contacting the service or they are unaware of its existence. Users will be easily discouraged from using the service if they experience problems in simply asking the question, irrespective of the quality of the response.

One way to facilitate ease of access to is have a central telephone number, preferably something which is easily remembered such as extension 3333. This method of easy access does of course depend on how enquiries are being handled within the information service (whether there will be one person always on the enquiry desk or whether the enquiries are handled by different subject or industry experts). If different staff are employed, the principle still applies but does mean that there needs to be several 'easy access' telephone numbers, all of which need to be publicised to the specific user groups. The clarification of staff responsibilities is particularly useful if enquiries are to be taken in person as it can be confusing and potentially embarrassing for users to walk into the information centre and talk vaguely to three different people who all seem to be incredibly busy at their PCs. It is much better to have a reception desk where the user is confident that whoever is sitting there will be ready to deal with his/her request.

This 'one stop shop' approach is particularly effective with users unfamiliar with using the service as they can be confident that they are talking to the right person who will ideally be able to answer the question themselves (or otherwise make an appropriate referral). If this 'reception desk' approach is not possible in the information centre, then perhaps the service needs to be marketed effectively showing individual responsibilities. For example, Person A is responsible for basic press searches while Person B can be contacted for book or journal ordering.

One final point about ease of access is for the enquiry service to be available at times which are convenient to the users. At the very least, a basic 9am to 5pm (or similar office hours) service should be provided with adequate cover over lunch. If staff resources allow, I would suggest some staff coming in early and others prepared to stay later as it is typically the most urgent enquiries that need to be answered at 6pm (ready for a big meeting at 9am the next morning).

KEY INFORMATION SOURCES

Any enquiry service, no matter how basic, needs to have access to a variety of information resources. For general information centres which are taking enquiries on a wide range of subjects and industries, I would suggest directories of business information sources such as *Croner's A-Z guide to business information sources*[1] or the *Aslib directory of information sources*[2]. These can be useful in indicating specialised industry-specific trade journals or research associations which may be worth contacting for initial enquiries. As experts in their fields, trade associations are also very helpful in either providing information themselves or suggesting potentially useful contacts. Key references works in this area include the *Directory of British associations*[3] or the substantially larger *Yearbook of international associations*[4]. *Willings press guide*[5] is also useful to identify the core journals in any particular industry or subject field. Even if the journal itself is not taken, it may be available via an online database or the editorial staff may be able to help with specific enquiries.

Many enquiries require socio-economic statistics such as the rate of inflation, UK population or average regional house prices. Most of this generic data is collated by the Office for National Statistics so it is often useful to have the *Official statistics*[6] to hand. The key source of statistical information on specific companies is provided by their annual accounts – if the information centre works for a specific sector such as financial services, it is worth ensuring that annual reports for all major players in that industry are available. Where the information centre does offer a particular subject specialisation, then the key reference works in that industry should also be available. For example, a management consultancy should at least have a copy of *The directory of management consultants in the UK*[7], an insurance company should subscribe to the Association of British Insurers'[8] statistical service and retail specialists should consider reports from Verdict[9] or Corporate Intelligence on Retailing[10].

In the 1990s, most corporate information centres will have neither the space nor the budget to have an exhaustive collection of hard-copy documents. Instead, use can be made of commercial online databases and the Internet. Many enquiries relate to recent company or market activity and therefore access to online newspapers and journals is essential. The choice of databases will depend on both budget and the types of information required. Services such as FT Profile[11], DataStar[12] and DIALOG[13] do not require an initial subscription fee and so it is sensible to have access to these as a basic minimum. Although connect time and document charges may seem high, they can be cheap when compared to the cost of storing large paper collections and the time it can take staff to locate relevant information. If there is sufficient demand, then perhaps a service like Reuters Business Briefing[14] could be considered. Although this carries a comparatively high monthly subscription charge there are no additional costs for data retrieved. This makes it an ideal database to offer to end-users which would relieve the information centre of many basic enquiries, allowing more time to perform more value-added research. Again, depending on the budget available, it may also be possible to purchase some CD-ROMs. This could be cost effective, for example, if there is a constant demand for company annual accounts across a variety of sectors and countries.

There will always be times when the enquirer is looking for information which simply cannot be obtained using existing internal resources. At times like these it is useful to be aware of various public reference libraries located nearby which may be able to help. In London, enquiries are often answered by a quick phone call to the City Business Library[15] or Westminster Central Reference Library[16] (which is particularly useful as it is an official deposit for all European Union documentation). Most large towns have similarly good central reference libraries – if not, some large libraries (notably the British Library[17]) offer good business information services for a fee. As well as the public sector, there are also several information providers who offer a brokerage service, in particular the London Business School's Information Service[18] and Disclosure's First Contact[19]. Although these information brokers offer a premium service, they are useful in providing access to sources which are unavailable inhouse and often have their own unique resources.

Finally, do not underestimate the importance of personal networks. It is vital to maintain contact with colleagues working in similar positions in a variety of organisations and industries where reciprocal arrangements can be developed. For example, any questions on case law would be difficult to answer without subscribing to either Lexis/Nexis[20] online or having a good collection of law reports. A reliable contact in the library of a law firm would be able to provide the information easily and quickly. Contacts can be made at all stages of an information professional's career, from university, through membership of organisations such as the Institute of Information Scientists[21], training courses or from social events held by specialist organisations such as the City Information Group.

WAYS OF TAKING ENQUIRIES

So, once the enquiry service has been set up, marketed to ensure potential users are aware of its existence and sources are ready to be consulted, the next step is to actually start receiving enquiries. There are a variety of ways in which this can be done which often depend on factors such as location, urgency and work styles. Some enquirers prefer to visit the information centre in person, feeling happier that they've talked through their needs with an information professional face to face. This requires excellent interpersonal skills. The enquirer needs to be confident that their request will be understood and handled expertly. Others prefer to telephone with their enquiries, from the convenience of their own desk. Where an enquirer is working away from the office (either working from home or at a satellite office location) it may be more convenient for the enquirer to use fax or e-mail. E-mail is becoming an increasingly common method of taking enquiries, both through a firm's internal e-mail facility or via external e-mail services such as CompuServe or Pipex. With enquiries received by e-mail, it can often be reassuring for the enquirer to receive confirmation of receipt of their e-mail as people can still be a little distrustful of methods where there is no paper backup. One final source of enquiries can be through a third party such as a secretary or an assistant. This can create problems where the enquiry is not as straightforward as it originally appears – it is usually easier to speak directly to the person who actually needs the information themselves.

TYPES OF ENQUIRIES

The information centre needs to be prepared to deal with enquiries on virtually any subject, even when there is a particular subject specialisation of either the firm or the client base. For example, working in a bank you would expect most enquiries to centre around the financial services market. However, always be prepared for the rogue enquiry (my own personal favourite while working in the financial services sector was to try and get the full score of the opera La Traviata in the original Italian).

One area in which the role of the enquiry service is definitely changing is in the shift towards not only providing data produced externally but also to cover internal data on the firm itself. This role is becoming more crucial with the increasing importance organisations are placing on 'knowledge management'. The information centre can play a key role in this process since, as a central resource, it is ideally placed to offer a 'one stop shop' enquiry service covering both external as well as internal information. The information service can collect data on the knowledge and experience gained from team based projects (and the various tools, techniques and methodologies used) or on key clients. Even if there is no specific internal data gathering function, a successful information centre will be seen as the source of knowledge on most internal company matters (some more relevant to the core business activity than others).

In the main, most standard enquiries will be either library related or requiring more in-depth research on a particular topic. Library related enquiries can be as basic as whether a specific book is available within the information unit or a recommendation for a key textbook or journal on a subject. Handling these enquiries will depend largely on the size and organisation of the information centre. Running a small specialised service will usually mean that the information professional is very familiar with stock held and the standard texts in the field. Alternatively, a larger information service may have to rely on an information retrieval system such as a traditional library catalogue to answer these questions. Where there is no subject specialist knowledge, then either:

- Key works such as *Willings press guide* or *British books in print*[22] will need to be consulted
- Professional book suppliers can be commissioned to produce a list of references
- A personal network of either subject specialists (within the firm) or other information professionals can be utilised.

The second common type of enquiry involves more in-depth research and the results will not necessarily be available from one single source. Most enquiries of this type tend to concentrate on either company or market information. Many requests for company information can be answered from annual accounts data and there is a variety of ways in which these can be obtained. The most obvious way is to contact the company direct and ask for a copy to be sent in the post or collected by courier (depending on deadlines). However, there are times when it may not be possible to do this perhaps due to the potential to break client confidentiality (some companies may ask why the annual accounts are needed and who requires them). If the original, full-text company accounts are needed regularly, then consider susbcribing to Disclosure's Laser D CD-ROM product or online databases such as InfoCheck[23] or ICC's[24] Juniper.

If these CD-ROMs/databases are unavailable, then Companies House[25] will have copies of the annual accounts (but require payment before sending out the documents) or organisations such as Disclosure may be able to help (which can be more costly). If the enquiry is for a particular financial detail about the company, then it may be necessary to use sources which have analysed the accounts such as ICC, Dun & Bradstreet[26] (particularly useful for private companies) or Extel[27]. All of these are available online either direct or through a third party provider such as DataStar[28] and will often produce specially commissioned reports if the data is hard to come by.

If the request for company information requires a bit more analysis of recent events, such as trends in the market, then it may be worthwhile obtaining a broker's report on the company (depending on budgetary restraints as these are often quite expensive). Broker's reports are a popular source of company information because of the added value element. Raw data has been supplemented with analysis, commentary and often forecasts. It is sometimes possible to obtain hard-copy broker's reports depending on who you are working for (for example if your company is a client of the relevant stockbroker) or the willingness of the broker to provide one (this can be particularly difficult!). It can be easier (but more expensive) again to rely on a third party provider, notably Investext. Investext[28] is available through many services such as DataStar and Profound[29] but, if possible, it is better to subscribe directly to their service as this guarantees full access to their database.

Another common type of company enquiry is for a basic summary of recent activity and, again, the means of answering will depend on the organisation of the information centre. Most should have access to some kind of online database and this is by far the easiest and most comprehensive method of tracking recent press and journal coverage of the company. It is a much more efficient use of time (and therefore cost effective) to search Reuters Business Briefing, for example, than to scan *The Economist* for the past three months. Online databases also have the advantage of allowing you to be either very broad or very specific in your search criteria. If searching for a very small company (particularly if it is not European/US based) then a general trawl through the Textline database ensures a good range of sources are covered. Alternatively, if searching for a large organisation such as the BBC then it is better to focus the search by limiting it by source and activity, for example. In addition to commercial online databases, the Internet is becoming an increasingly important source of data when answering this type of enquiry. Most companies' home pages include their latest press releases which give a good indication of their recent activity.

Another common type of enquiry is for market information. Inevitably there is a certain amount of duplication between market and company data. Enquiries on markets can range from "what are the recent trends in the banking industry?" to "who are the major players in the dry cleaning sector?". As with company information, a good starting place for a search would be in specific trade journals, either in the original hard copy (if the information centre is specialist enough to hold them) or via an online database. Reference works such as *Willings* can identify key trade journals to search for or databases such as Reuters Business Briefing can group them together under industry coverage. It may also be worth contacting the editorial team of the key trade journal to see if they are aware of any surveys done on this particular market.

If statistics are required on the market, it can be worth contacting the relevant trade association as they are often the key providers of data on their industry. The Building Societies Association[30], for example, produces a good variety of statistical publications containing most key statistics on the UK building society industry and the housing market. The ideal sources for these types of enquires are market research reports but, as with brokers reports, they are an expensive option and usage does depend on budget. It may be that a large project justifies the expense of purchasing a whole market research report in hard copy but, more usually, it is only one particular section that is required. Most market research agencies make their reports available online through services such as FT Profile and Profound (which is particularly useful when searching for market research information). Profound has very useful listings of contents pages and many reports are available in the original format using the Adobe Acrobat software which means that the original charts and graphs can be retrieved. Profound also has some particularly useful high level market briefing produced by Euromonitor[31] which are currently available free of charge.

As already mentioned, a third type of enquiry which is growing in importance (as organisations realise the value of leveraging their intellectual capital) concerns work previously performed by the company. This can range from the basic "have we ever worked for Company X?" to "what did we learn from the last big human resources project?". How this information is collected and stored is often a strategic corporate decision but it can be the role of the information department to organise the collection of data. Some firms are very well developed in their internal knowledge sharing procedures but for most organisations this is a relatively new area. Information professionals are ideally placed to become involved in the knowledge management function due to their expertise in storing and retrieving data and their abilities in handling enquiries. The most basic way of gathering internal knowledge can be to start collecting reports issued by each department. Sections of these reports can be used again for similar work, thereby avoiding 're-inventing the wheel'. A more advanced method could be to actually interview those working on a specific project to capture the learning points and to identify tools and techniques which were particularly useful.

THE REFERENCE INTERVIEW

All types of enquiries need a certain amount of questioning to clarify points (some more than others) or to refine specific information needs and most of the literature on the management of the enquiry service has centred around the importance of a reference interview. This is a very formal way of describing what can be, in essence, a very informal process of asking a couple of simple questions. The method of questioning will of course depend largely on the way the enquiry has been received. One obvious advantage with taking enquiries in person is that it gives the opportunity to question the enquirer if there are any ambiguities in their request. One of the classic examples of potential misunderstandings, cited by Tim Owen in the previous edition of this book[32] is "migration patterns in whales" and "migration patterns in Wales". Less ambiguity is likely to arise from written requests for information.

It is not necessarily true that the more complex the request, the more detailed the reference interview. Often, the enquirer has put a lot of thought into a complex request and is quite certain of precisely what they require. It is usually the more vague enquiries that need probing into, if only to clarify what is needed in the mind of the person asking the question as well as the information professional who will be looking for the answers. When the enquirer says "I need everything about Ford Motors over the past five years" the researcher knows from experience that this request will overwhelm the enquirer and is unlikely to be used. The key question to ask here is "do you really want everything or are you looking for something specific?" and so begins the process of the reference interview. Another function of the interview process can be to match the user's requirements with sources which the information professional knows are available (whether, for example, an article from the *Harvard Business Review* is acceptable to someone who is adamant that the answer should come from the *Sloan Management Review*).

When beginning to clarify what information is actually needed, it is worth asking if the enquirer has any data already. Often, the enquirer has the authoritative report on an industry but just needs to double check that s/he is not missing anything crucial. It is also worth asking if they are aware of any potential sources that you could try, particularly if they have a lot of experience in a sector which you know little about. Once the information professional has established what is currently available to the enquirer, it is time to start asking specific questions to clarify exactly what information is needed. Some basic questions which can be used include:

- What is the geographic scope of the enquiry e.g. is information needed only for the UK market or is there a European/international focus?

- What time period is appropriate? Does the enquirer need the most recent information available or should the search be concentrated around particular dates? The unwritten law of enquiry work is that the enquirer will always be wrong in their insistence that the information they need was in a specific source at a particular time.

- What is the budget for this work? If it is a low budget then it will be cheaper to look for press coverage instead of obtaining a market research report.

- What is the deadline for this enquiry? It can sometimes be worth negotiating on this point as "as soon as possible" can often mean "in time for my meeting a week next Thursday".

During the reference interview it is also worth agreeing the format for delivering results. If the scope of the enquiry really cannot be narrowed down using the suggested questions above, then it may be worth printing out a list of headlines for the enquirer to read through to select relevant articles. This ensures that the enquirer gets only the information they need and saves both time and costs for the information professional. It could also have the added advantage of making the enquirer realise that "everything about Ford Motors over the past five years" really is a very large amount of data which will encourage them to refine their requirements a little more in future requests. Alternatively, the enquirer may be happy for the information professional to scan through the information available and to select key sources of relevant data. However, this can depend on the relationship between the enquirer and the information professional and needs a certain level of trust in their judgement. A third method may be for the information professional to take the data retrieved and add value by either producing a written synopsis highlighting key issues and trends or, if it is statistical data, producing an analytical spreadsheet, possibly including graphs and charts. If the information professional is analysing the data in some way, it is very important that sources of data are always cited – firstly because it is a back-up procedure in case the validity of the report is ever questioned and secondly because you may be asked to update the data at some time in the future.

Whatever the format of the finished product, it is very important always to keep the deadline in mind. There is no point producing a perfect final report in three days when the information was needed in three hours; the quality of the finished product becomes irrelevant in that case. If there are to be any problems in meeting deadlines (for example, you are waiting for someone to get back to you or a particular database is unavailable) then it is vital that you keep the enquirer fully informed of potential delays. It may be that they can wait another day for the information but it may also be that if the answer is not available by 3pm then there is no point carrying on with the enquiry.

Whatever the style of the finished product, it is also worth agreeing the method of delivery. While some enquiries can be answered with a quick phone call (particularly the more basic questions such as exchange rates) often the results will run to several pages of data and an arrangement should have been made with the enquirer on the means of delivering the results. There is little point, for example, sending a comprehensive report via e-mail if the enquirer misses an important deadline because the results need then to be printed out.

Although there is a great deal of ground work and preparation which can be done when providing an enquiry service to enable most questions to be adequately answered, there will always be times when the information is simply not available. These are usually the enquiries that take the most time and cost the most money. It is relatively easy to produce a report on Ford Motors but much more difficult to research a private firm based in Bangkok. For this type of enquiry, where experience and knowledge of sources suggests that the research will be difficult, it is a good idea to manage client expectations by warning them of potential problems in advance, ideally when taking the original enquiry. In a situation where little or no information is retrieved, it is very important to keep an information audit showing which sources/organisations/contacts have been used and what the results were. At the very least, this will satisfy the enquirer that all possible efforts have been made to find the information and may prove a useful record to answer similar enquiries in the future.

ETHICS

As with most commercial activities, there are certain ethics involved in providing an enquiry service. While most enquiries concern data on companies and markets which are publicly available, there may be times when the enquirer needs data which is not in the public domain. This can often be the case where competitive data is required, for example, when a brochure is needed from a rival company to see how they are marketing a particular service, or when comparative data may be required on the client's competitors. The question for the information professional then is how far are they willing to go to get the answer and this is something which is up to each individual. My own personal preference is that I would never hide the name of the company I was working for and would always identify myself if asked directly. This may cause difficulties for your end-user. However, a solution to this dilemma is by using neutral third party information brokers such as Disclosure's First Contact or the London Business School's Information Service. One obvious problem with such outsourcing is the cost. Alternatively, the information centre can provide address details and telephone numbers for the relevant companies and let the end-user contact them direct.

MONITORING ENQUIRIES

Monitoring enquiries handled by the information centre provides a key source of management information and can be used in a variety of ways. The easiest way to do this is to use an enquiry form. Enquiry forms should be easy to use and should therefore be kept to a simple format. The form should be used as a tool to help the information professional by prompting for certain key information (such as the job number to charge costs incurred) and to provide data for management information analysis. Information should only be recorded if it is to be of value later. The enquiry form should not be designed as a perfect document to be completed perfectly in best handwriting. A simple form should include sections for name and department of enquirer, contact details (phone number, voicemail etc.), job number (and whether costs are to be recharged internally or to an external client), date, deadline, whether the enquiry was successfully completed (to the satisfaction of the enquirer) and if not, why not (this information can be used to identify where there is a potential gap in sources held or subscribed to). It should also record which resources were particularly useful as this information can be used again at a later date. Last but not least, there should be plenty of room left on the form to record details of the enquiry.

Once the information has been entered onto the enquiry form and the enquiry completed, these forms can be used to analyse both the level of use and effectiveness of the enquiry service. The best way of collating statistics based on the enquiry form would be to enter information using a spreadsheet package such as Lotus 123 or Excel. Depending on the structure of the information centre, the data entry could be done by a junior member of staff with the Information Manager carrying out more complex analysis. The key purpose of this spreadsheet would be to measure the level of usage of the enquiry service by simply looking at the number of enquiries handled, identifying trends and analysing potential reasons behind any increase or decrease in demand (for example, the impact of a new member of staff or a new way of handling enquiries). Trends in the numbers of enquiries can be very effectively shown using a series of graphs generated by the spreadsheet package. The data could also be used to monitor usage by particular departments of the firm and could be the basis of a marketing campaign to target those who are infrequent users. This data can also be used to assess the value of different sources. There is little benefit in subscribing to an expensive database if it is only used once or twice each month. Similarly, if the same types of enquiries are failing to be answered satisfactorily then clearly the information centre's resources are insufficient and this needs to be addressed. Finally, one key way in which the enquiry form can generate worthwhile management information is in monitoring the number of enquiries which are recharged and can therefore be seen to be income generating. While this data may also be available through accounting systems, this may not necessarily give the whole picture. For example, the accounting system may show 10 rechargeable hours out of 20 giving a utilisation rate of 50% whereas the percentage of enquiries which are actually chargeable may be 80%, with the non-chargeable ones taking the longest to research.

CUSTOMER SERVICE FOCUS

Enquiry work requires a positive attitude towards the service culture. The enquiry service exists to support the organisation to perform its function as effectively as possible and so the information service needs to maintain a reputation for accuracy and reliability. The importance of maintaining contact and dialogue with users cannot be overstated and this can be achieved in a variety of ways. On a basic level, the enquiry form should monitor the level of satisfaction with the way enquiries are handled. Depending on the size of the firm, dissatisfied users should be approached for their comments. Some enquiries may have failed for reasons which are unavoidable (for example the enquiry was a particularly difficult question to answer). Constructive feedback and analysis of unsatisfactory enquiries may result in positive improvements to the information centre such as the purchase of new data sources or extra training for staff. On a broader scale, it may be useful to hold occasional meetings with regular users of the enquiry service to see if they have any ideas for improvement. Where the users of the enquiry service are working remotely and do not often visit in person, it may be possible to organise informal get-togethers (over lunch for example) where they can meet the enquiry service staff and also network with other colleagues working in similar industries or situations. Non-use of the service should also be investigated.

A good way of indicating a commitment to offering a high quality service would be to set some guidelines or benchmarks. For example, the information centre could guarantee a turnaround time for enquiries of one working day (unless otherwise agreed or the enquiry is particularly urgent). Also, depending on staffing resources available, individuals within the information centre could be given responsibility for dealing with enquiries from specific departments, so that users would usually deal with the same person. This would also allow a greater degree of subject or sector expertise to develop, resulting in a more effective service. Other guidelines could cover the different prioritisation given to chargeable and non-chargeable work or demonstrate the importance of work performed for clients outside the organisation compared to enquiries relating to internal practice development. Although these guidelines and benchmarks would vary according to the type of organisation, the intention remains the same, to ensure high standards of service are consistently maintained.

PRE-EMPTING ENQUIRIES

Anyone providing an enquiry service over a period of time will be able to identify the common themes and questions which occur repeatedly. One way of managing the workload of the information centre would be to have pre-prepared answers to these common questions. If exchange rates or interest rates are frequently requested, it would make sense to have a recent listing to hand (this could also have the added advantage of marketing the information centre and 'trailers' for other useful data sources could also be included). Fact sheets could be prepared to answer a range of common enquiries and are particularly useful when dealing with members of the public who may use the service. The fact sheets could either be compiled in the information service or by appropriate experts elsewhere in the organisation. This information could also be posted on the organisation's intranet in the form of 'FAQs', 'frequently asked questions'.

Where the information centre has a particular sector specialisation it may be worth monitoring the activities of key players in that industry. This could be done either electronically through regular searches on a press/journals database and key articles circulated to interested users or via a hard-copy press cuttings service which could either be provided inhouse or outsourced. The advantage of producing this 'client watch' is that frequently requested information is always to hand.

LEARNING FROM EXPERIENCE

It is vital to the smooth and efficient running of an information service that the experience gained in answering enquiries is captured in some way for use in handling similar requests in the future. The development of a 'corporate brain' or 'information manual' is particularly useful to train new recruits or temporary members of staff. If the information centre is dealing with a wide range of requests, then it may be more practical to restrict this data to very broad or general subject areas or to concentrate on 'hard to find' material. Conversely, if the information centre (or part of it) has a subject specialisation then the information manual can be as detailed as possible, covering potential sources of information for all aspects of the industry. The format of the sourcebook can either be in hard copy or in electronic format depending on personal preference. If held electronically, then perhaps the manual could be stored using groupware such as Lotus Notes (or held on the intranet) which would allow several users and editors to access the data simultaneously. Holding the information electronically allows instant updating and the ability to conduct a free-text search throughout the whole document. Alternatively, the data could be managed using text retrieval software to enable more effective searching.

THE FUTURE

The role of the enquiry service has changed radically over the past decade from being a book based service to a research facility exploiting a vast range of online data sources. The rapid expansion in electronic information means that data can be easily sent via e-mail, which is especially useful in meeting the needs of a growing band of remote or distributed users. The increasing use of online sources is reflected in the number of database providers who are introducing packages specifically aimed at end-users who are encouraged by the rapid development and popularity of the Internet and the World Wide Web. However, while the growth of 'free' data via the Internet is a positive development, there is a real need for information professionals to manage user's expectations and remind them that valuable information is just that – valuable and worth paying for. This increased ability of users to conduct their own basic searches has two other major implications. Firstly, it can free up the information professional to do more complex work that adds real value to the organisation by performing more research or analysis rather than simply providing raw data. Secondly, information professionals need to develop their IT skills to handle the next generation of computer-based information services and to provide training and support for end-users to perform more of their own data retrieval.

Finally, I have already touched on what I feel to be of growing importance to the information professional, namely the development of the 'learning organisation', the need to capitalise on the internal knowledge and expertise of employees. The information centre can play a key role in this strategic development and the development of a knowledge management function is a natural extension of the information unit's role.

REFERENCES

1. *Croner's A-Z of business information sources,* Croner Publications Ltd, London (1996).

2. Reynard, K. W. and Reynard, J. M. E. *The Aslib directory of information sources in the United Kingdom,* Aslib, The Association for Information Manangement, London (9th edition 1996).

3. Henderson, S. P. A. and Henderson, A. J.W. *Directory of British associations.* CBD Research Limited, Beckneham (1994).

4. *Yearbook of international organisations.* KG Saur, Munich (1995/1996).

5. Crossfield, C. et al. *Willings press guide.* Reed Information Services, East Grinstead (1996).

6. *Guide to official statistics.* HMSO, London (1990).

7. Irwin, H. *The directory of management consultants in the UK.* AP Information Services, London (1996).

8. Association of British Insurers, 51 Gresham Street, London EC2V 7HQ. Tel: (0171) 600 3333.

9. Verdict Research, 112 High Holborn, London WC1V 6JS. Tel: (0171) 404 5042.

10. Corporate Intelligence on Retailing, 51 Doughty Street, London WC1N 2LS. Tel: (0171) 696 9006.

11. FT Profile, 13-17 Epworth Street, London EC2A 4DL. Tel: (0171) 825 8000.

12. DataStar, Knight-Ridder Information, Haymarket House, 1 Oxendon Street, London SW1Y 4EE. Tel: (0171) 930 5503.

13. DIALOG, Knight-Ridder Information, Haymarket House, 1 Oxendon Street, London SW1Y 4EE. Tel: (0171) 930 5503.

14. Reuters Business Briefing, 85 Fleet Street, London EC4P 4AJ. Tel: (0171) 250 1122

15. City Business Library, 1 Brewers Hall Gardens, London EC2V 5BX. Tel: (0171) 638 8215.

16. Westminster Central Reference Library, St Martins Street, London WC2H 7HP. Tel: (0171) 925 0870.

17. British Library Business Information Service, 25 Southampton Buildings, London WC2A 1AW. Tel: (0171)-323 7454.

18. London Business School Information Service, Sussex Place, Regents Park, London NW1 4SA. Tel: (0171) 723 3404.

19. Disclosure First Contact, 26-31 Whiskin Street, London EC1R 0BP. Tel: (0171) 278 4243.

20. Lexis/Nexis, Halsbury House, 35 Chancery Lane, London WC2A 1EL. Tel: (0171) 400 2823.

21. Institute of Information Scientists, 44 Museum Street, London WC1A 1LY. Tel: (0171) 831 8003.

22. *Whitaker's books in print*. J. Whitaker & Sons, London.

23. Infocheck Equifax, Godmersham Park, Godmersham, Canterbury, Kent CT4 7DT. Tel: (01227) 813000.

24. ICC Information, Field House, 72 Oldfield Road, Hampton, Middlesex TW12 2HQ. Tel: (0181) 783 1122.

25. Companies House, 55-71 City Road, London EC1 1YBB. Tel: (01222) 380801.

26. Dun & Bradstreet, Holmers Farm Way, High Wycombe, Bucks HP12 4UL. Tel: (0161) 228 7744.

27. Extel Financial, 13-17 Epworth Street, London EC2A 4DL. Tel: (0171) 251 3333.

28. Investext, Aldgate House, 33 Aldgate High Street, London EC3N 1DL. Tel: (0171) 369 7860.

29. Profound, M.A.I.D., The Coomunications Building, 48 Leicester Square, London WC2H 7DB. Tel: (0171) 930 6900.

30. Building Societies Association, 3 Savile Row, London W1X 1AF. Tel: (0171) 437 0655.

31. Euromonitor, 60 Britton Street, London EC1M 5NA. Tel: (0171) 251 8024.

32. Owen, T. Enquiry services. In: *Handbook of special librarianship and information work*, edited by P. Dossett, Aslib, The Association for Information Management, London (1992).

FURTHER READING

Abels, E. G. The E-mail reference interview, *RQ*, 1996.

Bopp, R. E. and Smith, L.C. *Reference and information services: an introduction*, Libraries Unlimted Inc., Englewood (1995).

Grogan, D. *Practical reference work*, Library Association Publishing, London (1991).

Lavin, M.R. Improving the quality of business reference service, *The Reference Librarian*, **48** 1995.

Owen, T. Success at the enquiry desk: successful enquiry answering – every time, Library Association Publishing, London (1996).

Serials Management

Lyndsay Rees-Jones

INTRODUCTION

The problem with writing anything about the complex issue of serials management is knowing where to stop. There are any number of variations and approaches to the subject. Consequently there is tremendous scope for individual flair in the provision of serials as part of the overall special library or information service.

Selecting a starting point can be tricky too, as the whole process is so cyclical. Simplistically the cycle is as follows: research is undertaken; a paper is written and submitted to a publisher; the paper is published in a journal; the journal is subscribed to by a multitude of institutions and individuals; the paper is read and influences further research, is cited in a subsequent paper, and the whole process begins again. The whole nature of this cycle imposes a structure on libraries who act as distributors of, and repositories for, this information. The information must be made available, and disseminated, and stored for future reference. This is all fine for what is referred to as the 'learned' journal. What about the more newsy, esoteric journals? These are often the titles which corporate institutions depend on to keep informed of world events, competitors' activities and public opinion. They may not have the same shelf life, but they are crucial for their currency.

Define 'serial'! Hazel Woodward and Stella Pilling[1] settle on the following definition: "A publication in any medium in successive parts bearing numerical and chronological designations and intended to be continued indefinitely. Serials include periodicals; newspapers; annuals (reports, yearbooks etc); the journals memoirs, proceedings, transactions etc of societies; and numbered monographic series."

In the past, a serial was commonly thought of as a 'print on paper' product, produced on a regular basis over a period of time. As defined here, the term must now encompass CD-ROMs and electronic journals. The effect of alternative formats on serials management can often be underestimated, even though it can have significant implications for the library and its service.

In this chapter I shall endeavour to look at serials and their relevance to the modern library. How are they selected, acquired and managed? What issues should the librarian or information professional consider when developing serials as a core element of information provision to the host company or organisation? If I fail to answer any of the questions adequately I apologise. Serials can be a confusing issue, but my intention is to take an informal stroll through the topic in order to offer some practical constructive guidance, rather than produce a learned dissertation.

THE ROLE OF SERIALS IN A LIBRARY AND INFORMATION SERVICE

Do serials in a special library play a different role from that of serials in any other sort of library, or are the issues common to all environments? What does the information published in this form add to the overall service provision of the library? These questions can be looked at from two angles. Firstly, is the information that is available in serial format, a valid information resource for the library and its clients? I shall use two examples of companies in order to emphasise a point; a pharmaceutical company and a public relations company. The mythical pharmaceutical company would be rather naïve to ignore the considerable stream of literature on medical issues. Developments in this field are disseminated via learned journals, where scientists need to publish to achieve recognition of their work. These publications are usually costly and their acquisition can result in cuts elsewhere in the service.

On the other hand, an information unit attached to a public relations company may be more concerned with the activities of products and their rivals. This information is rarely available in learned journals, but is found in the more newsy ones. Serials of this nature are frequently on free circulation, and although there will be administrative resources involved in their receipt and distribution, their inclusion will not cut swathes into a budget. Although they may use or present the information in different ways, neither organisation can afford to ignore the information published in serials without jeopardising the development of the business.

Secondly, as serials form just one element of the overall information provision, is the time involved in their management disproportionate to the input? In our pharmaceutical company, medicine is one field of science where there has been a dramatic development in the range of material available in electronic format. A library in such a company cannot afford to be without access to this information, and this will have considerable implications on a library. Apart from the quite significant impact on the budget of acquiring a large number of titles (including multiple copies of some of those titles), the whole IT infrastructure needs to be able to cope. For example, Internet access, networked CD-ROMs, and client access to conventional online sources may all be required. The public relations company will be very interested in these new media, but from a different angle. The Internet's increasingly commercial feel opens up vast potential markets for their clients' products and services. Again, the commitment to this resource will be significant, and often at the expense of more esoteric information sources.

Libraries in all sectors need to consider these issues, but it is often the case that serials have a particularly important role to play in special libraries where they often merit a greater share of the budget.

SELECTION

Selection is subjective. I was about to write that it "can be", but reviewed my thought process, and came to the conclusion that even with the very best intentions no two individuals would interpret an organisation's needs, and therefore its library's, in the same way. Most experienced librarians would also admit that the process of selection will vary from year to year, indeed as it should. No company stays still, even the most complacent information manager knows that events outside their control will affect internal decisions. At the risk of sounding clichéd, change is inevitable. How does the librarian work with this change to ensure that the serials provision is valid and continues to pay its way?

What is so difficult about choosing a few titles, buying them, and including them in the stock of your library? It is not as straightforward as popping along to your local newsagents, browsing the shelves, and picking a few titles. There is no 'one-stop shop' for serials in the same way that traditional library suppliers and bookshops provide the opportunity to see monographs before you buy. Although sample copies can be obtained, the whole process of selecting titles is generally based on a range of activities rather than one single procedure. For instance, the organisation's subject fields may indicate some key titles (the pharmaceutical firm cannot afford to ignore the latest issues of *The Lancet*, *Pharmacogenetics*, or the *British Medical Journal* and anyone working within the field of marketing will subscribe to *Marketing Week*). Such titles identify themselves, but the information professional would need to trawl the subject indexes of serials catalogues to identify other possible purchases, and then find some method of refereeing their usefulness to the organisation. The whole process can be a minefield of decisions, and as long as it is appreciated that no decision will be set in stone, it is also a valuable learning experience.

Selection is not just about what journals or CD-ROMs to subscribe to but also about how you will acquire them once selected, and how you will administer them once they begin to arrive. These are significant issues in themselves, and will be covered in more depth in the following sections.

A librarian taking on the responsibility for a company's library will either be setting up a new unit, or taking over an established one. Both have their attractions. The challenge of joining an organisation and starting from scratch must be appealing to most professionals. Alternatively, taking over an established library allows the information professional some time to learn how the host company operates and how the management thinks, and to institute gradual change.

A serials selection policy will need to accommodate a range of needs and subject interests. These interests will have evolved over time to mirror changes in direction imposed internally by development and progress, and externally by market pressures and technological advancements. A policy will need to consider all these issues, especially if the process has become formalised, such as in terms of a more formal split of the subject areas or rigid adherence to a share of the serials budget between different departments.

When devising a policy for serials the following points may be useful:

- Is there a company mission statement which influences the direction the library must take, in terms of coverage?
- How broad is the range of topics which library clients need support with?

- Has previous (if existing) practice been based on a structured approach, with a selection policy (as referred to above), or has it been ad hoc, i.e. flavour of the moment?
- Who pays?

The librarian can be prescriptive and dictatorial when selecting serials material, or take advice and guidance from clients who are aware of developments in the business. Selection ideas will arise from routine library procedures. It is always advisable to keep thoroughly informed in relevant fields (by encouraging suggestions for additions to the serials list, and by canvassing opinion on new titles from the clients who are generally more able to judge the effectiveness and accuracy of the journal contents). Imagine not ordering the new journal which has just been heavily promoted at a conference attended by key figures in your organisation. They arrive back to work, all fired up with enthusiasm and are met with blank looks. At least if you can nod authoritatively and announce "it is on order", you will retain some credibility.

There are other issues in the selection process. Consider the following questions:

How broad is the subject range which the library needs to cover?

Should you opt for a few in-depth titles, or the broader coverage of several titles? There may be a significant number of core titles in relevant subject fields, or alternatively the library may need to subscribe to titles covering a range of subjects. The budget will play a significant part in focusing the decision making process, but it should not be the prime criterion. Certain subject disciplines have core titles priced in thousands of pounds (such as chemistry), whereas others (such as information technology) are significantly cheaper. This may make good coverage of the subject area(s) harder to achieve and will depend on the information manager's ability to combine primary (i.e. direct subscription for the library) supply of serials information with secondary (i.e. via interlibrary loans, or agreements with other libraries).

How many journal titles are subscribed to, and how many copies of those titles are required?

The information manager must identify how frequently they are published, and how quickly the information can be disseminated around the organisation. What happens to back issues? Are they stored or binned on return? How many staff are available to deal with the serials? This will impact on how the serials are managed when they arrive in the library. With low staff numbers it may be impossible to do much more than check in the journals and shelve for reference, rather than circulate them.

How big is the serials budget?

Budget restrictions will generally impose a rationalisation on the listing each year, by virtue of the fact that it would be impossible to maintain the current expenditure.

ACQUISITION OF SERIALS

Should you use a subscription agent? This is an important decision, and although nothing is set in concrete, it is wise to consider all the pros and cons before deciding how to acquire your carefully selected journals. Much will depend on how many titles you subscribe to, and whether you wish to benefit from the range of services which agents are providing and are planning to provide. In the main, libraries will obtain their serials either directly from the publisher, or via an agent. Occasionally there will be reciprocal arrangements with other libraries and institutions, swapping 'house' titles for example.

Depending on the number of titles, and the range of publishers, it may be preferable to deal directly with the publishers themselves. This will enable the library to benefit from the numerous discounts and special offers which can be very attractive to a library on a tight budget. For example, many publishers will offer a special price to libraries which commit to two or three years advance subscription. Dealing with a large number of publishers however, and a significant number of titles, all with different renewal dates, can be extremely time consuming and a waste of limited resources.

Subscription agents act as intermediaries between the publisher and the librarian. The relationship is a relatively straightforward one, with the librarian submitting a list of titles, which are published by a variety of publishers. The agent then arranges for the supply of the serials to the library on a subscription basis, with all the invoicing and paperwork being dealt with via the agent. Depending on the preferred payment method, this can mean just one invoice a year, as opposed to numerous invoices, and can save dramatically on administration costs. It can also simplify issues relating to exchange rate fluctuations and differing subscription years. The agent earns income from savings via the publishers, and/or via a small percentage charge on the subscription cost of a journal. Apart from helping to simplify the complex process of serials administration, the agents provide various value-added services to customers, such as access to their inhouse databases and catalogues.

Procedures for ordering will vary depending on the organisation. Your organisation may impose strict internal stock ordering guidelines. Whereas most agents, and many publishers, will accept orders electronically, it may not be possible for the library to make use of this method, due to internal procedures and/or systems. Subscription agents are flexible enough to be able to proceed with an order as long as they have some formal confirmation.

Invoicing may have similar restrictions. Serials are generally paid for on an annual basis, in advance, although on occasion short runs can be arranged if needed (such as for a specific project). The accounts department of an organisation may need to be informed of the fact that serials are paid for in one financial year, and then 'consumed' in the following financial year. This may have a bearing on whether a library will use an agent. The 'one line invoice' benefit offered by agents, which simplifies a very complex procedure, is one of the main reasons for choosing them.

This 'one line invoice' enables a library to pay for the entire serials list on one invoice, and is usually sent at the beginning of the summer. As many prices may not be available at that time, the agent bases the charge on the current price plus a percentage to account for inflation (and exchange rate fluctuations where relevant). If this invoice is paid in advance of the annual round of serials renewals, there will generally be a discount available on the total invoice. The earlier the payment is made, the larger the discount, with the incentive diminishing at regular intervals until the annual renewal round is reached, generally in October for the next 12 months. The following year, the library will receive a 'definite' invoice, which lists the actual prices of each title (once the increases and exchange rate fluctuations have been taken into account). This may mean a refund to the library, or an additional charge. The benefits for the library are predominantly administrative. On the alternative system – pay as you go – there are often adjustment invoices for titles as prices rise and agents need to pass on the charge, which can result in innumerable small invoices which actually 'cost' a disproportionately high amount to administer.

RECEIVING SERIALS

How are serials to be dealt with once they begin arriving, and what impact will this have on existing clerical and administrative routines? The choice between using manual or electronic systems for managing the subscriptions will depend on staff availability, the existing or potential IT infrastructure and the budget.

The aim of checking-in serials is to monitor receipt; that they arrive on time, are the right titles, and are arriving in sufficient numbers. This can be a labour-intensive job, which will need to be undertaken each day.

Once received, are the titles placed carefully on the shelves in the library for predominantly reference use, or are they allowed out on loan? This depends on the fundamental issue of what role the serials play. If there is a need to get the information to the users, the most effective method is to circulate the journals. Restrictions of copyright make the circulation of tables of contents (where they are sufficiently useful to use as a current awareness service) subject to the agreement of the publisher. There is no consensus among publishers on the issue, with views ranging from the negative to the positive (who take the stance that circulation of the contents page is good publicity).

The problems which are associated with circulating serials (which range from losing issues, to dealing with sensitivities about the relative 'position' on a list), are outweighed by the positive benefits. At the simplest level, circulating journals has a drip-feed effect on the awareness of personnel within an organisation, with eye-catching circulation slips and library identification on the journals themselves (for when the slips are 'accidentally' removed) ensuring that the 'Library' lands on their desk regularly. The renewals exercise refered to earlier is also a useful promotional tool and the need to ensure circulation slips are updated is a relatively simple means of publicising library activity.

To ease the burden of serials management on a day-to-day basis, the subscription agents offer a Consolidation service. The following components comprise the service:

- Order, receipt and check-in of subscriptions at the agent's base
- Option of circulation slips and library identification being added to the journals
- Online access to the agents' inhouse systems to update circulation lists and review holdings
- Automatic claiming for missing journals
- Speedier supply of overseas titles.

Frequency of delivery can be suited to the library, but will affect the service charge. The main advantage of this service is the release of the most precious resource, namely the staff.

ARCHIVING OF SERIALS

In large academic institutions archiving journals will be second nature and a crucial element of the service. In general, these libraries have significant space to store back-runs of core titles. At the opposite end of the spectrum, many special libraries are without the luxury of archive storage, with the notable exception of some of the larger research institutions, and companies.

Regardless of the space issue, it is important for the library to draw up a retention policy. This policy may be quite detailed, listing years, volumes and issues for each title, or it may be as simple as how many issues can be stored in the file box(s) allocated for that title.

When deciding which serials will go straight into the bin, when returned from circulation or, if reference, when subsequent issues are received, and which are allocated precious space on limited shelving, the librarian will need to consider the following:

- How current is the information (weekly, quarterly)?
- How frequently are previous issues referred to?
- Is the serial available in electronic form? (for example, *The Economist* on CD-ROM is produced quarterly, in which case copies need only be stored for a three month period if the library can afford to switch archive storage into an alternative medium). Many titles are available full-text via online or the Internet after a delay beyond hard-copy publication.
- Is the title available quickly and easily via interlibrary loans?

As a general rule, the more frequent a title, the more ephemeral.

The balance between access and holdings needs to be finely tuned. Is the storage available to the library onsite or offsite, and is it accessible at all times or must arrangements be made to get access? Again the crucial thing to remember is that if systems are flexible enough in design, they can adapt to changes in demand, so that as the serials subscribed to follow changes in the organisations' areas of interest, so the retention policy can mirror any changes.

EXPLOITING THE SERIALS COLLECTION

The best publicity is often the most subtle, which can be achieved by wide circulation of the serials around the organisation (all with a library label attached advertising where they began their journey). This needs to be supplemented by a good serials list which is updated regularly so that old subscriptions are removed, and new ones added. An automated serials management system can help tremendously in simplifying the process, however a value-added list (with brief description of the content and subject coverage of a title) can be worth the additional effort. This list should be widely available both in the library and also circulated throughout the organisation and, if possible, accessible over the network, depending on the sophistication of the IT infrastructure.

When the renewals list arrives from the serials agents in early summer, or when the publishers' reminders begin appearing in the post, the opportunity should be taken to contact everyone on the journals' circulation lists. These may be titles that are seen via library circulation, or it may be that these are subscribed to directly on behalf of the user for their retention. Sending a memo or e-mail to everyone, with a list of the titles they see (asking for confirmation of their current requirements) is a useful exercise for rationalising the list and reaffirming interests. In order that due attention is paid to the memo/e-mail, a suitably worded threat can reap rewards, for example "if no response is received by [date] it will be assumed that you no longer wish to see the journals listed and you will be removed from the circulation lists".

Is the serials management system, if automated, accessible in the library and/or via the local area network or intranet? If so, the users can access serials data directly. These procedures should form part of the normal library induction programme given to all new staff. Direct access to the system is a useful facility for users to check the most common questions, such as, whether the library subscribes to a specific title and if a particular issue is in stock.

SUPPLEMENTING THE SERIALS COLLECTION

An important inclusion to the library's selection policy is the extent to which external sources are used for the loan of serials which are on the periphery of the organisation's interests, but which are still necessary on occasion. Unfortunately national collections are subject to the same budgetary restraints as everyone else, so that it is not wise to assume support will be available. Local liaison schemes, formal and informal, as well as the networks built up by individual professionals, are also useful supplements to serials provision. Even where a membership charge may be levied, the union catalogues produced by liaison schemes provide a very useful back up to the service.

TECHNOLOGICAL DEVELOPMENTS: ELECTRONIC JOURNALS

A professional approach requires the information manager to keep abreast of new technical developments and how those new developments and initiatives could enhance the library and information service. However, there is a danger in becoming over enthusiastic about potential future changes while ignoring all the implications for existing services. Technological advancement has to be handled gradually. Unless the library is in a position to update overnight, it may have to follow other organisational developments. Many large companies are still wary of access to the Internet, thinking that it leaves their own internal networks vulnerable, and that it is a big 'time waster'. Stand-alone access can be a compromise, but this reduces the opportunity to fully utilise the potential of electronic journals, which are taking centre stage in discussions on the future of serials. Hardly a conference goes by without reference to e-journals or digitisation (the conversion from paper to electronic formats, as opposed to journals published directly onto the Web). By the end of 1997 there will be approximately 2,500 Internet accessible peer-reviewed journals. This figure is likely to rise to nearer 10,000 by the year 2000.

To fully utilise the potential of the new media, there will be a need for new equipment, training and support in addition to new library procedures. Permanent ownership of hard-copy against access rights to e-journals should be considered, but all the issues are in the melting pot, and copyright matters have yet to be resolved.

Most serials agents are offering customised services to ease the problem of libraries dealing direct with a multitude of access platforms and passwords. Until there are enough titles to make it worthwhile, this will probably remain the domain of academic and the larger special libraries. The agents are planning to act as intermediaries to inform, facilitate and support, and, in effect, to act as a 'one-stop shop' for the supply (not selection) of electronic and hard-copy journal provision. Most of these services are in an embryonic stage, and there needs to be much discussion between the publishers, the intermediaries and the librarians.

CONCLUSION

It is impossible to conclude such a rapidly evolving topic. The traditional provision of serials information which I have sketched out, will continue for some time to come, although will gradually decline. Continuing in parallel, and at a sharply gathering pace, will be the new electronic approach. However events develop, it is certain that serials will continue to be a crucial element of the overall information provision of a special library and information unit.

Serials are a vast area, and I have skimmed through a very broad topic, and one which is undergoing revolutionary change in terms of format and delivery provision. It is very exciting, and will see the information professional continuing to play a most significant role.

REFERENCE

1. Woodward, H. and Pilling, S. (eds) *The international serial industry*, Gower, Aldershot (1993)

Records Management

David Haynes

INTRODUCTION

Why records management?

In recent years there has been increasing convergence between different aspects of library and information work. Records management has emerged as a profession in the last 10 years and with its emergence a recognition that the skills required to effectively manage documents are a part of the core competencies of the librarianship and information science. Evidence of this includes the overlap of members of the professional bodies covering librarianship, information science and records management, and common initiatives such as the information and library services (ILS) lead body for national vocational qualifications and the establishment of the Library and Information Commission.

In many organisations there has been a move towards integration of information services. Increasingly, librarians and information managers have responsibility not only for library and information services, but also for document management. Many organisations have recognised the benefits of good document management and of bringing common activities under a single, integrated management structure. This provides economies of scale as well as greater consistency and access to a wider range of skills within an information group. Records management is now an option on many information science courses and will continue to be an important part of the range of specialisms available to librarians and information scientists.

Scope

This chapter is intended to provide an overview of records management with pointers to more detailed sources of help and expertise. Just as it is not possible to learn librarianship purely from reading a textbook, I do not presume to teach in this chapter everything there is to know about records management. However at the end of reading this chapter, or delving into the relevant parts of it I hope that you will have some ideas about how to address the particular challenges that your organisation faces. I also hope that you will be aware of the wider issues that need to be kept in mind when establishing a records management service. The chapter encompasses good records management practice and is based on experience in government departments (adhering to the principles of the Public Records Acts), and commercial organisations in the private sector driven by business needs.

Records management as a discipline has grown to cover a range of activities and information handling products and this has made defining the limits more difficult. In this chapter we concentrate on management techniques, although we provide some background on the technology that is used for records management. In this chapter records management includes document management, electronic records management, and, document imaging systems.

Driving forces

There are many driving forces for the introduction of good records management procedures within organisations. Some of the reasons are driven by negative factors such as liability, disaster recovery, and protection against breach of intellectual property rights. Others are positive, such as more effective operation of administrative procedures, continuity, and more efficient use of resources such as people and space.

Statutory requirements

We can start with legal obligations. Government departments and many non-departmental public bodies are required to keep records to a particular standard under the Public Records Acts. All limited companies are required to keep basic business records under the Companies Acts and particular industries such as the oil industry, pharmaceutical companies and financial advisers are covered by specific regulations which govern record keeping.

Protection against litigation

Companies that sell services or manufacture products for sale to the general public are increasingly aware of the dangers of litigation that can arise if a product is implicated in injury or death of a customer. In many cases the defence against litigation is centred around records that can demonstrate that the company was not negligent and that it was working to the best practice of the time when the problem occurred. This protection against litigation is becoming increasingly important in the public sector as government departments and agencies are becoming more accountable to the general public.

Intellectual property

Some industries are based on intellectual property whether this be music, written work, videos, trade marks or patents. Protection against theft of intellectual property depends almost entirely on keeping the relevant records and protecting them against damage. Ownership of property depends on written title deeds. Contracts are another valuable asset that need to be managed and kept in suitable conditions.

Disaster recovery

A key role for records managers in many organisations is protection of vital records. This helps to ensure effective recovery from disasters. This is especially important in information intensive activities such as finance, research and development, sales and marketing. Precautions such as keeping off-site copies of documents, and adequate protection against fire, flood and theft fall within the remit of records management.

Continuity

For many organisations the only tangible evidence of their past existence is the business records and archives. The history of a company can play an important part in its ongoing sense of identity and records can play a significant role in this process. The benefits of this sense of continuity may not be as easy to qualify but they are nonetheless important. Minutes of board meetings and of departmental groups and committees can provide a useful commentary on the company and an indication of its future direction. These factors can be particularly relevant during a period of change, such as that following a merger, take-over or change of ownership.

Corporate memory

Finally, records management is a key to effective use of resources within an organisation. They can provide a way of revisiting previous decisions and can help to avoid similar problems in the future. Provided an adequate record of former activities has been kept it is possible to save time and effort of unnecessary repetition. Effective records management is not only about the retention of key documents it is also about disposal of ephemeral material and duplicate documents. A good records management system ought to save space.

Definition

Before we proceed any further we should agree a definition of records management. For the purposes of this chapter we will take the following general definition taken from the *Records management handbook*[1]: "records management is the management of any information captured in reproducible form that is required for conducting business."

RECORDS MANAGEMENT STRATEGY

The important point to bear in mind is that there is no one correct way of devising a policy and it is vital to adopt an approach which is appropriate for your organisation. Development of a records management strategy should incorporate the following steps:

1.   Determine needs and audit resources
2.   Construct policy
3.   Consider constraints
4.   Develop strategy
5.   Allocate resources
6.   Implementation.

Determine needs

A useful starting point for the development of any information service is the requirements of users. This applies to records management services with the proviso that by users we mean organisational users. The starting point for a records strategy must be the organisational and business requirements. The requirements study should be carried out in conjunction with a records audit (described later), so that the requirements are in the context of what is available and achievable.

The techniques for carrying out an audit are similar to those of an information audit. An appropriate sample of individuals should be selected for interview, based on the different functional areas, business groups and levels of seniority within the organisation. There will be several possible views of requirements, the most common ones are:

- Operational requirements – What records are required for an individual to do his or her job properly?
- Record creation – What records are generated as a result of specific tasks or activities?
- Strategic requirements – What are the organisational priorities and requirements for record keeping including statutory requirements and legal protection?
- Future plans – Developments that might change the records management requirements of the organisation.

Within each of these areas, issues such as requirements for retrieval, speed of access to records, length of retention, and record format should be explored. The line of questioning should focus on the activities of the individual being interviewed and the responsibilities of their working group. This can be extended to consider how the findings would apply to other members of the group represented.

A useful technique is to compile a list of requirements and ask the respondent to rank them. This can help to overcome the problem of 'wish-lists' and can provide a basis for resolving conflicting interests. This is especially important when it comes to making difficult decisions about resources.

Construct policy

The requirements provide the basis for a records policy. This may be part of a more widely-ranging information policy. The elements of a records policy should include the following:

- Legal requirements
- Operational requirements
- Strategic requirements
- Role of records in the organisation
- Responsibilities for records management.

The culture of the organisation will determine how this policy is put into practice. There has been a move among many organisations towards a more consultative or 'democratic' approach to decision making in which case it would be appropriate to circulate a policy document of this type for comment. In a more controlled environment, or where legal or statutory requirements are the main driving force for records management, for instance, general consultation will be less important and expert opinions of specialists within the organisation will take precedence.

Consider constraints

Inevitably there will be constraints placed upon the records management function that will mean some hard choices on priorities. The constraints are mostly driven by the availability or lack of resources.

Space is often a critical factor in the implementation of a records strategy. Lack of space may affect the retention policy, and it will certainly have a bearing on where records should be kept. Off-site storage becomes an important consideration where office space is restricted. However this has to be weighed up against security and ease of access to materials. Alternative media for storage of records may provide a solution and technologies such as document image processing (DIP) and microfilm are possibilities.

Technology is another major constraint. If the organisation has not invested in an appropriate IT infrastructure the cost of providing access to digitised images of documents may be too great. The prior existence of systems for microfilming or scanning and digitising images may make these approaches more viable for some organisations.

Technology on its own will not solve records management problems. People are needed to manage and run the systems and to ensure that material is retrievable. The availability of suitably qualified and experienced staff may offer one avenue for development. However if additional staff are required to implement or run a system this could be a major limiting factor – especially where there is a freeze on recruitment. Alternatives are transferring an existing member of staff from another area and training them up, or contracting in staff on a temporary basis in order to keep the establishment figures down.

Developing a strategy

There are a number of different approaches to the development of a strategy for records management. Each organisation will have its own unique requirements and it is not possible or necessarily desirable to be prescriptive about the strategy. The records collection may be organised according to one or more of the following criteria:

- Level of use
- Location
- Subject content
- Security classification
- Document type.

Level of use

The level of use of records may form the basis of a definition of active records versus inactive records. For instance, an inactive file might be one which has not had any papers added to it within the last 12 months. Alternatively, a record may become inactive following a particular event such as the closure of a retail outlet or disposal of property or other asset. The record associated with that item may no longer be required or used as regularly and could therefore be held off-site. We should emphasise that there is only a point in classifying a record 'active' or 'inactive' if this in some way affects the way it is handled or where it is stored. The most common reason for classifying records by their level of use is so that the inactive records can be stored off-site or microfilmed so that the paper originals can be disposed of, thus saving space.

Location

Another approach to handling records is the decision to centralise or decentralise the record collections. By this we mean central location of records rather than central co-ordination of records which we will deal with later. Central location of records may be required where security is an issue, or where the records themselves have an intrinsic value. It may also be desirable where records need to be kept in special conditions, protected against fire for instance. For records that are required by specific individuals or groups of individuals on a daily basis, it may be more appropriate to store them near their users. This principle can be extended to localising the operational control of the records. This is an approach adopted by many UK government departments. One department may have numerous registries each with its own record manager. There is still central co-ordination with a Departmental Record Officer who is ultimately responsible for all record keeping within the department.

Subject content

In knowledge-based organisations such as law firms and management consultancies, the records may contain unpublished material and internal documents that represent the expertise of the firm. This can provide a valuable knowledge base that supplements the published information that may be found in a library. In many cases this internal information is what gives the firm an advantage over its competitors. In such cases the organisation of information in the record collection may need to reflect a subject-based approach. It may be necessary to actively index records and to arrange them physically so that material on the same topic is grouped together. However this approach may make it more difficult to manage the collection using retention schedules. Many records managers have also come up against the dilemma of librarians trying to decide where to shelve a book that covers more than one topic. Consistent indexing plays an important role in ensuring retrieval of relevant material.

Security

Security is expensive. A document that has been classified as 'confidential' or 'secret' will need to be more carefully monitored and managed. This costs staff time and other resources. For instance, secure cabinets are generally more expensive and certainly more bulky than ordinary filing cabinets. However, where there is a strong case for documents to be kept securely it will be necessary to devise a system for classifying the security level of the document, who has access to it and how it is handled. This will also determine where classified documents are kept and what special measures need to be put in place to protect them.

Document type

Document type is one of the most common ways of arranging records. For instance invoices may be kept in one place. They may be arranged by date or by creditor name. Where the documents have a standard format, they may be internally generated forms for instance, it may be easier to handle them all together. Many of the Document Image Processing Systems were originally designed to handle a specific category of document and experience suggests that they work best in that kind of environment. With a particular category of document there is usually an obvious arrangement which may also reflect the main point of access. For instance, invoices may be arranged by date where this is the main way of retrieving them. If an additional point of access such as company name is required, it will be necessary to index them accordingly.

Allocate resources

Allocation of resources to records management should be based on the strategy. There are two aspects to this: the resources required to implement the new system, and the resources required to run the service on an ongoing basis. This is an important distinction because for many organisations (especially those in the public sector) there are different procedures for obtaining funding for once-off expenditure (such as that associated with implementation) and funding for recurrent expenditure, such as staff and running costs.

It is also important to be able to assess the on-going costs of a new system before making a decision. Low initial costs may be offset by high running costs. In making a case for the allocation of resources, it is important to consider the benefits. For instance, savings may result from the implementation of a systematic approach to records management. The savings may be difficult to quantify, if they are in terms of staff time saved looking for records or information, or increased productivity. More direct benefits such as storage space reduction and lower running costs are easier to quantify.

The following checklist indicates some of the headings under which costs may be allocated. These will vary from organisation to organisation but will usually include the following components:

Implementation costs

- Staff time (internal staff)
- Consultancy costs
- External expertise (records audits and systems implementation)
- Hardware and software procurement
- Installation costs

- Retrospective conversion (e.g. labelling, classifying, indexing, data entry)
- Building work and office refurbishment to accommodate records
- Transfer of records to the new location (may include cost of weeding files and labelling boxes).

Running costs

- Staff
- Office overheads
- Administrative overheads
- Purchase of external services such as use of off-site storage facilities
- Supplies (printer consumables, computer consumables, stationery etc.)
- Maintenance contracts for equipment and software
- Cost of transfer of records to and from the repository.

Implementation

Planning the implementation requires project management skills. This is beyond the scope of this book, but the references listed at the end of this chapter provide more detail. The elements of project management that apply here are analysing what needs to be done and then determining the resources necessary to complete the tasks. The resources we have discussed already and include staff time and expertise, equipment and financial resources. Time is a critical element in project management. Further techniques such as critical path analysis may also be necessary to determine the order in which tasks must take place – and how much time must be allowed for the entire implementation process.

It is essential that users of the records management system are involved in the implementation process. Training is a good starting point and it is usual to include staff training as an essential component in the implementation of a new system. Training can range from briefings for senior staff to practical sessions for those who will make direct use of the new system. Records management training should also be included in induction programmes for new staff.

RECORDS MANAGEMENT TECHNIQUES

Records management has grown up from a number of different disciplines, including librarianship, information science, business administration, archive management and information technology. Each of these areas has brought a range of techniques and skills to the records management field. This section deals with some of the more commonly used records management techniques. This is not a comprehensive list but does include some of the key methods in records management today:

- Records audits
- Retention schedules – document lifecycles
- Indexing – subject retrieval
- Records management software.

Records audits

As part of the review process a records audit may be necessary. It provides valuable information on the extent of a records collection and the type of material held within the collection. It allows the records manager to quantify the problem and to allocate appropriate resources. The steps in conducting a records audit are as follows:

Identify the different types of record held

The record type may be defined in terms of medium (e.g. microfilm), or use (e.g. invoices), or by owner (usually department). These parameters need to be agreed before the audit takes place and should be chosen in such a way that they will contribute to the planning for the new system. For instance, if it is agreed that individual departments will be responsible for their own records, then a departmental breakdown of records should be established during the audit. If, on the other hand, another criterion such as security level (e.g. confidential and secret documents) is used this should be audited. In many cases the categories used for the audit will be based on existing classifications and it may not be possible to use an alternative categorisation.

Record the location of the record types

The audit form should include the location of the records. If the records are in unmarked cabinets or dispersed in a number of different locations, it will be necessary to label the cabinets or to use an agreed method for numbering the rooms where the records are held. The usual method of auditing is by location. Each cabinet or location (this applies to electronic records as well) is examined in turn and the contents are listed on the audit form.

Assess the volume of records in each category

The volume of records will be measured in different units, depending on the records and on the way in which they will be managed. For instance, it may be useful to indicate the number of individual folders there are as well as the amount of shelf-space they occupy. This is particularly important for planning storage requirements for physical files. However if a document scanning system is being implemented for storage of digitised images, it is critical to estimate the total number of pages (individual sides of paper) rather than the number of file folders. It may also be necessary to record the size of the individual pages and in some instances the state of the material (is it well preserved and will it stand up to some of the paper handling systems that might be used?). It may be necessary to estimate the total volume of records by sampling different locations. One technique is to count the average number of file folders per metre of shelf space and then count the number of pieces of paper per folder. This can provide a factor for estimating the number of papers in a given collection. Different types of record may require different factors, so it may not be advisable to use a single factor for all parts of the collection.

Determine the age of the records

Later we come on to discuss retention schedules. Where possible the review process for records should be a routine operation triggered by the age of a document or by a specific event. Estimating the age of individual records can be useful for planning. It may, for instance, identify records that need to be reviewed and weeded, or suggest candidates for off-site storage.

Retention schedules – document lifecycles

The idea that each record has a lifecycle which is determined when it is created has become common currency in the records management profession. Retention scheduling (or disposal scheduling if you want to look at it the other way) saves a great deal of unnecessary work by defining the length of time that a record is retained for and the review points during its life. Provided the records can be easily identified by their date of creation (either by colour coding, or by the order in which they are shelved, or by use of a computer-based document management system), it is possible to make document review and disposal a routine operation. Figure 1 below shows an example of a document lifecycle. This is a generalised model and will vary depending on the specific documents covered:

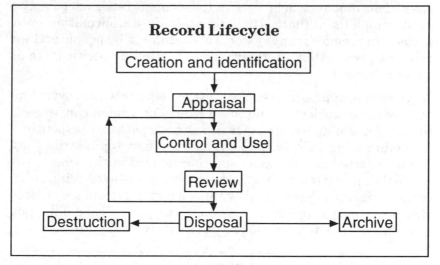

Figure 1

Indexing – subject retrieval

Many records systems depend on the record type to determine where they are located and how they are retrieved. This is especially the case for DIP (document image processing) systems. For instance invoices, lend themselves to this type of treatment. They will almost certainly be arranged by date, but they may also be categorised by supplier or by type of product. Ensuring accurate retrieval may be relatively simple for this type of application.

However, many records management systems contain records that are arranged by subject. Subject classifications are notoriously difficult to maintain unless there is rigorous control on the creation of new subject headings and everyone is trained to apply the categories consistently. For instance, many UK government departments operate a system of themes for their files, based on broad subject categories. Where there is a dedicated records manager with some discretion and control over the creation of new files the system works well. However if individual members of staff make unilateral decisions about the creation of new file themes the system can fall apart, as individual topics may be spread across several themes. A recent records survey in a financial institution identified 12 different sequences of files relating to projects managed by one department. This made it very difficult to locate a specific document or to be sure that document retrieved gave the most complete, authoritative and up-to-date information on a project. In practice many systems are mediated by people and we rely to a great extent on their recall of where a specific piece of paper is located.

A systematic approach to subject retrieval is one way to overcome some of these problems. A subject classification scheme can be used, provided it is simple and easy to use and one person is responsible for maintaining it. This means that when new topics arise they can be inserted into the most appropriate part of the scheme. In manual filing systems it may be better to separate the filing order (which is usually determined by the file number) from the subject classification. For instance a group of company files can be put into a number of different sequences as shown in Figure 2.

Classification	Sequential	Alphabetical
C.1	2	Action with Communities in Rural Areas
C.2	7	Advisory, Conciliatory and Arbitration Service
C.3	8	Aslib, the Association for Information Management
C.4	1	Association of British Chambers of Commerce
C.5	5	Banking, Insurance and Finance Union
C.6	6	British Association for Open Learning
C.7	3	British Library Business Information Service
C.8	4	Business in the Community

Figure 2

In the above example the files can be arranged by classification (not recommended), in sequential order (the order in which the files were created), or alphabetical order. One of the most common mistakes is to set up a classification sequence based on alphabetic file titles. Apart from being redundant, the classification scheme does not allow for expansion. To add a new organisation to this list will disrupt the classification. For instance to add 'British Computer Society', which would be no. 9 in the sequence, you would have to create a new code between C.6 and C.7. But the only way of doing this is to make the code more specific e.g. C.6.A, which could suggest to a user that the British Computer Society is a subsidiary of the British Association for Open Learning, which it is not. With the widespread availability of database systems, sequential filing systems work very well, because the primary point of access is the database, not the shelving order.

Individual records can be indexed, but consistency is even more important because of the considerable variation in the use of terminology. Synonyms (different words with the same meaning) are a particular problem. Where there is more than one way of describing a concept it is important to have some way of guiding users to the correct term. The traditional approach is to keep a list of controlled terms. This list can be developed into a thesaurus so that a synonym will lead into the controlled or preferred term. Most file management systems have a field for additional indexing terms or key words. These can be restricted to terms that appear in the thesaurus. An alternative approach is to restrict words in the file titles to preferred terms in the thesaurus. If this approach is used, it is important that the thesaurus or authority list is regularly updated to take into account new words and concepts.

An example of synonym control can be see with the following sample entries:

Computing

Synonyms

Data processing

Information management

Information systems

Information technology

Information Resource Management

Synonyms

Information management

Information science

Librarianship

With the widespread use of databases and the introduction of computer-based document management systems it is now possible to incorporate a thesaurus into the retrieval. This allows use of uncontrolled vocabulary to describe a file and the system will in some cases automatically switch to the controlled term and identify all the relevant files. This still requires some control to be exercised by a database or thesaurus manager, but it is a powerful technique that makes things easier from the user's point of view. For instance, in the above example a search on librarianship would retrieve records indexed under 'information science' and 'information resource management', and, more problematical 'information management' which is also synonymous with 'computing'.

Records management software

Software specifically designed for records management has been around since the early 1980s. Products currently on the market have been designed to handle routine operations associated with records management, such as creation of review lists and destruction lists, and improve the retrievability of records. Some of the systems include sophisticated interfaces that allow users to identify records by a number of different criteria including date of creation, originator, file title, keyword, and department.

The software on the market has been developed from several different sources. Some are based on library management packages and have been adapted to the records management environment. The idea is that there are many routine operations that are similar in a records centre and in a library. Other systems have evolved from text retrieval packages and are based on the powerful text searching features of these packages. This is particularly useful for files with extensive titles and which may have short descriptions or summaries associated with them. Still other packages are based on relational database systems (as indeed many library management packages are themselves). These are well suited to the complex range of tasks that a large records centre might be engaged in.

There is no one preferred route for automating records management. It is important to draw up a specification based on your requirements. These requirements can then be prioritised into essential and desirable features. This will make searching for an appropriate records management package much easier and will save a great deal of the effort wasted on reviewing bids from suppliers of unsuitable packages.

For further information on records management software see the *Records management software survey*[2] which contains a listing of some of the main packages and a short description of their features. Other useful sources are the *Document management guide and directory*[3] from Cimtech, and the *Software users' yearbook*[4] (also available on CD-ROM).

STORAGE

There are three main options for storage of records:

- Paper-based documents
- Microfilm
- Electronic storage of digitised images.

These media can be used for documents that were originally produced on paper. There is a fourth option – storage of electronic documents, which is dealt with later on in this chapter.

The choice of storage media will depend on the anticipated level of usage of the documents, their suitability for storage on different media and the costs associated with conversion. Other considerations such as security and disaster recovery also need to be taken into account.

Paper-based documents

There is a considerable choice of storage equipment for paper documents. Four-drawer filing cabinets are widely used in offices. Although they are not particularly efficient users of space, individual cabinets are small enough to fit into most offices. Although they allow for denser storage, lateral filing cupboards are bulky and are not as easy to fit into many offices as four-drawer filing cabinets. There are a number of proprietary systems for handling files with colour coding for rapid location of individual files.

Where there is a large volume of files and space is at a premium, mobile racks can be installed. The floors may have to be specially strengthened to support the weight of files in a mobile racking system. This type of system is expensive in terms of equipment and installation costs and is usually used when there is an over-riding reason (such as high security or frequency of use) for keeping the paper records on site.

Less active records, which nevertheless may be needed occasionally can be kept off-site in warehouses. Off-site storage works when a delay of up to 24 hours in retrieving a file is acceptable. Normally the files are put in boxes and rather than retrieving an individual file, an entire box is recovered. There are several specialist companies that provide off-site storage facilities. The charge may be by the number of boxes, plus a handling charge for each retrieval, or there may be a flat fee for a closed collection which includes an agreed upper limit for the number of retrievals made. The *Records Management Society's membership list*[5] includes a directory of suppliers.

A universal measurement of filing capacity is linear metres of shelving occupied by A4 documents filed laterally. This measure can be used to compare the relative space utilisation of different storage equipment. Figure 3 below shows these comparative values. For a given floor-area, mobile racks are able to store the greatest linear meterage of files, followed by the lateral files. The four-drawer filing cabinets are relatively inefficient users of space. As a general rule of thumb, lateral files have twice the storage capacity of four-drawer filing cabinets and mobile racks have twice the capacity of lateral files for a given floor area. The density of filing is expressed in the number of linear metres of files per square metre of floor space. The floor space includes the working area needed to gain access to the files.

File storage	Floor area	Total work space	Capacity (linear metres)	Density
Four-drawer filing cabinet	0.3 m²	0.7 m²	2.0 m	2.9 m/m²
Seven-shelf lateral file	0.5 m²	1.1 m²	6.3 m	5.7 m/m²
Mobile racks (5 x 6-shelf racks)	2.4 m²	2.4 m²	27 m	11.3 m/m²

Figure 3

Microfilm

Several years ago microfilm was seen as a declining medium that would be superseded by document image processing technologies.

However, promotion of the new technologies has led to greater awareness of the critical nature of documents and the importance of keeping them. This has helped to stimulate the market for microform which has seen something of a resurgence. It is a long-established and mature technology and there are common stand-ards for the format and quality control of microfilm images and it offers a number of advantages over other media.

Microfilm is stored in two main formats that allow for reading of the images with a variety of equipment provided by different manu-facturers:

- Microfilm rolls
- Microfiche.

Microfilm is available as 16mm and 32mm rolls; 35mm file can also be held in cartridges, for ease of handling and storage. The microfilm rolls are normally 30-76m long.

Microfiche are rectangles of microfilm 105mm wide. Each micro-fiche typically holds 98 A4 pages. A variation of this is microfilm jackets which are cards the size of a microfiche with sleeves into which individual strips of 16mm microfilm can be inserted. Com-puter Output on Microfilm (COM) is often produced as microfiche.

The following international standards govern the archiving of records on microfilm:

Photography-processed photographic film for archival records sil-ver-gelatin type of cellulose ester base – Specifications (ISO 4331)

Photography-processed photographic film for archival records – sil-ver-gelatin type on poly(ethylene terephtholate) base – Specifications (ISO 4332).

Proprietary computer-aided retrieval (CAR) systems allow users to identify individual documents from a microfilm collection. This type of approach is popular because it allows for additional index-ing of images and encourages the use of sequential filing systems which make best use of space.

Image storage

Digitisation of images or document scanning has emerged as a key technology in records management. There are many well-publi-cised examples of effective use of imaging technology, or document image processing (DIP) for storage of records and paper-based in-formation. Two of the UK's major political parties have well-docu-mented cases of use of leading products in this area to improve their responsiveness to emerging news stories and public issues. The key to this technology is the creation of a scanned image from the original document. This scanned image may be stored on optical disk or (increasingly) on magnetic disks (as the price of magnetic storage continues to fall).

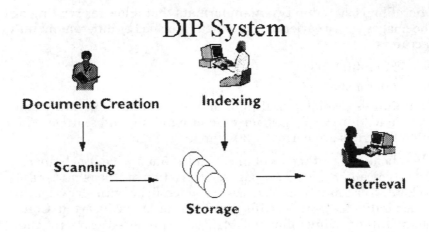

Figure 4

An operator has to index items that are put on the system, although some products are capable of processing any scanned text and converting it into searchable text. Once the image is available on the system a user can then interrogate the database and retrieve the scanned image. Many of the most successful applications have been concerned with a single category of document, such as customer orders, invoices, and forms filled in externally by customers or applicants. Where there are several different types of document on the system, indexing becomes more of an issue. Expert indexers or information professionals are needed to maintain the indexes and ensure that indexing is consistent. Figure 4 shows the main components of a DIP system.

Summary of storage options

Figure 5 below shows some of the comparative advantages and disadvantages of different storage media.

Option	Advantages	Disadvantages
Paper-based system	Proven system Stable technology No conversion costs No intermediary technology necessary	Bulky High storage costs High retrieval costs Need to transport material Security
Microform	Established technology with widely-used standards Proven life of over 100 years Precedent for legal admissibility Compact Easy to secure	Expensive to film Quality control is essential to ensure readability Retrieval of images is cumbersome Costs of printing images in bulk
Scanned images	Very compact storage Very rapid retrieval Sophisticated retrieval Easy to secure Easy to distribute via a network	Technology still developing Rapid changes to proprietary systems available Expensive to scan images Migration costs as technology develops Costs of printing out records
Electronic documents	Very compact storage (typically 10x that of scanned images) Flexible retrieval Free text searching Easy to secure Easy to distribute electronically	Control of system to ensure outputs are representative of inputs Need to introduce control procedures to ensure that archived documents are not changed Migration costs as storage media and software become obsolete

Figure 5

COMPUTER-MEDIATED SYSTEMS

Computer-based technology is widely used to improve the quality and speed of retrieval of paper records. Computer-based enhancements are also available for microfilm and computer retrieval is an essential component of document image systems. Some of the different technology components that are used are described below.

CAR – Computer-Aided Retrieval of microfilm

This is usually in the form of a database that contains an index of documents and their location within the microfilm collection.

COLD – Computer Output on Laser Disk

COLD technology has emerged with the development of DIP. Instead of scanning in an image, electronically held data is output directly onto laser disk. Where there is a consistent document layout, a template is scanned into the system and this is merged with the data at the point of retrieval to give a facsimile of a document, rather than the image of an actual document. An example is purchase orders produced by a sales department. The format of the purchase orders is consistent and so the variable data is stored with one image of a blank order form. The data and image are merged to produce the document at the point of retrieval.

COM – Computer Output on Microfilm

Data in electronic format such as in a database can be output directly onto microfilm or microfiche. This saves the expense and effort involved in printing out a paper-based document and then photographing it to make the microfilm. This is commonly used for library catalogues and for large printed directories. COM has the advantage of lower production costs, and compact storage.

DIP – Document Image Processing

This technology is based on scanners which are used to digitise images of documents and store them on optical or magnetic disks. A number of suppliers have devised integrated DIP systems. Others put together systems based on equipment and software from several manufacturers and producers.

Document management software

Database software has been developed and adapted for use by records managers to help them control the creation and circulation of records. These are primarily designed for paper-based systems and parallel some of the library management systems that are on the market.

ELECTRONIC RECORDS

The development of office automation and the widespread use of word-processors to generate new documents means that most paper-based documents have an electronic equivalent. Some estimates suggest that 90% of documents currently created originate as machine-readable documents. These electronic documents need to be managed. The traditional route has been to ensure that all significant documents, including e-mails are printed out and held on a paper-based file. However this is time-consuming and wasteful of space. An alternative approach is to manage documents in their original electronic format.

Electronic documents come in a variety of forms and definitions will vary from organisation to organisation. As well as word-processed documents there are spreadsheets, graphical presentations, databases and database reports, electronic mail messages, and graphics images.

Text retrieval provides one avenue for ensuring retrieval of electronic documents based on their information content. Some groupware systems have a text retrieval capability. However additional problems of consistency in use of indexing terms arise and these need to be addressed. Techniques such as the development of synonym lists or thesauri can provide a way of enhancing retrieval.

There are special considerations that arise from the management of electronic documents:

- Version control
- Document lifecycle
- Back-up and data archiving.

Version control

It is easy to generate multiple versions of a single document. This is compounded if the document is circulated to several different individuals and each individual makes changes to the document. The problem is in establishing what is the official or definitive version of the document. This is a management problem, but document management software can help by keeping track of versions and providing information on who made what amendments and when. One approach is to circulate a draft document and then save the final version in such as way that no further changes can be made to the document (by controlling the read-write access to the document, for instance).

Document lifecycle

Retention schedules are often created for paper-based documents, but they can be applied just as effectively to electronic documents.

There is a cost associated with keeping an electronic document, and if there is a clear lifecycle for that document then it should be possible to devise an appropriate retention schedule.

Back-up and data archiving

A feature of computer-based systems is the need to have in place a disaster recovery strategy. The commonest disaster is a system crash where one of the hard disks becomes damaged or corrupted. If that happens the data on that disk may be irrecoverable. It is therefore necessary to make regular back-ups of the system. A common scenario is for a partial back-up every evening – only of these files that have been added to the system or amended since the last full back-up. A full back-up may be done weekly and this ensures that everything on the system including programs and settings are copied onto an alternative medium. Off-site storage of the back-ups is a key feature of any back-up regime. In the long term it may be necessary to transfer the electronic data onto new media as existing media become obsolete. For instance there is no guarantee that optical disks of today will be readable on tomorrow's equipment.

An even more critical issue is the survival of file formats. File formats for documents created with existing software may not be accessible in the future because of changes to the software used for producing and reading documents. It may be necessary to put in place strategies for migration of data to new software systems.

INTRANET, GROUPWARE AND WORKFLOW TECHNOLOGY

The Internet/intranets

The Internet has had a profound effect on people's perceptions of information handling and retrieval. The technology associated with the communication of information via the Internet is being incorporated into a number of office automation or groupware products. This means that organisations or groups of users can communicate using the same protocols as the Internet via their internal networks. This is known as intranet technology. Intranet technology means that documents incorporating Hyper-Text Mark-up Language (HTML) standards provide the basis for communication. This overcomes some of the difficulties associated with incompatible word processing software (different packages or different versions of the same package, for instance).

The Internet technology has recently been extended to 'applets' or small software applications that are embedded in documents. These applets may generate simple graphics within a document, or may incorporate moving images, or they may be applications that the user can interact with. Programming languages such as Sun Microsystem's Java and Microsoft's ActiveX have been designed for generating documents incorporating these miniature applications.

The standards that have been established for accessing Web pages on the Internet have become so widely used that many organisations have adopted them for internal information systems. Software packages for reading Web documents are widely and cheaply available. There are now a number of products that support intranet standards and allow for distribution of information within an organisational network. Intranet technology is described in more detail in the case studies at the end of this handbook.

Groupware

Groupware technology became established during the early 1990s with the development of Lotus Notes. Groupware technology allows people within an organisation to exchange and share information. It is normally based on a local area network where there are common resources that can be accessed by different groups of people. Electronic messaging is at the heart of most groupware products. Some of them offer productivity tools for group work, such as scheduling software. Groupware technology can also be used for distributing and collecting information and for pooling resources in databases.

In 1996 there was the first signs of convergence between groupware and intranet technology with several products that are marketed as bringing the two technologies together.

Workflow

Workflow is a development that has been widely used in conjunction with DIP systems and increasingly with electronic document management systems. High-volume transactions that have documentation associated with them lend themselves to workflow analysis. It provides a systematic view of the flow of documents and information necessary to complete a task. There is specialist software that can be used for mapping these flows graphically. These flows can then be redesigned to eliminate unnecessary steps and improve the effectiveness of document systems.

LEGAL ASPECTS

Most organisations are required to keep certain classes of document under the UK *Companies' Act 1985*[6]. Basic financial information such as invoices and receipts have to be kept for up to seven years and to be available for inspection by the Inland Revenue. Company records such as minutes of board meetings and share registers also need to be preserved. An excellent guide to the retention of documents summarises the main laws that apply to the retention of documents[7].

Individual sectors and industries are affected by legislation regulating their areas of activity. The largest single group is the government and its agencies. Records generated in the course of government have to be kept according to the guidelines within the *Public Records Act of 1958*[8]. The well-known 30-year rule relates to the release of key government documents into the public domain after a fixed period. The Public Record Office is responsible for policing the Acts and for acting as a repository for government records. In practice they exercise considerable discretion about what should be kept and what should be disposed of. The majority of records (some suggest 98%) are disposed of before they ever reach the Public Record Office. Criteria such as historical importance and uniqueness are applied when selecting records for retention. Although the PRO is actively investigating different technologies for long-term preservation of records they still use paper as the preferred medium. Whatever individual government departments might be doing about electronic document management, they are required to use paper as the main storage medium.

Particular industries such as the petrochemical industry and pharmaceutical industries are required to keep documents to minimum standards of preservation and retrieval as a condition of being allowed to operate and market their products. Safety considerations are the primary concern. Within the pharmaceutical industry *Good laboratory practice*[9] and *Good clinical practice*[10] stipulate the standards to which documents need to be kept by the companies.

Apart from legal requirements, many organisations keep extensive documentation to protect themselves against litigation. The ability to demonstrate that they were not negligent and that they were operating to the accepted standards of the day have been found to be effective defences against actions taken by litigants. In order to be admissible in court, a record has to be the best available copy – preferably the original. There is still considerable debate about the admissibility of electronic documents in court. The debate seems to revolve around the issue of being able to demonstrate that a copy is a true record of what occurred and that it has not been altered or tampered with since it was created.

The *Data Protection Act, 1984*[11] is intended to protect data subjects against abuse of personal information, and to protect their privacy. The act originally applied to computer-held records containing personal information. There are currently proposals under consideration to extend this protection to manual records. Until now there has been a disincentive for many organisations to automate these types of records.

Good records management is a key element in many quality assurance procedures. Some industries such as architecture and management consultancy depend on effective record keeping and documentation in order to qualify for quality certification. *ISO 9000*[12] is the standard for quality assurance.

REFERENCES

1. Penn, I.A., Pennix, G. and Coulson, J. *Records management handbook*, Gower, Aldershot (1994, 2nd edition).

2. Parker, E. *Records management software survey*, Records Management Society, Princes Risborough (1997, Issue 3).

3. Broadhurst, R.(comp.), *Document management guide and directory*, Cimtech Limited, Hatfield (1997, 8th edition).

4. *The Software User's Yearbook*, VNU Business Publications, London (1997).

5. Records Management Society, *Membership list of the Records Management Society 1996,* Records Management Society, Princes Risborough (1996).

6. *Companies Act, 1985*. The Stationery Office, London (1985). ISBN 0 10 540685 6

7. Hamer, A.C. *A short guide to the retention of documents*, Institute of Chartered Secretaries and Administrators, London (1996).

8. *Public Records Act, 1958.* The Stationery Office, London. ISBN 0108 501 221

9. *Good Laboratory Practice.* SI 654, The Stationery Office, London (1985). ISBN 011 0641051

10. *Draft Directive on Good Clinical Practice.* Directorate General III of the European Commission. Document 5778/96, Brussels (1996).

11. *Data Protection Act, 1984.* The Stationery Office, London (1984). ISBN 0 10 543584 8

12. *Quality Management and Quality Assurance Standards.* (A series of standards) BSEN ISO 9000. International Standards Organisation.

FURTHER READING

Books

Australian Archives, Keeping electronic records: policy for electronic recordkeeping in the Commonwealth government. Australian Archives (1995). [URL: *http://www.aa.gov.au/AA_WWW/AA_Issues/KER/KeepingER.html*]

British Standards Institute, *Code of Practice for legal admissibility of information stored on electronic document management systems,* British Standards Institute, London (1996). (DISC PD 0008 1996. ISBN: 0580257053).

British Standards Institute, *Guide to preparation of microfilm and other microform that may be required as evidence,* London: British Standards Institution, London (1984, BS6498:1984).

British Standards Institute, *Recommendations for the processing and storage of silver-gelatin type microfilm,* British Standards Institution, London (1975, BS1153:1975).

British Standards Institute, *Processed photographic film for archival records,* British Standards Institution, London (*BS5699).*

Cook, M. *Information management and archival data,* Library Association Publishing, London (1993).

Good Laboratory Practice Monitoring Authority Code of Practice, GLP Monitoring Authority, London (April 1997).

Reiss, G. *Project management demystified: today's tools and techniques (2nd Edition)*. E&FN Spon, London (1995).

United Nations (ACCIS), *Management of electronic records: issues and guidelines*, United Nations, New York (1990).

United Nations (ACCIS), *Optical storage – overview of the technology and its use in the UN*, United Nations, New York (1994).

United Nations (ACCIS), *Strategic issues for electronic records management*, United Nations, New York (1992).

Young, T. L. *Planning projects: 20 steps to Effective Project Planning*. The Industrial Society (1993). ISBN 0 85290 879 2

Young, T. L. *Leading projects*. The Industrial Society (1993). ISBN 0 85290 878 4

Young, T. L. *Implementing projects*. The Industrial Society (1993). ISBN 0 85290 880 6

Journals

Business & Technology, Dennis Publishing Ltd, 19 Bolsover Street, London W1P 7HJ.

Document World, Powerhouse Solutions Ltd, 19-21 High Street, Sutton, SM1 1DJ.

Inform, Association for Information and Image Management, 1100 Wayne Avenue, Suite 1100, Silver Spring, MD20910, USA.

Information Management & Technology, Cimtech Ltd, University of Hertfordshire, 45 Grosvenor Road, St. Albans, AL1 3AW. Tel: (01727) 813651.

Managing Information, Aslib, The Association for Information Management, Staple Hall, Stone House Court, London EC3A 7PB, UK Tel: (0171) 903 0000

Records Management Bulletin, Records Management Society, Woodside, Coleheath Bottom, Speen, Princes Risborough, HP27 0SZ. Tel: (01494) 488599.

Organisations

Cimtech Limited, University of Hertfordshire, 45 Grosvenor Road, St. Albans, AL1 3AW. Tel: (01727) 813651.

Records Management Society, Woodside, Coleheath Bottom, Speen, Princes Risborough, HP27 0SZ. Tel: (01494) 488599.

Society of Archivists, 40 Northampton Row, London ECIR OHB, UK. Tel: (0171) 278 8630 Fax: (0171) 278 2107.

Dissemination of Information

Stella Trench

INTRODUCTION

Dissemination of information is the timely distribution of relevant information of high quality within an organisation to meet the needs of the user community. It may be tailored to the needs of a particular group within the organisation and it will use the most appropriate distribution method for that organisation.

The success of an organisation now and into the 21st century will increasingly depend on how it uses information. Both internal and external information are key components in gaining a competitive edge in industrial, scientific and commercial environments. Information can be moved around and utilised as never before with better and cheaper technology. Information on products, markets, the legislative environment, customers, technical data and standards, political and economic situations, competitors, internal know-how, staff and staff expertise, training and development documentation, internal management information – these are all examples of the kinds of information upon which an organisation depends in order to be successful within its field of operation.

With exceptions within the special libraries environment, there is rarely a library collection that is set up in order only to preserve information. More usually the collection has been set up to meet the research and information needs of the organisation and simply acting as a storage facility will mean that these needs are not met. Thus, the dissemination of the information held within that collection is one of the most important purposes of the special library and if it does not carry this out, it is unlikely that it will remain in existence for very long. There are very few organisations that can carry the expenditure of a library collection without it being seen to be useful to the organisation.

This chapter demonstrates the role that library and information centres play in the dissemination of information within organisations. The use of wide area networks (connected mainframe computers) and local area networks (PCs linked by servers), satellite and dial-up connections have all made the dissemination of information a much more immediate process and this will be discussed in some detail. In addition, recognising what skill sets information staff carrying out these duties need is key.

SOME PRINCIPLES OF DISSEMINATION

The adage 'the right information to the right person at the right time in the right format and of the right quality' never rings more true than when it is applied to dissemination services. There are some long-standing golden rules which it is worth reproducing and discussing in a little detail.

*   Information must be pertinent to the needs of the individual or organisation to which it is sent. It will be judged entirely upon its relevance to the individual user. In a definition by Foskett,[1] a pertinent document is "that which adds new information to the store already in the mind of the user, which is useful to him in the work that promoted that request."

*   The information has to be timely. It is of no use producing a high quality product if the information is out of date or after the event or misses a deadline. At the outset it is important to establish the frequency of update needed and whether or not there is a business deadline that will drive the deadline of the information provided.

*   The quality of information is key. This sometimes has to be balanced against timeliness. Facts may have to be verified and choices made about the most reliable and reputable sources. It may be necessary to check with subject specialists as to the validity of information.

*   A large quantity of information should not be mistaken for a quality service, sometimes the most relevant information is contained in one figure, one line or one article. A survey published by Reuters[2] found that most managers suffer from information overload and this is a major source of stress in the workplace. Anything that condenses information rather than adds to overload is helpful. Librarians and information specialists have traditionally been most concerned with

comprehensiveness but, especially in a commercial environment, information professionals have to take many more decisions on behalf of their users as to what is relevant.

- The format and presentation of the information is important and may have to vary depending upon the audience. The electronic delivery of information may be appropriate but in some circumstances hard-copy material may be preferred.

- A back-up request service is important if more information is required on an item sent out, or a hard copy of a journal article of which a summary was prepared. In some cases it is possible to use the requests for follow-up as a measure of how relevant the initial information was.

- Especially in a small library or information service, the department itself may not hold all of the relevant information or have enough staff to provide a comprehensive dissemination service. External sources may have to be used to supplement what is held internally. This might take the form of contracting out abstracting services, using commercial online databases, using a back-up library for journal article requests etc.

- It is essential to reassess constantly what is provided as the interests of individuals and organisations change with time. What was appropriate at one time, may need modification to keep abreast of current needs. A company may acquire a new business and it becomes necessary to extend coverage to encompass information relating to it. Woe betide the information department that continues to provide information on a subject which is no longer of interest because the company sold that particular part of its business.

- It is up to the information professional to try and interpret the often poorly expressed needs of the user into a meaningful service. Some users are less information literate than others and may request a familiar information product by name rather than discuss the nature of the information they really need.

- The cost of providing a dissemination service should be equal to its usefulness and will need to be constantly assessed. Simply put, does the service offer good value for money? New ways of providing a service may become available that are cheaper or more efficient than a previous method and so the information professional needs to constantly re-assess the service.

IDENTIFYING USERS AND DETERMINING THEIR NEEDS

The users within an organisation are likely to be diverse, carrying out differing jobs with differing levels of information already available to them from informal networks and their own information sources. The following list is representative of possible users of an information dissemination service within an organisation:

- senior management
- scientists
- engineers
- production staff
- technical support staff
- geologists and exploration staff
- marketing departments
- new product development managers
- sales forces
- general managers
- planning staff
- other key decision makers e.g. deal makers
- financial managers and accountants
- mergers and acquisition specialists
- loan or portfolio managers
- underwriters and brokers
- stockbrokers
- investment managers.

The list is endless and each of these potential users will have differing information needs, sometimes radically different. The latest research developments in electronic measuring equipment may excite the technical research manager but may not interest the sales force director. The marketing group may need regular data, for example on housing starts or consumer prices or on competitor activity. The mergers and acquisition specialist may need information about deals being completed and prices paid for businesses. The engineer may need to know about new standards to which he has to adhere. The scientist may need to know about new processes and research carried out in his area of specialism.

The stockbroker will need to monitor his chosen industrial or commercial sector in minute detail.

The senior management group has deliberately been placed at the top of this list, for the library and information service needs to successfully service this group successfully in order to gain support and backing for the activities it wishes to carry out. Most industrial and commercial organisations are not democracies so the concept of equal service to all may not apply. The information specialist has to be prepared to influence the most important people in order to obtain resources to carry out his or her business.

It is up to the information specialist to determine who are the key people within the organisation that need a dissemination service. This can be done by obtaining department and staff lists from the human resources department and talking to the line manager to whom the information specialist reports about relative importance and roles. Obtaining any organisation structure chart, if one exists, is useful. Within large public companies or other regularly reporting organisations, using the annual report will give a good idea of the constituent key companies and managers. Sometimes there will be less obvious service areas that also need information – the human resources department may need information about salary surveys, the legal department may need help in identifying the progress of legislative changes.

The first step is getting to know the business. There are many ways of doing this, for example, using internal induction and training courses, getting to know staff, taking external courses in relevant subjects, reading basic text books on core subjects, reading internal newsletters (both current and past editions), reading planning and strategic documents if possible, reading relevant professional journals. Sometimes the hardest part of joining an organisation is finding out how the organisation itself operates, especially if it is a large, multinational, multi-product organisation. A well-known professional in the insurance information field[3] in the United States went so far as to gain an insurance underwriting designation by study and examination in order that she could understand the business of the organisation for which she was working. It is not so uncommon for senior information managers to gain an MBA or other higher degree in order to become more familiar with the language of business and communicate better within the organisation.

By getting to know the business of the organisation, the information specialist will then find it easier to identify potential users of a dissemination service. These can then be canvassed as to what types of information are useful to them. It is worth remembering that some people are not used to using information or expressing needs, so the information professional may find it helpful to talk to individuals about their jobs, having them describe what they do and from where they currently obtain any information key to their role. It may be possible to conduct an internal questionnaire if there are already services in place and there is a need to assess their effectiveness. However, a half an hour conversation with a key manager of an area may actually be more useful in determining both his needs and those of his staff. It will also give the opportunity to allow the information specialist to describe the type of information dissemination service that might be possible within the context of the organisation and let them know generally what the library and information department does. Some people have very little idea of what a professionally run information service can do to enhance their effectiveness.

If a needs analysis study has been carried out within the organisation, it may be useful to circulate this to managers in order to generate discussion, further ideas and feedback.

IMPLEMENTING A DISSEMINATION SERVICE – WHAT FORM WILL IT TAKE?

Dissemination of information can take many forms and be a fairly simple process or a highly structured and complex service. Below is a list of the types of dissemination that may take place:

- Journal article photocopies
- Journal article lists
- Newsletters
- Abstract bulletins, including short summaries of journal articles
- Acquisition newsletters listing new information sources available
- Journal circulation
- Patents and standards bulletins

- Bulletins containing information about forthcoming events
- Tailored news for individuals – selective dissemination of information
- Press cuttings services
- Data on a particular subject of common interest
- Report writing and summarising of information
- Electronic delivery of journal articles
- End-user searching – putting research and information tools onto users desks.

Acquisition lists

A very common practice is for libraries in organisations to produce a list of recent acquisitions to the stock. This will alert users of the service to new materials which may be of interest. All kinds of materials can be included in such a service: new journal titles, books, reports, standards, conference proceedings, market research reports and so on. Sometimes the recent acquisitions list is incorporated into some other type of newsletter. For example the Chartered Institute of Bankers includes recent additions in its regular magazine for members. The publication of such lists can mean that buying duplicate copies of an expensive publication is avoided.

Journal circulation

A common practice within scientific or technical environments is to send periodicals on a circulation list of readers who wish to read particular publications on a regular basis. Rather than buy multiple copies of a journal, expenditure is reduced by sharing copies. However this reduction in cost has to be offset against the length of time the journal takes to reach the last person on the list. Also, during circulation the actual location of the journal may be difficult to assess should it be needed urgently and somebody has to be on the bottom of such a list. There are many organisations where there are regular discussions about the position of readers on such a list. A delay in reading the journal may not be such a problem in some research environments but, where time is critical, it is more satisfactory to arrange for multiple subscriptions of popular titles. A list with more than about six names on it is going to take too long to be read by everyone.

Journal article services/press cuttings services

At its most basic, libraries and information services may offer photocopies from the collection of journals, books, reports and ephemeral documents which it has collected and organised. With due regard for copyright issues, the service may select journal articles which it knows to be of interest to the organisation and distribute titles or enhanced titles of these articles from which users can select items of relevance and request original articles. In the scientific and technical field, the journal titles may be very descriptive and the user can make informed selections. In the business or social sciences field, it may be necessary to enhance the title in order to make the subject matter more obvious. An example is the title "Payback from a winning personality",[4] which actually discusses the use of celebrities such as comedian John Cleese and footballer Eric Cantona in advertisements to successfully promote intrinsically dull products.

Abstracts services

Another possibility in terms of service is the preparation of abstracts. Library and information staff will select items of relevance from journals or reports and write abstracts or short summaries describing succinctly the main points of the article, often using key words and phrases from the original article. The writer of the abstract will be assisted if s/he has some knowledge of the subject if it is of a technical nature. These can be arranged in broad subject order and disseminated to users who will be alerted to useful subject matter. This may lead to requests for the original full-length article.

In both of the above cases, article requests may be generated and, provided adequate copyright permissions are in place, the article may be photocopied. The article may also be obtained from services such as the British Library or Blackwell's Uncover, either in hard-copy or electronic format. These are already copyright-cleared.

Commercial current awareness services

There are information companies that provide a tailored abstracting and information service for organisations that do not wish to employ in-house abstracting staff. One such is Esmerk Information[5]. The information department can specify the subject areas to generate a profile of interests for the organisation. Esmerk then scans the relevant journals, creates abstracts and sends them in either hard-copy format or, more usually, electronically on a daily, weekly or monthly basis depending upon needs. These can be distributed internally by electronic or other means and, for a further fee, they can be databased to create an archive of information.

There are organisations that specialise in particular narrow subject areas, offering an abstracting service. One example is Legal Information Resources, now owned by Sweet and Maxwell, based in Yorkshire, who provide an abstracting service in the legal and related fields. Their information is available in various formats including CD-ROM. One professional association, The Institution of Mining and Metallurgy, provides specialist information on extractive metallurgy and mining and provides the results of searches from its IMMAGE database on diskette which has the search engine provided with it. Kluwer offers a variety of alerting services in the business and legal fields through its well-known Croner imprint. These are now available in diskette form as well as hard copy and there are associated newsletters. *Croners Reference Book for Employers* is one of the best known. This supplies information relating to all aspects of employment law in an easily digestible form.

Use of online services in current awareness

Most online services now offer the possibility of using their databases to create a current awareness service. As well as reacting to specific requests for information, the host provides the opportunity to set up and save search strategies which can be run on a regular basis. These can be run so that they carry out the search, and select information added to the database since the last time the search was run. This is possible within hosts such as DIALOG and more business oriented services such as Reuters Business Briefing. This is extremely useful for monitoring quickly changing and time-critical information. One company uses Tenders Electronic Daily to monitor invitations for competitive tenders emanating from the European Union which have a deadline as to when the tender has to be submitted. An insurance company uses press information about notifications from foreign governments about loans extended to new infrastructure projects in order to tender for the insurance opportunities. Other ways of using saved searches include looking for information appearing on a company's competitors on a regular basis.

Rather than simply printing the results of searches, all commercial online hosts allow the possibility of downloading search results. This gives the opportunity to present the information in better formats, to remove irrelevant articles, to insert headers and generally enhance the clarity of the results. The use of downloaded information is subject to contractual agreements between the database hosts and the information suppliers and the information professional has to check the contractual situation in each case. Most hosts allow the temporary storage, for example for up to 30 days, of downloaded data, but require royalties if that data is to be kept for longer and form part of an in-house database.

The use of electronic databases allows the incorporation of images into current awareness services. Many hosts use viewers such as Adobe Acrobat to allow graphs and images to be incorporated so that the document looks like the original hard-copy format. Corporate Profound from MAID PLC, for example, uses this technology so that drawings, graphs, tables, and other formatting detail are available. Reuters in its Briefing Products also uses Adobe Acrobat and, in addition, has a photographic library available online. These can be useful for incorporating a photograph of an event or person into a presentation or document to enliven the copy. Chemical structure can be searched, viewed and printed from several online databases such as CAS Online (DIALOG). In the business arena again, the CD-ROM or optical disk services of providers such as Disclosure allow the downloading and printing of images of annual reports of public companies. This can obviate the need to keep large collections of hard-copy annual reports which take up valuable and expensive shelf space.

Report writing and summarised information

Increasingly, information departments are becoming involved in activities which were thought to be outside their traditional role. Senior management within organisations may be offered a report writing service where information from a number of different sources is analysed and summarised. This requires an extended skill set for the information professional and may take a considerable amount of time. The reports may relate to competitor activity, to an industrial sector or to background information on a country or region. More technical reports may mean the writer having in depth knowledge of the subject area.

PRESENTATION OF INFORMATION

The look of a piece of delivered information is very important if it is going to be easily read and taken seriously by the recipient.

Photocopies should be clear without cutting off important information. Journal articles should have full references added by the information professional (if there is no reference at the bottom of the page). Bulletins should be professional looking with clear section and subject headings, an index page, information about where to go for additional information and help. Word-processing software is very sophisticated and high quality output can be achieved with graphics and spreadsheets integrated into the bulletin.

For downloaded searches, it is good practice to put a descriptive heading at the top of the search and to tidy up the output. When putting together the results of several searches it may be necessary to group information by subheading or date and to re-number entries. Pages can be numbered, unnecessary messages from the host deleted, duplicate records removed, headings emboldened and footnotes added. All of these relatively simple tasks can greatly improve the appearance of an online search. Numerical data can be presented using spreadsheets such as Microsoft Excel or Lotus 123. For example, a time series of price information looks more professional if the columns align and the information is properly centred across a page.

DELIVERY OF INFORMATION

The basics

At its most fundamental level, delivery of information might be done personally. There is nothing wrong with hand delivering a much needed piece of information to a requester as this gives the opportunity for instant feedback on whether or not the information meets requirements and also establishes personal contact.

In many cases, this approach is not possible because the requester is distant or because the information is needed in another format.

All information centres should be able to post documents, send them by express courier if urgently needed and have a high quality, fast, plain paper fax machine.

Electronic mail

Many organisations use electronic mail to deliver information. E-mail consists of message handling software and a central mailbox to which registered users are given access.

Short messages can be typed out and sent using standard e-mail packages such as MSMail or MS Exchange or Lotus Notes. Longer documents requiring more specialised formatting can be sent as attachments to an e-mail. Spreadsheets, databases and word-processed documents can be sent as attachments which the reader can click on when s/he receives the e-mail to launch the relevant software package and read the item. Many organisations can receive and send external mail direct from their internal e-mail package. It is possible for example to have Internet e-mail directed into the company e-mail system.

Groupware, Internet, intranets and extranets

One area that has seen rapid change over recent years is the development of standard platforms within organisations for the delivery of information. Up to five years ago, many organisations had already adopted groupware such as Lotus Notes in order to deliver large amounts of information quickly and easily and to allow the sharing of information and databases particularly within large organisations with a wide-spread work force. Lotus Notes versions of various online databases have been developed by information providers. Information can be created in one place and replicated and used elsewhere within the organisation by linking Lotus Notes servers. One down-side of this development was the high initial cost of buying and installing the software across a large organisation.

Knowledge databases have become somewhat common in certain professions that rely upon selling the expertise of their staff. A good definition of knowledge management was given by Remeikis of Booz Allen & Hamilton, management consultants.[6]

"Simply put, it is the creation, capture, exchange, use and communication of a company's intellectual capital – an organisation's best thinking about it's products, services, processes, markets and competitors. Closely related to a company's other information activities, knowledge management involves gathering internal information, such as financial and marketing data, and combining it with related external data, such as competitive intelligence."

Information is stored as to projects previously carried out, staff specialisms, case notes, information gathered previously in order to carry out an assignment. The information specialist may play a large role, along with the Information Systems Department and other areas, in the development, maintenance and usage of such a Knowledge Database. Firms of management consultants, solicitors and accountants have developed knowledge-based systems; one such is the solicitors Linklaters and Paine.

Recently there has been an explosive growth in the use of the Internet and the World Wide Web to search for and share information. The Internet grew out of academia with university professors and students alike sharing information. With the development of Web technology and browsers such as Internet Explorer and Netscape Navigator, usage spread out from the academic field. Now many companies use the Internet to advertise their products and as public relations platforms. Almost all public companies publish their financial results on the Internet along with company histories, press releases, and product descriptions. With the advent of more secure data encryption to protect personal information such as credit card numbers, more and more products are being sold over the Internet. Pressure groups, government departments, professional associations all have a presence and more sophisticated search engines are being developed in order to find useful data.

The Internet has presented new challenges to the information professional who must not only be aware but must keep ahead of developments. The Internet has enabled many non-information professionals to carry out their own searches for information cheaply. The special librarian's role is clearly one of being expert in this area and being able to assist first time searchers to find what they are looking for or to offer alternative sources of information when it is found that the Internet cannot solve all information problems. Many organisations are providing Internet enabled PCs at every desk.

Information providers met this challenge upon their traditional markets by developing Web versions of their products. These were often simplified forms of their online service and they are now reaching new markets of people who have not used their command-led search engines. Dun and Bradstreet, Knight Ridder and MAID are examples of providers who have developed Web front ends. Some companies have developed products that are only available on the Internet. One example is Internet Securities which specialises in offering press and financial information on markets such as Eastern Europe, Central and South America, and China (in both English and the original language). Some companies have appointed Internet information officers whose job is to identify relevant information sources and enable their usage within the organisation, offering training, user guides and advice. One such is British Telecom.

Healthworks, the medical information supplier, offers US and UK users free Internet access to a range of medical databases, including Medline. The producer generates revenue via the Internet through copyright payments made when users request the full-text of articles and from subscriptions paid by those outside the UK and the USA.

It was just a short jump from the growth of Internet technology to the use of Web technology being adopted to organise and connect information within organisations themselves. Using the same Web browsers but with the information residing on internal computers instead of linking outside the organisation, internal information storage and provision is being revolutionised. Intranets contain vast amounts of information about an organisation. Within a large company or organisation, different subsidiary companies and departments provide information to enhance communication and provide a standard and easily accessible platform for disseminating news. For example, Unilever announced an intranet news system to broadcast corporate messages to staff across Europe.[7] A 1997 study[8] surveying 737 large companies, showed that, while only 4% of large UK organisations have built an intranet to completion, a third of them are in the process or preparing for one. The main reason for doing so was ease of access to all types of information. Research by IDC[9] suggests that Internet and intranet technologies are set to grow at a rate of 50% a year until 2000.

There is now a growing market for off-the-shelf intranet applications. Microsoft have launched a set of free templates, The 60-Minute Intranet Kit, designed to help users quickly and easily bolt an intranet together.[10] Soutron, the software solutions company, offers products called DB3/Text WebPublisher and DB/TextWorks to allow non-experts to set-up an Internet or intranet site very easily. One of the features of the software is the ability to convert to HTML automatically.

With the growth of Internet and intranet usage, there is the need to move between the two environments easily. Corporate intranets often allow passing through a security fire-wall to the Internet to allow usage of general information therein and the usage of fee-based services being developed by information suppliers such as Dun and Bradstreet. For example, Reuters have a product called Reuters News Explorer, a personalised news alert service which pushes news and information onto the desktop using probability analysis techniques to select relevant news items by matching news to a personal information profile. This is known as 'push technology'.

The role of the information officer or librarian in the facilitation of intranet and Internet solutions is a key one. This role takes the librarian into regular contact and working relationships with systems staff and information suppliers. The librarian often remains the best judge of an information source and knows the information needs of the organisation within which he works. Thus the librarian can provide an important liaison in order to use the intranet as a platform to disseminate the library's own materials and newsletters or as a conduit to bring external information into the organisation. The question of who should be involved in such a project has been discussed[11] since such developments require input from across the whole company.

Extranets link organisations with selected external organisations in order to allow sharing of information and communication in a seamless manner.

BACKUP SERVICES

Many dissemination services offered and discussed above give the full text of articles or reports. In this case, the librarian may find that backup services mean providing further information on a topic in which the user's interest has been stimulated. A single article may not give all the details required and the librarian may have to identify other useful items on the same topic.

In the case of an abstracts service, the librarian has to be prepared to provide full text of the original articles. This may be achieved using either online retrieval of articles or photocopies of the articles from journals that are held in stock. Copyright rules have to be observed in this case. An alternative is to subscribe to a service such as the British Library to supply original articles.

An easy method of making requests for back-up information is advised. A tear-off sheet can be used for a hard-copy newsletter, making reference to an item number in a bulletin to save the user from having to give details of the item. One must also be prepared for the busy executive to rip off the page with the item upon it and for him to scribble a note on this with his request. Accepting requests by e-mail and fax is standard procedure. In the case of an organisation with an intranet, the library may have its own home page and have set up a department e-mail address to which requests can be made. In this case it is important for the library to check the e-mail on a regular basis to retrieve requests.

USER FEEDBACK AND EVALUATION OF SERVICES

Whatever services are offered, it is important to constantly re-assess them to take account of changing circumstances and needs. A research organisation may be launching into a new field of work, a manufacturing unit may move into another production area, a commercial organisation may use a different distribution method. Does the information you provide reflect this? Users leave and join organisations. It is important to keep accurate and up-to-date information about the people to whom information is sent. It is not good practice to continue to send newsletters to a person who retired or moved on several months before.

Some libraries use regular questionnaires to canvass opinion about their services. If this is done, it is important to give feedback to users and what changes to services are planned as a result of the information they supplied. More informal feedback is also important. A simple question about whether or not the information matched the request can be asked when you next see the user. A response form appended to individual requests for information also works. Within my own organisation, the research department carried out a survey of users for one month, asking for feedback on specific pieces of information sent as to timeliness, quality, quantity and format.

User feedback can be used to help justify new services or justify the continuance of current services. Library services within commercial and industrial organisations can easily be the target of cut-backs in times of corporate hardship. Keeping track of specific successes where information contributed to the success of a particular project or process is important. Although it is difficult to assign specific monetary values, knowing that a piece of information helped to win a contract worth £3m is important.

CONCLUSION

Dissemination is a fundamental part of the information management function. The way information is packaged, processed, analysed, presented and delivered can have a major effect on its significance to the organisation. Dissemination services allow the information intermediary to offer important value-added benefits and so create a range of high quality service options for the users and at the same time increase the worth and visibility of the library and information function.

REFERENCES

1. Maureen Strazdon whilst at the College of Insurance in Philadelphia, USA

2. Foskett, D.J. A note on the concept of 'relevance'. *Information Storage and Retrieval,* **8** (2), 1972, 77-78

3. Lewis, D. *Dying for Information: an investigation into the effects of information overload in the UK and world-wide.* Reuters, 1997, p350.

4. Payback from a winning personality. *Financial Times,* 4 January 1996.

5. Esmerk Ltd, Benham Valence, Newbury, Berkshire, RG20 8LU UK.

6. Remeikas, L.A. Knowledge management – roles for information professionals. *Business and Finance Division Bulletin,* Special Libraries Association. **101**, Winter 1996, 41-43.

7. Stammers, T. UK: Unilever backs Intranets. *Computing,* **21** May 1997, p2.

8. *Evaluation of intranet development solutions,* UK. Slough: INPUT, 1997. INPUT, Cornwall House, 55-57 High Street, Slough, Berks, SL1 1DZ. Tel. 01753 530444

9. Gens, F. *How big is the Internet/Intranet Market?* IDC, 1997.

10. *The 60-Minute Intranet Kit.* Available from *http://www.microsoft.com/office/intranet.*

11. Gibson, P. UK – Focus on Intranets. *Information World Review*, **5**, May 1997, p21.

Copyright

Graham Cornish

INTRODUCTION

The idea behind copyright is rooted in certain fundamental ideas about creativity and possession. Basically, it springs from the idea that anything we create is an extension of 'self' and should be protected from general use by anyone else. Coupled with this is the idea that the person creating something has exclusive rights over the thing created, partly for economic reasons but also because of this extension of 'self' idea. Copyright is therefore important to ensure the continued growth of writing, performing and creating. Copyright law aims to protect this growth but, at the same time, tries to ensure that some access to copyright works is allowed as well. Without this access creators would be starved of ideas and information to create more copyright material.

Copyright divides into two main areas: economic rights and moral rights. In the UK the emphasis has always been on economic rights, i.e. what economic benefit can rights bring in terms of royalties, sale of all or part of copyright, licences and so on. Moral rights include the right to be named as the author, the right not to have another person named as the author instead, the right not to have works falsely attributed to oneself and the right to prevent the mutilation of the work which includes adding bits on and chopping them off or changing the meaning of the text.

Libraries are in a unique position as custodians of copyright material. They have the duty to care for, and allow access to, other people's copyright works. This places special responsibilities on all those working in libraries, archives and the information world generally. Librarians and information intermediaries in the widest sense of the phrase, practise their profession by using this property so they should take all possible steps to protect it, whilst, at the same time, ensuring that the rights and privileges of users are also safeguarded.

Because copyright is such an intangible thing, there is often a temptation to ignore it. Those who take this approach forget that they, too, own copyright in their own creations and would feel quite angry if this were abused by others. Some of the restrictions placed on use by the law may seem petty or trivial but they are designed to allow some use of copyright material without unduly harming the interests of the creator (author).

The 1988 Copyright Act[1] differs substantially from previous legislation and even this basic legislation has been considerably modified since it was introduced in 1989. Many definitions have changed, new rights have been introduced, lending and rental now play a much more prominent role in the law than previously and licensing as a concept is firmly established by the Act.

The rapid growth in the dissemination of information by electronic means has had the effect of heightening awareness of the subject, making people more keen to know their rights and privileges and generally creating an atmosphere of extreme caution in case anyone puts a foot wrong and ends up in court. Whilst this is no bad thing, nobody should become too paranoid. Although there has been a recent tendency for copyright infringement cases to be heard in criminal courts, this is usually where important commercial considerations apply such as republishing or reproduction in bulk for commercial purposes. Most infringements of copyright by individuals are dealt with through the civil courts so that the rights owner must take legal proceedings if it is thought an infringement has taken place. As there are no cases at present involving libraries as such, it would be reasonable to assume that a similar route would be taken, given that libraries are not, or should not be, involved in mass reproduction for commercial gain.

The existing legislation has been the subject of considerable analysis by many authors and there are useful monographs on the subject for library and archive staff[2,3]. We should all know what the law says (even if we do not always know what it means!) so there is scope to develop services outside the exceptions which the Copyright Act makes by talking to the licensing agencies and other rights' owners' organisations to negotiate use of material in return for royalties. Those working in the information industries should view this as a real way forward when the law inhibits the introduction of new services without the owners' consent. Therefore, although the privileges given by the law to users and libraries should be stoutly defended, it is important not to lose sight of the exciting possibilities that may be achieved in co-operation with copyright owners.

This chapter seeks to examine some of the major issues in copyright law to determine where the information intermediary stands and what can and cannot be done in broad terms for individual users.

DEFINITIONS

One of the great pitfalls of taking any legislation at face value, and certainly copyright law, is to assume that the words in the Act or instrument mean what you think they mean. Current UK legislation abounds in words which are not defined and are therefore open to various interpretations. On the other hand, some words are defined in a way that defies understanding by the normal English-speaker! Some important examples are discussed here, not just to emphasise the point, but because these terms are of major importance in interpreting what information intermediaries may do.

No work is protected by copyright unless it is "original"[4] nor is copyright infringed unless a "substantial" part of the work is copied[5]. These then are the first two questions: is it original and have I copied a substantial part? No guidance is given and professional judgement must be used to determine the answer. One learned judge said "If it's worth copying, it's worth protecting"[6] which seems reasonably fair. The word "reasonable" and its derivatives occurs many times in the Act but is never defined either. For example, librarians may make copies of reasonable proportions of non-periodical works[7]. All we know about a "reasonable" proportioning in this context is that it must be a substantial part because there is no infringement if a substantial part has not been copied. An undefined term defined in terms of another undefined term! Likewise a "librarian" is not defined although the law gives a number of privileges to this group of people. On the other hand, some terms are defined very clearly. For example, an "article" in a periodical is defined as "an item of any description"[8], therefore including contents and title pages, indexes, letters to the editor and even advertisements.

Owners, their rights and their limitations

Ownership of copyright is a complicated issue. Although the author is usually the first owner, that ownership often passes immediately to an employer if the work is created as part of normal employment[9]. In addition, parts of copyright can be transferred to others by sale or contract while the author retains other parts or sells them to different people. Owners' rights extend far beyond straightforward copying [10]and include issuing copies to the public (which itself embraces lending, rental and electronic distribution), performing, playing or broadcasting and adapting and translating a work. These rights are exclusive to the copyright owner and, because they form a type of monopoly, have to be limited in some ways to ensure that users have access to copyright material.

The limitations on these rights are provided by quantity, time and use. Quantity is essentially the idea that less than a substantial part can be freely copied as discussed above under "definitions"; in addition copyright is limited by the time it lasts. As a rule of thumb copyright lasts for 70 years from the end of the year in which the author dies[11] or 70 years from creation or publication if there is no author. There are special rules for sound recordings, films ,videos and computer-generated works as well. If the work was first published outside the European Economic Area (EEA) then copyright may last for only 50 years depending on the rules in the country of origin. The third limitation is the use to which copies of a work may be put.

Copying

To limit the copyright monopoly the law permits limited amounts of copying by individuals and libraries/archives. Individuals may copy from any type of work [12] provided that, if challenged, the individual doing the copying could say they considered it fair ("fair dealing"). There are no limits stated and each action of copying must be judged on its context and merits. The only purposes allowed for this type of copying are research and private study; criticism or review; and reporting current events.

Libraries (and in some circumstances, archives) are given specific privileges[13] provided they stick to certain predetermined limits. Although these often seem rather narrow, they have the advantage that, if adhered to strictly, libraries cannot be challenged when making copies, whereas individuals are always open to the charge that what they do is not fair. Libraries are essentially allowed to copy one article from one issue of a periodical or a reasonable proportion of any other type of work but this privilege does not extend to artistic works such as charts, plans, maps, photographs and similar works. Given the definition of "article" mentioned earlier, this has serious implications for information units offering current contents or SDI services. As the contents page of a journal is an article it cannot be copied unless requested by a reader. Once that reader has received the contents page from an issue the same reader cannot then have a copy of any article in that issue.

Any copying by libraries must be accompanied by a statutory declaration[14] from the reader relating to the purpose of the copy and that no copy has previously been supplied. Again, this limits the services that a library can offer. Any idea of copying an article for someone on the basis that it is of interest to them without their having asked for it is prohibited by the law. Library copying for individuals must be reactive not proactive. In addition, the reader must pay for the making of the copy and contribute to the running costs of the library. This ensures that the exercise of this privilege does not fall on the public purse but comes out of the reader's own pocket.

Libraries may also copy material in their reference collections for preservation purposes[15], provided the work cannot reasonably be purchased, and most publicly-funded libraries can also copy material for each other, either to enrich collections[16] or replace items in each other's reference collections when material has been lost or damaged[17]. Again there are strict limits on the amount to be copied and payment must be made.

There are also special rules for copying for examinations[18], copying in the classroom[19] and copying for public administration[20]. This latter, although defined in broad terms (judicial or parliamentary proceedings or statutory inquiry), leaves much room for argument. At what point do judicial proceedings actually start, for example?

Lending and rental

Until 1988 lending and rental were not part of copyright law, neither was the Public Lending Right Scheme operated in public libraries in the UK. The 1988 Act introduced limited lending/rental rights for owners of the copyright in audio and visual materials[21] and also prohibited the lending of such items through public libraries except under licence[22]. Under the 1996 regulations on lending and rental, all rental and lending of copyright materials become an exclusive right of the copyright owner. Rental is defined as for commercial benefit, whereas lending brings no direct commercial or economic benefit although charging the operational cost of a loan is allowed. Although this right will apply to all materials, copyright owners will not be able to prevent lending of any material by "prescribed" libraries (essentially publicly-funded libraries) with the exception of public libraries. In the case of the traditional public library, lending is restricted to material purchased before 1997 and *books* covered by the Public Lending Right Scheme[23]. As this scheme does not include anything that is not print, nor periodicals, artistic works of any kind or electronic materials, public libraries power to lend will be severely restricted.

The proposed "publication right"

In the UK anyone who publishes a work has a an exclusive right over that particular edition for 25 years from the year in which the work is published regardless of whether the content of the work itself is in copyright[24]. Therefore anyone preparing a new edition (not just a reprint) of Shakespeare's plays has a right in that edition. This does not stop anyone else from preparing their own new edition provided it is done independently. However, the EU has introduced a Directive which requires legislation to allow anyone who first publishes an unpublished work which is out of copyright to have an exclusive right over that work for 25 years. This would mean that anyone who first published an unpublished manuscript which is out of copyright but kept in a library or archive, would have an exclusive right to publish or copy it for 25 years. This could be a reader who obtained a photocopy of the work and the library would lose all rights to make copies of that work even for research and private study. This would be a serious impediment to the free-flow of intellectual information[25]. Fortunately, such legislation for the UK is likely to be a dead duck even before it quacks. The reason for this is twofold: firstly because of the transitional provisions of the 1988 Copyright Act all unpublished material in the UK, of which the author is dead, is protected until 2039; secondly, the legislation also allows publication of such material only if the owner of the physical document allows it. This would enable libraries and archives to enter into any such contract as they wished when releasing material for publication. A limitation on the exclusive right of the published work could be put in place to allow the library/archive to continue to provide copies for research and private study, for example.

Computer software

Computer software is treated in many ways as a literary work and protected as such. However, the very nature of computer software and the way it is used required specific legislation to be introduced. For example, it is virtually impossible to use software without copying it, yet copying is an exclusive right of the copyright owner! There are also clear problems with vulnerability and it is desirable to make a back-up copy in case a fault occurs or a virus is subsequently introduced. Again this would be an infringement of copyright. There are also problems with the fact that one piece of software may be needed to design or run a completely new application (e.g. windows-type applications). To do this requires the technician to get into the software to see how it works and make the necessary adjustments to the new application. Again, this process, known as reverse-engineering, is an infringement of copyright. To avoid these difficulties the EU introduced new legislation which has now been implemented by the UK[26]. An interesting feature of this legislation is that, if the copyright owner tried to introduce clauses to prohibit these actions, such clauses would be null and void.

Moral rights

Moral rights have been mentioned earlier. In an electronic environment these are crucial as it is so easy to undertake any or all of the actions defined as moral rights with very little detection. Authorship, provenance, content and meaning can all be changed and material added and deleted with very little difficulty. Ironically, it may well be these rights which play the most important role in the electronic world as scholars are as anxious as authors that the works which they receive are intact and their integrity has been retained. Obviously how one views a report on lung cancer from the Tobacco Research Council will be different to how one views a similar document on the same subject from the Medical Research Council.

The electronic environment

There are several areas which need consideration because of the challenges which technology and copyright law present. Libraries will need to provide access to materials in electronic form, although to talk about "acquiring" them may be misleading. Such access raises the challenge of the fairly obvious one of format. The hardware and software which is now being used to create digital images will not be around in 10 years, or even five years' time. There will be a need to be able to change from one format or program to another. However libraries may not have the right to do this because of the ownership of the digital images which have been created. But it also has to be faced that actions which are considered normal in the paper environment are rapidly becoming viewed with great suspicion by copyright owners in the electronic world. Even viewing is seen as a potential infringement of a work because to load the documents onto the screen means making a copy of it and this is not allowed in law.

Similarly, to transmit a work to somebody else would effectively make a further copy of it and this again would not be permitted by any copyright owner. This even extends to the fact that where electronic documents are sent to a remote user they are not allowed to view them before they download them. Otherwise, they might view the document and decide this is not the one they want and therefore send it back again (whatever that means in electronic terminology!) therefore a delivery would have taken place or a copy made but to no benefit to anybody who owns the copyright material. Similarly, browsing is seen by many copyright owners as a potential threat because it means that there may be multiple access to the same document whereas in the paper world browsing must be restricted to one person at a time.

Because of all these problems there is considerable research into the mechanisms for protection which look at the possible technology for controlling and managing copyrighting documents. They all revolve round the idea that "the answer to the machine is in the machine". Models have been developed which would enable the copyright owner to monitor, inhibit or control the use of documents and also to set royalty payments which might vary between different types of user and even within the same document. To overcome the more extreme elements of this sort of technology the European Commission have established a European Copyright User Platform (ECUP)[27] which is trying to strike a balance between owners and users. Nevertheless we need to be aware that the documents which we create or cause to be created, may pose serious copyright problems in the future.

SOME SOLUTIONS

To deal with some of these issues the European Commission has funded a number of projects on electronic copyright management systems (ECMS). This is the catch-phrase of the moment. As far back as 1989 a major project called CITED (Copyright in Transmitted Electronic Documents)[28] began to design a model for the management of copyright in the electronic environment. This model has subsequently been taken into other projects with such names as COPICAT, COPYSMART and COPEARMS. COPICAT (Copyright Ownership in Computer Assisted Training) has developed technology to handle copyright protection for distance use, while COPYSMART is working on the use of Smartcard technology to control access and collect royalties. COPEARMS (Coordinating Project for Electronic Authors Right Management Systems) is a EU-wide project to develop a standardised approach to the implementation of the CITED technology. A further major EU project, IMPRIMATUR (Intellectual Multimedia Property Rights Model Universal Terminology for Universal Reference) is charged with the task of building a worldwide consensus on standards and methods of copyright management without indicating a specific type of software//hardware solution.

The results of all these different projects is that there are embryonic systems available for dealing with many of the problems which have just been outlined. However, we have to realise that the interests of libraries and, indeed, academic publishers, are very small fish in a very, very large pool. The real driving force for many of these developments will be the entertainment and leisure industries such as music and video. Some of these projects do have partners from such industries but the span of such interest is very wide which is demonstrated by the fact that one project focuses exclusively on the textile design industry.

Databases

In the UK a database is already recognised as a literary work protected by copyright but this is not the case in many countries, and definitions of what is "original" (as stated earlier) vary considerable. To try to harmonise the situation the European Commission has introduced a directive on databases which recognises that a database, regardless of the content, shall be regarded as a copyright work provided that sufficient investment has been made in it by the creator in terms of data collection, verification or arrangement of the material to make it a new work. Thus, even if the content is not of itself copyrightable, then nonetheless the database can be. An obvious example is the telephone directory where each entry is not a copyright item because it is a statement of fact but the compilation is regarded as a copyright work. In this case the Commission has given the protection of 15 years for such databases. This is called a *sui generis* right as it is not actually copyright but analogous to it. It is a right found only in databases, hence its Latin name. It is important to notice that the EU definition of a database is not restricted to an electronic document but can be any type of compilation[29]. However, in the United Kingdom they are almost certainly protected under the doctrine of "sweat of the brow" which is part of the originality test. In America, a different decision was reached when one telephone company took the entries from another telephone directory and used them as part of their own database. The American Court ruled that the mere telephone directory arranged by family name could not be a copyright work because it is the obvious way to arrange such a work. The doctrine of "sweat of the brow" was not considered sufficient.

The important thing to note is that even where a series of documents are old and probably out of copyright, turning them into some sort of compilation, whether in paper or electronic form, will mean that the publisher of this collection has copyright in the overall total package even though not in individual items within it. This is already the case in the United Kingdom and is also linked to typographical copyright, mentioned earlier.

Licences and contracts

The 1988 Act sets the framework for licensing agencies[30] and licences generally to become much more widespread. As copyright is a property right it can be traded like any other property and therefore the owner can allow anything to be done under contract or licence which the owner wishes to permit and can, at the same time, agree the terms for such actions. Most electronic publications are currently supplied with a clearly defined set of parameters for what can, and cannot, be done. Such actions as downloading, retransmitting, networking, printing onto paper or incorporating into other documents, are all allowed or not as the case may be. By agreeing to such a contract the purchaser agrees to abide by the limitations set out. These may be more or less generous than the exceptions given under national legislation but anyone subscribing to a CD-ROM or online database should always study carefully the terms of the contract under which it is supplied.

Licensing for some aspects of copyright, namely neighbouring rights, has been established in the UK for many years in the shape of the Performing Rights Society but this concept has now been extended to all forms of copyright use. Probably the best known is the Copyright Licensing Agency (CLA) which offers licences to copy a wide range of published material provided that it is in paper format. Licences exist for education (separately for schools, colleges and universities), government departments, law firms, industry and commerce and special licences for such activities as document supply can be negotiated. But other agencies are playing an increasingly important role, and there is now a scheme to license the use of newspapers, offered by the Newspaper Licensing Agency. Other agencies include Christian Copyright Licensing (for the words of hymns), Educational Recording Agency and Open University (for off-air recording for educational use), Design & Artists Copyright Society (for slide collections), as well as the long-established Performing Rights Society (for public musical performance) and the Mechanical Copyright Protection Society (for recording music on to any medium).

International treaties

Quite often references can be found to "international copyright law". Copyright law is, in fact, national in character and is framed within the general context of international conventions. There are, in effect, three of these. The first and oldest is the Berne Convention which requires, amongst other things, no formalities before copyright can be claimed and a minimum protection (as at December 1996) of 50 years from the end of the year in which the author dies. The Universal Copyright Convention requires a shorter period of protection and the use of the famous © in order to claim copyright protection. The third international treaty is the Agreement establishing the World Trade Organisation which requires those taking part to put in place legislation for the protection of intellectual property of which copyright forms a part. This latter has considerably increased the number of countries enjoying reciprocal copyright protection with the UK[31]. The result of these treaties, in broad terms, is that works published in any other country which has signed them are protected in the UK as if they were UK publications, except that the length of that protection in the UK will not be longer than that granted in the country of origin.

Demythologising

Copyright is a fast-moving target. Therefore it is not surprising that copyright law abounds in myths, most of them based on a smattering of knowledge often obtained a long time ago when the law, technology and society were rather different. So perhaps it is appropriate to attempt to dispel some of those myths once and for all.

Legal deposit

Once known as 'copyright deposit' because there used to be a requirement to deposit a copy of a work with a named organisation (Stationers' Hall, British Museum Library, etc.) in order to claim copyright. This requirement disappeared when the UK signed the Berne Convention in the late 19th century but the myth persisted because the legislation requiring copies to be deposited with certain libraries (the British Library, Oxford and Cambridge Universities, National Libraries of Scotland and Wales and Trinity College Dublin) is enshrined in the 1911 Copyright Act[32]. This deposit has now been renamed 'legal deposit' to try to avoid the confusion and has no relevance to copyright law at all. Copyright subsists whether or not a copy is deposited. As at December 1996 there are proposals to reform legal deposit with its own legislation which may finally kill this myth.

Copyright symbol

This was mentioned under the section on international treaties. This symbol has no meaning in UK law nor in any other country which has signed the Berne Convention. It was widely used in the USA until that country signed the Berne Convention and can still be found in a number of developing countries' publications.

Copyright registration

It should now be clear that there is no such thing as registering copyright. Patents, designs and trademarks can, and must in some cases, be registered but no such system exists for copyright.

ISBNs and ISSNs

For some incomprehensible reason there is a rumour abroad that works without either of these identifiers are not copyright. These numbering systems are devices for the book trade, which have been hijacked by the library profession for its own purposes, but which have nothing whatever to do with copyright.

World Wide Web

"If it's on the Web, it's not protected." This is a statement of hope rather than reality. Just because a work has been mounted on the World Wide Web or another other publicly-accessible information service, this does not change its copyright status. Certainly there are many WWW sites which state that works may be freely downloaded or copied but this does not mean they are not protected by copyright and increasingly websites are becoming protected by passwords and other devices as the real value of the information provided through them becomes evident. One day someone is going to be too free with another person's copyright material on the Web (republishing it or retransmitting it as if it were their own) and the original owner will take action which may help dispel this myth too!

THE FUTURE

The future of copyright is assured despite many prophets of doom and gloom who see its days as numbered. Some experts say that copyright will be replaced by contracts but there are two major difficulties to this: firstly there will always be a need to define what is protected and therefore owned and this will continue regardless of the technology; secondly there is a need to define the rights that owners have and how they need to be limited and this cannot be left to individual private contracts. An example of how the law can be used to limit rights is the Computer Programs Regulations[25] which permit certain actions even if the copyright owner tries to impose a contract preventing them. There are also other pressures to ensure that copyright not only continues but extends its scope. Commerce and industry need a system of protection for a growing segment of their intellectual property rights as exists for inventions (patents) and indicators of quality and origin (trademarks, service marks).

Paradoxically technology, seen as a threat to copyright by many, is the very reason copyright is becoming more important. On the one hand networking and digitisation present major challenges and threats to copyright material, on the other hand the same technology offers the possibility of being able to control use of material and receive payments for it. This is an attractive possibility for owners who are less concerned to prevent access than obtain payment for use. The value of much electronic information is such that investment in high technology to protect it may become worthwhile. The increasing internationalisation of information also means that laws need to be harmonised to ensure that information provided in one country is protected in another and therefore offers a 'level playing field' for information providers. This is the motivation for much EU harmonisation and also the increasing pressure on the World Intellectual Property Organisation (WIPO) to amend the Berne convention to broaden the scope of owners' rights.

CONCLUSION

Copyright was once seen as a dull and almost irrelevant area of law relating to information provision. It has now become central to all that libraries, archives and information centres wish to do. Far from being dull it has become one of the most dynamic and fast moving areas of law. For a real intellectual challenge which will continue to affect all that information professionals want and need to do - watch this space!

REFERENCES

1. *Copyright, Designs and Patents Act,* 1988.

2. Wall, Raymond, *Copyright made easier,* Aslib, London (1993) (new edition due 1998).

3. Cornish, Graham, *Copyright: interpreting the law for libraries, archives and information centres,* Library Association, London (1997, 2nd edition).

4. *Copyright, Designs and Patents Act,* 1988, s.1(1)(a).

5. *Copyright, Designs and Patents Act,* 1988, s.(16)(3)(a).

6. Petersen, J. *University of London Press Ltd v. University Tutorial Press Ltd* [1916]2 Ch 601 at 610.

7. *Copyright, Designs and Patents Act,* 1988, s.39.

8. *Copyright, Designs and Patents Act,* 1988, s.178.

9. *Copyright, Designs and Patents Act,* 1988, s.11.

10. *Copyright, Designs and Patents Act,* 1988, s.16.

11. *Duration of Copyright and Rights in Performances Regulations 1995* (SI 95/3297)

12. *Copyright, Designs and Patents Act,* 1988, s.29.

13. *Copyright, Designs and Patents Act,* 1988, s.38-40.

14. *Copyright (Librarians and Archivists) (Copying of CopyrightMaterial) Regulations* (SI 89/1212).

15. *Copyright, Designs and Patents Act,* 1988, s.42(1)(a).

16. *Copyright, Designs and Patents Act,* 1988, s.41.

17. *Copyright, Designs and Patents Act,* 1988, s.42(1)(b).

18. *Copyright, Designs and Patents Act,* 1988, s.32(3).

19. *Copyright, Designs and Patents Act,* 1988, s.32(1).

20. *Copyright, Designs and Patents Act,* 1988, s.45-50.

21. *Copyright, Designs and Patents Act,* 1988, s.18A.

22. *Copyright, Designs and Patents Act,* 1988, Schedule 7, 8.

23. *Copyright and Related Rights Regulations 1996* (SI 96/2967) reg.10.

24. *Copyright, Designs and Patents Act,* 1988, s.15.

25. *Copyright and Related Rights Regulations 1996* (SI 96/2967) regs.16, 17.

26. *Copyright (Computer Programs) Regulations 1992* (SI 92/3233).

27. See regular news of ECUP in *Information Europe,* Belshon Publishing, London.
28. *CITED Final Report*, British Library, Boston Spa (1994).
29. *Directive 96/9/EC on the legal protection of databases,* section (14) and article 1(2).
30. *Copyright, Designs and Patents Act,* 1988, ch.VII.
31. *Copyright (Application to Other Countries) (Amendment) Order 1995* (SI 95/2987).
32. *Copyright Act 1911,* s.15.

Data Protection and the Information Manager

J. Eric Davies

INTRODUCTION

The issue of data protection impinges on the library and information service manager's sphere of activity in a variety of ways, since the staple commodity in the manager's activity is information, much of it related to people. It is therefore important that the scope of data protection legislation is appreciated and that steps are taken to ensure that operations are conducted within the law. This chapter seeks to explain the broader principles of data protection, describe the current UK legal situation, and discuss the approach to general good data protection management practice.

WHAT IS DATA PROTECTION?

A fairly comprehensive definition of data protection would be:

> A legal, technical and social or managerial framework through which are achieved the objectives of ensuring that information held (usually electronically) about identifiable persons is obtained, stored, used and transmitted in such a way that it cannot be consulted, exploited, altered or disposed of without appropriate authorisation and safeguards to avoid detriment to a person's interests.

The entire issue surrounds respect for a person's privacy and affording confidentiality to personal information; but it goes further than that to embrace the concepts of reliability of any information and its fair and legitimate use by those who have proper access to it.

THE LEGAL BACKGROUND

It is worth sketching briefly the background to the enactment of data protection legislation in the UK to provide a perspective for the manager.

The move from regarding computers simply as swift and clever calculating machines (number crunchers) to devices for manipulating large amounts of information – any information – provided an entirely new perspective for society. The combination of this phenomenon with speedy and reliable telecommunications offered an IT scenario with remarkable possibilities, but it also engendered some attendant anxieties. As information technology applications became more widespread and sophisticated throughout the globe there was a perception that processing data about people by computer presented a serious threat to their privacy and lifestyle. Although there was little real evidence to support such worries, there was a mood abroad that such activity should be controlled. The implications for trade in, and exchange of data on the international scene was also recognised because movement of personal information from one nation to another could be inhibited without adequate safeguards.

Notable landmarks in the development of data protection legislation in the UK are the Report of the Younger Committee on Privacy[1] which was published in 1972, and the Report of the Lindop Committee on Data Protection[2] which appeared in 1978. On the international front, two important initiatives which provided an impetus for development of legislation in the UK and abroad were the establishment of a Convention (or Treaty) from the Council of Europe[3] and the publication of Guidelines from the Organisation of Economic Co-operation and Development[4]. These all contributed to the design of legislation in the United Kingdom, which, after a few false starts with private members' bills and a governmental bill overtaken by a general election, culminated in *The Data Protection Act* [DPA] of 1984[5].

Since 1984, *The Data Protection Act* has governed the use of personal information processed by computer in almost any context. More recently the European Union has passed a Directive[6] which is intended to harmonise data protection within the member states. The Directive differs from the existing legislation in several ways and the UK, in common with other nations, will have to amend its law accordingly. It is within this framework that the manager must plan and operate.

A reminder

The aim of the Chapter is to summarise, with reference to the current legislation, the salient points of data protection for the manager. It should however be stressed that there is no substitute for first-hand reading and understanding of the original texts of legislation and related official material – especially for anyone closely involved with the issue. Readers are therefore urged to consult the primary material to acquire a full understanding of the situation.

HOW DOES DATA PROTECTION WORK?

The DPA prescribes acceptable activity and provides the means for identifying, monitoring and regulating the use of personal data in IT systems. It is designed to protect the interests of the individual by limiting the possibility of their being harmed by wrongful use of data whilst at the same time allowing the legitimate and proper use of such data. It should be noted that the DPA does not generally seek to prevent the holding or use of personal information, nor to guarantee complete privacy for an individual, but to ensure that acceptable standards are followed.

Definitions

Words in legislation are used in a precise way and the DPA has its own vocabulary with which it is important to become familiar. Below, summary definitions of some of the terms used are provided:

- *Data* - information recorded in a form in which it can be processed automatically
- *Personal data* – information or opinions relating to a living, identifiable individual, but not a data user's intentions towards them
- *Data subject* – an individual about whom personal data relates
- *Data user* – *a* person or an organisation holding data that is processed or to be processed, or who controls the contents and use of a collection of data

321

- *Disclosing information* – making available information, or extracts of information, of data held; the medium of disclosure may be oral, hand-written, printed or screen display, or otherwise

- *Computer bureau* – person or an organisation who processes data for data users, or allows data users the use of equipment for such processing (note that the definition extends beyond commercial computer bureau businesses)

- *Processing* – amending, augmenting, deleting or rearranging data, or extracting the information constituting the data, *but excluding simple word-processing.*

- *Data equipment* – equipment for automatic processing of data or for recording information to enable it to be so processed.

The Data Protection Principles

Acceptable activity is described in eight Data Protection Principles enumerated in the Act. They specify how personal data is to be managed. They are as follows:

Personal data held by data users:

1. The information to be contained in personal data shall be obtained, and personal data shall be processed, fairly and lawfully

2. Personal data shall be held only for one or more specified and lawful purposes

3. Personal data held for any purpose or purposes shall not be used or disclosed in any manner incompatible with that purpose or those purposes

4. Personal data held for any purpose or purposes shall be adequate, relevant and not excessive in relation to that purpose or those purposes

5. Personal data shall be accurate and, where necessary, kept up to date

6. Personal data held for any purpose or purposes shall not be kept for longer than is necessary for that purpose or those purposes

7. An individual shall be entitled:

a) at reasonable intervals and without undue delay or expense

(i) to be informed by any data user whether he holds personal data of which that individual is the subject

(ii) to access to any such data held by a data user

b) where appropriate, to have such data corrected or erased.

Personal data held by data users or in respect of which services are provided by persons carrying on computer bureaux:

8. Appropriate security measures shall be taken against unauthorised access to, or alteration, disclosure or destruction of, personal data and against accidental loss or destruction of personal data[7].

A further condition appears in a section devoted to the interpretation to the Principles, which permits, with safeguards, the retention and use of material as an archive for historical or statistical research, thereby enabling longer term research and scholarship to flourish.

Use for historical, statistical or research purposes

Where personal data are held for historical, statistical or research purposes and not used in such a way that damage or distress is, or is likely to be, caused to any data subject:

a) the information contained in the data shall not be regarded for the purposes of the first principle as obtained unfairly by reason only that its use for any such purpose was not disclosed when it was obtained

(b) the data may, notwithstanding the sixth principle, be kept indefinitely[8].

The Data Protection Registrar

The function of identifying, monitoring and regulating activity is undertaken by the Office of the Data Protection Registrar – a Crown appointment with a range of powers to direct and influence personal data use. A mechanism for appeal against the Data Protection Registrar's decision exists in the form of a Data Protection Tribunal which is open to users of data, but not individuals whose information is being used.

Central to the regulation of activity is the compilation of the Data Protection Register in which Data users' activities have to be formally recorded. The registration process will be dealt with more fully later. The Register is available on the Internet and is regularly updated.

The powers and responsibilities conferred upon the Registrar include:

- Compilation of the Register of Data Protection including acceptance or refusal (in particular circumstances) of registration

- Making information in the Register publicly available

- Issuing a Deregistration Notice (in particular circumstances) which will prohibit a data user from continuing to process data by having been removed from the Register

- Issuing an Enforcement Notice directing a data user to undertake a particular course of action if the Principles are being or have been contravened

- Issuing a Transfer Prohibition Notice which will prohibit the movement or 'export' of data elsewhere

- Institute court actions against data users

- Enter and search premises and examine and seize material (where appropriate and necessary) with a Warrant from a Circuit Judge

- Promoting the observance of the Principles by data users and computer bureaux

- Consider complaints from persons about the Principles and the law

- Disseminating information about the Act and its operations and providing advice

- Encouraging the creation of codes of practice regarding data protection management.

Exemptions

Some exemptions to the regulatory and other requirements of the legislation are specified for certain circumstances or types of information use. They are summarised in an appendix to this chapter. They range from almost 'total' exemption – not requiring registration of data use, data subject access, nor limitations or disclosure – to more limited dispensation from the provisions. Many are of a specialised nature and few are really appropriate to the LIS manager's realm of operation. Those that are, include:

payroll and accounts systems and distribution lists, both of which are almost fully exempted. It is important to note however that the scope of these systems should not stray beyond what is specifically exempted. For example, incorporating assessments of performance in payroll and accounts systems would take them out of the exemption.

THE LIS BACKGROUND

A wide range of personal information applications in the typical library and information service (LIS) falls under the ambit of the DPA. Some may be covered by the tightly defined exemptions noted earlier. Below are outlined some examples:

- 'Membership' records of clients and their interests
- Material issue/circulation records
- Records of services provided, and to be provided to clients (including records of searches run for clients, stored searches, and stored SDI profiles)
- Specialist information files on people and organisations (for example, consultants and researchers, officials of local institutions)
- Local catalogues of material (for example, OPACs with personal authors' names)
- . Local World Wide Web pages incorporating personal information
- Staff/personnel files
- Payroll files
- Accounts/Invoice files
- Orders files (for example, orders for books with personal authors, requested by individuals, and/or purchased from individuals)
- Electronic databases (bibliographic and factual)
- Centralised cataloguing data records
- Catalogues of material from other institutions
- Booksellers' databanks
- Publishers' databanks
- Expert systems
- Electronic mail/messaging systems

- Internet WWW pages from other locations.

These applications may include information on a variety of people. Some examples include: clients – past, present and potential; authors, and similar creators of material; individual specialists, consultants, researchers and advisors; individual secretaries of organisations and institutions and similar contact names; individual suppliers, vendors, contractors and donors of material and services; staff – past, present and prospective; and even more generally, prominent individuals such as scientists, industrialists and politicians.

Though it may be slightly blurred in practice, a distinction of sorts can be made between those types of application relating to *internal* factors where most material is compiled inhouse and those relating to *external* factors where material is 'imported' in some way into operations. The latter category presents some additional problems in terms of authenticating and verifying the data being used. In short, it should have a 'clean bill of health, as far as it is possible, before it is introduced into the local environment. There is perhaps a parallel here with the need to safeguard an operation against the introduction of viruses and other rogue programmes.

With this array of personal information available in a library and information service, the overall management of data protection matters requires a careful and considered approach.

MANAGING FOR DATA PROTECTION

The LIS manager's role in data protection will vary with the nature and size of the organisation of which he or she is a part. A constant, however, will be the need to ensure that data protection policies, procedures and integrity relating to the LIS environment are appropriate and complete.

A large organisation may well have a full time data protection officer whose role will be to ensure compliance with the law and to develop good practice through training and supervision within the organisation. The LIS manager will need to liaise with, and take advice and direction from such an officer. At the same time responsibility cannot and should not be abdicated for the conduct of data protection within the LIS manager's parameter of control.

Moreover, the role of data protection officer may in some cases fall upon the LIS manager as an additional responsibility.

An information specialist in a small operation (such as an information partnership, or voluntary body) or working as a freelance consultant will face quite different circumstances and demands. More of the data protection management issues, responsibilities and procedures will have to be addressed directly.

COMPLYING WITH THE PRINCIPLES AND THE LAW

The manager will need to establish and maintain policies, practices, procedures and systems which ensure compliance with the Principles and good data protection practice generally. There are a range of management implications here, including strategic decisions to be made, the design and operation of systems, supervision, training and security. It should be noted that the DPA places an onus on directors and managers of an organisation should they, through neglect or wilfulness, create a situation where the law is broken. The Principles of Data Protection embody the fundamental approach to the way affairs are to be conducted. Some observations will be made on managing operations with reference to the Principles.

Collecting fairly and lawfully

The first Data Protection Principle requires that information be collected fairly and lawfully. Clearly, information must not be obtained by breaking the law or by getting others to break the law. Data obtained from third parties, for example, must be obtained in circumstances where it is legal for them to disclose it, so their data protection registration must describe disclosures appropriately. Much data will be acquired directly from the data subject and must be obtained fairly. Reasonable steps should be taken to ensure that the data subject is made fully aware of what is happening and what will be done with the information. This can be fairly simply achieved in appropriate documentation and notices to LIS users and others.

A safe and sensible policy is to employ as much candour and transparency as possible in dealing with data subjects, especially when information is being gathered from them. Moreover it cannot be assumed that they are expert in this field so it is wise to approach the situation at the level of knowledge of 'the average person in the street'.

The provenance of 'externally' acquired information should be established and its integrity verified as far as possible. Appropriate qualifications on the origin and reliability of data may be necessary. Vendors supplying data should be asked to confirm its data protection status and as far as possible its reliability. The important issue is to avoid being left open to the challenge that procedures and practices were unfair or unlawful because of inadequate management.

Purposes and the registration process

The Principles specify very clearly that personal data shall be held only for specified and lawful purposes, and further that it shall not be used or disclosed in any manner incompatible with those purposes.

The mechanism for specifying the purposes to which data is put is through formal registration with the Data Protection Registrar's Office. It is the duty of data users to register activity involving personal data unless an exemption appertains to their particular circumstances or purpose for using information.

Registration is effected by providing information to the Data Protection Registrar's Office. Formerly, this exercise was undertaken by submitting the details of activity on a standard form which could be obtained from Crown Post Offices. More recently the Data Protection Registrar's Office has modernised and streamlined the procedure under the DUIS – Data Users Information System. Under this system a preliminary contact is made with the Office which then verifies the data user's scope of operations and collects and collates the user's details online. 'Pre-filled' documentation is sent to the data user for verification, and amendment if necessary. This documentation is then returned to the Office with a declaration. To complete the registration a fee, currently £75, must be paid. A registration may be taken out for up to three years. Clearly a temporary and short term information application should be registered for a shorter period. Registration may be renewed, provided details have not changed, and a further fee is paid. Registrations can also be amended if circumstances or details change, and no fee is payable. In addition a registration may be cancelled if a particular application is discontinued.

Details which have to be furnished upon Registration include:

- The purpose for which data is held or used (why is data held, why is it used?)
- The sources of the data (where or from whom the user intends to obtain information?)
- The types of data subject about whom information is held or used (what kind of people are described?)
- The types of personal data (what kind of information about people is held or used?)
- Disclosures of data (the people who will be shown or given all or part of the data)
- Overseas transfers of data (any overseas territories or countries to which the data user may wish to move all or part of the data).

It needs to be stressed that the approach to identifying data use is *purpose* driven. That is – what is it that is to be accomplished by using the personal data? An example would be lending and hire administration or, put more simply, issuing and returning books and all the attendant procedures. It is sometimes a temptation to think in terms of *files* held rather than *purposes* achieved, but one purpose may involve several files, and equally one file may fulfil a number of purposes especially with current integrated 'housekeeping' systems. Though it is open for any user to describe in his or her own words what the purpose or purposes are, there are a set of precoded standard purposes which can be used and into which a vast number of operations fit easily.

By way of illustration some examples of standard purposes are noted below:-

- P001 Personnel/employee administration
- P002 Work planning and management
- P008 Purchase/supplier administration
- P009 Business and technical intelligence
- P014 Lending and hire services administration
- P016 Research and statistical analysis
- P017 Information and databank administration

- P018 Trading in personal information
- P022 Education or training administration
- P067 Health care administration
- P073 Citizens Advice Bureau administration
- P074 Software development, test and demonstration.

Clearly the manager's first priority will be to ensure that operations for which he or she is responsible are properly registered under the DPA. Where this is undertaken in the organisation is, in a sense, less important than making sure that it is properly undertaken. The LIS manager should know precisely what, within his or her area of operations, falls within the scope of the DPA, and check accordingly. A sensible precaution, if someone else is responsible for registration, is to ask to see a copy of the documentation *confirming* the registration with the Office of the Data Protection Registrar. The old adage of "Don't leave it to someone else – someone else is leaving it to you!" is worth repeating!

Another important consideration is to work precisely within the specified registration. Any extension or modification of activity will require an amendment to the registration, or in some cases an entirely new one. Such action should be taken *before* new work starts.

Extent of data held

The fourth Data Protection Principle requires that data be adequate, relevant and not excessive for performing the purposes declared by the user. Some aspects of this may be open to conjecture – what may be adequate, relevant and not excessive in one context may be considered quite the opposite in another. The type and amount of data held is, to some extent, up to the judgement of the manager. However, the manager must be able to defend and justify fully the extent and nature of the data held. There is to be no gathering of data 'just in case'. The test should be – what data is really needed to perform this function/purpose properly and accurately?

Accuracy and up-to-dateness of data

The accuracy of data is crucial to successful operations in any application and it is therefore in the manager's interest to ensure its integrity. There is added impetus to achieve this with personal data because the DPA Principles very clearly specify the necessity for information to be accurate and up-to-date. In many instances this will entail the co-operation of a data subject who will need to inform a data user of changed circumstances such as an address, occupation or subject interests. This process should be rendered as easy as possible through, for example, providing a standard form for reporting amendments to personal details. It is wise also to seek assurances regarding the quality and accuracy of data obtained from outside agencies. In addition, routine processing of whatever kind should follow the highest standards of practice to maintain data quality.

Duration of holding data

Similar considerations hold good regarding the duration for which data should be held. The manager needs to exercise judgement but there are some factors to help in the assessment. Firstly, information regarding business transactions need to be held for at least as long as is necessary for audit and taxation purposes. In some circumstances it may be important to keep an information archive to track the evolution of a project or process – not least to establish priorities in intellectual property issues. Staffing information may need to be kept even some time after an employee has left an organisation in order that reliable references for future employers and prospective employers can be provided.

Data may be accumulated to monitor the use of material and services with a view to developing and improving them to be more client-oriented. In some cases however it will be sufficient to keep the information in a form in which it is 'depersonalised' since it is the service or material rather than the specific user that may be of interest. The special provisions in the DPA regarding the use of data for historical, statistical or research purposes, noted earlier, are also relevant to decisions regarding the retention of data.

Dealing with data subject access requests

The DPA makes provision under Section 18 for individuals to ascertain whether data is held about them and if so, to receive and examine a copy of it. Further provisions cater for the correction or erasure of data found to be inaccurate – a court may order the rectification or erasure of information. Furthermore, a data subject may take legal action to seek compensation for damage and distress caused by inaccurate information. Normally 40 days are allowed for the data user to furnish data, though it may not be modified or interfered with (other than as part of routine processing) in the interim. An example of continuing routine processing would occur say in a circulation system if the data subject continued to borrow and return material. There would be little point in not updating the data in such circumstances.

Data users may charge a fee for data subject access – it is currently £10 per registration. Moreover they may ask a requesting party for information to help find data if that is felt reasonable. For example, a manager might ask of someone making a request for data "Were you ever a user of this information service, or were you ever a supplier of goods or services?" There is also provision to overcome 'nuisance' requests because the DPA specifies that unreasonably frequent requests need not be complied with. This is a grey area however as what is unreasonably frequent is open to interpretation.

Material provided in response to a request must be in a form which can be intelligible to the recipient. Therefore coded information must have a key provided to render it decipherable.

The data user is obliged only to give a requester that information to which he or she is entitled by law. Material covered by exemption does not, therefore, need to be disclosed. Neither does the fact that an exemption is being used have to be stated. If material is only partially exempted from data subject access then the appropriate amount must be disclosed.

It is highly recommended that a formal procedure should be in place to deal efficiently and correctly with data subject access requests. The procedure need not be complex, especially in view of the relatively low volume of requests that may be expected according to past evidence. It should however cover stages from initial receipt of a request through to its processing and the final delivery of information. And it should be the province of a knowledgeable and senior supervisor. Some procedures for handling complaints arising out of the exercise should also be available. The time to decide what to do is not after the first request (or worse still, the first complaint) has been received.

Of particular value is maintaining a log of requests and their fulfilment. This is a useful aid regarding any queries and problems which may arise later. In addition, dated receipts should be taken for data provided in response to a request. Where complaints do arise regarding the data disclosed, the ideal is to resolve the situation courteously, speedily and amicably. This restores confidence in the operation and is good public relations. Where matters cannot be settled so amicably, legal advice should be sought with some urgency before matters become too fraught and litigation (which is almost always costly) is resorted to.

A crucial factor is establishing the true identity of a person requesting data subject access. After all, disclosing information to an imposter is a sure way of compromising data protection. The task is made easier in many situations nowadays with the introduction of company identity cards and similar documents. Alternatively driving licences, passports or even correspondence can be used to prove identity. Circumstances where a person's agent or representative is seeking data have to be dealt with carefully and some proof of authorisation should be sought.

In some circumstances it may be helpful to establish a routine whereby data subjects are, at intervals, automatically supplied with output of data held. For very large organisations this is probably not feasible since the cost of mailing material would be prohibitive. However, it offers several advantages for organisations which can undertake it.

It is a useful procedure for verifying the accuracy and up-to-dateness of data – recipients can be sent a pro-forma to notify any updates or corrections. It therefore represents good public relations with data users, since candour and openness is readily evident. Moreover, a data run can be timed for the data user's convenience so as to avoid peak loads in processing and staff absences.

Security

The eighth Data Protection Principle requires that adequate security be accorded to personal data. The topic is a wide one and embraces a whole range of issues. Moreover the approach to security is to some degree subjective rather than absolute and must take into account the potential hazards and risks that apply. It is pertinent to note that the registration procedure does not include the need to specify the nature of security which is applied to a particular purpose or application.

In brief, factors influencing security include: the environment in which operations take place, the personnel who have access to operations, the technology and systems (hardware, software and telecommunications) employed, and the overall management regime. Elements contributing to security threats include; natural hazards, man-made hazards, accidents, criminal behaviour, misuse of systems, carelessness and inexperience in the operation of systems. Thus data may be lost through flood or fire at one extreme, or through miskeying on the other. Data may be compromised and improperly disclosed through eavesdropping or 'simply' failing to keep material locked up, or out of sight. In addition, it may be damaged by computer hacking or a systems fault. Reasonable precautions to avoid loss or damage need to be taken and procedures to effect speedy recovery of data instituted. Elements in controlling the vulnerability to loss, disclosure and damage include: access control to installations, secure locks on vulnerable areas and equipment, the use of passwords and, if appropriate, encryption, maintenance of adequate backup data, random checks, audit trails, adequate supervision and training, and complete documentation and instructions. Thus it is possible to think in terms of providing security through physical protection, technical protection, and sound personnel management.

Another crucial aspect of computer security involves the development, maintenance and regular rehearsal of a disaster recovery plan designed to cope with contingencies that arise. Organisations may also take out insurance against security breaches and it may cover the cost of litigation arising from incidents as well as loss of materials and business.

TRAINING, AWARENESS AND SUPERVISION

A great deal of the integrity of data protection relies on people within an organisation. The way they operate systems and provide services will be important. Staff at all levels need to be apprised of the need to handle personal data with care and have some appreciation of the consequences of failing to do so. New staff in particular need to be made aware, but it is easy to become complacent, so regular updating training and continuous supervision are also important. This points to the need for formal training for those who handle data, or manage operations in any way. The training need not be extensive but it needs to be effective. The author has examined the process in greater depth elsewhere[9].

A survey [10] of academic library and information services conducted by the author in 1995 revealed that fewer than half of the institutions from which replies were received feature data protection awareness in induction training. The proportion fell even lower when ongoing training was considered. In addition, the great majority of respondents regarded their own awareness of data protection matters, and that of the staff generally as 'adequate'. Few claimed it to be 'good'. The situation was capable of improvement and arguably, needed to be enhanced in view of the way in which IT now pervades deeply into operations.

Effective supervision is also a key factor in good data protection practice. There need to be clear lines of responsibility regarding the procedures for handling personal information. Moreover such matters should be clearly described and documented, perhaps with a local code of practice if appropriate. These factors simply reflect good management practice but their importance in this context needs to be emphasised.

EUROPEAN UNION DEVELOPMENTS

As noted earlier, the European Union has passed a Directive[11] which promises to alter the data protection picture significantly. However, at the time of writing the way forward in legislation is not clear. The existing DPA may be modified by a Statutory Instrument – a device used already to modify and add detail to the DPA legislation. Alternatively a new Act may be introduced, but this will absorb much valuable parliamentary time. Managers are strongly advised to keep a watching brief on this issue. The excellent regular 'LISLEX' column in the *Journal of Information Science* is one good source of relevant and specific information; the Office of the Data Protection Registrar is another. (Further general sources of information and advice are detailed in the next Section).

Member States of the European Union are obliged to implement the Directive through their own national legal systems within three years of its original adoption. In this case the UK Government will have to create appropriate legislation by October 1998. Article 1 of the Directive describes its objectives in two paragraphs as follows:

1)   In accordance with this Directive, member states shall protect the fundamental rights and freedoms of natural per-

sons, and in particular their right to privacy with respect to the processing of personal data.

2)   Member states shall neither restrict nor prohibit the free flow of personal data between member states for reasons connected with the protection afforded under paragraph 1[12].

The Directive retains the general approach already embodied in the DPA, with the specification of a set of principles and specific provisions together with mechanisms to identify and regulate activity operated by national supervisory authorities. The provisions of the Directive differ significantly in substance and detail however, and they go beyond the scope of the DPA in many ways.

One of the most important features of the Directive is perhaps that it applies to certain categories of manually organised files as well as those automatically processed through information technology.

There are other differences which, depending on circumstances and interpretation, become important. They include: the requirement for data subjects to give consent for processing; the specific requirement for data subjects to be informed of activity; the right of data subjects to be able to object to lawful processing; the stringent control over processing of 'sensitive' data such as that relating to race, religion and politics; and the introduction of an exemption to safeguard 'freedom of expression' which extends to protecting activities relating to journalism and artistic or literary expression. Another feature which is attractive to data users, is the possibility of selective exemption from, and simplification of, the registration process.

Whatever the final shape and detail of the revised legislation the need to manage personal data methodically and scrupulously will continue.

ADVICE AND FURTHER INFORMATION

The prime source of advice and assistance regarding data protection matters is of course the Office of the Data Protection Registrar. The Office has published booklets, leaflets and advice since the DPA was enacted. Readers are recommended in particular to read the helpful Guidelines publication[13]. The regular Annual Reports [14] of the Registrar contain useful information on the application of the legislation and problems that arise. In addition the

Office has a World Wide Web site on the Internet where much useful material is displayed and provided in downloadable form. The reader is strongly recommended to visit the site to keep up to date with developments in such area as the implementation of the EU Directive mentioned earlier – *http://www.open.gov.uk/dpr/dprhome.htm*

Another useful WWW site covering this and related topics is provided by the Strathclyde University School of Law *http://law-www-server.law.strath.ac.uk/*

Some relevant information can also be gleaned from the WWW pages of the Centre for Computing and Social Responsibility based at De Montfort University *http://www.ccsr.cms.dmu.ac.uk/*

The British Computer Society (BCS) is another source of useful information with a WWW presence *http://www.bcs.org.uk/index.html*

The National Computing Centre (NCC), based in Manchester, is also a reliable source through its WWW site *http://www.ncc.co.uk/*

Clearly, organisations such as the BCS and the NCC are primarily geared to disseminating information to members, or on a consultancy basis to others, and this should be borne in mind.

In more parochial professional terms the associations concerned with LIS professional matters in the UK, namely Aslib, The Library Association and the Institute of Information Scientists are worth approaching.

There are many useful books on the management of data protection and the following are a selection indicating the author's preferences [15,16,17,18,19]. The author has also produced a book focusing on the particular operations and needs of the library an information community[20]. Those wishing to explore more fully the philosophical and ethical issues surrounding data protection and the relationship between IT and society generally should turn to two volumes on the subject – one by Forester and Morrison, and the other edited by Kling[21,22]. A good general overview of computer security issues is contained in an excellent book by Hearnden which perhaps is now ready for another new edition[23].

CONCLUSION

This chapter has sought to provide a comprehensive yet succinct summary of the data protection issues as they affect the LIS manager. It has demonstrated that the proper management of personal information has important legal implications, as well as ethical and professional dimensions. As custodians and trusted stewards of information of all kinds, LIS managers should take responsibilities and obligations in this area very seriously.

REFERENCES

1. Great Britain, Committee on Privacy, *Report of the Committee on Privacy*, HMSO, London (1972, Command Paper No: Cmnd 5012).

2. Great Britain, Committee on Data Protection, *Report of the Committee on Data Protection,* HMSO, London (1978, Command Paper No: Cmnd 7341).

3. Council of Europe, Convention for the Protection of Individuals with Regard to Automatic Processing of Personal Data, Council of Europe, Strasbourg (1981, European Treaty Series No. 108).

4. Organisation for Economic Co-operation and Development, *Guidelines for the Protection of Privacy and Transborder Data Flows*, OECD, Paris (1981).

5. Great Britain, Laws, statutes, *The Data Protection Act,* (Public General Acts 1984 – Chapter 35), HMSO, London (1984).

6. European Union, Directive 95/46/EC of the European Parliament and of the Council of 24th October 1995 on the protection of individuals with regard to the processing of personal data on the free movement of such data, EU, Brussels (1995, In: Official Journal of the EU, Part (L), 23rd November 1995, p.31).

7. Great Britain, Laws, statutes, *The Data Protection Act,* Schedule 1, Part I, p.35.

8. Great Britain, Laws, statutes, *The Data Protection Act,* Schedule 1, Part II. p.37.

9. Davies, J.E. The importance of spreading the word: The Data Protection Act and staff training. *Training and Education: a Journal for Library and Information Workers,* **5** (1),. 1987/88, 3-22.

10. Davies, J.E. *Data protection and LIS management in academic libraries*, BLRDD, London (1996, British Library R&D Report No. 6248).

11. European Union, Directive. (*op cit.*)

12. (*ibid.*)

13. Data Protection Registrar, *The Guidelines: The Data Protection Act 1984*, Office of the Data Protection Registrar, Wilmslow, Cheshire (1994, 3rd series).

14. Data Protection Registrar, *Annual Report of the Data Protection Registrar: 12th annual report*, HMSO, London (1996, House of Commons Papers Series No. 574 Session 1995-96).

15. Evans, A. and Korn, A. How to comply with the Data Protection Act: policies, practice procedures, Gower, Aldershot (1986).

16. Gulleford, K. *Data protection in practice*, Butterworths, London (1986).

17. Pounder, C.N.M. *et al. Managing data protection*, Butterworth-Heinemann, London (1991, 2nd edition).

18. Savage, N. and Edwards, C. *A guide to the Data Protection Act: implementing the Act*, Financial Training Publications, London (1985).

19. Sizer, R. and Newman, P. *The Data Protection Act: a practical guide*, Gower, Aldershot (1984).

20. Davies, J.E. *Data protection: a guide for library and information management*, Elsevier International Bulletins, Oxford (1984, EIB Report Series No. 8).

21. Forester, T. and Morrison, P. *Computer ethics: cautionary tales and ethical dilemmas in computing*, MIT Press, Cambridge Ma. (1994, 2nd edition).

22. Kling, R. (ed.) *Computerization and controversy: value conflicts and social choices*, Academic Press, San Diego (1996, 2nd edition).

23. Hearnden, K. *A handbook of computer security*, Kogan-Page, London, (1990 rev.ed.).

APPENDIX

Summary of exemptions in the Data Protection Act 1984.

A. *Exemption from Registration and Supervision / Data Subject Access / Non-Disclosure Provisions*

1. Data held only for payroll and accounting purposes – subject to certain limitations on disclosure

2. Domestic, personal, family or related household affairs information or data for recreational purposes

3. Clubs, societies members' data – subject to the consent of members

4. Distribution lists – but disclosure limited by the consent of data subjects

5. Data held where the person holding the data has a statutory duty to make the information available to the public

6. Data used for safeguarding National Security.

B. *Exemption from Data Subject Access / Non-Disclosure Provisions*

1. Data used for the prevention and detection of crime

2. Data used for the apprehension and prosecution of offenders

3. Data used for the assessment or collection of any tax or duty

C. *Exemption from Data Subject Access Provisions*

1. Data relevant to making judicial appointments

2. Data covered by legal professional privilege

3. Data used for preparing statistics

4. Data used for carrying out research

5. Circumstances where providing subject access would expose the person complying with subject access provisions to proceedings for an office, other than one under the Act

6. Data kept only for the purpose of replacing other data in the event of the latter being lost, destroyed or impaired

7. Consumer credit data (Note however that this is accessible through consumer credit legislation).

and

Subject to an appropriate order qualifying the access situation issued by the Secretary of State

1. Physical or mental health information
2. Social work information (from local authorities *or* voluntary bodies)
3. Information for the purpose of discharging statutory functions regarding the regulation of financial services and activity and designed to protect members of the public against loss
4. Other data, disclosure of which is prohibited or restricted by any law, if it is considered that such prohibition or restriction should prevail

D. *Exemption from Non-Disclosure Provisions*

1. In circumstances where disclosure is urgently necessary to prevent injury or damage to health
2. In circumstances where disclosure is required by any law or by order of a court
3. Where disclosure is made for the purpose of obtaining legal advice, or in legal proceedings
4. Where disclosure is to the data subject or his representative, or by his consent
5. Where disclosure of the data is for the purpose of safeguarding national security even if the data is not already exempted for such a purpose from the various provisions applicable.

E. *All provisions of the Act*

The following may be regarded as being exempt from all its provisions having being 'defined-out' of the scope of the Act.

1. Information which is an indication of the *intentions* of the data user in respect of an individual

   Sect. 1, Subsect. (3)
2. Operations performed only for the purpose of preparing the text of documents. (Word Processing)

   Sect. 1, Subsect. (8)
3. As the scope of the Act is confined to 'automatically processed information', *manually* processed and organised

records are not *currently* subject to any control under this legislation. But the scope of legislation will alter as the relevant European Union Directive is implemented.

Liability for Information Provision

Phil Sykes

INTRODUCTION

The first part of this chapter, "How to get sued", outlines the circumstances under which an information broker or a company providing information might come to be sued for providing inaccurate information or otherwise failing a client. The second part, "How not to get sued", has the rather more positive purpose of advising on ways of minimising the risk of liability. The third part "Publishers' liability" looks at the special factors which come into play when information intermediaries cross the line to becoming publishers - a role which the Internet and other electronic distribution methods now makes alarmingly easy for LIS professionals to assume.

HOW TO GET SUED

How liability arises

There are two well established grounds of liability: contract and tort. These have been joined lately by a relative newcomer to the field called strict liability.

Liability in contract

Broadly speaking, contract is the relevant area of liability if money changes hands, and tort is the relevant area where information is provided for free. At its simplest, a contract arises when two people promise to do something for one another. For example, an information broker may promise to provide information to company x in return for payment. There has to be a mutual exchange of promises for a contract to arise so if, for example, information is provided without charge no contractual liability will arise. There need not be a written record of a contract: a verbal contract is, in

343

most instances, legally binding - though the lack of a written record may make it difficult, in the event of a subsequent dispute, to prove that a contract arose or what its precise terms were.

Assuming that a contract has come into being through the mutual exchange of promises, what are the obligations of the parties to the contract? Broadly, of course, they are what the parties have agreed them to be. For instance, if it was agreed that information should be supplied by a certain date then that is a term of the contract. But the law also implies terms into contracts - that is, it causes certain terms to be part of a contract even though neither party has mentioned them or is even aware of them. The most important example of this, from the point of view of information providers, is found in Section 13 of the Supply of Goods and Services Act 1982. This implies a term into contracts for the supply of services that the supplier must carry out the service with reasonable skill and care. Although the act limits this provision to suppliers acting in the course of a business, it defines "business" to include a profession and the activities of any government department or local or public authority. So virtually anyone who supplies information commercially will be subject to it. Note, though, that the act will not apply in the absence of a contract so will not apply to situations where information is provided for free.

The 1969 case of Vacwell Engineering v BDH Chemicals[1], provides a relevant example of this principle in action. BDH, a laboratory supplier, negligently failed to warn Vacwell of the propensity of the chemical they were supplying to explode when it came into contact with water. A serious explosion occurred and Vacwell sued BDH. The case turned on whether BDH should have been aware of the dangerous properties of the chemical concerned. They claimed that they had done a literature search but had found nothing to alert them to the danger. It transpired, however, that they had not searched thoroughly enough. Some older material, which they had missed pointed out the hazard. Their defence failed, therefore, because they had failed to exercise reasonable care in ascertaining whether the chemical being supplied was hazardous.

To summarise: contractual liability arises either because one of the explicit terms of a contract has been breached - the promise, for example, to meet a specified deadline - or, more probably, because the *implied* obligation to use reasonable skill and care has been breached.

Liability in tort

Tort is the other main area from which liability may arise. Tort is simply lawyers' jargon for "wrong", and the wrong with which this section is concerned is the tort of negligence. The law of negligence is essentially the law of carelessness. It rests upon the assumption that we owe what is called a "duty of care" to those who might be affected by careless actions on our part. If we breach that duty of care in such a way as to cause somebody loss then we may have to provide compensation for that loss. Applied to LIS professionals that means, for example, that if we carelessly supply inaccurate information to someone who suffers loss as a consequence, then we (or more probably our employer) may be liable for damages.

Liability in tort is wider then liability in contract for two reasons. Firstly, there is no requirement of a mutual exchange of promises as there is in contract. So an information provider could, theoretically at least, be sued whether or not it is being paid to provide information. Secondly, in contract, liability is owed only to the parties to the contract. Third parties - people who were not involved in the contract - have no claims. In tort, the duty of care may be owed to a wider range of people.

Liability in tort is not quite as threatening as it may appear. Although theoretically very wide in its scope it is improbable, for public policy reasons, that the judiciary would be likely to apply it enthusiastically against the providers of free information. Even when a duty of care has, theoretically, arisen in a particular case, a court is allowed to consider whether there are circumstances which ought to limit the scope of that duty: a rule applied by Lord Wilberforce, for example, in the House of Lords case of Anns v Merton London Borough Council[2] in 1978. One such consideration might be the crippling effect it would have on voluntary information provision if damages were to be routinely awarded against providers of free information. Such a consideration was a significant factor in the decision in the Australian case of L. Shaddock and Associates v Parramatta City Council[3] in 1979. There, the Council negligently supplied inaccurate information about their development plans to a local builder who sustained losses as a result. They were under no statutory obligation to provide the information and did not charge for it. The court decided the case in favour of the council. One of the reasons for the decision was that an award of damages against the council might have lead to an undesirable restriction on voluntary information services provided for the public. Information professionals would presumably hope that the courts would extend a similar indulgence to them, but there can be no certainty about this. The Court of Appeal for example, maintained in the case of Riley v Tesco Stores Ltd[4] in 1979 that a Citizens' Advice Bureau could owe a duty of care to its users. This was only a subsidiary point in a case predominantly concerned with unfair dismissal, but it shows that there are no grounds for complacency in the information world.

Strict liability or "no fault" liability

In tort or contract an aggrieved client has to show that the information supplier was at fault in some way - that he has broken a contractual term or acted unreasonably. Recently, however, the principle of "no fault" liability has been introduced into this country via E.C legislation. It is almost inconceivable that this will be relevant to information intermediaries. There is, however, a remote possibility that it may affect publishers. This point is, therefore, considered more fully under "Publishers' Liability" later in the chapter.

How strict is the duty of care?

Can you be sued for the slightest lapse from perfection? Or will liability only arise if you make a really drastic error ? Both in contract and tort the answer lies in the word "reasonable". In a famous formulation of the duty of care in tort[5] Lord Atkin said "You must take reasonable care to avoid acts or omissions which you can reasonably foresee would be likely to injure your neighbour". As we have seen, the implied obligation in contract is also to exercise "reasonable skill and care". Usually the standard of reasonableness referred to is that of the average reasonable person - "The man on the Clapham omnibus" as one (sexist and regionalist) formulation has it.

Professionals, however, are judged by a severer standard: that of their fellow practitioners. The question would not be "What would a reasonable person have done in these circumstances" but "What would a reasonable information professional have done in these circumstances". This means, inevitably, that when a question of liability arises the issue of "good professional practice" will be relevant.

How difficult is it to prove liability?

The normal rule of proof in negligence cases is that the plaintiff - the person who claims to have suffered the damage - has to prove her case "on a balance of probabilities". That means the plaintiff has to prove that it was more likely than not that negligence occurred, but does not have to prove it beyond all reasonable doubt. Six years ago a draft EC directive (COM 90 482 final - OJ C12/8, 18 January 1991) proposed a change which would make it easier for a plaintiff to prove liability. Had it been accepted, a plaintiff would merely have to allege negligence, rather than being required to prove it. It would then be up to the service provider to rebut the allegation. As it turned out, the directive was withdrawn under heavy criticism, largely because it was unclear which service providers would fall within its provisions. That is unlikely to be the end of the story though. It would be surprising if it does not resurface in some other guise over the next few years.

HOW NOT TO GET SUED: MINIMISING THE RISK OF LIABILITY

Good practice

Negligence is about carelessness and making mistakes. The best way to avoid being sued for negligence is to avoid making mistakes. This is a counsel of perfection of course but, if you are in a high risk area, it may be wise to adopt procedures for checking, or rigorous codification of working practices of the kind required by BS5750 accreditation, so that you systematically reduce the likelihood of error. It is also essential for staff to keep their subject and technical knowledge up to date. "Reasonableness" is not an immutable standard: in all professions practices which were once perfectly acceptable can become outmoded through developments in technology and knowledge, and persistence in such practices could in itself help a client establish grounds for a negligence action.

Exclusion clauses or disclaimers

This is an area around which a great deal of legend has accumulated. Typically, an exclusion clause consists of a statement - either incorporated in the written record of a contract or notified to the recipients of a service by means of a publicity displayed notice - saying that no responsibility is accepted for certain types of error or failure of performance. A common example is "We accept no liability for losses arising from negligence on our part". The touching faith in the efficacy of such formulae exhibited widely by the information profession is both simplistic and dangerous.

There is both a professional and a legal objection to the use of exclusion clauses of the "We accept no liability for anything" variety. The professional objection is that it seems to make a mockery of the central claims of our profession: we negate the value of what we do by saying we do not adhere to any standards in doing it. The legal objection - a fairly devastating one - lies in Section 2(2) of the Unfair Contract Terms Act 1977 which says that exclusion clauses are subject to a test of "reasonableness". In other words they will not work (they will not be legally effective) unless they are reasonable. One cannot, of course, always anticipate what a court will find reasonable or not reasonable, but it is fairly certain that it would find unreasonable this kind of wide-ranging disclaimer because it negates the central point of the contract.

Recently, the provisions of the Unfair Contract Terms Act have been supplemented by European legislation. The Unfair Terms in Consumer Contract Regulations (SI 1994 No. 3159) brought into force a 1993 European directive and lays down a rule - more general than the provisions of the Unfair Contract Terms Act - that unfair terms should not be binding on consumers. Unfair terms are defined as "...any term which, contrary to the requirements of good faith causes a significant imbalance in the parties' rights and obligations....". It should be noted, however, that the Act applies only to consumers. Business and corporate users of LIS services would not be protected by the regulations.

What kind of exclusion clause could information providers use which might pass the test of reasonableness? There are a number of possible exclusion clauses listed in Table 1. The first is a clause excluding liability for errors in sources used. This would seem to have a fair chance of success. It would clearly be unreasonable, for example, if every item of financial information derived from Jordan's or Dun & Bradstreet had to be independently verified. The second is a point which is obvious and reasonable to information providers - that we cannot guarantee to find all relevant information on a particular subject - but is not always apparent to some of our customers who may attribute a greater degree of infallibility to our magic devices than we ourselves do.

The last example given is a clause preventing liability to third parties - that is to those who are not themselves parties to the original contract. It may be that the information provided to a client is passed on to a third party and that the third party suffers loss as a result of its inaccuracy. Though the third party cannot sue in contract, because they were not party to the contract, they may have a claim in tort. It seems prudent to at least try to stop this liability arising in the first place by stating that the information is provided only for the use of the direct client.

Insurance

Exclusion clauses, then, have to be used judiciously. Even then the protection they afford may be partial and uncertain. Insurance is a more reliable method of protection against the consequences of liability and is much more widely used by information providers. It is a mistake to imagine, however, that no thought need be given to it. An insurance company needs a full and accurate picture of activities and the types of claim that may be brought against any company it is ensuring. If there are inaccuracies in the proposal form which forms the basis of the contract between a company and its insurers, or if key facts about its operations have been omitted, then the insurance company may, in certain circumstances, repudiate the contract. That is, it could refuse to pay out.

PUBLISHERS' LIABILITY

The legal risks run by the primary producers of information - publishers and database suppliers - are greater than those run by intermediaries. The two categories are not mutually exclusive. In the age of desktop publishing and the Internet we are almost all publishers.

At this point the likelihood of liability leaps several orders of magnitude. Although there are, as yet, no directly relevant English cases, there are enough American and European cases to give grave cause for concern. In Saloomey v Jeppesen[6], a United States case, the publishers of an aircraft navigation chart were found liable for a mistake in one of their charts which led to a plane crash. In Gribinsky v Nathan[7], the publishers and the author of a book on wild fruits and vegetables were found liable when a user of the book died because the book failed to distinguish sufficiently between the edible wild carrot and the inedible, indeed poisonous, hemlock. Perhaps the most important case from our point of view concerns a name with which we are all familiar. In Greenmoss Builders v Dun and Bradstreet[8], Greenmoss successfully sued Dun and Bradstreet because they mistakenly told Greenmoss's bankers, with whom Greenmoss were negotiating a loan, that Greenmoss had filed for voluntary liquidation.

So it is clear that if you become an information provider you run a definite risk of incurring liability, though in the cases described above the negligence (carelessness) of the service provider had to be proved. This is worrying, but not as worrying as a recent line of argument that information providers might be subject to the principle of "no fault" liability or "strict liability" as it is more commonly known. Under strict liability an aggrieved client merely has to show that he suffered damage from a defective product. He does not have to show that the manufacturer acted unreasonably or that the defect was the manufacturer's fault. "No fault" liability is quite common in the United States and an EC directive of July 1985[9] is gradually bringing it into effect in EC member states. It became part of UK law with the passing of the Consumer Protection Act in 1987.

Whether information provision is covered by the Consumer Protection Act largely turns upon whether information is regarded as a product or a service. The CPA generally covers tangible, physical products and the damage that may result if those products malfunction in some ways. While books and CDs are physical and tangible, any damage which results from them is likely to be because of the intangible, non-physical information they convey, and not a consequence of their physical makeup. It therefore seems improbable to the author that they would come within the scope of the Act. Other views, however, have been advanced on this subject.

CONCLUSION: WHAT IS THE LIKELIHOOD OF LIABILITY ARISING?

The likelihood of an information professional incurring liability is still limited. Even in America, which spends an astonishing 3% of its GDP on legal actions, there have not yet been cases of LIS professionals working as information intermediaries being sued for negligence or breach of contract. Other areas faced by the information professional are probably still more fertile sources of legal trouble: copyright, data protection, and the legal areas of employment, occupiers' liability and health and safety which any employer has to be aware of. It is also worth remembering that an individual employee is unlikely to be personally sued for negligence. It is far more likely that the employer - who is jointly liable for negligent acts committed in the course of the employee's duties - will face legal action. Not that this offers much comfort to the employer.

However, as the section above demonstrates, liability for publishers is a reality, and the hitherto clear boundary between publishers and LIS professionals is rapidly being eroded by the ease with which original information can be disseminated. Nor should the absence of case law for information intermediaries be regarded as a guarantee of future safety. Commercial information provision, by the standards of the ancient professions, is still a relatively small and comparatively new sector. As more organisations come to rely upon market and environmental information the risks will grow. Here is a series of questions about your activities:

- Do you provide information for money? Do you aim at profit?
- Do you provide specialised - e.g. medical - information to a professional group?
- Do you supply information which, if inaccurate, could cause physical injury?
- Do you know that the information you supply is likely to be relied on to make important decisions?
- Are you beginning to publish information, as opposed to merely mediating information published by someone else?

If you answered "yes" to one or more of these questions you should consider adopting some of the preventive measures outlined above. Bear in mind that a general article such as this cannot provide solutions to individual legal problems. This chapter may form a useful starting point in your deliberations about liability and how to protect yourself from it, but there is no substitute for advice about your particular circumstances from a qualified practitioner.

REFERENCES

1. Vacwell Engineering Co Ltd v BDH Chemicals (1969) [1971] QB 88, [1969] 32.All ER 1681.

2. Anns v Merton London Borough Council [1978]AC 728, [1977] 2 All ER 492.

3. L. Shaddock and Associates Pty Ltd v Parrammatta City Council [1979] 1 NSWLR 566.

4. Riley v Tesco Stores Ltd [1980] ICR 323, [1980] IRLR 103, CA.

5. Donoghue v Stevenson [1932] AC 562, [1932] All ER Rep 1.

6. Saloomey v Jeppesen & Co. 707 F.2d 671 (1983).

7. Gribinsky v Nathan (T.G.I,1er, 28/5/1986, p1987,1R,3R).

8. Dun & Bradstreet Inc v Greenmoss Builders Inc. 472 US 749 (1985).

9. 85/374/EEC, 25 July 1985.

Managing People

Susan Hill

INTRODUCTION

There are so many books written on management. They cover every aspect from self management and motivation, through project and function management, to team and people management. These can be in the style of the "One, Two or even Five Minute Manager", through to the much more serious, in-depth view of management by the current flavour of the month management guru. Some of these are aimed at the special library and information market. In any general library and information journal there is likely to be at least one article addressing a specific issue of management. Some journals are dedicated to the subject (such as *Library Administration and Management)*.

Beryl Morris of Hudson Rivers, Management and Training Consultants, has written a review chapter of the literature of staff management published in 1996 for *Librarianship and Information Work World-wide*[1]. I recommend this review as a good starting point to further reading for any library and information manager, for either newly appointed staff or experienced practitioners. It covers literature published in the English speaking world in 1996, predominately Great Britain and North America, with some Asian and Australasian influence and input.

Equally, there are many courses offered on all aspects of management. General management courses are run by specialist centres such as Ashridge Management College, Henley Management College, and any one of the business schools. Other providers are the professional associations such as the Institute of Personnel Development, the Industrial Society and those more specifically addressing the special library and information sector. These include open courses run by library and information training specialist companies and associations (such as Aslib, the Library Association and TFPL) and inhouse or tailored courses from library and information training consultancies (for example Hudson Rivers or the Burrington Partnership).

Many of these courses are dedicated to people management while others cover just an element of this as part of a wider brief. A calendar of training events is usually available either from the organisations mentioned, or appears in the many specialist information and librarianship journals. It is important that you develop a good awareness of what courses are available, and through networking find out which ones might be effective in your specific circumstances.

The intention of this chapter is to highlight some of the issues of people management that arise with both candidate and clients, as seen through the everyday work of a recruitment consultant. Our candidates can be either managers or people being managed, whereas our clients are more likely to be library and information managers or human resource departments. Those issues that are important enough to lead to a decision to change jobs are regularly highlighted when we talk to new candidates and take new jobs from our clients. Given the space constraints of a single chapter one could not hope to do justice to the complete subject of people management. It is important to make the time and provide the effort to continue your own professional and personal development by exploring the subject further. Ideally this should take the form of reading and practical instruction. Reading a book such as this is a good start.

SEEING THE GALAXY OR SEEING THE ATOM?

The ultimate responsibility of a manager is to drive their department (or company) forward and to ensure that the right people, tools, environment and support are in place for effective progress to be made. High on the list of priorities should therefore be effective people management resulting in optimum effort and output from all staff.

The way in which people are managed very much affects their working lives, from the first day of work, throughout their career until the day they retire. It can also reflect on the private life of the individual. Just as a manager often feels there is room for improvement in the individuals or teams working to them, so too do individuals feel that the way in which they are managed could be improved. When this is not addressed in a satisfactory way it is a frequent reason given for wanting a job change. A little like the cry "my wife/husband doesn't understand me", except that we hear something like "my manager doesn't understand me." Interestingly the reverse is rare "my staff don't understand me!" All too often if someone is unhappy at work it tends to overflow into their private life.

In the confidential atmosphere of the one-to-one interview (recruitment consultant and candidate) many of the issues of both good and bad management are aired. Continual professional networking, often with senior managers from the special library and information sector, includes discussion of current people management issues and ideas. I shall outline the most predominant issues, the ones that I feel have the most effect on the working life of the individual, but first a visit to the dictionary.

Management: The art, manner, or practice of management.

- Executive ability
- Administration
- Skill in contriving, handling etc
- The art of acting or managing
- Manner of directing or of using anything
- Skilful treatment.

Manager: One who controls or directs.

- One who organises other people's doings.

Just a selection of some of the 'interesting' dictionary definitions to be found and in my view, particularly in this day and age, not all are accurate. A management consultant would describe a manager as someone who makes things happen.

I have often said that a good and successful information specialist needs to be a delicately balanced combination of communicator, salesperson, negotiator, diplomat, technologist, politician, to have an endless supply of information, initiative and knowledge, coupled with business, management and administration skills.

With some tweaking this could be altered to produce a good definition or a useful memorandum for a manager, to read: "a good and successful information people manager needs to be a delicately balanced combination of communicator, salesperson, negotiator, diplomat, technologist, politician, to have an endless supply of information, initiative and knowledge, coupled with business, management and administration skills, a sprinkling of enthusiasm and understanding of individuals and the desire to empower them for their futures and the future of the organisation."

THE BENEFITS OF BEING A GOOD PEOPLE MANAGER

The special library and information service is an excellent environment in which to be a manager. There is little, if any, emphasis on rigid hierarchies or bureaucracy. The challenge of management can range from a one person unit, with some part-time or non-professional assistance, to that of a large department with team members of all levels, and a mix of skills and job functions. For some library and information managers with ambitions above and beyond the library and information world, it can provide the first steps into a broader management role within a company.

Whichever type or level of people management you are embarking on, it is sound practice to work on the principle that managing people should mean encouraging and empowering them to produce their best. In other words giving and getting the best from people, and at the same time also giving and getting the best from yourself. This is by far the most positive aspect of managing. Seeing the individual grow and develop features prominently in the list of rewarding aspects of management of every manager I know.

THE ISSUES AFFECTING PEOPLE MANAGERS

Some of the major issues facing people managers in the special library and information sector today are change management, technological development and time pressures. These all have a tremendous impact on the individual manager and team. So too do financial resources. The major issues that affect the individual being managed are more likely to be communication, motivation and professional and personal development. A manager who is decisive, consistent and yet flexible, who can provide a sound framework in which the individual can progress and experiment, who encourages people to face challenges and extend their boundaries by inspiring confidence and encouragement can create a powerful and motivated team. Above all, an effective manager respects people as individuals and realises that they are also often busy and under pressure.

MANAGING CHANGE

This decade was originally dubbed "the caring nineties" but the recession and the escalation of the pace of technological change has meant that the predominant issue for managers and the individual has been managing change. Managing turbulent change is a key issue for senior people working in or with organisations today. As John Harvey Jones has said: "Without question, the most desirable management skill for the nineties will be the ability to manage change. This is one of the rarest and most difficult skills to learn."[2]

Whether we are management or staff, how we view these changes and challenges very much affects the way in which we deal with them. We need to learn to live effectively with continual change - to constantly reassess ourselves, our skills and our jobs. Quite simply, if we fear change, find it threatening or fail to cope with it then we (individuals, teams or departments) could sink, without trace. People fear change, and therefore may resist it, because they see it as a threat, either to their job, their status, sometimes their earnings, and even to the loss of familiar surroundings. Above all they may be afraid that they will be unable to cope with the different conditions, working practices or the inevitable reorganisation that change will bring.

It makes sense to plan changes and the resultant effects as far in advance as possible. It is essential to outline and explain the need for the changes and to consult those who will be affected. This consultation can provide valuable input on factors you may have overlooked, and will give the individual a chance to appraise you of their anxieties (and the reasons for them) while allowing you to take them into account in your planning.

Winning their consent and understanding in advance of, and throughout, the periods of change, will provide powerful, positive motivation for everyone concerned. Where possible, provide specific detail and instruction in writing. Remember too that debriefing is a valuable follow-on to change. It may be that further changes and adjustments will need to be made to the newly introduced working practices and systems.

RECRUITMENT AND SELECTION

Selecting the right people is vital for good management. Selecting the right people is as important when recruiting temporary and contract team members as it is for permanent staff. The roots of this start in the thinking through and production of a good sound job description and personal specification. These are not legally required in the UK (although a job title is), but they do provide a solid basis for successful, effective recruitment. They give you a chance to sell the opportunity and potential of the job to individuals and provide a part of the framework for the interviewing and selection process in conjunction with the candidate's own CV. Choosing individuals with the right personality and fit for the job and company is also essential. Ultimately you can give people technical skills or enhance existing ones. If they have enthusiasm, intelligence, and a desire to continually develop, then you can train them.

You need people who see the rapid changes in the special library and information sector as a positive challenge. People who will be able to cope with the fact that resources now change all the time. New products and services are constantly being developed and introduced into the market, some successfully, some not. New approaches to information delivery are being continually embraced, particularly with the development of the company intranet. You want to be sure that your team members see that the changes brought about by information technology are challenges, not threats. A positive approach is partly dependent on the personalities of your staff and partly down to the way you manage your department.

The recruitment process will depend on your company procedure. However, in the special library and information sector this is usually the responsibility of the manager of the department. If you have not recruited before, then make sure that you use the facilities and backup provided by your human resources or personnel department. If there is not one, and you are using a recruitment agency, then take advantage of their expert knowledge and help. Most agencies that specialise in this sector will provide you with a ready made short-list of pre-interviewed candidates, provided that you have filled your part of the bargain and put together an appropriate job description and specification.

When you plan your first budget, try to include some external recruitment and selection training for yourself, if this is a new area to you. At the very least, ensure that you are familiar not just with current legislation, but also with company policies. For example, you would not want to unwittingly break any discriminatory laws, and perhaps your company has a policy of positive age discrimination - seeing the value in the 50 plus candidate.

Now that you have recruited good staff, how do you keep them motivated and ensure that they perform to their best effect?

KEEPING THE RIGHT PEOPLE

Training, learning and continued professional development

A point that I have made since the mid-1980s, when first asked to talk about skills in the library and information sector, is that good people are the most valuable asset you have. Ongoing education and training are very real necessities and ignoring this is a false economy.

A fear that many managers have, is that if they invest in training in new developments and systems, their staff will then leave for better paid jobs. This is not necessarily true, and even if it is, it is an acceptable risk to take. You need to keep people motivated and one of the best ways to do this is to give them pride in what they can do. Training should never be seen as something you only get when you have a problem that needs correcting. It should be an open door leading to new skills and abilities. A good external training course currently costs in the region of £200-£350 per day per person. Ideally you should try and budget £1,000-£1,500 per staff member per annum (three or four man days of training). If this is not possible, do not lose heart. Use your lateral thinking skills to devise other ways of ensuring your staff are fully conversant with new skills and technologies. Many product and service providers provide 'free' training in the form of updates or via their approach to customer services. Take advantage of this, plan such sessions into your training schedules. Inhouse courses, tailored to meet the specific functions and requirements of your department, can have a much lower cost per head and have the benefit of simultaneously updating the skills of all or a good proportion of the team.

Before you choose training courses it is very useful to set good objectives, in writing. Start by identifying (or auditing) the skills of individuals within the department. Then establish a written list of skills in short supply and who would best benefit from training in specific essential skills. You can then use this list as a basis for planning training. Then establish a procedure for monitoring the training and its usefulness to the individual and/or department. This helps you to decide whether to use that particular method or provider of training in the future and whether the time and effort invested has had benefit to both the department and the individual. Sit down with each team member and explain to them what you expect them to get from the training, and ask them what they hope to achieve. To avoid any disappointment do make sure that you both have the same, or very similar, objectives.

The benefits of good induction training should never be overlooked. In larger organisations this is often addressed on a company-wide basis. Whilst you want to get your new team member working effectively from day one, if they are to be really productive they will need to know as much as possible about the organisation and its ways of working. This should be backed up with departmental induction providing a sound introduction to the purpose, procedures and functions of the department.

An extended form of induction could take the form of mentoring, by experienced and capable individuals or perhaps work shadowing. Along with this can come one-to-one instruction of the individual by an appropriate person. This could be you, the manager, or a team member who is a particular specialist or expert in this area.

IDENTIFYING TRAINING NEEDS

There are different ways in which you can identify the training needs of individuals in your department

- Through appraisals and performance reviews
- Noting errors or shortcomings
- Introduction of new technologies
- Asking individuals if there is specific training that they feel would help them
- Changes in procedures, or perhaps legislation

- Keeping aware of current issues in information work (i.e. copyright)
- Changes to job responsibilities or staffing levels.

Evaluating the impact and usefulness of training will comprise a number of aspects:

- Was the level right? If not: did you choose the wrong level or was it incorrectly promoted?
- Was it clear and structured and backed by good course notes?
- Did the individual enjoy it and come away with a positive feeling?
- Given sufficient elapsed time, has the individual been able to implement the practical aspects?
- Again with time, has their behaviour or approach to work been noticeably different?

Remember that sometimes training is not necessarily just about learning new things. It can also mean having the skills and abilities that have been learned informally (through professional participation and development) reinforced in a formal way. It can also be vital for updating and broadening existing skills. Coming away from a course feeling confident that the things you have been doing are appropriate and effective can be more powerful or beneficial than coming away having learned too many new things.

There are many different ways in which you can implement training, and it need not necessarily be through external courses. The larger your department or company, then the more potential trainers you have. Do not overlook skilled individuals within your department. They may not have given training courses before, but with some help from you (or another suitably qualified individual) they could put together a half-day course which would be of benefit to others in the department as well as enhancing their own skills.

REAP THE BENEFITS OF KEEPING THE RIGHT PEOPLE

Continuing professional development

The provision of flexible learning, distance learning and open learning courses by the many institutions involved in the provision of library and information training is a boon to continuing professional development. Along with these, there are the many specific professional meetings run by associations and their special interest groups (such as IIS, CIG, AIOPI, AAL, ICLG, CoSL, UKOLUG: see list of organisations at the end of this chapter). The IIS runs regular evening courses aimed at providing professional development and their Southern Branch has an evening meeting each month (as does ICLG) with an informed speaker providing an introduction, update or expanding on a current hot topic. CIG has six to eight evening meetings on a specific theme or topic each year, and four social events that allow informal networking and information interchange. Encouraging your team to belong to these organisations and circulating details of these meetings (and hopefully being in a position to pay or subsidise payment of their subscriptions to these associations and groups and/or attendance at the meetings) can bring benefits to the whole team.

The Continuing Professional Development Framework, introduced by the Library Association in 1993 encourages individuals to take responsibility for their own personal and professional development. It is particularly useful to encourage the habit of recording and analysing work and training. S/NVQs could also be looked at as a route to further development for some team members.

There are nearly 20 library and information schools in Great Britain and Eire. They constantly reassess their educational programmes and nearly all now offer distance and modular learning programmes. Some of the courses being developed are extremely interesting and can enable your staff (and you) to keep ahead of the times. Many other institutions offer distance learning that could be relevant to the work of the modern information professional. Encourage your staff to take charge of their own professional development and investigate the possibilities that these courses may hold for them.

PERFORMANCE MANAGEMENT FOR THE TEAM AND INDIVIDUAL

Appraisals

As a manager, you must budget 'time' into your people management schedule. Time for the team, and time for the individual. Hopefully your organisation has an appraisals system well established. In most organisations this is a once per year exercise. It should be taken as an opportunity to discuss an individual's requirements and development without any censure on your part. It is vital that you encourage a very open and positive approach to the appraisal, not one of fear.

Some managers in the library and information sector, feel that the effects on staff of the rapidly changing technology make six-monthly appraisals more appropriate. It may be that these are backed up with monthly meetings with individuals. It is no good laying out a plan of development and work for the individual and then addressing the issues only once a year, particularly if development is not proceeding as either of you envisaged. Appraisals are not the place for addressing 'big' problems either. Faster, more specific action is vital in those circumstances. Appraisals are a very effective way to highlight the minor issues (on both sides) and to provide an opportunity to work to a positive solution.

Developing good working relations through appraisals and team meetings will often encourage individuals who see a problem or an issue developing in the department, to tell you about it. This can give you the opportunity to deal with the issue fast and effectively. Such open communication should be encouraged, but care should be taken not to 'name names' or develop favourites.

TEAM MEETINGS

One of the things that I have found most invaluable as a manager, and as a team member, is a regular forum for ideas and information interchange. This forum can also be used to give and receive project updates, to give guidance and advice, whilst distancing yourself and leaving the authority where it is invested - in your team.

The need may not be so obvious when there are just two in the department. If you work in close physical proximity then much of what is happening is seen and overheard. However, too often the time pressures, the phone, and other urgent interventions can take away the opportunity for the two of you to interact (such as days when you are barely able to even finish a sentence). Make time for interaction and communication, such as once a month outside the office, or at least locked in a room for 30 minutes with no interruptions. If that habit is developed early on in your people management strategy, then you will find it so much easier when you have a bigger team.

In a larger department, you will find that the more junior or less confident team members may not possess the confidence to contribute to these meetings. Do not make the mistake of allowing such meetings to be dominated by more senior or confident team members. Often younger, newer graduates are more up-to-date in certain developments and can make valuable contributions. The seemingly quiet member may be a thinker, one who needs time to think through an issue and formulate their answers. Develop a strategy where you ask each team member in turn for their contribution. Open questions can be just as effective in this situation as in an interview. "What is your opinion about product X?" will elicit a more confident response than a question that requires a "yes/no" or "I like it/I don't like it" answer. A positive response to their contribution ("that's a good point, I hadn't thought of that") will encourage them and increase their confidence. By all means start the proceedings, but don't hog the limelight. If an individual fails to produce at these meetings or is always beaten to the ideas and suggestions by the others then remember that and ask them first next time. You will need to address the issue if this doesn't work. Perhaps work with them outside of the meetings to help them develop their communication skills. For some the fear of speaking up in front of colleagues can be all pervading. Once dealt with it will be a good experience for both of you.

Asking a team member to give a brief (five or ten minutes) presentation on a training course, evening meeting (or other professional development event that they attended) can have two benefits. Providing them with a chance to practise presentation skills, while at the same time informing other team members of a new or interesting development in the special library and information world. It can also help you, the manager, assess the usefulness of the course or meeting and make a decision on whether to continue exploring this subject.

One of the benefits of voicemail is that it can allow you to take the necessary 30 minutes out for such meetings, without imposing a burden on others to take messages. Think about a social team meeting once in a while as well. If alcohol is not banned within the building, perhaps a wine tasting one Thursday or Friday at 5.00 or 6.00pm. Why not invite the team for coffee and croissants at a starting time 30 minutes earlier than usual? Alternatively offer them breakfast, before work, in a nearby café. They will grumble, but they will all be there for 8.00am.

Keeping the team aware of what is going on both inside the department and the company as a whole, is vital. You should take care to ensure that negative or potentially worrying news is handled sensitively and with care. However, even in difficult times, honesty and reassurance are vital. One information manager told me that she was always able to keep her team abreast of developments within the organisation as a whole and used the weekly and monthly team meetings to do so. When I said how impressed I was with the open communication within her organisation, she laughed and said that the only reason she could do it so effectively was because her department was the focal point for receipt of the external press clippings service. Her lateral thinking had allowed her to use this vital resource to keep her team informed, and also to ensure that the information department was seen by others in the organisation as the place to go for internal news and information.

MOTIVATION

Why motivate your staff? Think of those days when you feel an energy coming from within, an enthusiasm, and positive forward motion. When you are certain that you can and will do what needs to be done to achieve a result. Did you think you were just having a good day? Most likely you were well motivated. Creative energy seems to flow particularly well when one is positively motivated.

Motivated people are much more likely to achieve personal, departmental or corporate targets, and achieving those targets or goals will further motivate individuals. Motivated people take less time out. Your users will benefit from the positive atmosphere that well motivated people create around them. Their energy, enthusiasm and confidence created by their positive motivation will enable them to cope better and accommodate change. They will also work better within the team and with their colleagues. Undoubtedly more work will be achieved and better quality work at that. Poorly motivated people will show apathy and indifference to their work, probably accompanied by bad time-keeping, a lack of co-operation in the work environment and inevitably resistance to change.

To maintain a good level of motivation among your staff, it is important to keep the lines of communication open. Listening skills are important but it is also important to observe moods, flows, cycles and even body language. Your own enthusiasm will be transmitted as much through your body and mood language as through your actions and words. It may be that some of the things that affect motivation may be outside your control (most likely salaries, general terms and conditions of employment) but showing the individual that you recognise their efforts, giving them responsibility and challenging work, whilst maintaining good communication with the individual or team will keep them well motivated. The way in which you motivate you staff will depend on the size of the department and the number and levels of people that you manage.

Junior, inexperienced staff will require different strategies to senior, experienced people. Be aware of, and acknowledge, the sometimes menial attributes of their job, but give them deadlines and targets and be firm with them. Ensure that they are made aware of the importance of their role in the grander scale of things.

THE TEAM

Equally as important is knowing your team. The strengths and weaknesses of each individual. This in an ideal world would be a changing scenario with different aspects of an individual's strengths and skills coming into play at different times. You do need to remember that you are the 'boss', so although you may feel strongly that you are very friendly with individuals your ultimate relationship should be that of boss and subordinate, and undoubtedly they will see their relationship with you in the same way.

You will find it useful to establish some knowledge of the different private lives and potential effect these have on office life. On the personal development front, a skills audit within your department can bring surprising benefits. This can be incorporated into the appraisal routines, or made the subject of the regular team meetings. The idea here is not just to identify who can search which databases, design an intranet and speak fluent Greek, but to find seemingly non-relevant skills, or professional skills that extend beyond the current job and department requirements. These skills may be useful at some stage in the future. These might be artistic, design, marketing, or similar skills. It is up to you to elicit the skill, identify it and calculate its potential for the department.

THE PERSONAL ISSUES

You may not want to be an agony aunt, but in most offices, this is often necessary. The personal lives of your team can impact on their working lives. There is an etiquette to dealing effectively with bereavement or terminal illness of near and dear ones and difficult though it may be the effort is very much appreciated. This can have a positive effect on helping the individual at a very difficult time. Some organisations are now implementing company wide bereavement policies which can include the services of trained counsellors. Check what your organisation is prepared or able to do.

Other issues may need careful thought on your behalf as to how involved you wish to become. In my time as a manager, I have counselled on bereavement, separation and divorce, and most traumatic of all (for me) ensured that a very inexperienced and naïve 18 year old, pregnant but far too afraid to tell her mother, received appropriate and independent advice on all sides of the adoption versus abortion issue. A completely different and yet equally difficult case arose recently for a fellow manager when he had to deal with the effect of a substantial lottery win on the work of a key team member.

REMUNERATION

Surprisingly, remuneration is not such a big issue. This is more likely to apply to longer serving team members and you will need some creative approaches to prevent problems arising. Any new recruits will have accepted the job for what it offered them in terms of potential satisfaction and development. They will have thought through the money issues. Occasionally frustration will arise when the team members look outside the department at the pay scales of others in the organisation. This is especially difficult in the financial services sector, where other company employees appear to receive as much in an annual bonus as an information specialist might earn in five years.

Most people will make comparisons with their peers in another organisation, friends in the same types of jobs, or advertisements.

To many people, recognition of a job well done, or a promotion (such as a grading change within the organisation) is as important as the salary earned. As a manager you should always be aware of current salaries in the sector. Contributing to salary surveys is one way of keeping abreast, another way is to contact a recruitment consultant who specialises in the sector.

TIME MANAGEMENT/DELEGATION

As a manager I find it easy to promote the values of time management, but like many busy managers I often fail with my own time management. Delegation is a difficult art, but for many staff, being given a responsibility (either as a task or a permanent addition to their job description can be a joy). You should be sure in your own mind that the work is delegated for positive reasons, and that you use the time that is created effectively. It is vital that you, as the manager, find time to address the issues of people management, to do your creative and developmental thinking, so think about it next time you have a busy week, a full in tray and nowhere near enough hours in the day - do it, dump it or delegate it!

So many of the things I have mentioned link in with each other and have a knock on effect. Well prescribed job descriptions and person specifications enable you to recruit better staff. Good, skilled staff, with the right motivation achieve well defined targets, strive to further develop their skills and knowledge, and carry departments, and therefore companies, forward.

Take the time to get it right. Our working life could last from the early 20s to the early 60s, about 40 years. In each 24 hours, up to eight will be spent asleep and an average of 10 in preparing for, travelling to, or at work. Over 60% of our waking hours are in some way work related. Is it too simplistic or idealistic to aim for a good proportion of this time to be uplifting and giving satisfaction?

How can we achieve that for ourselves - and for our staff?

- Recruit suitable people
- Ensure the individual is aware of what is expected from them
- See that they understand their key responsibilities

- Keep them well trained and motivated
- Give regular feedback on performance
- Praise/reprimand when appropriate
- Be aware of the effects of change
- Keep up-to-date with information as well as people management developments
- Take time to enjoy the benefits.

As a manager you become a dual professional. Not only do you owe it to yourself and your team to keep abreast of developments in the information and special library sector, but you must also familiarise yourself with personnel management issues. Those of your company and those where knowledge is required by law.

At the beginning of this chapter, I mentioned the many books, courses and articles on the various aspects of management. I did not set out to read and regurgitate other people's (often very good) ideas. You are an information person, you can find those books, articles and courses and dip into the ones that have relevance and appeal. Chances are that no one book will address your needs perfectly. Work on the principle that if you learn one new thing, then it has been a good day. Whatever facet you have decided to adopt, incorporate it into your working practice and tailor it to be effective in your situation. It will take time - persevere.

People management, when well planned, is one of the most enjoyable aspects of management. Treat your people as you would a garden. With constant care and attention and nurturing. The reward will be to see the individual grow and blossom and others look at you with impressed envy, in turn providing them with the motivation to do the same in their 'garden' when their time comes. Every manager that I speak to will always mention that seeing and being able to influence the growth and development of their team is the single most rewarding aspect of managing people.

REFERENCES

1. Librarianship and Information Work World-wide, 1996, Bowker Saur, London (1997).
2. Jones, John Harvey, *Managing to survive* (Library Administration and Management).

ORGANISATIONS

AAL (Association of Assistant Librarians),

c/o Rosie Mercer, Curlough House, Caledon, Co. Tyrone, BT68 4XP. Tel: 01232 240503 Fax: 01232 231907

AIOPI (Association of Information Officers in the Pharmaceutical Industry),

c/o Janet Davies, Director of Medical Services, Bristol-Myers Squibb Pharmaceuticals Ltd, 141-149 Staines Road, Hounslow, Middx, TW3 3J. Tel: 0181 572 7422 Fax: 0181 572 7370

Aslib, The Association for Information Management,

Staple Hall, Stone House Court, London, EC3A 7PB. Tel: 0171 903 0000 Fax: 0171 903 0011

Ashridge Management College,

Berkhamsted, Herts, HP4 1NS. Tel: 01442 843491 Fax: 01442 841209

Burrington Partnership,

33 Green Courts, Green Walk, Bowden, Altrincham, Cheshire, WA14 2SR. Tel/Fax: 0161 928 6240

CIG (City Information Group),

PO Box 13297, London, E1 9TY. Tel/Fax: 0171 702 2121

CSL (Circle of State Librarians)

Honorary Secretary, c/o Prison Service HQ Library, Room 224, Abell House, John Islip Street, London, SW1P 4LH. Tel: 0171 217 5253 Fax: 0171 217 5209

Henley Management College

Greenlands, Henley-on-Thames, Oxfordshire, RG9 3AU. Tel: 01491 571454 Fax 01491 571635

Hudson Rivers Management and Training Consultants,

    13 Arlington Road, Woodford Green, Essex IG8 9DE. Tel/Fax: 0181 505 9453

ICLG (Industrial and Commercial Libraries Group),

    c/o Elizabeth Dwiar, Theodore Goddard, 150 Aldersgate Street, London, EC1A 4EJ.

IPD (Institute of Personnel and Development),

    IPD House, Camp Road, Wimbledon, SW19 4UX. Tel: 0181 971 9000 Fax: 0181 263 3333

IIS (Institute of Information Scientists),

    44-45 Museum Street, London WC1A 1LY. Tel: 0171 831 8003/ 8633 Fax: 0171 430 1270

Library Association,

    7 Ridgemount Street, London, WC1E 7AE. Tel: 0171 636 7543 Fax: 0171 436 7218

TFPL Training,

    17-18 Britton Street, London EC1M 5NQ. Tel: 0171 251 5522 Fax: 0171 251 8318

UKOLUG (UK On-line Users Group),

    c/o Christine Baker, The Old Chapel, Walden, West Burton, Leyburn, North Yorkshire, DL8 4LE. Tel: 01969 663749

Marketing the Information Service

Bridget Batchelor

"Marketing is 90% common sense."

I particularly like this definition of what over the years has been set up by its practitioners as a pseudo-science, full of its own jargon and requiring experts to do it. Certainly, the marketeers managing a major brand such as Dulux paint have big budgets and a lot of responsibility for maintaining the integrity of the brand. They need analytical structures and recognised marketing techniques. But for those of us simply concerned with ensuring that our customers' needs are met effectively by our product or service (rather than someone else's), common sense is the main talent required.

The ability to do jigsaws is also useful. There are a number of interlocking facets which together make up effective marketing, and fitting them together into the right pattern for your library, at this time, with this budget and these resources takes a certain amount of careful thought and creativity.

Marketing is also fun. It appeals to those who are analytical, working with market research data to draw up well-supported plans for how to satisfy customers' needs. It also allows creative souls to generate ideas for different ways of attracting customers, or informing them how good our service is.

Finally, marketing is about survival. As my colleague Helen Coote (author of Aslib's Know How Guide on marketing[1]) is wont to say "No marketing, no customers, no library – so no job".

There are three iterative stages in marketing a special library service. These stages are marketing strategy, service delivery and implementation of the marketing plan. You will see that I do not include selling (and one or two other activities which you will find in a classic text-book on marketing). That is because I am only going to cover those activities about which the manager of a special library needs to know in order to do some effective marketing among all the other duties.

STRATEGY

Many people start marketing by thinking about promotion. This is a fundamental error, because promotion cannot be effective unless you have thought through who are the targets for your brochure or newsletter, and what message you want to put over. Having a strategy is therefore a crucial activity for any marketing person. Let me say *straightaway* that I am not talking about fat tomes of analysis which languish on the shelf unread. Efficient marketing planning means understanding your marketplace in sufficient detail to draw up an action list of what you are going to do within a defined time period to match your service to your customers' needs and expectations within your objectives (and budget).

Ideally, your objectives should be related to what you want to achieve in the marketplace, for example to increase the number of customers from a specified part of your organisation, or improve the response time by X% (if customer surveys have shown this to be necessary). Objectives which are introspective – such as to reduce the cataloguing backlog to X weeks – are not helpful to the marketing effort, since they are not related directly to users' needs. All objectives should be SMART – Simple, Measurable, Achievable, Realistic and with a Timescale.

In the old days, people supplied what they produced or stocked, and the customer had to lump it. This attitude is summed up in the famous story about Henry Ford offering to supply any colour of car as long as it was black. Nowadays the motto is "Have what will sell, not sell what you have." What will sell is what the customer wants and/or needs. There is a difference, as all the librarians I have worked with instinctively understand from their experience of reference interviews. An enquiry which runs along the lines "Where do I find information about Mongolia?" is an expressed *want*. The enquirer's *need* could be for information on anything from the climate to the number of yaks exported per year.

Users

You need to understand three things about your users. Firstly, their information needs: this covers not only the subject matter of enquiries, but also issues such as the timing of particular types of enquiry (are some sorts of information more in demand at business-planning time, for example), or the need to keep readily available data going back over a number of years. From this will flow decisions about the nature and size of the stock, the way it is made available, access, opening hours – anything which relates to the service you offer.

But not all users have the same needs. People work different hours, they do different jobs, need different types of information, are comfortable with different types of output. The first marketing planning exercise is therefore to break down your customer base into *segments*. A segment is a group of users who have a number of needs and characteristics in common which are meaningful for your service. For example, you could segment your users by their leisure pursuits (providing you had the information to do so). This is in principle a perfectly valid segmentation, but unless you are going to stock a range of sports journals for use at lunchtime, it would not be useful to you. It would not tell you anything about your users which will enable you to provide a service more effectively tailored to their information needs at work.

The classic ways of segmenting the market are

- Geographic, i.e. region, urban/rural
- Demographic, e.g. age, occupation, nationality, religion
- Psychographic, e.g. social class, personality type
- Behavioural, e.g. product usage (light, heavy), brand loyalty (none, high).

These examples are taken from Fast Moving Consumer Goods (FMCG) marketing, which is where the bulk of marketing theory originates. But it is not difficult to translate them into special library terms. For example:

- Geographic – those in different buildings or locations
- Demographic – function, discipline, speaking a different language
- Psychographic – level of management, knows their mind/ditherer
- Behavioural – service usage, access (personal caller or user of telephone/fax/e-mail), browser or focussed searcher.

Segmentation enables you to provide different people with a service which fits their needs as closely as possible, thus increasing the likelihood of them becoming regular users.

Example

> The newly-appointed librarian of CAD Partnership, a multi-disciplinary construction consultancy with five UK offices, one in Berlin and one in Hong Kong has segmented her market primarily by discipline (architect, civil engineer, quantity surveyor etc), location and market sector (e.g. public sector, commercial, hotels and leisure). The majority of enquiries are made by telephone, although there are some 'regular' users who come in person. Two of the five headquarters divisions are medium to high users of the enquiry service, but the others are predominantly borrowers of books and journals. The Hong Kong office makes virtually no use of the service at all, and only one person in the German office speaks fluent English.
>
> On the basis of this information, the librarian has restructured the Current Awareness Bulletin by discipline and market sector, and has put it up on the newly-installed intranet. She has also set up an arrangement with an EIRENE member to provide an equivalent service in German for the Berlin office.

The second category of information you need about your users is their Critical Success Factors (CSFs). What criteria will they apply in deciding whether you are a reliable information provider? Typical examples include speed of response, helpfulness, understanding of their type of work, currency of stock. Different segments (and in extreme cases, different individuals within a segment) will have different CSFs, which they will apply to all possible sources of information at a particular time. By understanding CSFs and meeting them, you can ensure that users get their information from you, rather than the recesses of their own memory or from colleagues down the corridor.

Analysis of the CSFs of the customer segments you have already identified enables you to define further the way in which you organise your information service.

Finally, you need to understand what your users expect from an information service, and how they perceive your particular one. You can largely control the latter, by the type of service and the you way provide it (see the section on 'Service Delivery'). Unfortunately, you have much less influence over users' expectations, which are based on past experience of both your LIS and others, how others have fared ('word of mouth advertising') and what happened in similar situations but different circumstances. For example, a potential client whose only direct experience of librarians is in a local small public library on a Saturday morning is likely to have a low expectation of the professional expertise of a corporate information service. Similarly, their expectation of any sort of telephone enquiry service will be affected by the service received from direct insurers or Railtrack.

Users' expectations of a service and their actual experience seldom coincide, unless they are regular users and know what to expect. Usually their expectations are higher, and effective management of the consequences of this gap can play an important part in establishing the reputation of your information service. If you give them a little more than they expect, in whatever way (speed, courtesy, quality of information or the way it is presented), they will not only use you again, but may also be likely to mention their experience to others. Conversely, a poor experience is almost guaranteed to be talked about in the canteen or the corridor.

A group of American researchers[2] have established that people have a perception of an ideal service, as well as a perception of the service with which they actually deal. Instinctively, we compare the ideal and the reality, and so understanding the nature of this "perception gap" plays its part in marketing planning. Once you know its nature and extent, you can take action to narrow the gap.

Example

> Following a series of meetings with key customers, the CAD Partnership librarian has drawn up a number of matrices to record her understanding of the characteristics of some of the customer segments. She has drawn up a list of CSFs, which she has listed in priority order for each segment. Together with her conclusions about their perceptions and expectations, this information forms the basis of her marketing action plan.

Data collection

All this understanding is based on information about your users. Ideally, it is information gathered and analysed systematically through whatever means are appropriate. There are five basic ways of collecting market data.

- Structured questionnaire, where someone asks a sample of people a set series of questions, either by telephone, face-to-face or on paper/e-mail

- Semi-structured interview, where the interviewer has a checklist of subject areas, but the conversation is more free-flowing and responsive to the answers given

- Focus groups, where small groups of people are asked for their views by a facilitator who structures the conversation without leading it

- Mystery shopping, in which you test the quality of a competitor's service – or your own! – anonymously. (Try telephoning your own help-desk with a spurious enquiry to test the helpfulness of the response)

- Face-to-face conversation, perhaps at the end of an enquiry, or by pre-arrangement ("I would like to come and talk about how the Infrmation Service can help you more effectively").

The quality of the conclusions you draw from any market research depends on how representative the sample is, the thoroughness of the data-gathering exercise and how intensively it is analysed. A 'straw poll' taken in the staff restaurant may give you a broad feel for the likely reaction to a new service, but it is no substitute for seeking input from likely customers at an early stage. But you should be wary of straining for too great a level of accuracy – once some clear trends emerge, it is more efficient to get on and implement sensible actions based on partial information than spend unnecessary time in validation.

Customer selection

Finally, I come to that aspect of customer assessment which many find difficult, especially inhouse service providers who feel that they are tied to their customers. Demand management (or too much to do and too few people to do it with) is a fact of 1990s life for most managers, of whatever sort. Many librarians have told me that they hesitate to undertake too much marketing because they are afraid of generating a demand which they cannot handle.

I answer them in three ways. Firstly, marketing is not just about promotion and selling, i.e. those activities which lead directly to demand. Strategic marketing is about balancing the needs of your users with your LIS's ability to deliver. This includes designing a portfolio of services which reflect current market demand (which may include phasing out services which are no longer 'profitable'), and adopting policies which will generate the type and level of demand which you are able to handle within available resources. Some of these policies amount to rationing (such as premium pricing). The marketing skill lies in presenting the package in a positive light so that the information service's reputation remains intact.

Secondly, marketing is no longer about getting more and more customers in through the door. It is about developing long-term relationships with high-quality customers, who see you as partners in achieving shared objectives. (Approach summarised in Adrian Payne's article *Relationship marketing – making customers count*[3]. The advantages to the librarian are that:

- Following the Pareto principle, by focussing on the 20% of customers who provide 80% of your business, demand for the bulk of your core services is more predictable and manageable

- The information service is involved early in projects and are therefore able to add greater value, and earn greater respect in the organisation.

Implicit in this is the concept of selecting users. Virtually no-one in any industry or profession has the resources to sell into all available marketplaces, and choosing which marketplaces to serve, and what service to offer in them, is an integral part of marketing planning. Based on their *attractiveness* to you, and your *ability to compete*, you can assess:

- Which of your customers are most important
- Which services you are going to offer them.

This enables you to allocate your priorities accordingly. While this is not an easy task, particularly for corporate librarians who are expected to serve the whole company, it is a practical necessity. Once the decisions are made (and agreed as appropriate), your marketing effort can be directed on that basis.

Thirdly, you are likely to be the first in line for the cuts unless you not only offer a service of value to your organisation, but are seen to do so. An element of marketing therefore must be promotional about who you are and what you do to make your organisation successful.

Why do clients use your LIS?

A simple answer may be the mountaineer Mallory's classic "Because it's there", but that is not enough for a marketeer! People use a service because it will bring them some *benefit*, directly in terms of usefulness (e.g. a car is a means of independent transport) but also in terms of how that purchase will make them feel (e.g. a Porsche puts you one up over the neighbours). Car salesmen are therefore selling independence and personal image – they should not be selling the *features* of a car such as its engine capacity, colour, passenger-carrying potential etc.

What are the benefits which *your* LIS brings to its users? I hope that, this far through this chapter, your answer starts "It depends . . ." because different segments of your client base will look for different benefits. Many of them simply want solutions to problems. But others will want confidence which comes from knowing that they are acting on the latest information available; or be able to work undisturbed on important research; or know that you can find out obscure facts through your network of contacts. Only you can define the benefits which you can use to sell your LIS effectively.

Exercise

It is not always easy to identify the benefits, because we are used to thinking in terms of the features of a product or service. So try this: make a list of all the features of your LIS (opening hours, number of serials, qualifications of staff, IT facilities etc etc). After each feature, write "which means that", and add the benefit(s) which that feature brings. For example: "Our Keynote Market Reports on CD-ROM are updated quarterly which means that you always have access to the latest information".

Clients also use your LIS because it is *different* in one or more important ways from the alternatives. It may be convenient (right by the lifts), or have a better range of relevant stock, or the staff may be friendlier or more knowledgeable. It may of course be 'free'! Again, you will need to identify which differences appeal to which users, so that you can emphasise them in your promotion and selling efforts. The differences are often related to the CSFs.

Example

> The main CSFs of the architects working at CAD Partnership's HQ on public sector work are timeliness of information, understanding of public sector requirements and the ability to produce very detailed answers to enquiries. The librarian has written an article for *Input* (the house journal) describing three recent queries which demonstrated these qualities, and highlighting the contribution of one of her staff, newly-recruited from a government department. It concluded "Celia's three years of specialised support for the Construction Directorate of the Department of the Environment has given her a detailed knolwedge of how their minds work (FEATURE). This means that she can help you get under the skin of DOE-funded schemes quickly, and prepare bids which are more in tune with their hidden agendas (BENEFIT)".

Competition

The essence of marketing is persuading the right number and type of users to come to you for their information needs. This inevitably means taking account of the competition. Many inhouse librarians have said to me that they do not need to think about competitors, because their users are not allowed to go anywhere else. That does not mean that they do not face competition.

Competition is anything which encourages a customer to do other than use your LIS. Users always have a choice – even if it lies between dialling your enquiry number and doing nothing, or making do with whatever information happens to be around.

Exercise

> Write down all the alternatives open to your customers (actual or potential). Your list should include non-information sources, such as colleagues, as well as sources which your customers can use themselves without your help.

> Once you have identified the sources of competition, you need to assess how likely your target users are to use them, so that you can counter the attraction. Draw up a matrix which rates your service and those of the main sources of competition against the users' CSFs, on a score of 1 – 5 (low to high).

This will identify where you are relatively strong and weak, and enable you to take action. This action could include changes to the nature of your service (in marketing jargon 'service development') to overcome the relative weaknesses, and/or promotion of the strengths, by emphasising the benefits to users of these features of the service.

Much marketing practice is based on comparisons with the competition. I have already talked about selling the ways in which your service differs from the competition, and the importance of understanding your users' expectations, which will, to a certain extent, be based on their experience of other libraries. It is unlikely that special librarians will be concerned with direct tests of how you rate against the competition, such as market share, but comparative positioning should form part of your marketing planning.

Positioning is all about how you are seen in your marketplace, in relation to the competition. Do you provide a top-quality service, quicker, faster, friendlier (or whatever is important to your users)? Or are you average, relying on certain key differences (such as convenience) to attract and retain your clients? Are you Harrods or M&S? Each of those has a clear positioning in the department stores marketplace.

Every supplier has a position by default. The marketeers' job is to decide what positioning their information service should have and manage the various factors which contribute to it to implement that decision. These factors include not only marketing tools such as the marketing mix (see below), but also all aspects of the customer's experience of the LIS, especially service delivery.

SERVICE DELIVERY

I have already looked at the importance of never forgetting that your users have a choice, and of differentiating your service from the alternatives available to your users, in ways which make your service more attractive. One of these ways is to design the service delivery package against users' established needs and expectations with as much care as the basic service itself. This is an integral part of marketing, since it has a direct impact not only on the positioning of the information service, but also on the level of useage.

Satisfied users are more likely to remain loyal to their infomation supplier, and may become positive advocates of the service to others. Such customers are an asset to any supplier, but to an inhouse service provider they are invaluable. Not only do they bring their own custom, but by positively advocating your qualities, they are influencing the climate in which you operate. This makes it more likely that the more rewarding types of work will come your way, but is also a protection against corporate raids on your budget, because you are known to be of value. This approach to doing business, called 'relationship marketing', envisages that a supplier can, by taking positive action, move a customer up a 'ladder' from being someone who has no loyalty to a particular supplier to being a full partner. Managing the service provided, the way it is delivered and the quality of every interaction is a fundamental part of this approach.

Service, like beauty, is in the eye of the beholder. It is as good as the user decides it is. The standards against which service is judged not only change with time and circumstances, but also vary between clients. As with other aspects of marketing, service management starts with the user's needs and expectations. Standards are set on the basis of what is important to the customer, with appropriate ways of measuring performance. Many organisations have set standards without finding out what service levels customers are looking for.

Example

A business information library set itself the standard of responding to all enquiries by fax. In a subsequent customer satisfaction survey, it transpired that only 60% of their customers required that level of service routinely – the remainder were content with first class post. This enabled resources to be deployed elsewhere, without loss of customer satisfaction.

Research[2] has shown that of the 10 determinants of service quality which are important to customers, the most important is *reliability*. However, a totally reliable service which is not easily accessible and not supported by acceptable levels of, say, *courtesy* and *responsiveness* will not necessarily have loyal clients, who do not look elsewhere. (The remaining six determinants are communication, competence, credibility, knowledge, security/freedom from risk or doubt, and tangibles.)

Individual customers will rate these determinants variously at different times in different circumstances, and possibly in relation to different services. The trick is to devise service levels which manage and meet this variety of expectations.

The quality of a product is (relatively) easy to check, control and manage. However, a service is intangible, may be of inconsistent quality because it is delivered by imperfect human beings, is perishable and cannot be owned by the consumer. Linking these characteristics to understanding of customer needs and expectations enables the right service and service delivery to be designed.

Intangibility

It is not possible to touch or handle the quality of an information service (or any other service) before using it. Customers must therefore trust the librarian to a greater degree than a product retailer, or find other ways of assessing the service in advance. Judgements tend to be made on:

- Recommendation by others
- Tangibles associated with the service, such as the decor or signage
- Their experience of dealing with the organisation during the time they are deciding whether to use its services.

Inconsistency

The providers of a service are human beings, not robots. They will have different personalities, skills and ways of communicating. Controlling the quality of the service so that it meets a consistent standard can therefore be difficult. This is especially so in a library where high levels of interaction with users (who also have different personalities, skills and ways of communicating) are involved. In addition, because services are provided by people, users may not:

- Distinguish between the service itself and the person providing it
- Recognise that they themselves contribute to the quality of the output by providing sufficient detail about their enquiry.

It is for this reason that a section on people is essential in the marketing plan of service providers. For example, it enables you to pinpoint and justify the training needed to overcome identified service delivery weaknesses.

Perishability

Most services cannot be stored for future use. You cannot answer queries before they are made, or compile a current awareness bulletin before the information is available, to avoid work piling up during peak staff holiday times. This leads to peaks and troughs in demand and supply which have to be managed within resource constraints without damaging customer service.

Service delivery is the way you put all the understanding and analysis into practice. It is about having the right people in the right place, saying the right things, supported by the right systems and equipment, so that customers receive the service they want in a way which they perceive is at least acceptable, and preferably 'delightful'.

A customer usually has more than one contact with an organisation while using its services. Often called 'Moments of Truth'[4], these experiences affect:

- His/her decision whether to use the service (if there is a choice)
- Whether they use it again
- What they tell their colleagues

and consequently

- The reputation of the service, and how many others use it
- Customer expectations and satisfaction.

Exercise

A useful starting point for analysing service quality is to chart this 'customer journey'. Identify who is in contact with customers, about what and what role that contact plays in satisfying the customer. You should

- Look at the journey from the customer's point of view
- Establish what is good and bad about each of the contacts
- Identify all the components of each contact, i.e. all the people and processes which are involved, directly or indirectly.

The result is a picture of what it is like to be a customer of your LIS, warts and all.

On the basis of this analysis you can set service standards to ensure that each 'Moment of Truth' at least meets the customer's expectations, and preferably exceeds it. They should be:

- Small in number, so that staff are not confused or overloaded
- Focussed on the customer's priorities, not those of the organisation
- Specific, so that they are not open to different interpretations
- Communicated effectively, so that everyone understands what is expected of them.

Service performance can be measured in a number of ways, and this is not the right place to go into them in detail. But one of the most important feedback mechanisms are complaints, for two reasons. Firstly, research has shown that effective handling of complaints can have a positive effect on customer loyalty. Secondly, they provide a way of spotting problem areas, if a number of similar complaints are made. Once you know something is wrong, you can take action to put it right. Complaints are therefore of direct interest to the marketing person, who is concerned both with the reputation of the LIS and with the design of the services it offers.

THE MARKETING PLAN

The classic marketing plan used to have four elements, dealing with the aspects of the product which a brand manager is able to control directly to differentiate it from the alternatives. Usually called the '4 Ps', they are product, price, place (sometimes called distribution or channel to market), and promotion. There are other 'Ps' – positioning for example – but 'people' is now becoming generally recognised as the fifth 'P'. It is absolutely necessary for service providers such as librarians to think about people. I have described the theoretical basis for their inclusion under 'Service Delivery', but it is actually obvious. Despite the growing use of IT and the telephone in information work, most library customers still deal with a person to a greater or lesser extent. The quality of library staff, and the way they approach their jobs, play a vital part of the effective marketing of the service.

Product

A more accurate description than 'product' is 'portfolio of services', since very few if any LIS offer only one. The collection of services will be a mixture of core services, without which you cannot reasonably claim to be a LIS (such as an enquiry-handling service), and peripheral services, which are nice to have, but not fundamental to the role and objectives of a LIS (such as doing photocopying). The portfolio will also be a mix of services which make different contributions to the overall viability of the LIS. The marketing plan needs to look at the mix of services, and develop the optimum mix, based on users' needs, wants and expectations, and the objectives set for the LIS in its business plan.

Portfolio planning was pioneered by the American guru Peter Drucker[5] some 30 years ago, but it was popularised by the Boston Consulting Group in the early 1970s. Their 'growth-share matrix' became one of the most popular management tools ever, primarily because of the apparent ease by which it can be completed. Done properly, it should be based on large amounts of market data, but it can be done intuitively, as an aid to thinking. In a four-box grid, the service portfolio is divided into:

- *Rising stars* – a popular service for which demand is growing. These will include CD-ROMs and other IT-based services, which are 'toys' as well as producing useful information for users, and will repay investment because of the increase in custom which they will attract

- *Problem children* – a service which is under-used, although the demand is there. The question to be addressed is why people are not using the service. If it is the way it is provided/presented, more resources will be required to remedy the problem; will the investment be recouped?

- *Cash cows* – popular services for which demand is now static or growing slowly. These are the 'old favourites', for which people constantly return

- *Dogs* – unpopular services for which demand is static and may be declining, these consume resources for little positive return.

Once each service has been categorised (however roughly), a number of fundamental questions can be asked. Why are the problem children and dogs unpopular? Are they out of sync with customers' current needs and expectations? Can anything be done to overcome the problems, and will it be worth the return? Assuming that none of them are fundamental core services, should you be drawing up plans for withdrawing them, in a positive and managed way? If any of them are core services, the plan must look at the remedial action needed, lest the viability of the LIS is questioned.

Example

> After a review of services, the CAD Partnership librarian concluded that professional expertise was not required to manage the purchase and distribution of journals, other than those retained for reference in the Information and Resource Centre. She has therefore started negotiations with several suppliers to set up a bulk purchase contract, under which individual Business Units will order what journals they like from their own budgets. This will release 20% of the time of one of her staff.

On the positive side, what needs to be done to capitalise on the popularity of cash cows and rising stars? Can the life of a cash cow be extended by up-dating it in some way (cosmetic or otherwise?) What needs to be done to nurture the rising stars so that they become established features of the portfolio, on which users depend, and which will ensure long-term customer loyalty?

Portfolio management needs to be undertaken in the light of the basic user segmentation already done. Different groups of customers will give different priority to the various services, and their likely reactions to proposed changes need to be weighed carefully and, where appropriate, plans drawn up for handling them.

Deciding to withdraw a service can be hard. But, given limited resources, there are only two ways of making room for new developments: by cutting out or reducing in scale an existing service, or working more efficiently. Eventually, there is no more scope for efficiency savings, and cuts are inevitable. It is better to do so on a planned rational basis, rooted in customer demand, existing and predicted. Having in place a structured marketing plan can play a vital role in budget negotiations. It should:

- Collect and analyse data about your users
- Provide for necessary as well as appropriate developments in your service
- Promote an image of the LIS which reflects what customers want and will support.

The second aspect of portfolio management is consideration of services which are needed but not currently provided. This may be because customer need has developed in a particular way, or there have been technological or other changes bringing new services in their wake. Examples are the introduction first of online services, and subsequently of CD-ROMs. The cost of introducing these services must be calculated and written into the plan, together with an assessment of the impact on customers and their perception of the LIS. How does it fit with the positioning?

Pricing

This is of course only relevant if you are operating a charged service. It is a marketing issue because the price of a product or service can affect demand, and/or positioning. Since people tend to value what they pay for, charging extra for a service will reinforce a presentation of it as a high-quality or premium product (such as charging extra for rapid turn-round). But charging premium rates for an average service will simply get you a reputation for being expensive, rather than high-value.

Problems often arise if charges have to be introduced for a previously free service, perhaps after a policy change within an organisation. Cost recovery is a common basis for charging in these circumstances. If you are required only to charge for services for which you have to pay (such as online charges, or Companies House searches), the only issue is how you are going to present the introduction of charges. Careful preparation of the ground, with explanations of the background, will minimise any adverse impact.

However, if you have to start hard charging for your time, there are a number of ways in which this can be done. Careful understanding of the cost basis you are required to use will be necessary, such as whether it includes full overheads, or only salary-related costs. Once you have done the calculations, there are three basic approaches to charging:

- Virtually all time charged for, apart from dealing with simple factual enquiries such as "Do you have a particular reference book?"
- A certain amount of time free (e.g. 10 minutes), thereafter a fee is charged for a set period of time (e.g. 15 minutes)
- Subscription entitling members to free (or reduced fee) access to the service. These schemes can become very complicated, with several levels of subscription for different types of service.

The decision about which type of charging regime to go for will depend on the type of library, its relationships with its customers and the circumstances surrounding the introduction of charging. A marketing plan should consider whether the right regime is in place, and whether the objectives would be better met by any changes, either in the type of charges for the various services, or the level.

Place

This section of the marketing plan deals with the ways in which your service is 'distributed', in other words how customers access the LIS and get the information they need. It therefore covers:

- The quality and adequacy of the communication channels with your users – telephone, fax, e-mail as well as face-to-face contact
- Availability, including opening hours
- Location and staffing of the enquiry point
- Layout, shelving etc
- Ease of use and accessibility of the catalogue
- Environment of the library including furniture, lighting and decor.

Your aim is to make your LIS pleasant and easy to use, so that customers will both come back and also spread the word that this is the best way to get the information they need to do their jobs. Many of the issues considered in this part of the marketing plan will involve expenditure. If you can show that your proposals are based on responding to customer needs (which by definition they will have been, as part of a marketing plan), and that you have prioritised and scheduled the work which needs to be done, your proposals have a better chance of being accepted at budget time.

Example

> A two-person businesss information service has decided that its customers should be able to talk to a person, rather than a machine, if at all possible. They therefore have two cordless telephones with a range of 500 yards from the basestation, enabling them to take calls away from the desk. These are set to transfer calls to a mobile 'phone for times when they are both out of the office or with a client. Calls are only taken by an answering service if the mobile 'phone is unanswered.

You will of course need to strike a balance between the demands of your users (who between them might for example want the LIS to be open from 7.30am to 8.00pm) and what is either practical or cost effective. The main thing is that you have thought through how to organise this aspect of the service, taking into account customers' known views, the attractions of alternative sources of information and what is realistic. Telling people about the results forms part of your promotional plan.

Promotion

Although I have been at pains to point out that there is more to marketing than promotion, it is nevertheless an essential marketing activity. If people do not know what you can do, they will not come and ask you to do it.

I will cite my own experience as the user of a particular corporate library. I used to do all my own research, merely using the reception desk to ask where particular types of books could be found. I was never given any indication that the library staff had the skills in searching for information which I now know they had. They sent me journals on circulation and bulletins listing recent acquisitions, but they did not come to talk to my division to understand our needs or explain what they could do. Both my expectation of libraries in general and perception of this one in particular were low.

Promotion comes in many shapes and forms. It is highly unlikely that you will need to use all of them. The purpose of the promotional plan is to select those most appropriate for the level of awareness you want to achieve, and to integrate them so that there is a continuous flow of information about the LIS, what it offers, who the staff are, and the values and the standards it works to.

There are two important things to remember about promotion. Firstly, whatever method you use, it must reinforce the positioning you have decided on. Ideally, every form of promotion should be easily recognised as coming from the LIS. There are several ways of achieving this. One is a logo, and consistent use of a particular type-face and prescribed formatting. It is not necessary to have outside experts in to devise this corporate identity – the most important thing is that, once agreed, it is followed all the time, by everyone.

Example

> The CAD librarian has decided that the LIS needs to present itself in a way which fits better with the positioning of the company. She wants the staff to be recognised as professionals in their own right, since her customers value professional standards highly. As a start, she has ordered printed covers for the current awareness bulletins, to replace photocopied front sheets. She held a competition for the design of a logo and the cover to encourage interest, particularly among the younger staff. She has taken down the old posters from noticeboards, some of which were dog-eared, and has asked the designer of the bulletin covers to extend his design concept to an outline poster which can be used for advertising special events.

Secondly, before starting work on any form of promotion, think through who your target audience is and what message you want to get over. Apart from factual publicity such as a poster giving details of an event, the wider the target audience, the more difficult it is to give a clear message. This is because you will be trying to address the interests of different customer segments through one mechanism. Wherever possible, it is better to produce several different types of material which you can tailor to different user groups, and direct it to them specifically. Modern IT, especially e-mail, makes this much more practical than ever before.

It is unlikely that special librarians will need to use paid public advertising or will have much regular contact with the mass media. The three main types of promotion which are most useful to a special librarian are:

- Pure promotion of the LIS
- Products which demonstrate the quality and usefulness of the LIS work
- Awareness events such as induction tours for new members of staff, in-library teaching sessions for example on a new database and open sessions.

Pure promotion

The basic promotional vehicle is the brochure. First and foremost, this should emphasise the benefits to be gained from using the LIS. Its main purpose should be to encourage people to visit, or at least to contact the LIS, so it does not need to comprise an exhaustive list of features such as opening hours, types of stock and available databases. Remember that many users want information to help solve a work problem, and may not be interested in how that information is held or accessed. Use your 'corporate' colours and style, have it professionally printed if possible and distribute it widely. However, two words of warning. It can be very tempting to order large quantities because the unit cost can fall dramatically. Large quantities of brochures can last a long time – well past the time when you want a new brochure. Secondly, do not include information which may go out of date during the lifetime of the brochure.

Newsletters keep users in touch with LIS activities, developments and successes and are an excellent form of promotion, as long as they:

- Are produced regularly, so that people learn to expect them (and hopefully look forward to their arrival!)
- Are lively, written in a style which will make people want to read them
- Have a dynamic visual style, without using every trick available on your word-processor or DTP kit; use your corporate colours and style
- Give information which the reader wants to have.

Newsletters can easily be e-mailed, which means that you can tweak the style and/or content to match the interests (or prejudices) of different users. You may, for example, write about basically the same thing in different styles for top management and younger staff.

Posters are a simple way of publicising events and the introduction of a new service. They can be easily produced, but you must take care not to leave them up too long, because people will stop 'seeing' them, and they will begin to look tired and old.

Products which promote

These include awareness bulletins, fact sheets and abstracts. Like newsletters, they can easily be targeted to the most interested audience electronically – assuming that you have done the basic data collection about the needs and interests of different people. Few people have time to wade through a pile of extraneous junk to reach the few bits of information which interest them – they will think better of you if you do the sorting for them. By doing this, you will give a good impression of customer awareness which will encourage people to bring you their enquiries.

Awareness events

These bring people into the library and for that time they become a captive audience. But (apart from induction tours, which are organised for those involved) people come voluntarily, so there has to be a good reason from them to give up precious time. This can be because they will get something from the content of the event, such as a teaching session on a new database, or because you have offered some incentive (usually free drinks or food). As before, you should think carefully about who you want to attract and why, at this particular time, and then organise the style of the event, the timing, duration etc and the publicity/invitations to be attractive to that particular target audience.

People

People are included in the marketing mix because they are an integral part of the LIS service, and are vital to the success of the marketing plan. They are the means through which the service is delivered, and they directly affect customers' expectations and perceptions.

You will need to consider issues such as:

- The mix of experience and qualifications, in relation to current and foreseen customer needs
- Interpersonal skills, particularly for those dealing regularly with customers
- Understanding of the positioning of the LIS, its aims and values, so that they can behave in accordance with them consistently in all dealings with customers
- Any additional skills or attributes, such as knowledge of an unusual language which can be capitalised on in the marketing campaign.

In your first marketing plan, you may find that there are a number of weaknesses which need to be addressed, for example through specific training. These can be fed into the routine appraisal process, and identified as actions in the marketing plan. The advantage of dealing with these issues in the context of marketing is that the remedial action can be presented in a positive light, as contributing to the future success of the LIS.

Monitoring and evaluation

As with any planning in business, the marketing plan should be regularly monitored. In order to do this, you should identify a small number of key performance measures to establish the success of the action you are taking. These should relate to the objectives you have identified for the plan, and include means of assessing things which are important to your customers.

Example

The CAD Partnership librarian has discovered from a survey that people are more interested in the speed of response relative to their needs, rather than the absolute time taken to deal with their enquiry. She has therefore instituted a system under which a timetable is agreed for detailed research enquiries, following discussion about real need and the reality of delivery. These contracts are monitored on a monthly basis, and she intends to publish the results. She has talked individually to the heads of those sections who are frequent users and designed this aspect of the service in the light of these discussions. She plans to continue the dialogue with the intention of developing the service in partnership with regular users, so that they will take more responsibility for managing their own demands, and the service can thereby improve under its own momentum.

The marketing plan should be a dynamic part of managing the LIS. Its aims and assumptions should be clearly thought through and stated, enabling swift reassessment and change if circumstances alter. Its effectiveness should be positively monitored, and corrective action taken if things are going off track.

FINALLY

I have words of comfort for those of you for whom this all sounds a bit structured and bureaucratic. The most effective form of marketing will always remain the delivery of a high quality service. The big difference which these marketing techniques can make is that by taking the time and trouble to understand the needs, wants and expectations of your customers (actual and potential), you can design a service and the way it is delivered that is more likely to be viewed as adding value. The LIS which is seen to be a valuable asset to its organisation will always have a future.

REFERENCES

1. Coote, H. *How to market your library service effectively, (2nd Edition)*, Aslib, London (1997, Know How Series).

2. Parasuraman, A., Zeithaml, V.A. and Berry, L. L. A conceptual model of service quality and its implications for future research, *Journal of Marketing*, **49** (Autumn) 1985, 41-50; and [by the same authors] SERVQUAL: a multiple-item scale for measuring consumer perceptions of service quality, *Journal of Retailing*, **64** (1) 1988, 1 2-40.

3. Payne, A. Relationship marketing – making customers count, *Managing Service Quality*, **4** (6) 1994, 29-31.

4. Carlzon, Jan, Moments of Truth. Ballinger Publishing Company (1987). Key excerpt in McKinsey Quarterly, Summer 1987.

5. Drucker, P. F. *Managing for results*, Heinemann, London (1964).

Towards the Electronic Library?

Charles Oppenheim

INTRODUCTION

What do people mean by the term 'electronic library' (often called 'digital library' in the USA)? They usually mean a library in which all, or virtually all, of its holdings are in machine readable form; furthermore such a library is fully connected to telecommunication networks; by implication, users of such a library are not in any way restricted in its geography. It could be down the corridor or 1,000 miles away. All a user has to do is log into it from a terminal at home, in a hotel, or wherever, and search its holdings, view the results on screen, download the material of interest, annotate it, file it in a private filing system, and so on. It is confidently predicted by some that most business, academic or professional library users will routinely search for, and obtain information in this way in the next 10 years.

As electronic libraries develop, it is further argued, they will become interlinked, and so not merely will users have access to the material of their own library, but also to the holdings of any or all other libraries in the world. One should not just think of text in machine-readable form. Graphics, photographs, video and so on would also be available in this way. This sounds wonderful, and when it does come about, it certainly has the potential to be wonderful, but there are many things holding back the development of the electronic library at the moment, and I will come on to these later in this chapter.

THE CURRENT LIBRARY MODEL

The current model of a library is relatively straightforward. The library is the interface between the users and the vast amounts of published and unpublished information available. The user comes in, gains access to the information by means of inspecting the library's holdings, or by means of interlibrary loans or a document supply service if the material is not available there. Besides its patrons, libraries deal with other types of bodies - publishers, bookshops and subscription agents to obtain materials directly, or other libraries for interlibrary loans. In turn, of course, the publishers deal with the authors of original materials.

In the electronic world, the scene is more complex, because the possibilities for direct contact are far greater. A user may deal directly now with a publisher or an author, for example. It is a fast changing scene, with, for example, subscription agencies moving into the abstracting and indexing business, and publishers moving into the bookshop business, or document supply business. By "moving into", I mean either developing their own business, or acquiring an existing business in the new sector.

It is not clear in the medium term who in the industries will survive and who will not, and whether completely new types of entrepreneur will emerge. It may be that, for example, bookshops become the major source of electronic information and supply to users, or they may get completely squeezed out; the same, of course, applies to librarians.

What is clear is that an increasing amount of material, particularly in the scientific research area, is now appearing first, or only in electronic form. This growth in electronic publishing is a result of authors putting up material directly on the Internet, traditional print publishers moving into the electronic publishing business, and other companies never associated with publishing before moving into electronic publishing as a new venture. So, come what may, libraries will have an increasing proportion of the new materials they are adding to stock in machine-readable form; in addition, digitisation of older print material into machine-readable form is accentuating this trend.

I am not suggesting, incidentally, that there will be no requirement for print published materials by individuals, or by libraries; what I am suggesting is that, particularly in fast moving scientific subjects, print will rapidly become unimportant over the next decade. I am also suggesting that the current model of relationships of supply of materials will inevitably change, and that no player's future role can be taken for granted.

ELECTRONIC LIBRARY RESEARCH

The vast bulk of research and development work in electronic libraries is being led by academic libraries, particularly university libraries. Why is this? Firstly, in academic institutions, librarians are expected to attract research funding, do their own research and get publications. Secondly, in the corporate sector (with the exception of R&D intensive industries such as the pharmaceutical industry), libraries are seen primarily as service institutions, there to help achieve corporate goals, but with relatively little funding or freedom to do things that are speculative.

Four countries lead in the field of electronic library research - Japan, the USA, Netherlands and the UK. The USA is the most active simply in the numbers of experiments underway, but the UK leads the way in its co-ordination of effort and joint venture research. This is because of its eLib programme, funded by the Higher Education Funding Councils. This £25 million initiative funded about 60 research projects involving universities, publishers, learned societies and hardware and software companies. Some of the projects are very large, involving millions of pounds, and others cost as little as £20,000. The projects are mostly due to end in about 1998. The projects are designed to fit into one another and between them cover most of the areas that need exploration. The intention is not to end up with electronic libraries, but rather to identify the issues and problems, and possible solutions, for a future generation to then develop fully. Particular areas the programme has homed in on include new digitisation techniques and the digitisation of useful printed materials, the development of new electronic journals, the development of electronic pre-print archives, novel document supply services including on-demand publishing, the training and education of librarians, academics and students, tools for searching the Internet, storage and retrieval of images, and preservation and copyright issues. The long term aim is to engender a culture of change and acceptance of the electronic library within the higher education community, and the industries, such as the publishing and bookselling industries, that serve them.

FACTORS PREVENTING THE DEVELOPMENT OF ELECTRONIC LIBRARIES

In my view there are five areas that need addressing before the electronic library can become a reality. These are: technical issues; legal issues; economic issues; psychological issues; and educational issues.

Technical issues

The electronic library cannot become a reality until a number of technical issues are resolved. These include questions regarding the development of efficient searching, retrieval and dissemination tools; the development of methods for the compression and decompression of images, both still and moving; the indexing of images is at a rudimentary stage and needs much more work; the development of widely agreed and accepted standards; the development of widely accepted cryptographic encoding tools and the development of well established and cost effective digitisation and error correcting tools. The problems are well understood, and many of the solutions are in hand. However, much work still needs to be carried out.

Legal issues

The electronic library cannot take effect, even if the technical issues are resolved, unless issues to do with copyright, privacy, etc are dealt with. The copyright issue is particularly problematic. Copyright owners (typically at the moment the publishers) are sometimes reluctant to allow libraries to digitise their materials, and then let those digitised materials loose on networks, as they are concerned about the considerable potential for copyright infringement that could so easily occur under such circumstances. Publishers have responded to the challenge by sometimes refusing to give libraries permission to do such digitisation, and threatening to sue anyone who does such digitising without permission, whilst at the same time attacking on two fronts.

The first is to attempt to gain changes in the law to make it explicit that browsing on screen, and sending material down a network are both restricted acts that require the copyright owners' permission before they can be done. At present the law is sufficiently ambiguous that it is not explicit that doing these things without permission is infringement. Secondly, the publishers are supporting the development of a variety of hardware and software tools to protect their data. These range from encrypted materials, through to Electronic Copyright Management Systems (ECMS) that control the access to material, keep records of who has accessed the materials, and provide for charging mechanisms for those that do access the material.

All these efforts by the copyright owners have only been partially matched by user developments. Some user organisations are attempting to fight the proposed changes in the law; they were successful in the US and at a diplomatic conference at the end of 1996 but there is still a feeling that the law will eventually change. Other users have objected to the development of ECMS, but their voices are unlikely to be heard. The most interesting user reactions have been to press authors no longer to assign all their copyright to publishers when they create items, to demand further royalties from their publishers, if and when their materials are distributed electronically, and to develop Codes of Practice on what is, or is not, permitted for users in an electronic library.

Unfortunately, there is a risk that the users and publishers will move to opposed and entrenched positions, a situation that will do neither any good and will delay the development of the electronic library, or else result in an electronic library that has large gaps in its collections.

Economic issues

These are being considered at last. The question of how one should price, and charge for information in an electronic library has yet to be resolved. This is an issue that has been addressed, and resolved, by other industries, such as the online industry, the CD-ROM industry, the real-time financial information industry, and the software industry. The pricing and licensing strategies they have come up with vary considerably, but all have one thing in common - they involve an element of trusting the client to do only what the client says it will do. It is a pity that this sort of trust is not yet much evident in the debates on pricing of electronic materials for libraries.

Each of the algorithms one can think of for charging in an electronic library environment has its pros and cons, and it is clear that there is no one single best solution. The fundamental question is whether users are willing to pay at point of use, or whether libraries retain their general principle that most services are free to users. If they decide to charge users, there are a variety of models they could adopt; these may or may not reflect the charges the library bears for offering the data.

Clearly, somewhere money has to change hands. A fundamental part of that is the question of whether this is based on pay per use, on a subscription with unlimited use, or some combination of the two (so much to join the club, and then so much to use). If one decides to charge by use, then further questions arise. On what basis are the charges made? On the time spent? On the number of items retrieved? On the number of bytes downloaded? Whatever model is adopted will favour some types of users and penalise others. We have a long way to go to understand the economics of electronic publishing, yet pricing decisions made now will set the trend for the future. The uncertainty about the economics of electronic publishing, the pricing models to be adopted, and how libraries and users will adapt to them, is certainly hindering the development of the electronic library.

Psychological issues

These have hardly been considered, and yet could have an enormous impact on how well electronic libraries are used. How do people select and use information? How do they like it displayed? How do they react to electronic material rather than print? Would they prefer the electronic library to look and feel like a traditional library? The limited research done so far has mainly concentrated on user-friendliness of interfaces, but the issues go far deeper than that. For example, even highly computer literate students still feel more comfortable with print if they are given the choice. Why is this? It is clear, too, that people prefer to read items on the train, at home and in the bath rather than in a work environment. If the electronic library is to succeed, it must deliver information in the way that people feel most comfortable, rather than forcing people to read at a PC terminal on a desk. I am arguing that people come first, and that attempts to force people to read on screen when the system is not appropriate for that purpose will lead to resistance or resentment.

Another psychological issue is the depth of information needed. Some people want simple answers, others complex ones. The ideal system will recognise these needs, and supply results according to those needs; but how will the computer system recognise those needs? It implies highly intelligent retrieval engines, with a lot of sophistication hidden under the surface that the user is not aware of. Much research is also needed in this area.

In my view, the psychological factors have not been studied sufficiently, or given sufficiently high priority. The research that has been carried out so far gives us some inkling of the problems we have to overcome before people feel comfortable with the electronic library.

Educational issues

Print on paper is so commonplace that it almost appears natural to know what to do with the artefacts based on this technology. This is not the case for an electronic information source. Methods of training and educating users have to be developed. People also need to understand the implications of the electronic library for their life, their work and their leisure. This is clearly a set of issues far greater than the electronic library itself, but even the simple act of training people in how to access and use electronic information routinely is an enormous task. We do not yet know the best way of achieving this aim.

THE INTERNET

To some people, the digital or electronic library and the Internet are synonymous. This is somewhat misleading. It certainly does seem, however, that the Internet has become so popular and pervasive, that electronic libraries will make sure they are compatible with its protocols and software. This in turn implies that every person who uses electronic libraries will also expect to have access to the Internet, and that the electronic library will look and feel just like any other Internet source. So, issues relevant to the Internet will apply to all digital libraries.

The Internet has been hugely hyped. Quite why this is, I don't know, but its growth rate, sheer anarchy, the problems of privacy, of pornography, and of libel on the Net must be part of the fascination. Statistics show that the millions of Internet users represent the most affluent in our population - for example, figures show that the average income of UK people who had access to the Internet in 1996 was £45,000 p.a.

This group of affluent corporate and private users (and the figures seem to show there is a fairly even spread in use between working hours and evenings and weekends) represents an enormous potential market for suppliers of goods and services. This group greatly outnumbers the number of clients for traditional online services, such as Knight-Ridder, FT Profile, etc. Services such as Compuserve and America Online are already far more familiar to the population than the names librarians have traditionally dealt with.

There are, in my view however, some problems that inhibit major commercial use of the Internet. These issues will also have be resolved before the electronic library, linked into the Internet, becomes a reality. The first problem is retrieval and navigation software. The Internet is an anarchic mix of services, and it is very difficult to find your way to what you want, and to eliminate the junk. There are a variety of software tools, such as browsers, to help you. These browsing, search and retrieval tools are often slow, inefficient, and often produce results that are unusable. This is because the sites have changed their coverage, have moved, the information is only accessible to internal users at the sites, or the information has been mis-indexed.

Typical cases include a search using a webcrawler for the term *construction* (this was a genuine search for WWW (World Wide Web) home pages on the construction industry), which resulted in thousands of hits to irrelevant WWW pages that happened to be "under construction". The second case was a search on alligators. One of the first hits to be picked up was a totally irrelevant home page of a US student; at the bottom was the message "See you later, alligator". I invite readers to run a search using one of the standard Internet search engines on their own name. The results are likely to be entertaining.

There is a crying need for better navigation and retrieval tools. Clearly there are not the resources to prepare a hand carved index for every new item that appears on the Internet, and it would be foolish to try to ask the authors themselves to index in a sensible fashion. What we need is a robust and reliable method of automatically indexing full-text documents. This is an issue where surely the skills of librarians and database producers can be brought to bear. Another area where we need progress is reliable deduplication of hits, so people are not forced to read the same item repeatedly.

Fortunately, many companies are developing improved Internet search tools, and although none at the time of writing offer as high quality searching as (say) DIALOG does, there is hope for the future.

The second problem is *security*. By its very nature, the Internet has been designed to be an open system for free exchange of materials. Therefore, no one should be putting material up if they are worried about its value and are worried it may be copied illegally. It is very difficult to prevent breaches of security.

There is also the concern that if a third party can log into your own WWW home page they may then be able to slip across into other computer systems maintained in the organisation containing sensitive data. Everyone has heard of firewalls for preventing this, but no one is sure how reliable they are. Thus, whilst commercial companies hoping to sell information such as online hosts will be happy enough to go up on it, as they *want* people to log into them, companies say, entering tender negotiations will be worried that someone will be eavesdropping on their electronic communications, or else using their Net presence to hack into computers holding confidential information.

People are rightly cautious about putting any sensitive data up on the Net, or connecting computers holding such data to the Net, and are therefore attracted to the idea of using cryptographic techniques to make their materials secure. However, there are problems with using cryptography. The US government is anxious that the Mafia, terrorists, drug smugglers, money launderers and so on cannot communicate with each other without it being able to eavesdrop. It has therefore banned the use or sale of highly secure cryptographic softwares. This is a problem area that can be resolved by politicians, but is at present holding up the development of secure communications on the Internet.

The third problem is *copyright*. It is easy to download items, and send that material around free of charge to all and sundry. There have been a number of cases of copyright infringement actions taken against individuals who have posted material, usually either software or soft porn pictures, to large numbers of bulletin board clients without permission. If you are charging for information, you will be worried about this, and this may well inhibit your willingness to put material up for sale on the Internet, as you fear you will be ripped off. The work in the field of ECMS to control what people can do with copyright material is obviously of relevance.

The fourth problem is *quality*. The quality of the information on the Internet is extremely variable, and this problem is compounded by constant addition and deletion of sources and sites. The main problem is that there is too much information, most of which is redundant or inaccurate. There is no centralised control on the Internet. The individual information providers themselves, often amateurs or academics rather than commercial organisations, decide what information is made available. Compare this to the world of print publishing or online, where the publisher acts as a quality filter, deciding what will sell. No doubt, people will recognise the good sources and ignore the poor ones, and quality assessments, along the lines of a BSI kite mark, or the AA rating system for hotels, will mature. Then, in turn, we can hope that the browsers and search engines will have the flexibility to confine themselves to just searching the good quality sites.

The final problem is *payment*. Since 1994, the Internet has been increasingly used by business. However, commercial services on the Internet will not become a major business until the issue of digital cash is resolved. There is a curious psychological factor at work here. Most of us do not hesitate to quote our credit card number over the phone, even though we know it could be abused or intercepted. Most of us are happy to use an ATM hole in the wall machine even though we are entering a password into a network that might be intercepted. However, few of us are willing to type in our credit card number over the Internet.

Statistics tell us there is a higher incidence of credit card fraud through people misusing a card number from the phone than from using one intercepted on the Internet, but our perception of the risk is different. This means that business on the Internet where money changes hands is far less than has been predicted. The work undertaken by companies such as Digicash in developing safe, robust and trusted methods of transferring money over the Internet is therefore crucial if the Internet is to be used for buying and selling information or other services or products. It may be some time before this work reaches completion.

CONCLUSIONS

I hope this chapter has made it clear, therefore, that there is a lot more to developing and running an electronic library than simply scanning in texts and saying to the users "off you go!" There are many issues to be addressed, and some of them are likely to prove to be major obstacles to the development of the electronic library. However, I hope this chapter has also made it clear that librarians and information scientists have a key role to play in overcoming these problems, and that no amount of effort should be spared in getting to grips with the issues that this chapter has raised.

The Development of an Intranet at Scottish Media Newspapers

Ian Watson

INTRODUCTION

The explosion of the World Wide Web in the early 1990s heightened public awareness of the computer as an information appliance rather than a simple word-processor or number cruncher. The Web of course simply provides a very flexible and friendly graphical user interface (GUI) to the technologies and protocols underpinning the Internet, the global computer network which dates back as far as the 1960s. The Internet allows data and information to move from one computer to another regardless of its make or location.

The same technologies can be applied to any network whether it be global or local, open or closed. The term 'intranet' has been coined to refer to a computer network built upon Internet technologies but one in which access is restricted to a particular group of users, typically employees of a company. Thus the Web has brought to the business world an inexpensive way of distributing corporate information to employees, business partners and customers.

At its simplest an intranet offers a client/server cross-platform solution to information management problems. In other words it provides a uniform way to access information regardless of where or on what platform it resides and regardless of what kind of computer is sitting on the user's desktop. In its most basic form an intranet is made up of just three pieces of software: a Web server, Web browser, and firewall to keep unauthorised visitors out. A fourth component – a search engine – is also essential as the volume of information to be managed grows.

This case study describes how Glasgow-based Scottish Media Newspapers, part of the Scottish Media Group, adopted the intranet approach to improve the quality of its information services as part of its multimedia publishing ambitions. Established in 1783, *The Herald* (formerly Glasgow Herald) is one of the oldest English language newspapers in the world and, with a daily readership of 380,000, is Scotland's leading quality broadsheet. The *Evening Times* is Scotland's best-selling evening newspaper with a daily readership of about 400,000, mostly in the greater Glasgow area.

INFORMATION ASSETS

Next to its journalists a newspaper's most valuable asset is the information it holds in its archives. For many years the primary activity of the typical newspaper library was the maintenance of newspaper cuttings files. In the 1980s the increased availability and sophistication of full-text retrieval software paved the way for the creation of digital text archives. In 1989 a digital archive of the editorial content of *The Herald* and *Evening Times* came online using *Basis* retrieval software from Information Dimensions[1]. In theory this should have provided a better service to journalists by removing the reliance on cumbersome cuttings files which were always subject to the vagaries of classification procedures, misfiling and even loss. Now, the archives would be searchable from the journalists' desks which ought to have been a very welcome development.

In practice things worked out somewhat differently. The link from the production system (Atex) to the Prime computer which ran the archive was not reliable and the command-line interface was never popular except with a very small number of journalists. Attempts to simplify the interface with menus and prompts were largely unsuccessful in overcoming the inherent difficulties with systems based on arcane command languages. This mirrored the problem faced by online database hosts in their attempts to make their systems attractive to the end-user rather than the professional intermediary. The problem was that the user interface, quite acceptable to the information professional, was visually dull and not very intuitive for the non-professional or occasional user.

Meanwhile newspaper production technology had moved on and by 1993 page make-up at Caledonian was fully automated using *Quark Xpress* running on Apple Macintosh machines. The text and picture archiving processes had to be upgraded and integrated into the production system. A key requirement of the new system was that it would not only allow but also encourage journalists to use the archive from their workstations, whether Apple Mac or Windows-based PC. Desktop access to the archive using a friendly GUI would not only be a major boon to the journalist, it would also free library staff from routine searching and allow them to concentrate on the management of information resources.

It was a relatively straightforward job to migrate the existing news archive from the old Prime platform to *BasisPlus* (the successor to *Basis*) running on dual Sun Sparc20 processors with a 12Gb Sun RAID sub-system. *BasisPlus* combines the relational features of an SQL database with the full-text retrieval and sophisticated document handling capabilities. Crucially it also offered a Web server which automatically adds HyperText Markup Language (HTML) coding on the fly.

Around this time the World Wide Web was emerging from the shadowy world of the Internet aficionados to become almost a household toy. Instead of persevering with proprietary front-ends we suddenly found a perfect solution in the form of *Netscape*, a platform independent interface. With the *BasisPlus* Webserver in place sitting on top of the *BasisPlus* database, all we needed was a *Netscape* browser on every user's desktop machine, whether Macintosh or Windows. Adding *Netscape* and the appropriate Internet protocols (TCP/IP) was a relatively straightforward task. Users would then use the now familiar method of pointing and clicking with a mouse to find relevant information.

Using software developed inhouse, stories are extracted from the *Quark* pages and loaded to the *BasisPlus* database. Journalists can search from their desktop using a very simple *Netscape* form. Many were already familiar with *Netscape* from their use of the World Wide Web, so they did not have to grapple with unfamiliar tools as was the case with the old command-line interface. Although our newspaper journalists use Netscape on Macintoshes, it was no problem to extend access to colleagues at Scottish Television where the platform is Windows running Microsoft Internet Explorer. ISDN provides the link between the two sites. In the near future the system will be extended to handle photographs as well as *Adobe Acrobat* view files of the complete pages so that journalists will be able to see the context of the original story.

TOWARDS AN INTRANET

With the technology in place it was a relatively simple step to create a dynamic information system. The *Netscape* browser can be customised by information services staff with a minimal knowledge of the UNIX operating system on which it runs. Even this level of knowledge will be unnecessary as the use of Web authoring tools becomes more widespread. Nonetheless, with a minimal knowledge of HTML it proved quite feasible to set up an embryonic intranet.

The first step was to add information and advice files: a guide to information services; catalogue of information available on CD-ROM; new services, and a directory of personnel. The next step will be to add company policies and practices. Information held centrally can be updated once without concerns about replacing out-of-date paper copy. Information services staff can concentrate on organising information confident that there is a very simple dissemination method. For example, a rapid facts database has been established: library staff traditionally kept notebooks or card files containing regularly required information, such as the date the first man landed on the moon or the number of people killed in various disasters. Once this information is transferred to a database mounted on the intranet the whole company can access this information. This simple intranet is already showing some benefits. A simple listing of CD-ROMS helps promote an understanding of what kind of information is available. A 'What's new' file keeps the page fresh and helps maintain interest in the information service.

Communicating with users has ever been a challenge for managers of information services. Educating users about what the service is and what it can do for them is a challenge especially in the face of the widespread perception of the library as a passive service. In the newspaper world this is compounded by a notion that the library is mostly a filing system for cuttings and the job of the librarian is to cut, file and fetch packets of mouldy paper.

As the librarian emerges into a more proactive role, the intranet offers a highly effective way of pushing information at the user. We know that when a major story breaks most writers will need to check historical facts. For example, major accidents require historical information on similar accidents, casualty rates etc. This information is available on databases but the librarian can compile the statistics once and put them on a current information file on the intranet. There is nothing new in compiling such information packs, what is new is the distribution channel.

In 1996 Caledonian Newspapers, as the company was then known, invested £500,000 to set up a seven-server Web site as part of a diversification into electronic and multimedia publishing. As part of this diversification the company has recruited a strong team of specialist designers and software engineers whose skills will be employed to develop quality interfaces and high quality Web pages. Creating a simple Web site is simple but a combination of information management and design skills are vital to making the service work efficiently for users. Intranet and Internet developments will in time combine to offer a wider range of information services not only to employees but also to customers.

While intranet technology is relatively simple, its management is not without its headaches for information technology departments. Administration can become unwieldy as intranets lead to a proliferation of devices and addresses and decentralised systems can have high maintenance overheads. Intranets also have the potential to increase traffic significantly which can cause bandwidth problems. Care had to be taken therefore to make sure that the information available could and can be handled by the network. Some technology managers are reported to be concerned that bandwidth for vital business applications is being squandered by less than vital intranet data. This is the kind of problem that can be resolved by an information services staff who are aware of how to manage and structure information. There has to be an awareness that an intranet should not become an information free-for-all. The key problem is managing a vital resource called information. This does not mean allowing everyone in the company unlimited access to the intranet whether for retrieving or publishing information. It does mean making it available to those who need it when they need it.

For information services staff the intranet offers a wonderful range of technologies on which they can develop their skills as information managers. The modest intranet at Scottish Media Newspapers has begun with internal publishing of important information and we are feeling our way towards greater interactivity. We see it as a flexible tool which will enable us to provide a better and more responsive service and which will act as a model for a much more extensive system operating across all of our expanding multimedia group.

The intranet is another step in the direction of becoming proactive as opposed to custodians of dusty old cuttings and the low status which accompanied such a role. It is not insignificant that the intranet development has been accomplished by a redefining of the staff roles and attempts to change the image of information services away from the passive librarian towards the dynamic research specialist.

So far the intranet has proved very popular with journalists as a simple way of accessing information held in the text archive. Much of the popularity derives from simplicity of use, in the same way that use of the Internet has been stimulated by the arrival of simple GUIs. It is noticable also that the traditional online vendors now see the Web as the way of at last achieving the holy grail of end-user searching. There are, however, signs that users are becoming more sophisticated and demanding more of the system. The challenge will be to keep ahead of these demands and ensure that the retrieval capabilities of the search engine are at least equal to the kind of functionality that users will find when they point their browsers at the Internet rather than the intranet.

REFERENCE

1. Information Dimensions *http://www.id-london.co.uk*

Introducing an Intranet at the Institute of Health and Care Development

Bob Bater

ON YOUR MARKS

Track record

The Institute of Health and Care Development (IHCD), previously the NHS Training Division, is one of a number of 'new wave' trading agencies re-born out of the NHS reforms instigated by Margaret Thatcher's government in 1991. The Institute's mission is to facilitate the implementation of NHS training initiatives in England and Wales.

The IHCD comprises a quite heterogeneous collection of activities, from operating an awarding body for health-related NVQs, administering training bursaries and producing a comprehensive (electronic) database of NHS-related training resources, to the commissioning and publication of training support materials, organising conferences and exhibitions and undertaking research and consultancy on specific training and development issues.

In the past, the organisation had several sites throughout the country, but it is now concentrated at a single site in Bristol. Permanent staff number about 65, supported by an assortment of specialist contractors, most of them on short-term project-based contracts, but some on longer-term contracts to provide central services. InfoPlex Associates currently provide the Information Management and Technology (IM&T) Services to the Institute.

Despite its small size, the IHCD has a considerable corpus of internal information which must be made available to staff. Some of this is concerned with ensuring that they are aware of the rules, regulations and benefits attached to their status as public sector employees. Much of the rest exists either for internal management purposes, or to support day-to-day dealings with the disparate and geographically distributed customer base – the 500-odd NHS Trusts and Health Commissions and sundry other organisations which constitute the NHS in England and Wales, and their million-plus employees.

A better perspective

The IM&T Services function had always maintained a capability to build custom information systems to support specific departmental needs. But this had never been considered to include the information on rules, regulations and benefits which applied throughout the organisation. Instead, this was dealt with in the conventional way, through the production of a range of handbooks and guidance notes, imaginatively word-processed, but distributed as hard copy.

It was only when the organisation became aware of the Information Resources Management (IRM) approach, that all of the Institute's previously fragmented information sources, services and systems were viewed in the same perspective. In the early 1990s, this triggered a number of attempts to stress the strategic role of information, to focus on the 'I' of 'IT' rather than the 'T', and to introduce Information Management (IM) procedures and techniques. Progress was made, but problems were soon encountered, both cultural and technological.

The cultural problems existed on two levels. At the operational level, it was one of enabling staff to appreciate the important contribution quality information could make to improving customer service through better performance of their roles. At the strategic level, it was the problem of getting management to include information among the organisation's strategic resources, and to manage it accordingly.

The technological problem was simply that, while the Windows interface offered easy access to the tools required for preparing and processing information, it seriously lacked any means of searching for and retrieving information once it existed. Attempts were made to overcome this barrier by converting some information resources into Windows Help files, held on a central server and accessible from any desktop PC. But this method was not applicable to all resources, and it was only the advent of Internet technology – and the intranet concept in particular – which presented a solution to the technological problem and, as a bonus, to the cultural problems as well.

GET SET

Just in case

Once an IHCD intranet was deemed appropriate, it was realised that it could serve to crystalise the concepts of information management – and IRM – around it. No less than any other information resource, an intranet rapidly loses value if it is not managed and maintained. But the need to manage its information resources is implicit in the intranet, inherited from its Internet parent where global internetworking demands precise management of each individual node, if not of the whole. The IHCD intranet therefore not only offered a means of making information readily available, but could also serve as a vehicle for the introduction of effective information management.

Previous attempts to gain management committment to IM and IRM had lacked a focal point, a gap which an intranet could admirably fill. The approach adopted was therefore to build a small prototype intranet within the available resources, and to demonstrate this as part of a presentation to senior management on the Institute's information strategy. The specific advantages of an intranet could thus be highlighted in a highly practical way, whilst stressing the need for it to be geared to organisational objectives through proper information management procedures.

To provide a starting point, a Baseline Information Inventory was undertaken which catalogued some 40 discrete resources, both paper-based and electronic, maintained independently by different departments. Further examination revealed that around 30-40% of the content of these overlapped, and that a third were either no longer used or had been forgotten about. The information strategy made a number of recommendations for dealing with this situation, the most urgent of which were presented as a series of 'Action Brief' papers to management, containing the business case and any other information that enabled them to make an informed decision. The first paper dealt with the need for an intranet under the heading of 'Information Sharing'.

Practice and action

Information Sharing began by discussing relevance, quality and availability as the prime objectives of information management, what these mean in practice, and how ready access to information supports a shared corporate knowledge-base and vision which contribute both to internal effectiveness and to better customer service. Pointing out that much of an organisation's information is 'locked-up' in personal or departmental filing cabinets, desks and drawers (and of course, in the organisation's IT systems) the paper proceeded to compare the advantages and disadvantages of paper-based and electronic documents, and to explain how an intranet could 'unlock' all of these resources, make them readily available in an easy-to-use more manageable way, and incur lower costs and less staff time in the process.

Finally, the paper presented a four-phase Action Plan, proposing an evolutionary approach tackling the issue of corporate documentation first, then recommending ways of developing the intranet into further, more strategic realms. The first phase, resulting in an *IHCD Corporate Handbook*, was envisaged as occurring over three months, while the remainder would need 12 to 18 months. The four phases, each involving a post-implementation evaluation stage, are:

- Corporate documentation
- Operational intelligence
- Corporate knowledge and skills
- Strategic partners and customers.

The *Information Sharing* and other Action Brief papers were discussed during a three-hour Information Management Workshop involving the IHCD's Executive Management and senior Business Managers in October 1996.

GO!

Keeping it simple

The initial attempt to build the prototype intranet immediately ran into resourcing problems. Firstly, although the TCP/IP communications protocol could readily be implemented on all workstations and servers, there was no budget for the Web Server software it would need to talk to. Secondly, much of the content planned for the *Handbook* existed as a dozen or so loose-leaf ring binders, already beautifully word-processed well beyond the formatting capabilities of Hyper Text Markup Language (HTML), and demanding a level of resources to convert them to HTML which was simply not available. These two major headaches were resolved when it was realised that we had naïvely believed the propaganda disseminated by the big intranet solutions vendors.

On further investigation, we discovered that Web browsers can utilise 'file URLs', which address files via the standard DOS/Windows path names, and that for smaller intranets therefore, TCP/IP and Web Server software were not essential. Moreover, the 'helper application' facility in modern Web browsers would allow us to consider alternative ways to incorporate the documentation legacy, rather than translating it all into HTML.

The prototype intranet therefore utilised only one of the conventional components of Web technology – the browser. This provided access to a number of pages containing general information on staff issues and the Institute's various business units, re-authored in HTML from the original word-processed documents. Where re-authoring was impractical, Adobe Acrobat was used to produce exact electronic analogues of the original documents in Portable Document Format (PDF), enhanced with the hyperlinks and other navigation facilities Acrobat provides. By designating Acrobat as a 'helper' application in the browser, the Acrobat Reader program was automatically invoked when a link to a PDF document was clicked.

Acrobat was also used to provide access to an organisation chart. The original A4 landscape hard copy was recreated over several portrait-oriented pages in Microsoft Powerpoint, then processed into the equivalent PDF documents, together with the hyperlinks leading from one to the other. Finally, by using the 'helper' facility again, several Windows Help files – one a summary of the Data Protection Act, and the other a 'test' on the same topic – were incorporated into the *IHCD Corporate Handbook*, to provide a truly comprehensive set of information resources accessible via a common interface – the Web browser.

Getting involved

The prototype *Corporate handbook* received enthusiastic approval from management, so long as it could be accommodated within current budget guidelines. However, prior to full implementation, it was agreed that ways of involving staff in the provision of its content needed to be developed, so that it was not regarded as yet another system for top-down communications from management, but one which was owned and contributed to by everyone.

A structure has therefore been devised which assigns overall editorial control initially to a Personal Assistant in the Executive Management section, with the longer-term intention of broadening this function to include Business Unit representatives by means of an Editorial Board. Each unit representative will commission content from among his/her unit's staff, and oversee the unit's total contribution, ensuring it is updated as appropriate. Initially, Web page design and coding will be undertaken by IM&T Services, but during 1997, tools will be introduced allowing the direct conversion of word-processed documents into HTML. This development will allow the units to undertake their own content preparation and publishing, with minimal involvement of central IM&T services.

The principles on which the IHCD intranet is being built – an evolutionary approach, keeping it simple, and getting staff involved – are not just common sense; they are considered to be the only way in which an appropriate information culture can be encouraged and enabled to develop, amongst staff and management alike. Then, when the further phases make their demands on resources, it is anticipated that the IHCD intranet will have proved itself well worthy of them.

Electronic Publishing at the Association of Commonwealth Universities

Colin Hewson

INTRODUCTION

The *Commonwealth Universities Yearbook* has been produced by the Association of Commonwealth Universities since 1914. The bulk of the 2,500-page *Yearbook* consists of 450 chapters, one for each ACU member university. Each chapter contains address and contact information, lists of academic staff arranged alphabetically by department, and lists of selected groups of administrative staff – some 250,000 staff names in total. The book also contains essays on the higher education systems in Commonwealth countries, and two indexes.

In 1993 the ACU decided to computerise publication. Before computerisation, production was a traditional cut-and-paste operation. A copy of the previous year's university chapter was cut out and pasted on to paper. Any queries for the compiler were written on by hand and the whole sent to the university for revision. When the chapters were returned, they were edited and the copy annotated, also by hand, before being sent to the typesetters. Page proofs were then returned to the ACU for checking. The text of the book was held electronically by the typesetters and it was not possible to perform any type of electronic search or to produce any dataset other than the *Yearbook*. The book had several indexes, most compiled manually, but thorough searching was very time-consuming. The book also had typographical inconsistencies. Textual information could appear under different headings in each chapter, so searching for the same piece of information across several universities could be extremely difficult. As chapters were –

and still are – largely edited separately from each other (though with well-developed editorial guidelines) and as the book had grown and developed over many years, these inconsistencies were not surprising.

The ACU had already gained some experience in the computerised production of directories. In 1990-91 several smaller publications were computerised using CAIRS-IMS (information management software). IMS, produced by CAIRS Ltd, was already used inhouse as the Library's information retrieval package, and although other packages were investigated, IMS was found to be the most suitable for producing these directories. The data in each of these publications was already well structured, and could straightforwardly be broken down into separate fields. Computerisation has meant that queries for compilers are held on the database, and downloaded with the entry when it is sent for revision. Proofreading can now be undertaken as soon as the database had been updated. After editing is complete, the text is downloaded with appropriate coding – desktop publishing flags or a markup language – embedded automatically in the text by the report generator. We are also able to run inhouse searches and to produce ad hoc lists as required[1].

Although a fine package in many ways, IMS was clearly unsuitable for producing the much larger and more complex *Yearbook*. We began to look around for suitable software.

SPECIFICATION FOR THE DATABASE

The most important requirement for the new database was that it should be able to produce the *Yearbook*. However, the package had to be flexible. We did not want to buy a package that could produce the *Yearbook* and nothing but the *Yearbook*. We wanted to be able to produce mailing labels from the data to sell commercially and for our own publicity purposes, and to be able to use the data for other purposes as well. The diverse information in the *Yearbook* required a series of separate, but linked, databases capable of handling a mixture of data, including short, coded fields and larger essay-length articles.

The *Yearbook* has a 40% update each year. Much of the information in the book consists of lists of staff and it was crucial that the editors should be able to edit records in context. We wanted the package, as far as possible, to allow the editors to work their way sequentially through a university chapter as they would if they were editing it manually. Staff for each department needed to be presented for editing together: we did not want the editors to have to scroll through large numbers of records for individual members of staff in order to find the one required. We wanted the package to have good editorial features, including cut and paste, default entries into fields and other labour-saving features, and to have devices to maintain consistency and data integrity on data entry.

The database had to have good indexing techniques and powerful search capabilities. The report generator had to be capable of manipulating the data both for the *Yearbook* and for other report formats, such as mailing labels.

We also wanted the system to be capable of producing the publications that had already been computerised. There was scope for rationalisation here. On IMS, each database is self-contained – although cross database searching is now available – so that on the ACU's IMS system a single address might be held in four different databases. We wanted the database to be able to handle bibliographic data as well, so that we had an integrated package capable of handling a range of data about the university systems in the Commonwealth.

Several packages were investigated, but we decided to upgrade to CAIRS' new package, CAIRS-TMS (text management system). We knew the company well, but, far more important, CAIRS was the only company to demonstrate an appreciation of what we were trying to achieve. We also knew that we would be able to develop the system after we had taken delivery of it: experience with IMS had demonstrated the importance of being able to make changes to database structures and report formats ourselves.

DATA ANALYSIS AND DATABASE DESIGN

The project began at the micro level, by designing the academic staff database, after analysing the information held on individual members of staff in the *Yearbook*, and adding several new attributes that we wanted to collect, such as gender. We then moved up a layer and devised a departmental database to contain textual information about each individual department. A TMS database consists of up to 26 separate databases, called document classes, which can be linked, or which can be self-contained.

The links between the departmental database (DOCD) and the academic staff database (DOCA) are the departmental name, which is entered in the DOCD record and all corresponding DOCA records, and the unique code for the university. The code consists of two elements: the first signifies the country and the second the university name. For example, the code for the University of Adelaide is AU ADE. The codes are for internal editorial use only and are not reproduced in the *Yearbook*. They mean that it is possible to avoid typing often lengthy university names when editing or searching. They are assigned to ensure a correct sorting order, so that the University of Adelaide sorts under *A* and not under *U*.

We then moved to the macro level to try to devise an overall database structure that could cope with the many different university structures throughout the Commonwealth. Some universities have separate campuses or colleges, and the structure of some universities is unique. The solution was to devise a hierarchy with sufficient levels to be able to accommodate every university. Thus, although there are fields on the database labelled *Campus / College, Faculty, Department* and *Sub-department,* in some cases the data in them may belong to a different type of hierarchy.

The text of the previous year's book was retrieved from the printer. The staff data was highly structured and consistent. CAIRS wrote a data conversion program that restructured the data into the DOCA and DOCD formats. Some data was also converted from our IMS databases. Some data did have to be input manually, but much of this was new administrative staff information that was being collected for the first time.

EDITING

Crucial to the choice of TMS for the new database was its menu facility. Menus can be programmed to perform any number of tasks, including searching and the presentation of data on screen. Editors choose the university they want to edit, and then the type of data – usually staff and departmental records. As they make these selections the editors move through a series of static menus. In the background TMS is developing a search profile according to the options the editor has chosen. Finally the list of departments at the chosen university is displayed dynamically on screen. The editor can now edit the departmental record, or can call up the staff records and edit them. A new record is created by selecting an existing record to be copied. The university code and departmental information are read automatically into the new record and do not have to be typed afresh each time.

These menus are written in CPL, the CAIRS Programming Language, which has similarities to Basic. CPL can also be used in the report generator. Although reports can be written using simple commands, all reports used to output *Yearbook* data are written in CPL, which is a powerful tool, for manipulating, reformatting and conditionally outputting data.

Proofs are now downloaded overnight and data for the *Yearbook* is downloaded with formatting codes for conversion by the printer into typesetting instructions embedded in the data. As a consequence, the need for editors to make frequent decisions about typographical style has been eliminated, and consistency of style has been achieved. A word-processing macro is run on each chapter after it has been downloaded, and some manual amendments may be required to incorporate future changes about which we have been informed, so that the data included in the book is correct at the time of publication.

FURTHER DEVELOPMENTS

Computerisation has transformed our ability to search for and use the information in the *Yearbook*. We are able to generate mailing labels for our own publicity purposes, and a commercial mailing list service has been launched. Production of a CD-ROM is currently under discussion.

The Library's IMS databases have been migrated to TMS and integrated into the *Yearbook* system. An OPAC has been developed using menus written in CPL, enabling users throughout the office to run complex searches without any knowledge of how the data has been structured.

REFERENCE

1. Robinson, E. and Hewson, C. Data markup and directory publishing: experiences of using CAIRS-IMS at the Association of Commonwealth Universities, *Program*, **27** (3) 1993, 237-248

Computer Assisted Learning at Forest Healthcare

Anne Weist

The Forest Healthcare NHS library in the Medical Education Centre at Whipps Cross Hospital has extended its role by taking advantage of the opportunities that new computer technology and an innovative Medical Education Director/Clinical Tutor have created. This should be no surprise because, historically, the best access to computers for postgraduate doctors has been in the Education Centre's Library. Although, largely funded for medical staff, we have increasingly been able to provide information support and advice across the Trust. The Trust's recognition of our important role in accessing both management and clinical health information has led to better funding and to a place for the Librarian on the Trust's Research and Development Committee.

Currently we have two whole-time equivalent information professionals and a full-time library assistant. Though a relatively small department, we have always embraced computer technology: first, through DOS-based online database access via Knight Ridder and inhouse databases and, secondly and more recently through CD-ROM and the Internet. Postgraduate doctors have used the Library to get help with basic word-processing. We have now expanded the range of IT support and training further into postgraduate medical computer assisted learning using CD-ROM technology, and the Internet.

THE INTERNET

We have had an Internet connection via Demon since January 1995. We were the first department in Forest Healthcare to have a link and one of the first NHS libraries in the North Thames Region to be connected. This meant that the Librarian was invited to be a representative on the North Thames Internet Planning Group and that she was involved in early regional training initiatives.

The Internet connection provides easy e-mail access to important professional discussion lists. The Mailbase lists that we currently subscribe to include: Lis-Medical, Medical-IT, Medical Education, OMNI, and Evidence-Based Medicine. We are also on the North Thames Regional Library Network's and the BMIA's, now BHIA's (British Healthcare Internet Association), MED-DEV UK discussion lists. These forums have become a vital part of our existing networks and have provided many new sources of information. A practical example of this was the series of messages in November 1996 about the Government's new white paper, *A Service with Ambitions*. Vitally, they included the URL for the full text which was available free of charge. The Librarian was able to print out relevant sections for a GP Registrar who was going for an interview a week later. Another very useful discussion has been about 'free' access to the Medline Database via the Internet where some very obvious but highly pertinent comments were made about the quality of the interfaces available.

List members frequently highlight important new URLs and we are able to bookmark and begin to access them. We now have our own rudimentary 'virtual' catalogue of Internet resources and most people from the Forest Healthcare Trust come to us to find out more about the Internet. So far, representatives from all the following departments have sought Internet advice on more than one occasion: Press and Public Relations, the Research and Development, Clinical Audit, Nursing Administration, Medicine, Surgery, Anaesthesia, Obstetrics, Gynaecology and Paediatrics.

One of our senior registrars is able to run the fot-group, a Mailbase discussion list, focusing on new approaches to respiratory physiology, using our e-mail address. Promotion of such use is vital in demonstrating our intention to become innovative partners in near real-time medical communication. As well as benefiting medical staff locally, the fot-group also informs the UK higher education community as a whole by bringing in new information from abroad, and by providing a forum for discussion which is not appropriate for a journal. Currently there are 40 members of the group in 12 different countries[1]

HOME PAGE

It was the Library that started discussions about a local home page. With the help of North Thames Regional Library and Information Unit, the Librarian organised a series of meetings for those in Waltham Forest and Redbridge interested in posting information on the Internet. The result was the Medical Education Centre's Homepage. Loaded on London University Computer Centre's server, it includes information about all the advanced postgraduate courses run by the Forest Group of Hospitals Medical Education and Research Trust, details of guest lecturers, a description of library and CAL facilities, a link to all R&D projects currently taking place in the Forest healthcare Trust, and the Medical Education Centre's Diary Card. We believe that this is the first British Postgraduate Medical Centre page of its kind. URL: *http://www.nthames-health.tpmde.ac.uk/ntrl/mec/index.htm*.

Internet distance learning project for specialist registrars (SpRs) in respiratory medicine

This idea was inspired by a visit to Professor Stephen Heppell from Ultralab, Anglia University and his Masters Course in IT in Education which is delivered entirely across the Internet. Dr Michael Roberts drew up the proposal and has asked the Forest Healthcare Librarian to co-ordinate the home pages. The project went live in May 1997.

We intend to link up 40 specialist registrars on 16 different sites to enable them to communicate interactively with fellow students and teachers in North Thames (East). On 12 sites the NHS librarians are key to the success of the project because they can provide physical connections to the Internet and facilitate their use. We have been able to enlist their support and open up discussion with the universities about postgraduate medical access. A key role in all these negotiations is being played by the Regional Library and Information Unit.

Again, this new work can be seen as a development of NHS libraries' existing support role in postgraduate medical education. The opportunities for greater partnership are there in postgraduate as well as undergraduate education and undertaking them enthusiastically will highlight our value[2].

COMPUTER ASSISTED LEARNING (CAL)

The distance learning project for SpRs is part of a wider CAL project which has been driven by Dr Michael Roberts, Consultant Chest Physician and Medical Education Director/Clinical Tutor at Whipps Cross. The Medical Education Centre has had a dedicated postgraduate medical education computer/computer assisted learning (CAL) facility since January 1996. This facility should enable all doctors in the Forest Healthcare NHS Trust to become more computer literate and to take advantage of new learning technology.

So what is CAL? Put quite simply, CAL is the use of computer packages to facilitate learning. It exploits the latest computer technology moving beyond the text and images of books to include sound and video. In addition to being able to work with a variety of media, computers are also interactive. It is this interactive nature that makes a computer of such educational value. Users can respond to learning material on computer by self assessment and marking, searching for linked relevant material with ease, or printing off images or text which may be useful later.

CAL is quite developed in undergraduate education. A network of undergraduate CAL centres has been promoted through British Universities with Government support from the Computers in Teaching Initiative Centres (CTICs). Postgraduate Centres have not had the funding or support to promote similar innovations[3-7].

Much of the practical support for the Forest Healthcare project has come from Library staff. The initial work of finding out what was happening in CAL was undertaken by Dr. Michael Roberts, Clinical Tutor and Anne Weist, Trust Librarian. Using their respective contacts in the medical education field and library networks, they put together all the information they had gleaned. After deciding on the need for a dedicated Network Manager/ Training Officer it was logical for the Librarian to draw up a job description as the work was so closely linked to the Library's core function: the facilitation of postgraduate medical learning. The Library was assisted by the Trust's IT department and the Wellcome Centre's Information Officer.

We have always invested in not only the core textbooks and course books but also in print-based self assessment packages. Thus the move to computer-based packages is a natural progression. The standard of currently available CAL packages has, however, been disappointing. This has meant that the Medical Education Centre's CAL team has had to develop its own package. The CAL Officer is a key person. He is directly managed by the Clinical Tutor but gets day to day support from the Librarian, particularly on the Internet. We have already undertaken joint teaching sessions on the Internet where we focus on search engines and key sources and with the CAL Officer explaining more about more practical connection issues.

EVIDENCE-BASED PRACTICE

It should not be a surprise that one of the best and most frequently quoted definitions of evidence-based practice comes from a librarian, Ann Mac Kibbon: "An approach to health care that promotes the collection, interpretation and integration of valid, important and applicable patient-reported, clinician-observed and research derived evidence".[8]

Our involvement in regional training has improved our own retrieval skills and enabled us to ensure that, where it is available, we are better equipped to find 'research-derived evidence' and participate actively in a number of evidence-based practice projects. We have been able to promote the value of our traditional retrieval skills in the first two stages of evidence-based practice:

- Framing the question
- Seeking the data.

One notable venture is North Thames' Front-line Project. It has given our Maternity Unit a stand-alone Medline subset and the Cochrane Library on CD-ROM. Working with a team from the King's Fund, Clinical Audit and the Research and Development Department, we have been an integral part of a training programme and have provided technical support.

On both the library and maternity CD workstations, we have shown users how to use the excellent OVID software interface to search more sensitively. Where applicable, we have been able to promote the use of expert saved search strategies which enable end-users to filter the evidence more effectively[9]. Now, when evidence-based practice is discussed it is likely that our role will be recognised[10]. Currently we are helping the Trust's Maternity Unit to organise an evidence-based practice workshop for midwives in

North Thames. We are also participating in a research methodology training programme for local GPs.

It is an exciting time for us as we seize the developmental opportunities available to us in the following areas:

- Communication and information retrieval via the Internet
- Computer assisted learning, notably our network management role in the respiratory medicine distance learning project
- Use of the OVID Medline software interface to improve the sensitivity of our searches and the final quality of the evidence we retrieve.

REFERENCES

1. Macleod, D. *Managing a newsgroup on the internet,* February 1997, unpublished paper.

2. Rankin, J.A. Problem-based learning and libraries: a survey of the literature, *Health Libraries Review*, **13** (1) 1996, 33-42.

3. CTI Centre for Medicine, *Computers in Medical Education Conference 1995 Proceedings*, CTI Centre for Medicine, Bristol (1996).

4. Jelovsek, F.R. and Adebonjpjo, L. Learning principles as applied to computer-assisted instruction, *M.D. Computing*, **10**(3) 1993, 163-172.

5. Longstaffe, J.A. Using computer technology in support of teaching and learning, *Journal of Audiovisual Media in Medicine*, **19** (1) 1996, 33-36.

6. N'Gouaka, M. Roberts, M. and Weist, A. Computer assisted learning in the Medical Education Centre, Whipps Cross Hospital, Forest Healthcare NHS Trust, *IM & T Training News*, 1997 (in press).

7. Sotheran, M. and Millen, D. Resource centres for IM&T learning: enabling people flexibly, *The British Journal of Healthcare Computing & Information Management*, **13** (10) 1996, p.18. (Whipps Cross Hospital's Medical Education Centre).

8. McKibbon, K.A. et al, *The Medical Literature as a resource for evidence-based care,* Health Information Research Unit, McMaster University, Ontario, Canada (1995, Working paper).

9. Cumbers, B. and Wentz, R. *Using Medline to search for evidence: some background information and sample searches,* North Thames Regional Library and Information Unit (1997).

10. Batstone, G. and Edwards, M. Professional roles in the promotion of evidence-based practice, *British Journal of Healthcare Management,* **2** (3) 1996, 144-47.

FURTHER READING

Carmel, M. (ed.) *Health care librarianship and information work,* Library Association Publishing, London (1995, 2nd edition).

Cross-domain Database Searching at The Natural History Museum

Paul David Polly

INTRODUCTION

London's Natural History Museum contains an astonishing array of objects - the finches collected by Darwin and Fitzroy in the Galapagos, the fossilised remains of Miocene mammals from Kenya's rift valleys, rasterised reincarnations of Lankester's okapis, the bedlam of bibliographic references to millions of new species of beetle. The traditional task of computerised Museum catalogues is simply to keep track of the millions of items in its collections. The Library uses its catalogue to provide the locations of its books, journals, and archival materials to patrons. The science departments - Botany, Entomology, Mineralogy, Palaeontology, and Zoology - use their collections databases to process and track loans of specimens to other research institutions. The Photo Library maintains a database of digitised photographs and prints that are used in natural history publications around the world. Each unit has developed databases appropriate for its own unique holdings and curatorial techniques.

While administrative tasks are the *raison d'être* for most of the Museum's data holdings, they can also be used for research purposes. Collections databases, library catalogues, geographical information systems (GIS), and image archives can be used to answer many of the questions asked by natural historians. Ecologists typically need to know which species are associated in a particular geographic location and how those associations have changed through time. Scientists studying climatic change may want to know how the diversity of species through time is correlated with environmental indicators such as oxygen isotope excursions, which are often used to infer global temperature. Historians who are studying the impact of colonisation on science may want to know how many specimens were curated into natural history collections during the late 19th century and where those specimens were collected. Because our databases are divided along administrative lines, answering any of these questions would currently require laborious sifting through several information archives. If a single, complex query could be directed at all of the databases collectively, however, things would be simpler.

INFORMATION INTEGRATION ISSUES

Until recently, the primary impediment to an integrated data system within the Museum was that it would have required all of its databases to use a common format and be run on a common machine. While many of the systems do store similar information, such as geographic locations where specimens were collected, there cannot be complete overlap in design among our databases. By necessity, a different set of information is recorded in the palaeontology catalogue than in the botany catalogue—information such as geological age or library call numbers are pertinent for only some collections. Furthermore, each department requires efficient updating and retrieval of information. A centralised system would have made this more difficult because accessibility and response time would have been out of the control of the data owners.

But developments in Internet applications and technologies have created new opportunities. The widespread adoption of various open standards such as TCP/IP, HTTP, HTML, SQL, and Z39.50 allow diverse applications that are located on distributed computers to interact with one another over computerised networks. It is possible for a user to generate a query using one application, for that application to then translate the query into the appropriate standard and pass it along to other applications, and then to retrieve results, translate them back into the original query language, and return them to the user. Each distributed application continues to use its own appropriate standards for its own individual purpose; however, each application also answers queries from other applications that have different purposes. This means that data does not have to be integrated into a single application on a single computer to be queried, it only has to be held in applications that use open standards and that are capable of interacting over networks that use open protocols. We plan to use this flexibility to our full advantage.

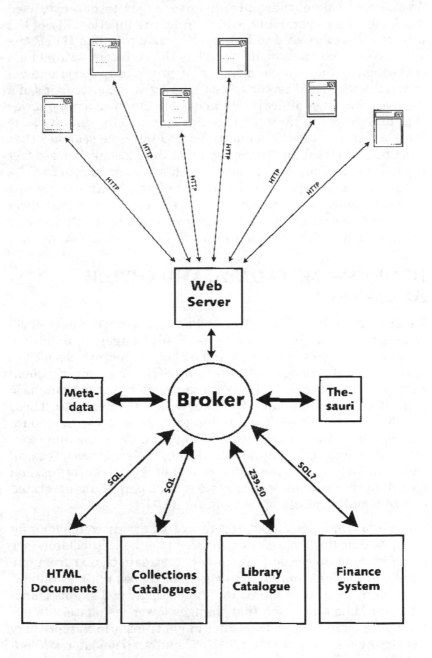

Figure 1 - Diagram showing system architecture

At the same time, there are disadvantages to decentralised databases. Interoperability is limited by the functionality of the protocols that are used to link applications together. HTTP, the World Wide Web protocol, is limited by the transient nature of its connections - there is no 'memory' of previous transactions between the client and server so that step-by-step construction of a database query is difficult or impossible. Furthermore, queries that are passed to multiple machines take more time because there are more network connections and multiple searches that must be performed. In developing IT at the Museum, we are trying to limit the number of packages that we use and to co-ordinate data structures to enhance interoperability among our systems whenever it is possible. In doing so, we are trying for a balance of centralisation and decentralisation that will allow us to get as many of the benefits as we can from both.

BROKERS, METADATA, AND OTHER BUZZWORDS

We are currently in the initial stages of integrating our collections catalogues, image libraries, WWW pages, and library databases using a semi-distributed model. We recently decided to develop our collections catalogues in an SQL compliant relational database system from Informix® and are planning the purchase of a Z39.50 compliant library system within the next year. These are the first two steps towards integration of the various data holdings in the Museum. Individually, each database and catalogue will continue to fulfill its traditional role; however, they all will be linked to users through a web of brokers, translators, and metadata that will allow each system to be part of an integrated research and administrative tool (Figure 1).

Translators, brokers, metadata, etc. are all trendy words for simple tools that link information sources together. Translators are pieces of computer code that convert a stream of text from one format to another and are analogous to the search-and-replace function in most word-processors. An example of a simple translator would be a program that changes lower-case letters to upper-case. A more complex translator might transform a proprietary word-processor document to HTML. Usually a translator can convert its material in both directions, hence its name. A broker is more complex than a translator because it makes decisions about what to do with requests and information. A broker receives a request for information, usually from an end-user, decides where to route the request, transmits it appropriately, and returns the results to the user. The broker may be able to route requests to a variety of applications and it may use translators to transmit and receive information. Decisions about how to route information are based on a collection of metadata about the applications and translators available to the broker. In this case, metadata contains information about the distributed resources available to the broker and the languages and protocols necessary for accessing them. Thesauri for expanding and parsing the user's query are another form of metadata. Metadata may also contain search indices of commonly queried fields in the larger remote catalogues. In all cases, metadata are information about 'real' data which helps the broker and/or the end-user to simplify and refine a search.

SEARCHING FOR STANLEY

A hypothetical user of the Museum's information system might want to locate information and artefacts associated with Sir Henry Morton Stanley's famous quest for Dr. David Livingstone. The user would simply type 'Stanley, Henry Morton' into the Author/ Collector field of the web interface and click the 'Submit' button. A request would be fired off to the web server, which would pass it on to the broker. The broker would then search its metadatabase to determine which databases and catalogues are likely to contain records with Stanley in either an author or collector field. Independent queries, formulated in the appropriate syntax, would then be sent to various applications - the library catalogue, the zoology catalogue, the image database, the botany catalogue, etc. - and would receive the returned results. These would then be summarised and returned to the end-user, who would receive a report to the effect that the Museum contains five books, one hundred letters, and 20 plants that were either written or collected by Stanley. A simple mouse-click would allow the user to see more detailed information about any of these holdings.

Because the Museum's users include biologists, geologists, historians, and other users, we can expect a diversity of queries. A user might want to locate museum specimens from a particular rain forest location in Belize as well as scientific publications on those specimens. Using the same interface, the user would submit the request, this time using a 'Locality' field. The broker would expand this query using a geographic thesaurus, which would determine the latitude and longitude of the location to match it with associated local and regional geographic names, such as Belize, British Honduras, Central America, etc. Using the metadata, the broker would again determine which resources are appropriate for this query, send it off, and send summarised results to the user.

EVOLVING INSTITUTIONAL MODELS

Every decade, every year, and practically every week, information technology changes in profound ways. At any given moment it is impossible to predict what possibilities and pitfalls are on the horizon. Developments in IT can quickly make institutional policies and procedures outmoded, but rethinking and retooling are time consuming and expensive. This is as true at The Natural History Museum as it is anywhere.

Decentralised information networks have distinct advantages and disadvantages for us. We do not have a large IT staff and it is impossible to keep information current centrally. Allowing information to be managed by the staff who are closest to its source keeps it fresh. At the same time, however, there are disadvantages to such a system. We often find that the same information is being compiled and held by staff in different departments. Such redundancy reduces the efficiency of the Museum as a whole and requires staff members to do work that could better be done centrally.

Issues surrounding the provision of information on the Internet also vex the Museum. For the past decade our funding base has slowly decreased and we have had to seek new ways of generating revenue to support our scholarly and public activities. The most publicly visible source of income generation is from the visitors to our public exhibitions. But the expertise of our scientists and the data on the natural world that we hold in our collections are other potential sources of income. At a time when most of the scientific world is moving towards free public access to scholarly publications and databases, the Museum must consider whether there are potential markets for such information. Should we charge for access to research information? Should we package information in CD-ROM and sell it to other institutions? If we do charge for access to our information, will we have to pay for access to others' data? These are questions with no easy answers, but we are increasingly pressed to come to grips with them as much of the world, especially the USA and Australia, are starting to insist on the free exchange of scientific data.

CONCLUSION

When it comes to making decisions about new technology, there are no easy answers. On the one hand, one can rush in without thought or planning and make so many mistakes in the choice of software, hardware, and protocols that everything must be ripped out and redone in a matter of months or years. On the other hand, one can investigate and plan *ad infinitum* as new technologies are unveiled and never reach the 'perfect' solution. We are moving ahead, but with some thought about where we are going. We are trying for a balance between easily-administered centralised systems and specialised distributed systems. We have not tried to make one system or one protocol do everything, but we have also tried to limit the number of different systems and protocols that we use. Hopefully the result will be an overall structure that is capable of meeting both specific curatorial needs and more general research and administrative ones.

Selection of an Integrated Automation System for the Public Record Office Library

Leonard Will

BACKGROUND

The Public Record Office (PRO) is the national archive for England, Wales and the United Kingdom. It supervises the selection for retention of records created by government, central courts of law and other public bodies, stores and preserves those records, provides access to them and promotes their use. It is thus a major primary resource for historical study.

The PRO has had a library of published and secondary material for over 150 years, but this was for the use of the staff of the Office and very little of it was available to the public. It contains about 150,000 items and receives about 340 current serials; about 200-250 new items are received each month. The library's catalogues and shelving arrangements were peculiar to itself, having been developed over its life to meet perceived local needs without much regard to standards used elsewhere. A system of unstructured subject headings was used and the alphabetical catalogue sometimes grouped related works together in a form reminiscent of an archival finding list rather than a set of unit records. There were three catalogue sequences: 'the Green Catalogue', in guard-book format, a card catalogue, and a rudimentary computer catalogue mainly used to print catalogue cards. Shelving was in a sequence of increasing 'foreignness': first the UK, then the British Commonwealth countries in order of seniority of membership, and then the rest of the world. It was difficult for even the library staff to find material.

NEED TO CHANGE

A change was clearly needed, and this was given added impetus by the Lord Chancellor's commitment to Parliament that the library should be opened to the public, following a recommendation of the Cabinet Office Efficiency Unit. A major physical reorganisation was in any case necessary to amalgamate the part of the collection that had previously been held in the PRO's central London office, now being closed. The library staff recommended that the new system should be as standard and mainstream as possible, taking advantage of all appropriate modern developments. It should form a sound platform on which future developments could be built, but should not contain any bespoke elements that would need continuing individual support.

PROJECT MANAGEMENT

The project was managed using the UK government's PRINCE[1] methodology. This ensured that the scope and deliverables of the project were clearly documented and approved, that the roles of the people concerned were defined, and that there were adequate controls and checks to ensure that the project plan was adhered to or updated if necessary. The work was split into two sub-projects:

- Choice and installation of an integrated library automation system, managed by Derek Breeden of the IT Department
- Retrospective conversion of the existing records, managed by Aileen Munro Cameron, Library Manager.

The retrospective conversion project was continuing at the time of writing, and will not be discussed further here. An external technical consultant was appointed through Aslib's Consultancy Service.

DEFINITION OF REQUIREMENTS

Interviews with staff of the library, internal users, and staff who dealt with public enquiries to the PRO confirmed that there were no special needs which could not be met, in principle, by features which should be present in a good modern library automation system. A technical specification was therefore drawn up incorporating the best modern practice. Each requirement was categorised as being mandatory, highly desirable, desirable or a request for information.

Much of the specification covered standard functions such as acquisitions, financial records, cataloguing, searching, loans and serials control. The following paragraphs pick out a few issues raised in the specification that are worth comment, as they have become more significant in recent years and they provide a useful way of discriminating between systems. As well as describing what was required, some notes have been included about the extent to which these features have been implemented in existing systems.

Database structure

The way in which data is stored is important both for efficiency and consistency. As far as possible data should be stored only once, so that repetitive input is avoided and variant forms do not arise. If a user has a clear model of the logical data structure it is much easier to understand how data entered at one point affects the output seen elsewhere. Suppliers proved very reluctant to provide clear data models for their systems; this may have been for reasons of commercial confidence, but it may also have been because their systems had evolved over time and the underlying structures were not very clear, logical or well defined.

Authority files

A specific aspect of the general point made in the preceding paragraph is that a system ought to maintain authority files for data items that may be linked to more than one bibliographic record. These are most commonly used for names of people and organisations, but can also be used for publishers, uniform titles, series titles, suppliers, and library users. Name authority files should provide for the storage of data about the people and bodies concerned, with links between related names that are clearly displayed as references to help cataloguers and catalogue users.

Authority files for subjects, including place names and form/genre terms, should maintain a thesaurus structure in accordance with BS5723[2], allowing for browsing and selection of terms from alphabetical or hierarchical displays. They should also allow generic searching for a term and all its narrower terms. None of the major systems on the market provide these functions in a completely satisfactory way.

MARC standards

The existing records were unsuitable for direct transfer to the new system, because they did not conform to any cataloguing standards. It was therefore planned that the retrospective conversion process would, as far as possible, use records obtained from elsewhere. These records would be in MARC format, and a choice had to be made between UKMARC and USMARC. Some system suppliers claimed to be able to handle both simultaneously, or to import from either, with internal storage in a non-MARC format, but this seemed liable to lead to risks and problems. A single entry in a name authority file, for example, could not match both the US and UKMARC subfield tags.

International discussions towards 'harmonisation' of MARC bibliographic and name authority formats were in progress at the time the system was being chosen, and it seemed likely that the resulting formats would be closer to USMARC than to UKMARC. There is also no UKMARC format for subject authority files. These reasons, and the US bias of the major system suppliers and retrospective conversion contractors, made US MARC appear the safest choice.

Links between records

The comparatively recent introduction to the MARC format of tags 76X to 78X provides an opportunity for improving the efficiency and consistency of data storage by allowing related records to be linked. These fields can be used, among many other things, to link earlier and later forms of title, and to link analytical entries to the host items that contain them. When an analytical record (for a journal article, for example) is retrieved, the display should dynamically merge details from the containing item (the journal), so that its current catalogue record, with shelfmark, loan status, and other variable information is displayed. This kind of relational data structure was not implemented in any of the systems examined.

Though the PRO library system was not intended to cover archival material, the full use of these fields would be particularly important in a system that was. Archival records often have a multi-level structure, and the inheritance of attributes from higher-level items is considered essential.

Subject access systems

In the light of its unhappy experience with a locally developed system, the library felt strongly that standard schemes of subject access should be used, and it decided to use the Dewey Decimal Classification and Library of Congress Subject Headings (LCSH). Not only do these schemes have substantial support and development teams, but also many imported records would already contain data in these forms. The weaknesses of LCSH were recognised, but there is no realistic alternative; the Library of Congress is gradually converting it to a proper thesaurus structure, as resources allow. A desirable requirement was that LCSH subdivisions should be indexed separately, so that they could be used in post-coordinate searching.

To supplement these subject approaches, it was also specified that users should be able to search the catalogue using incomplete information, such as words or phrases from fields determined by the library, including truncated terms and words containing wildcards. In future the library might add abstracts or other textual fields to records, and a system which incorporated good text retrieval functions would therefore be advantageous.

OPAC

The Online Public Access Catalogue interface is the most visible part of a library system, and vendors put a lot of work into making it look attractive and easy to use. Assessment of these interfaces was an important part of the evaluation process. They need to accommodate simple searches by beginners and complex searches by experienced users, with well-integrated help and guidance.

To allow use of a classified catalogue, a system should display an alphabetical index to the classification numbers that have been used, and should provide for browsing in a classified sequence of bibliographical records, with 'verbal feature' headings explaining the meaning of each classification number. Though this is the norm in good classified card catalogues with guide cards, none of the automated systems provided this type of display as standard.

Report writer

A special library has needs for flexible forms of output, both on screen and in printed form, and a configurable report generator is therefore an important part of a system. This should allow library staff to select, sort and print lists of records to serve as specialist bibliographies, current awareness bulletins or personalised SDI (selective dissemination of information) notifications as well as orders, claims, letters and management reports.

Some systems had many pre-formatted reports, but convenient and powerful formatting functions were hard to find. When they were present at all, they took the form of a fairly complex text-based programming system, an add-on report generator from another supplier, or the suggestion that data should be exported from the system and read into a word-processor for formatting. Most systems could not even generate a bibliographic record in ISBD (International Standard Bibliographic Description) format on the screen, much less a two-column formatted page of a bibliography with headers and footers.

Access from the PRO internal network and by external users

The PRO already has an internal network and the system was required to use this, though being otherwise self-contained. Some systems required their own client software to be run on each user terminal, while others provided HTML interfaces which could be used with standard Web browsers on an intranet or the wider Internet. When Z39.50 server and client software was also available this was an added advantage. External access to the system will not be provided initially, but it was desirable that any authorised user on the PRO network should be able to access the system; the use of standard browsers, or client software which could be freely loaded from the network, would facilitate this.

SYSTEM SELECTION

The estimated total cost of the system was not great enough to require an open advertisement in the *Official Journal of the European Union.* As a comprehensive directory of library systems in the UK[3] had been published recently, this was used to select a short list of seven suppliers who were invited to tender. Additional information from exhibition demonstrations and knowledge of systems in use elsewhere was used in making this choice. In fact only two suppliers submitted formal proposals; some of the others were too busy to be able to prepare a bid at the time required, and others may have decided that they could not meet all the mandatory requirements or enough of the desirable requirements to make bidding worthwhile.

An evaluation model was drawn up before any bids were received. This assigned a weight to each requirement (mandatory =5, highly desirable=3, desirable=1) and provided for the suppliers' responses to each requirement to be scored in the range 0 to 5. The weighted scores were totalled within groups, and these groups combined using two stages of higher-level weights, to ensure that the importance given to a group of requirements was independent of the number of items which it happened to contain. The groups and the weights allocated to them are shown in the table below. Scores were allocated on the basis of suppliers' proposals, technical discussions and demonstrations.

The cost of acquisition and running each system for seven years was calculated using discounted cash flow. The cost of each system was adjusted to allow for additional costs that would be incurred if the lack of any features had to be compensated for by extra staff time or other expenditure. The final conclusion was that the Unicorn system by SIRSI was the best value, and this was installed in January 1997.

ACKNOWLEDGEMENTS

I am grateful to the Public Record Office for permission to publish this case study, and to Derek Breeden and Aileen Munro Cameron for checking it for accuracy and for helpful comments. The successful completion of this project is due to the work of them and their colleagues.

	Second level weights %	Top level weights %
Features of the system		60
Library system functionality (e.g. acquisition, cataloguing, OPAC, loans, serials, reader records, standard reports)	30	
System characteristics (e.g. file structure, user interface, help functions, response times, report generation, customisation, sizing)	30	
System operations (transaction and batch processing, monitoring, system management)	20	
Constraints (hardware and software, compatibility of terminals)	20	
	100	
Service requirements		12
Implementation	30	
Training	20	
Documentation	20	
Support and maintenance	30	
	100	
Possible future requirements		2
Information about supplier		12
(Profile, background, experience, future plans, compliance with health and safety, standards and regulations, work practices)		
Project timetable and control		14
(Procurement programme, project management, arrangements for acceptance tests, methods and techniques, contractual requirements)		
		100

Summary of the higher level weighting schemes which were used to evaluate proposed systems

REFERENCES

1. Central Computer and Telecommunications Agency, *PRINCE version 1. New edition of PRINCE: Structured Project Management,* The Stationery Office, London (1996). A new version of the methodology, PRINCE 2, was released in 1996; information about PRINCE developments is given on the WWW page *http://www.open.gov.uk/ccta/prince/prince.htm*

2. British Standards Institution, *British Standard guide to establishment and development of monolingual thesauri,* BSI, London (1987). (BS5723:1987, ISO 2788-1986).

3. Leeves, J. with Russell, R. (comps), *Libsys.uk: a directory of library systems in the United Kingdom,* Library Information Technology Centre, South Bank University, London (1995).

Index

WITHDRAWN

GUILDFORD **college**

Learning Resource Centre

Please return on or before the last date shown.
No further issues or renewals if any items are overdue.

Class: 02 6

Title: Handbook of Special Librarianship

Author: Scammell Alison